Pentecostalism, Postmodernism, and Reformed Epistemology

Pentecostalism, Postmodernism, and Reformed Epistemology

James K. A. Smith and the Contours of a Postmodern Christian Epistemology

Yoon Shin

Foreword by J. Aaron Simmons

LEXINGTON BOOKS
Lanham • Boulder • New York • London

Published by Lexington Books
An imprint of The Rowman & Littlefield Publishing Group, Inc.
4501 Forbes Boulevard, Suite 200, Lanham, Maryland 20706
www.rowman.com

86-90 Paul Street, London EC2A 4NE

Copyright © 2022 by The Rowman & Littlefield Publishing Group, Inc.

All rights reserved. No part of this book may be reproduced in any form or by any electronic or mechanical means, including information storage and retrieval systems, without written permission from the publisher, except by a reviewer who may quote passages in a review.

British Library Cataloguing in Publication Information Available

Library of Congress Cataloging-in-Publication Data

Names: Shin, Yoon, author.
Title: Pentecostalism, postmodernism, and reformed epistemology : James K. A. Smith and the contours of a postmodern Christian epistemology / Yoon Shin ; foreword J. Aaron Simmons.
Description: Lanham, Maryland : Lexington Books, [2022] | Includes bibliographical references and index.
Identifiers: LCCN 2021043427 (print) | LCCN 2021043428 (ebook) | ISBN 9781793638748 (cloth) | ISBN 9781793638762 (paper) | ISBN 9781793638755 (ebook)
Subjects: LCSH: Smith, James K. A., 1970- | Pentecostalism. | Philosophical theology. | Reformed epistemology. | Postmodernism—Religious aspects—Christianity. | Christian philosophy.
Classification: LCC BX4827.S577 S55 2021 (print) | LCC BX4827.S577 (ebook) | DDC 289.9/4—dc23
LC record available at https://lccn.loc.gov/2021043427
LC ebook record available at https://lccn.loc.gov/2021043428

*To Esther, Ezra, Micah, and Sophia
Who have endured my absence with patience and love*

Contents

Foreword		ix
Acknowledgments		xiii
Introduction		1
PART 1: SMITH'S PENTECOSTAL EPISTEMOLOGY		**11**
1	Pentecostal Spirituality and Postmodernism	13
2	Pentecostal Epistemology	41
3	Pretheory, Theory, and Their Integrated Relationship	59
PART 2: SMITH'S POSTMODERN EPISTEMOLOGY		**85**
4	Postmodern Hermeneutic Epistemology	87
5	Smith the Relativist?	103
6	Against Narrative, Affective Knowledge	127
PART 3: REFORMED AND POSTMODERN EPISTEMOLOGY		**149**
7	Plantinga's Reformed Epistemology	151
8	Warranted Christian Belief	171
9	Reformed Epistemology, Postmodernism, and a Way Forward	189
Conclusion: Contours of a Postmodern Christian Epistemology		209

Glossary	217
Bibliography	223
Index	243
About the Author	255

Foreword

"The Views from Somewhere"

I once noted in a footnote somewhere that I thought there was important work to be done showing the ways in which Reformed Epistemology (RE) and postmodern philosophy were resources for each other. In that footnote, as I recall, I cited another footnote by James K. A. Smith who had said something similar calling for such work. Yoon Shin has written the book that Smith and I both said was needed.

What RE and postmodernism share, at their core, is an awareness of the situatedness of human knowing. Critical of all "views from nowhere," RE and postmodernism appreciate that we are always already somewhere. And, we *are* "there" before we *know* that we are. Life, both discourses realize, is the space of knowing. Accordingly, the goal of both RE and postmodernism is not to reduce life to the object of knowledge but instead to make knowledge adequate to the realities of finite living.

The initial difference between RE and postmodernism, however, is the seeming decidedly "religious," specifically Protestant Christian, commitments of the former, and the seeming decidedly "relativist" commitments of the latter. And, the all too common story goes, Christianity is a clear rejection of relativism and so anything like a full engagement between RE and postmodernism would face serious obstacles because it is like noting the similarities between oil and water—they are both liquids after all—and then, as a result, assuming that they will mix well. Perhaps the chemical, or in this case, confessional, structure, as it were, of RE and postmodernism are just incompatible. Accordingly, some have defended the importance of fighting against postmodern relativism in the name of the "absolute Truth" of Christianity. However, such accounts of absolute incompatibility reflect facile readings of both postmodernism and Christianity.

In response to such unsustainable readings, many others have offered more compelling proposals about the possibilities of this unlikely pairing between Christianity and postmodernism. Stressing the notion of epistemic humility called for as a result of the noetic effects of sin, and the relational form in which much of the New Testament is presented, scholars such as Merold Westphal, James K. A. Smith, and I, among many others, have long contended for the importance of postmodernism as a resource for better appreciating these aspects of Christian spirituality. In light of such an awareness, RE's confessional orientation should not be understood as necessarily localized to specific Christian claims, but understood to stand as a model for why lived commitments do not need to be abandoned in order to do philosophy. Instead, only by attending to such lived commitments, I would suggest, are we able to be philosophically rigorous. As such, RE should not be read as *necessarily* Christian, but as an epistemic proposal that makes possible confessionally specific lived identity, whether religious or not, as the context out of which any concern for evidence and warrant would then emerge. Only when we read RE as more broadly applicable in such ways does it offer the most substantive defense of the particular way that Christian belief and practice can serve as legitimate philosophical starting points.

Alternatively, postmodernism is not best understood as a metaphysical anti-realism at odds with Christian truth. It is only when interpreted in this flat-footed and ultimately incoherent way that claims such as Jacques Derridas's famous suggestion that "there is no outside of the text," Richard Rorty's sociological conception of truth, or Michel Foucault's proposal about the workings of power get read as rejections of all mind-independent states of affairs. Admittedly there are plenty of passages in the books of postmodern philosophers that might invite such interpretations, but they are ultimately uncharitable dismissals of the way that such thinkers are attempting to account for the humility invited by embodied life. Epistemic perspectivalism *does not* entail metaphysical anti-realism. Just because I can't get outside my, or my community's, hermeneutic frames doesn't mean that there is nothing outside of those frames. Indeed, to read postmodernism as a metaphysical thesis is to fail to appreciate its most basic epistemic gesture. If we can't get beyond our own perspectives, then there is no way to stand in the "view from nowhere" by which one could so easily reject metaphysical realism. Instead, open to a variety of metaphysical views (realist and anti-realist alike), postmodernism is best appreciated as a matter of epistemic humility occasioned by an embrace of existential risk.

When approached this way, we can see that RE can be grounded in Christianity insofar as the defenders of RE do draw heavily upon their own Christian tradition, without, thereby, requiring Christianity to be the only legitimately warranted option for epistemically responsible living.

Alternatively, we can note that postmodernism can be relativistic insofar as it appreciates the lived contexts in which all truth-claims are uttered, without thereby affirming anti-realism in all forms. This compatibility between RE and postmodernism is important because it strengthens the need for a more determinate inquiry into what it means to stand somewhere with confidence while still humbly recognizing that there are other reasonable places to stand.

In the attempt to think through the ways in which RE and postmodernism might be mutually reinforcing in relation to a specific historical, and religious, context, Shin impressively turns occasionally within the book to Pentecostalism as a historical example of how the postmodern epistemology he envisions might play out. His focus on Pentecostalism is significant because it does four things that are quite needed in the broader discourses of postmodern philosophy of religion, on the one hand, and Christian philosophy, on the other.

First, the consideration of Pentecostalism interrupts the narrowness that often characterizes so much of contemporary Christian philosophy. Far too often "Christianity" is understood within the philosophical literature as either Catholicism or Reformed Protestantism. Although both are important traditions that have each made significant contributions to philosophical history, there is a danger in not recognizing the diversity and dynamism in Christianity as historically practiced. Indeed, Shin's engagement with Pentecostalism is not the end of such expansive awareness but simply a step in the direction of increased inclusivity. "Christian" philosophy should never be synonymous with simply one Christian tradition, but instead allow for the plurality of Christian traditions: liberationist, womanist, Orthodox, and so forth. By offering the occasional engagement with Pentecostalism, Shin models the ways that RE and postmodernism should cultivate dialogical hospitality in light of epistemic humility.

Second, Pentecostalism is a global movement and, as such, increased philosophical consideration of Pentecostalism helps not only to add diversity to what counts as Christian philosophy, specifically, but also to invite more cross-cultural awareness in philosophy of religion, more broadly. In particular, by taking seriously the ways in which Pentecostal spirituality is often reflective of the sociocultural and historical spaces in which it gets lived out, we are likely to be more attentive to the ways in which abstraction is problematic as concerns embodied religious practice.

Third, the specific focus on Pentecostalism helps to overcome the latent cognitivist biases that are so often present within the mainstream debates in philosophy of religion. Pentecostalism is certainly a tradition that can, to some extent, be characterized by determinate beliefs and truth-claims, but it is also a tradition that appreciates affectivity as central to the relational dynamics of religious commitment. Shin's focus on narrative and affectivity in epistemology opens important spaces for future work on religious practice, liturgy, embodied cognition, and even identity theory.

Fourth, Pentecostalism has only recently received much philosophical attention, but for decades it has been the subject of sociological, theological, and historical analyses. Shin's work fosters room for significant interdisciplinary engagement as he adeptly navigates the fraught boundaries between analytic epistemology, postmodern philosophy of religion, Pentecostal theology, and cultural studies. In this way, Shin offers a stellar example of what I have elsewhere termed "mashup" philosophy.

This book is exciting because it announces where other books need to go. Even where I would disagree with Shin's specific claims on particular points, I enthusiastically support the new trails he is attempting to blaze. I look forward to hiking that trail with him because I think it offers new avenues in Christian philosophy, new opportunities in philosophy of religion, and new directions in postmodern epistemology. Ultimately, James K. A. Smith and I were both right to see the need for this work, but thankfully Yoon Shin was courageous enough to undertake it.

J. Aaron Simmons

Acknowledgments

This work represents years of thinking through Reformed and Pentecostal theology and philosophy. While the journey was filled with frustrations that accompany the research and writing process, it also led to self-discovery, new friendships, and greater understanding of God and God's wonderful creation. Bringing this work to fruition would not have been possible without friends and family who have encouraged me and gave critical feedback. With profuse apologies for being unable to include every person, I want to first thank my wife, Esther, who supported me at every step. Without her immeasurable support, this work would not have been possible. When you begin your own academic and professional journey, I hope that I can provide the same level and quality of support. I want to also thank my children, Ezra, Micah, and Sophia, who patiently endured daddy's work with love. Your daily examples of joy, love, and grace push me to become a better person.

There have been numerous mentors, friends, and colleagues who have encouraged me and critically engaged my ideas over the years. I am especially grateful for Philip Ziegler, Wolfgang Vondey, and J. Aaron Simmons for their extensive engagements. I have cherished my friendship with Ken and Melissa Archer. They not only helped me see Pentecostalism apart from my Evangelical lens, but I may have never participated in academic communities without their encouragement. I am also thankful for the friendship and mentorship of Bill Oliverio. His encouragements and critical feedback were critical to my development as a scholar. My dear friends Steven Felix-Jaeger, Aaron Ross, Lauren Raley, and Rick Wadholm Jr. were also instrumental for the development of my ideas and the resolve I needed to finish this project. I also leaned on the wisdom of the RE Facebook group for guidance. Especially helpful were Andrew Moon, Tyler McNabb, Joshua Sijuwade, Aaron Cuevas, and Frederick Aquino. With their inquisitive questions and feedback, my students have also played a key role in the direction of my ideas, especially those in the Plantinga reading group: Asia Lerner, Knowledge Washington, Justin Battles, Austin Spiller, Jordan Reed, and several others. You have bright futures ahead of you. And as this book was reaching its final stages, my students in the Graduate Systematic Theology course helped me battle through the struggles brought on by the pandemic with their enthusiasm and encouragement. With my apologies for being unable to name everyone, I want to thank Ilyne Deliquina, Joseph Hempfling, Steve Sipes, Morgan Sohl, Sid Ventura, Alex Capps, and Lisa Williams. Special thanks also go to my teaching assistants who read multiple drafts and provided important feedback. Asia Lerner, Courtney Krause, and Elizabeth Dykens, I could not have done this without you.

Two previously published articles appear here in revised portions, and I am thankful to Brill and the editors of *Pneuma* for their generous permission to reprint them here. The articles are "Pentecostal Epistemology, the Problem of Incommensurability, and Creational Hermeneutic: The Harmonious Relationship between Affective and Cognitive Knowledge," *Pneuma: The Journal of the Society for Pentecostal Studies* 40, no. 1–2 (2018): 130–49, DOI: https://doi.org/10.1163/15700747-04001005 and "Externalism, Warrant, and the Question of Relativism: A Plantingian Assist to Smith," *Pneuma: The Journal of the Society for Pentecostal Studies* 43, no. 1 (2021): 94–114, DOI: https://doi.org/10.1163/15700747-bja10006. The block quotation from George A. Lindbeck, "George Lindbeck Replies to Avery Cardinal Dulles," *First Things*, no. 139 (2004): 13–15 is reprinted with permission. I am thankful to Baker Publishing Group for permission to quote their email correspondence from November 9, 2016, in chapter 3.

Finally, thank you Lord for your abundant grace and mercy. You told me years ago that I needed to finish what I started. This is the fruit of that labor. My resolve came from you, so this work is not merely a product of my hands but is a gift from you. And to you, I give you this work. May you be glorified through it. *Soli Deo Gloria.*

Introduction

THINKING IN TONGUES: A TESTIMONY

Ever since I immigrated at a young age to the United States, I have inhabited the liminal space of identity that I later understood as the hybridity engendered by being a cross-cultural kid (CCK).[1] As I became more bilingual, I noticed that certain linguistic expressions of one language allowed for a fuller experience of the reality at hand than the other language, especially when the expression involved not only words but also intonation and bodily movements. In a sense, I "knew" the world at a deeper level through these embodied signs and acts. Moreover, my situated contexts and experiences, my hybrid identity, informed my knowledge in ways that differed from my Korean and Western counterparts.

In college, I was introduced to Van Tillian presuppositionalism. Drawing from its Dutch Reformed heritage, presuppositionalism teaches that knowledge is not neutral as it is the product of ultimate presuppositions. Knowledge, however, must reflect reality, and absolute reality that represents "the ultimate standard of meaning, truth, and rationality" is the absolute person of God revealed in Christian Scripture.[2] Unbeknownst to me, these twin ideas of perspectivism and realism prepared my postmodern turn.[3] At Reformed Theological Seminary, my introduction to James K. A. Smith and Radical Orthodoxy (RO) realized this turn. In RO, I found a thoroughgoing postmodern Christian movement that was not inflicted with the relativism that I was warned about by conservative Evangelicals. I was also able to move beyond the remaining modernism in Van Til's thought, the hermeneutics of totality, that seemingly made possible the attainment of absolute truth as covenant servant. As an egalitarian Pentecostal with some very different views at a Calvinist seminary, I was uncomfortable with the notion that the right (conservative Presbyterian) interpretation of Scripture clothed one to speak with the authority of God. Nevertheless, I am grateful for presuppositionalism, especially my professor, John Frame, whose thoughts prepared me for postmodernism. Presuppositionalism became my gateway drug to postmodernism.

Personally important in my discovery of Smith and postmodernism was Smith's Pentecostal identity.[4] Pentecostalism is not merely a set of supplementary doctrines that adds onto an established doctrinal system. Pentecostalism is a "glocal,"[5] polyphonic lived religion, a spirituality focused on the embodied encounter with the Holy Spirit. Implicit within the doxastic practices of Pentecostal spirituality are modes of knowing that are neither propositional nor quantifiable. This knowing otherwise highlights that knowledge arises from situated embodiment.

My conservative Evangelical-Pentecostal ecclesial traditions subsumed this situatedness in favor of absolute, neutral, and universal truth, which did not represent my hybrid identity and experiences. Smith's epistemology was the first systematic introduction to an epistemology that correlated with my life experiences and hybrid identity without losing the realism engendered by my faith. Since then, I have learned that Pentecostal spirituality naturally lends itself to this situated perspectivalism.

This work is the product of thinking through Smith's Pentecostal epistemology, appropriating, critiquing, and constructing where necessary. Early on in this research journey, however, I concluded that Smith's sketch of this epistemology is insufficiently Pentecostal. It is more accurately a postmodern epistemology that utilizes Pentecostalism as an example. On the one hand, this is expected since Smith purposefully narrows the scope of his epistemological proposal as a brief introduction and invites others to fill in the details. Part of this invited constructive work would inevitably require critique and modification.[6] On the other hand, Smith's various works that deal with epistemology provide a continuous but more developed epistemology without recourse to Pentecostalism. While developing Smith's epistemology in more explicitly Pentecostal terms was an option, I have decided to develop Smith's more robust postmodern epistemology. For his fuller account not only testifies to my identity as a Pentecostal but also as a CCK whose own Pentecostal identity has been greatly influenced by the Reformed tradition and the academic community. Although I am affiliated with the Assemblies of God (USA), a classical Pentecostal fellowship, my Pentecostal identity cannot be neatly categorized by sixteen propositional doctrines.

Reflecting my hybrid identity, I cannot rest easy merely utilizing Smith as my leading interlocutor. Upon recognizing areas of deficiency in Smith's epistemology, I saw how I could consistently and coherently appropriate the Reformed Epistemology (RE) of Alvin Plantinga and Nicholas Wolterstorff, as opposed to traditions that regard justification as a necessary condition for knowledge, to construct a more robust postmodern epistemology that incorporates the perspectivity of postmodernism, the realism of Christianity, and the analytic distinction between belief and knowledge. Given the continual misunderstanding of postmodernism within certain sectors of Christianity due to their modernist epistemological objectivism—the idea that objective knowledge can obtain absolute truth—there is a need for a realist epistemology that is sufficiently postmodern and Christian—postmodern due to its epistemological resources and the current milieu and Christian due to the importance of *pistic* commitments for knowledge, among other reasons. This work thus seeks to demonstrate that postmodernism and Christianity are not mutually exclusive.

Plantinga and Wolterstorff come from a long lineage of Reformed thinkers, such as Abraham Kuyper, Herman Bavinck, Herman Dooyeweerd, and Cornelius Van Til, who have creatively explored the implications of following the Augustinian dictum *fides quaerens intellectum* (faith seeking understanding). Notably, Plantinga, who received the 2017 John Templeton Prize and was once heralded as "America's leading orthodox Protestant philosopher of God,"[7] has worked tirelessly toward presenting Christian belief as rationally warranted without undefeated evidence or argument through his development of RE. Wolterstorff provides an account that shares an affinity with postmodernism's situatedness. Moreover, with their rejection of epistemic neutrality, postmodernism and RE seem, at first glance, good dialogue partners for a postmodern epistemology.

But why choose Smith as the primary interlocutor? Should not a book on postmodern epistemology primarily interact with the giants of French philosophy: Jacques Derrida, Jean-François Lyotard, or Michel Foucault? This is an important methodological question. The reason is that Smith, who specializes in deconstruction and phenomenology, is a superb exegete and synthesizer who has paved the way for his theological communities to reimagine and understand faith and reality more clearly through critical appropriation of postmodernism, especially by showing the Augustinian heritage of Derrida, Heidegger, and Camus.[8] In the construction of a *Christian* epistemology, then, Smith is an important and critical voice that cannot be ignored, especially for Evangelicalism and Pentecostalism that have widely viewed postmodernism as an insidious enemy infecting culture and faith with nihilistic relativism and moral decay. Their concerns are not wholly mistaken. The incessant postmodern critique, the deconstructing of preciously held commitments and beliefs, can seem frightening. But postmodernism is not a monolithic reality. This book is a way to help ease their concerns without capitulating to modernist assumptions and is an answer to Jerry Gill's point that postmoderns have not practiced the same amount of vigor in rectifying the problems of modernism.⁹ Given that Smith has been showing the positive contributions postmodernism can make to philosophy and religion, it is important to exposit and analyze his thoughts.

Smith is "fast becoming a major voice in the world of postmodern theology."[10] The renowned historian of religion Martin Marty considers possibly adding Smith to the collection of scholars who have influenced him, a list that includes luminaries such as Paul Ricoeur and Maurice Merleau-Ponty.[11] In Pentecostal philosophy, Smith, along with Amos Yong, is a Godfather-like figure, helping establish the philosophy interest group within the Society for Pentecostal Studies in 2000 and also editing Eerdmans' Pentecostal Manifestos series.

Importantly, the postmodern Pentecostal philosopher J. Aaron Simmons considers Smith's essay "Advice to Pentecostal Philosophers" as setting the agenda for Pentecostal philosophy.[12] Revealing his Heideggerian influence, Smith argues that Pentecostal philosophical methodology cannot start with some supposed abstract, neutral reason because philosophy is a theoretical, second-order reflection on pretheoretical lived experience. Thus, undergirding Pentecostal philosophy must be the embodied, lived faith of Pentecostal spirituality that provides the resources for theorizing in a manner consistent with its Pentecostal identity.[13] This situated, embodied emphasis has great affinity with continental philosophy, as evidenced in Pentecostal philosophy's prominent engagement with postmodern, not analytic, philosophy.[14] Such has been the influence of Smith. For Pentecostal philosophers, much of their philosophy must go through Smith, whether through appropriation, rejection, or creative and critical construction. This is because Smith set much of the agenda for Pentecostal epistemology (and, with Amos Yong and Nimi Wariboko, much of Pentecostal philosophy).[15]

The entrance into this work is thus through Smith, as it exposits and creatively appropriates Smith's postmodern Pentecostal epistemology while critically augmenting it with RE. This dialogue between continental and analytic philosophy, Pentecostal spirituality and the Reformed tradition, and perspectivism and realism represented by Smith and RE is an extension of the daily reality I face as a CCK. For CCKs, every day brings new "mashup" opportunities. In music, mashup brings different songs together to create a unique sound that blends without pure synthesis. This blending does not synthesize in such a way that the voices lose their distinctive features in the creation of the new. In a similar way, mashup philosophy takes cue from this musical genre and brings together different philosophies to form something new and original.[16] This work is a mashup project that synthesizes without negating the distinctive voices of the interlocutors.[17] However, despite their shared Reformed heritage, there are differences that could act as roadblocks for coherent synthesis. What are some of these differences?

First, while Plantinga has written extensively in epistemology, much of Smith's epistemology is embedded in his wider works in philosophical hermeneutics, philosophy of language, and philosophical anthropology that requires careful exegesis to clarify the details.

Second, Plantinga has predominantly written on noetic beliefs, whereas Smith's epistemology portrays knowledge as primarily and irreducibly narrative and affective, raising the question about whether they are addressing the same type of knowledge.

Third, while Smith finds himself at home with figures like Derrida, Lyotard, and Rorty, Plantinga finds much to reject in postmodernism, castigating its denial of objectivity and truth.[18] For Plantinga, postmodernism is "a kind of failure of epistemic nerve" due to its rejection of truth in the face of uncertainty that flows from the demise of classical foundationalism.[19] In this way, Merold Westphal's claim that "it is widely assumed, by friend and foe alike, that the central themes of the postmodern philosophers and the central loci of orthodox Christian theology are mutually exclusive" seems to capture Plantinga's sentiment.[20] Although Westphal believes that RE is compatible with postmodernism, he doubts Plantinga and Wolterstorff would accept the label "postmodern" to describe their thought.[21]

Fourth, Smith seems to relish in the qualities of postmodernism that Plantinga rejects. His supposed repudiation of realism and support for Christian relativism seem to represent all that is wrong with postmodernism.[22] In fact, his postmodern Pentecostal epistemology has invited criticism that of neo-Kantianism that results in narrative relativism and arbitrary adjudication.[23] Not only that, Smith criticizes Plantinga's epistemology, even its pneumatological aspect, as overly cognitive.[24] This emphasis seems methodologically antithetical to the primacy and irreducibility that Smith assigns to non-propositional, pretheoretical knowledge.

Given these differences, can this mashup even get off the ground? Must one agree with those who believe in the impossibility of rapprochement between continental and analytic traditions?[25] In the face of these concerns and questions, I propose that such a mashup is indeed possible and even valuable.

First, the acceptance of postmodernism has been growing, exemplified in Smith's own growing popularity.[26] Yet, misunderstandings of postmodernism and Smith abound, with Smith receiving charges of nihilistic relativism and non-rationalism. If Smith's representation of postmodernism is compatible with Christianity, then his postmodern, embodied epistemology should be taken seriously, especially by Christians. Smith's main epistemological themes correct reductive Enlightenment rationalism, revalues the integrity of perspectives, traditions, and the material, and develops non-propositionalist knowledge, which is often neglected in the field of epistemology.[27] This emphasis on situated perspectivity and embodiment better reflects embodied personhood and resists the hegemony of the mind.[28]

Second, Smith's postmodernism illumines the postmodern sensibilities of RE, such as the prioritization of properly basic beliefs, the ultimately *pistic* ground of metaphysical commitments, and contextual belief-formation. Moreover, the overt noetic element of RE complements the overt embodied elements of Smith's epistemology.

With these questions and possibilities, this book aims to provide a sound answer to an overarching question: Can Smith's postmodern epistemology inform a constructive, Christian epistemological vision in conversation with RE? I claim that this question can be answered affirmatively. With some repair, Smith's epistemology provides robust material for such a construction. Despite some dissimilarities, Smith's epistemology and RE can come together in a theory of knowledge that is faithful to postmodernism's emphasis on the epistemic perspectivism of being-in-the-world, embodied "know-how," and the warrant of non-propositional knowledge as well as to Christianity's commitment to truth and reality, which the gospel supremely represents. In this way, this modified epistemology reflects the reality of embodied lives. And even though my construction is motivated by my experience as a CCK, globalization and mobility have rapidly increased cross-cultural experiences and identities. To utilize Justo Gonzalez's verbiage for CCKs, we are all *mestizaje*.[29] Beyond my personal experience, Smith's reconstructed and augmented epistemology faithfully portrays the knowledge engendered by hybrid realities in our postmodern times.

BRIEF OUTLINE

The book builds its case through three parts. The first part on Smith's Pentecostal epistemology begins by defining Pentecostalism as an experiential holistic spirituality that integrates beliefs and actions in the affections. It then delineates Smith's understanding of a Pentecostal worldview in order to begin describing Pentecostal epistemology as narrative, affective knowledge and to situate the worldview as an instance of this embodied knowledge. Because Smith presents his epistemology as postmodern, the first chapter also describes a non-nihilistic postmodernism that provides the framework through which Smith's and my epistemology can be understood.

Building on the glimpse of Smith's epistemology provided in the previous chapter, chapter 2 provides an in-depth exposition, analysis, and critique of Smith's Pentecostal epistemology. Specifically, it critiques Smith's thin criterion for knowledge that harms the identification of his epistemology as Pentecostal and his subcognitivism that seemingly pays lip service to the role of theoretical thought. As repair, I suggest the distinction between narrative, affective construal as meaningful epistemic activity and narrative, affective knowledge, and the reciprocal relationship between noetic beliefs and affective understanding. The third chapter provides further support for this integrated, reciprocal relationship through the enlistment of moral psychology and philosophy of emotion.

The second part moves to delineating and analyzing Smith's postmodern epistemology. The first part argued that Smith's Pentecostal epistemology is insufficiently Pentecostal. In fact, the elements of Pentecostal epistemology are already present in his wider works that do not draw from Pentecostalism. Chapter 4 thus outlines the elements of Smith's postmodern hermeneutic epistemology and grounds it in Smith's embodied liturgical anthropology.

Chapter 5 introduces Smith's controversial promotion of relativism. The first section exposits his presentation of linguistic pragmatism as the rationale behind his embrace of relativism. Just as Smith presents Lindbeckian postliberalism as a Christian pragmatism, I demonstrate the lifelong trajectory of postliberalism in Smith's thought and provide a brief summary of postliberalism. I also show Smith's misunderstanding of postliberalism and demonstrate that Lindbeck is an ontological and epistemological realist whose performative-correspondence theory of truth accounts for categorial adequacy and intrasystematic coherence as necessary conditions for correspondent ontological truth.

Chapter 6 addresses Richard Davis's and Paul Franks's charges of relativism and arbitrariness against Smith. After summarizing their critiques, I demonstrate the importance of correspondence in their critiques, critique their presupposition of epistemological objectivism, and defend Smith as an ontological and epistemological realist. Furthermore, against the charge of arbitrariness, I propose that rational adjudication between different knowledge claims can occur by testing categorial adequacy and intrasystematic coherence, through *phronesis*, and utilizing immanent critiques and transcendental arguments. The chapter ends with an excursus on correspondence and the ethics involved in the immanent attempts to understand the transcendent Other by revisiting the relationship between pretheory and theory.

The third part pivots to RE. Chapter 7 introduces the trajectory of Alvin Plantinga's thought by first delineating his opposition to deontological justification, situating deontology in internalism and introducing externalism, and exposing his warrant criteria. I then provide commentary on proper basicality since it is the closest equivalent to Smith's notion of pretheoretical knowledge and argue for the reciprocal relationship between background experiences, inductive beliefs, and properly basic beliefs.

Again, following the trajectory of Plantinga's thought, the topic moves from warrant to warranted Christian belief. Chapter 8 interacts with

Plantinga's Aquinas/Calvin and extended Aquinas/Calvin models. The first section exposits the A/C model and highlights the ultimately *pistic* and circular nature of beliefs at the most basic level. Next, it addresses the charges that arise with this position, further adding to the modes of rational adjudication. The next section interacts with the extended A/C model. This model is especially important to this book because Plantinga comments on the importance of the affections. Importantly, I propose that Plantinga's affective analog of warrant can augment Smith's epistemology with robust criteria for affective warrant.

Chapter 9 brings postmodernism and RE closer by expositing Plantinga's compatibility with non-nihilistic postmodernism and Wolterstorff's postmodern RE. I argue that Wolterstorff provides a more dynamic picture of knowledge because he attends to its historical contingency and situatedness. In this way, Wolterstorff provides a more realistic picture of the standard knower as compared to the ideal knower of Plantinga without creating any opposition between the two. And, like Smith, Wolterstorff builds his notion of situated rationality on a situated anthropology.

After these expositions of RE, the chapter begins the constructive work by identifying areas of convergence, assist, and critique in order to augment Smith's postmodern epistemology with RE in a way that blends without distorting their unique voices. In such a way, while corrections are made of Smith and RE is utilized in new ways, the mashup epistemology should neither look foreign nor contradictory to the original voices.

The final chapter summarizes the work by offering seven succinct characteristics of my "Smithian" postmodern Christian epistemology and comments on its postmodern and Christian characteristics. The descriptions are brief since much of the details are offered throughout the book. If readers are suspicious about the possibility of a Christian epistemology being compatible with postmodernism, reading the final chapter to get a sense of the overall view may be helpful.

NOTES

1. A CCK is one who has inhabited two or more cultures for a significant period during his/her developmental years. See David C. Pollock, Ruth E. Van Reken, and Michael V. Pollock, *Third Culture Kids: Growing Up Among Worlds*, 3rd ed. (Boston: Nicholas Brealey Publishing, 2009), 43. I do not mean that my identity is hybrid only due to my third culture location. All identity is hybrid, multifaceted, and dynamic. Being a CCK highlighted my hybridity. See Jeannine Hill Fletcher, *Monopoly on Salvation?: A Feminist Approach to Religious Pluralism* (New York: Continuum, 2005), 82–101.

2. John M. Frame, "Presuppositional Apologetics," in *Five Views on Apologetics*, ed. Stanley N. Gundry and Steven B. Cowan (Grand Rapids: Zondervan, 2000), 207–31 (217).

3. James K. A. Smith is a presuppositionalist for these reasons. See James K. A. Smith, *Introducing Radical Orthodoxy: Mapping a Post-Secular Theology* (Grand Rapids: Baker Academic, 2004), 179–82. While agreeing with much of Van Til's epistemology, Albert Haig incisively argues that the metaphysics of Van Tillian presuppositionalism leads to univocal knowledge of creation despite Van Til's theory of analogy. See Albert Haig, "Modernity, 'Radical Orthodoxy,' and Cornelius Van Til: A Journey of Rediscovery of Participatory Theism," *Colloquium* 47, no. 2 (November 2015): 257–73.

4. It is standard practice for Pentecostal scholars to use "lowercase p" pentecostalism to refer to the multifaceted global movement. Wolfgang Vondey argues that "capital P" Pentecostalism can refer to the unity and diversity of Pentecostalism just as the designations of Catholicism and Lutheranism can refer to the unity and diversity within each tradition. See Wolfgang Vondey, *Beyond Pentecostalism: The Crisis of Global Christianity and the Renewal of the Theological Agenda* (Grand Rapids: Eerdmans Publishing Company, 2010), 11–12.

5. Glocalization of Pentecostalism indicates the interdependent relationship between global Pentecostalism and its countless local manifestations. Wolfgang Vondey, *Pentecostalism: A Guide for the Perplexed* (New York: Bloomsbury T&T Clark, 2013), 25–27.

6. Simo Frestadius's work on Pentecostal epistemology can be considered as following Smith's invitation even if Frestadius does not use Smith as one of his main interlocutors. Interestingly, he interacts with another Reformed epistemologist, William Alston. See Simo Frestadius, *Pentecostal Rationality: Epistemology and Theological Hermeneutics in the Foursquare Tradition* (London: T&T Clark, 2020).

7. Quoted by Philip Blosser, "God among the Philosophers," *New Oxford Review* 66, no. 9 (October 1999): 39–42 (39).

8. James K. A. Smith, *On the Road with Saint Augustine: A Real-World Spirituality for Restless Hearts* (Grand Rapids: Brazos Press, 2019), 34.

9. Jerry H. Gill, *Deep Postmodernism: Whitehead, Wittgenstein, Merleau-Ponty, and Polanyi* (Amherst: Humanity Books, 2010), 10.

10. Neal DeRoo, "Introduction," in *The Logic of Incarnation: James K. A. Smith's Critique of Postmodern Religion*, ed. Neal DeRoo and Brian Lightbody (Eugene: Wipf & Stock, 2009), xv–xxvii (xv).

11. Martin E. Marty, "James K.A. Smith's 'Cultural Liturgies,'" *Sightings*, November 12, 2018, https://divinity.uchicago.edu/sightings/articles/james-ka-smiths-cultural-liturgies.

12. Unsurprisingly, Smith reveals his Reformed influence in proposing Pentecostal philosophy as a confessional philosophy. J. Aaron Simmons, "Prospects for Pentecostal Philosophy: Assessing the Challenges and Envisioning the Opportunities," *Pneuma* 42, no. 2 (2020): 175–200 (185–87).

13. James K. A. Smith, *Thinking in Tongues: Pentecostal Contributions to Christian Philosophy* (Grand Rapids: Eerdmans Publishing Company, 2010), 4–6.

14. Simmons, "Prospects for Pentecostal Philosophy," 190–91.
15. Simmons, 185–89.
16. J. Aaron Simmons, "Introduction: The Dialogical Promise of Mashup Philosophy of Religion," *The Journal for Cultural and Religious Theory* 14, no. 2 (2015): 204–10 (205).
17. Using L. William Oliverio Jr.'s typology, this work falls under the umbrella of ecumenical Pentecostal hermeneutics because it not only draws contextually from the Pentecostal well but also from the Reformed tradition in the construction of a postmodern Christian epistemology. See L. William Oliverio Jr., "Theological Hermeneutics: Understanding the World in the Encounter with God," in *The Routledge Handbook of Pentecostal Theology*, ed. Wolfgang Vondey (New York: Routledge, 2020), 140–51.
18. See Alvin Plantinga, *Warranted Christian Belief* (New York: Oxford University Press, 2000), 424.
19. Plantinga, 437.
20. Merold Westphal, *Overcoming Onto-Theology: Toward a Postmodern Christian Faith* (New York: Fordham University Press, 2001), xi.
21. Merold Westphal, "Must Phenomenology and Theology Make Two?: A Response to Trakakis and Simmons," *The Heythrop Journal* 55, no. 4 (2014): 711–17 (711).
22. See James K. A. Smith, *Who's Afraid of Relativism?: Community, Contingency, and Creaturehood* (Grand Rapids: Baker Academic, 2014).
23. Richard B. Davis and Paul Franks, "Against a Postmodern Pentecostal Epistemology," *Philosophia Christi* 15, no. 2 (2013): 129–45.
24. Smith, *Thinking in Tongues*, 67n49.
25. See Anthony Quinton, "Continental Philosophy," in *The Oxford Companion to Philosophy*, ed. Ted Honderich (New York: Oxford University Press, 1995), 161–63.
26. His *Desiring the Kingdom* and *You Are What You Love* have won multiple book awards, such as the 2010 and 2017 *Christianity Today* book awards and the World Guild 2010 Canadian Christian writing award.
27. See Linda T. Zagzebski, *On Epistemology* (Belmont: Wadsworth Cengage Learning, 2009), 5; and Dru Johnson, *Biblical Knowing: A Scriptural Epistemology of Error* (Eugene: Cascade Books, 2013), 152–53.
28. Thus, Smith's embodied epistemology helps us better recognize how disability can initiate different modes of understanding. See Benjamin T. Conner, *Disabling Mission, Enabling Witness: Exploring Missiology through the Lens of Disability Studies* (Downers Grove: IVP Academic, 2018), 97.
29. Justo L. González, *The Mestizo Augustine: A Theologian between Two Cultures* (Downers Grove: IVP Academic, 2016), 15–18.

Part 1

SMITH'S PENTECOSTAL EPISTEMOLOGY

Chapter 1

Pentecostal Spirituality and Postmodernism

INTRODUCTION

Smith argues that embedded within Pentecostalism is a particular epistemology, a knowing-otherwise, that goes against the grain of the field of epistemology's propositional-mania. Without rejecting propositional belief as such, he argues that humans primarily know the world through a pretheoretical understanding that is more narrative and affective than propositional and cognitive. Expositing and analyzing this epistemology requires understanding the motivation and inspiration behind it. Since Smith identifies this epistemology as Pentecostal and postmodern, this chapter provides a survey of Pentecostalism as a spirituality and its worldview, and presents non-nihilistic postmodernism as the trajectory of Smith's own self-understanding.

PENTECOSTALISM AND SPIRITUALITY

True to his Pentecostal identity, Smith does not construct his epistemology upon abstract notions such as justification or warrant. As I explain later, Pentecostalism is not primarily a doctrinal movement. It is fundamentally a pneumatologically oriented, experiential spirituality motivated by the reality of Pentecost centered on Jesus. What makes an idea or act Pentecostal is this experiential ground. Smith recognizes that Pentecostal epistemology must not begin from an abstract idea but from this experiential ground. Therefore, understanding Smith's Pentecostal epistemology requires proper understanding of Pentecostalism.

Past studies of classical Pentecostalism tended to focus its analysis on doctrines with a methodology distinctly geared toward the exposition of doctrine.[1] However, Pentecostalism arose as "a thorough-going reformation of doctrine"[2] through what Amos Yong, Keith Warrington, Byron Klaus, and Wolfgang Vondey call Pentecostalism's heartbeat or hallmark: an experiential encounter with Christ through the Holy Spirit.[3] This emphasis on experience renders any essentialist view of Pentecostalism based on inadequate fundamental doctrines. Even though the doctrines of Spirit baptism and *glossolalia* are prominent for many classical Pentecostals, the launching of the Azusa Street Revival was realized through the experiential encounter with the Spirit. For Pentecostals, not only does experience precede theology, the pneumatological experience of Christ is "the heartbeat of development of doctrine."[4]

Importantly, due to its diverse global manifestations, there is wide acknowledgment that Pentecostalism is not a monolithic movement. Proper understanding of Pentecostalism requires an understanding of its specific (g)local manifestations. William Kay argues that the sheer number of Pentecostals in the majority world indicates the need for postcolonial definitions of Pentecostalism that rejects the privileged definitional normativity assumed by North American classical Pentecostals.[5] This need is made more acute by the emerging global voices that are challenging the doctrinal identification of Pentecostalism.[6]

That there can be no monolithic definition of Pentecostalism due to its variegated global expressions is evident. Global Pentecostalism demonstrates its flexibility, adaptability, and pragmatics by its creative enculturation in diverse settings. As Harvey Cox notes, "[Pentecostalism] was a religion made to travel, and it seemed to lose nothing in the translation."[7] The "lack of a fixed substance . . . its liquidity" aids Pentecostalism's successful global growth.[8] For Michael McClymond, this constant change and adaptation render the project of defining Pentecostalism difficult.[9] Therefore, Allan Anderson suggests that Pentecostalism(s) is a more accurate designator in the current pluralistic global context.[10]

With the difficulty of capturing the essence of Pentecostalism, Anderson wisely employs the Wittgensteinian idea of family resemblance to capture an imprecise but meaningful description of Pentecostalism. Family resemblance, for Wittgenstein, is not an essentialist concept. Instead, it describes similarities that overlap between varying forms of life.[11] For Anderson, this resemblance is Pentecostalism's emphasis on the works of the Holy Spirit.[12] Relatedly, the heartbeat of Pentecostalism, the personal, experiential encounter of the Spirit of God, is the best candidate to act as the central family resemblance of Pentecostalism. This does not mean that this experience of pneumatological encounter is essentialist or universal. Not only are the ways Pentecostals understand, seek, and experience the Spirit different, but experience is always already mediated, such as through Scripture, tradition, and reason.[13] Universal experience is impossible and neither is universal pneumatic encounter.

That the central family resemblance is experiential stresses that Pentecostalism cannot be understood primarily in doctrinal terms. Pentecostal scholars have thus argued that Pentecostalism must be understood as a spirituality.[14] And inasmuch as pneumatological encounter is embodied in Pentecostal praxis, Pentecostalism is an embodied spirituality. The picture of Pentecostalism as a hyper-spiritual and gnostic movement in popular lore is a caricature.

Spirituality

What, then, is spirituality? The Pentecostal theologian Russell Spittler defines spirituality as "a cluster of acts and sentiments that are informed by the beliefs and values that characterize a specific religious community" and notes the flexibility of the term due to the variety of ways that it can be expressed, unlike doctrine, which is more rigid by nature.[15] Likewise, Daniel Albrecht recognizes that embodied and affective sensibilities accompany Pentecostal rituals, and these sensibilities "act as both 'filters' through which worshipers experience and express their rites."[16] Alister McGrath notes that Christian spirituality is relational, existential, and pragmatic, which are related to belief, but not reduced to it.[17] According to Don Baker, spirituality includes attitudes and actions.[18] These definitions and descriptions indicate the centrality of embodiment in spirituality.

David Perrin provides a fourfold working definition of spirituality. First, humans have a spiritual nature, a fundamental capacity for immanence, which is the search of and engaging in creative expressions, meaning, values, and purpose through a variety of means. Second, humans have a capacity for transcendence. This is the awareness that reality is greater than one's life, which acts as the inner drive connecting persons to others, to care for the world at large in interdependence.[19] Third, Perrin connects spirituality with pretheoretical lived experience. Spirituality is a way of life that includes meaningful "attitudes, practices, rituals, and behaviors" in everyday existence. As a unified experience, it is not reduced to one area, such as doctrinal belief or noncognitive rituals. Any meaningful commitment, even those unconnected to divinity, has the potential to be part of spirituality. Finally, spirituality includes the theoretical study of itself. Spirituality is a way of life that must include theoretical reflection on the practices of spirituality, whether for personal improvement or academic inquiry.[20] These four features—capacity for immanence, capacity for transcendence, pretheoretical lived existence, and theoretical activity—constitute Perrin's holistic working definition of spirituality. They exemplify "the integration of all aspects of life in a unified whole."[21]

Pentecostal Spirituality

Steven Land's *Pentecostal Spirituality* is a seminal work that established Pentecostalism as a spirituality revolving around distinctive apocalyptic affections that act as the integrating core for beliefs and actions through which they are evoked and expressed. Land grounds this integrative spirituality in the Trinity, especially through the Holy Spirit who, as the bond of love, acts as the "agent of mutuality and interrelatedness in the Trinity and the church."[22] This integrative relationship between belief, affect, and practice is what John Frame calls triperspectival, according to which each aspect acts as a perspective that is integrated in the others. It is a perichoretic model that eschews balance for integration. That is, to fully and correctly understand the entirety of the relationship (i.e., Pentecostal spirituality) between the three aspects, each perspective must be understood in its relationship with the other two perspectives. While each can be highlighted and can play more prominent roles in particular contexts, ultimately, all three are "equally ultimate, equally important."[23]

This integrated relationship is evident in Land's understanding of theology as embodied and experiential, beginning from prayer, rather than primarily in rationalistic terms. Theology is second-order reflection on Pentecostal doxology that focuses on experience of the Holy Spirit and is only made possible by God first addressing the people through prayer.[24] "Theology begins in the prayerful response of persons to God."[25] The importance of this divine-human relationship in doxology is highlighted by Kevin Ranaghan who states that Pentecostal theology changed in order to keep up with developments in public worship.[26] Pentecostal belief (i.e., theology) thus is not primarily didactic, systematic, or propositional. It is an engagement of the mind evoked by an apocalyptic passion for the Kingdom of God due to having encountered the risen Lord. Through this encounter, the Holy Spirit drives and guides Pentecostals in their everyday participation in the divine life.

This lived theology is motivated by the experiential soteriology of Pentecostals that view salvation less in terms of removal of guilt and more in terms of participation in the triune life in Jesus through the Holy Spirit.[27] Whereas the Reformed soteriology of expiation and propitiation gives a static sense of one's standing with God and primarily promotes a noetic understanding of one's relationship with God, the more eastern soteriological understanding of participation recruits the whole person—mind, soul, and act—to now live out her relationship with God and God's creation. Real knowledge of God, therefore, engages the whole person. Knowledge of God cannot be reductively noetic. Knowledge of God is ultimately obedient knowledge, "to be in a right relation, to walk in the light and in the Spirit."[28] Pentecostal spirituality is aimed toward obedient knowledge in its emphasis on encounter.

For Pentecostals do not desire to seek mere encounter but desire transformation through the encounter in relationship with the Spirit.[29] The knowledge of the Spirit is obedient, transformative knowledge. Obedient knowledge is thus participatory knowledge, one that recruits the whole person: mind, soul, and body. This interplay between the distinctive beliefs, affections, and actions marks the character of Pentecostal spirituality.

Smith's descriptions of Pentecostalism as "an embodied set of practices and disciplines that implicitly 'carry' a worldview or social imaginary"[30] and "an affective constellation of practices and embodied 'rituals'"[31] resemble these definitions and likewise emphasize the importance of embodiment for spirituality. However, even though he utilizes Land's understanding of Pentecostalism as spirituality, unlike Land's triperspectival integration of *beliefs* in affections and actions, within Smith's understanding of Pentecostal spirituality is a tendency to overemphasize embodiment to the detriment of the noetic. In his Pentecostal philosophical methodology, Smith states that he will "read" the practices of Pentecostalism rather than its texts (theology) for his philosophical constructions. In this way, when he states that "Pentecostalism is not first and foremost a doctrinal or intellectual tradition,"[32] the distinctive Pentecostal beliefs do not even seem to hold secondary place in the construction. Rather, Smith seems wholly unconcerned with the ratiocinative elements of Pentecostal spirituality. But without the beliefs, how can Pentecostal spirituality remain Pentecostal?

Peter Neumann argues that Pentecostal spirituality stands in contrast to cerebrally oriented Christian spiritualities.[33] However, this argument ignores other spiritualities that are not cerebrally oriented. Pentecostal spirituality may be unique in its contents and praxis that push the bounds of the "dominant practices of the Christian tradition(s),"[34] but it is like other affective and experiential spiritualities. For example, Roger Olson's description of pietism's key characteristics resemble the descriptions of spirituality. Pietism is not cerebrally oriented but primarily experiential, relational, and devotional.[35] Daniel Castelo signals the similarity between Pentecostal spirituality and spirituality-like strands of Christianity by stating that classical Pentecostal spirituality is "a modern instantiation of the mystical stream of Christianity . . ., [and is] *a mystical tradition of the church catholic.*"[36] Harvey Cox broadens this similarity by pointing to humanity's primal spirituality, arguing that Pentecostalism's success is partly attributable to its ability to aid persons recover their primal spirituality. This primal spirituality is related to the *imago Dei* that deep cry for meaning and purpose that identifies humans as *homo religious.*[37] Primal spirituality thus identifies the shared universal sense of religiousness in humanity. Although Peter Althouse rightly criticizes Cox's modernist sense of universal religiosity that seemingly subsumes the qualitative distinctiveness of Pentecostal experience—and the distinctiveness of all religious experiences—it is not particular experiences, such as encounter with the Spirit, that mark spirituality as such.[38] Rather, the phenomenology of embodiment is a core mark of spirituality.

Given Smith's methodology of constructing his Pentecostal epistemology on its spirituality, this lack of distinction raises questions about the integrity of Smith's epistemology as Pentecostal. Although the loss of distinction does not invalidate his epistemology, the need for Pentecostalism for his epistemology is questioned. As I will argue later, Smith's epistemology is more appropriately a postmodern epistemology. While helpful for illustrating the contours of this postmodern epistemology, Pentecostalism is unnecessary for its construction. However, before investigating this issue more fully, the reasons why Smith understands his epistemology to be Pentecostal need to be identified. The answer lies in his Pentecostal worldview.

WORLDVIEW

Smith understands worldview in two senses. In one sense, rather than beliefs, it is the embodied doxological practices of Pentecostal spirituality that always already evoke a tacit, affective understanding or passional orientation whose contents represent the Pentecostal worldview. Worldview is a tacit understanding that affectively governs both pretheoretical and theoretical interpretation of and engagement with reality.[39] He draws this view from James Olthuis's definition of worldview, according to which a worldview is a "framework or set of fundamental beliefs through which we view the world and our calling and future in it."[40] As a fundamental framework, it acts as a comprehensive, pretheoretical, hermeneutical filter for meaning-making. Because it is pretheoretical, the beliefs are not cognitive, but imaginative, and they operate at the level of affections rather than thinking. More precisely, they operate prior to thought. Due to this emphasis on the affective, Smith considers Charles Taylor's social imaginary and Amos Yong's pneumatological imagination as apt terms to describe worldview.[41]

In another sense, Smith utilizes the term negatively because he considers the term to be burdened with cognitive bias. Smith distinguishes between worldview as a belief system and the more primordial, affective mode of being attuned to the world. While he does not reject worldview talk, Smith criticizes his own Reformed tradition for intellectualizing the concept.[42] The Reformed concept of worldview is important for bringing faith and reason closer together by demonstrating the *pistic* nature of ultimate beliefs, and Smith lauds the concept for challenging the reductionistic priority of ratiocination assumed by Cartesian anthropology. Nevertheless, the Reformed emphasis on belief is similar to Descartes's disembodied picture of "person-as-thinker" and individualizes faith by neglecting the role of the very material body of Christ, the church, in the life of faith. Thus, he states, "[I]f I bump into a 'thinking thing' and a 'believing thing' on the street, I don't think I'd notice much difference."[43] Against this priority of the cognitive, Smith presents an Augustinian anthropology that moves the centrality of human being from the mind to the heart. It is love, not thinking, that fundamentally orients humans.[44] Embodied, affective creatures primarily feel their way through the world.[45] The priority of the affective and imaginary is highlighted here once again. Smith's identification of worldview with the cognitive in *Desiring the Kingdom* reveals Smith's discomfort with the term in *Thinking in Tongues*, as he often surrounds the term with quotation marks in the latter work. For Smith, retaining the term "worldview" requires redefining it as affective, imaginary understanding that resides at a level deeper than cognitive beliefs.

Smith's misgivings about cognitive notions of worldview are not idiosyncratic. In his magisterial work on worldview, David Naugle highlights the deeply affective nature of worldview, arguing that it is rooted in the heart. He establishes this view on the central role the heart plays in the *imago Dei* as testified in Scripture. Both Testaments continually describe "the 'heart' as the central, defining element of the human person."[46] Thus, Naugle proclaims that "human existence proceeds 'kardioptically' on the basis of a vision of the heart."[47] As the root of personhood, the heart acts as the foundation and guide for pretheoretical believing and thinking. Despite Smith's criticism of the Reformed notion of worldview, Naugle, who is also Reformed, does not fall trap to the '"person-as-(cognitive)believer" anthropology. Instead, consistently following the Reformed emphasis on the myth of religious neutrality, Naugle argues that people are fundamentally worshipers, highlighting the innate affective longings that drive human existence.[48] Thus, even though neither Naugle nor Smith engage each other in their works, their views on worldview parallel each other.

Another Reformed scholar who has made an important contribution to worldview studies is James Sire. Like Smith and Naugle, he defines worldview as "a commitment, a fundamental orientation of the heart."[49] Worldview is not a set of propositional beliefs. It is utterly pretheoretical and presuppositional. That is, it is the grid through which one believes or thinks, and one cannot ultimately prove it even though she can think about it and critique it. It is a commitment that acts as the bedrock of one's beliefs.[50] However, unlike Smith who defines persons and their worldviews ultimately as affective, Sire argues that the biblical notion of the heart encompasses the intellect. Nevertheless, while this difference may seem to be a point of departure from Smith, they are similar in their view that worldviews direct the conscious mind and include an affective element even if they disagree on the role of the affections.[51]

Pentecostal Worldview

Given the embodied and affective root of worldview, it is unsurprising that Smith's mission to identify a Pentecostal worldview leads him to the ethnographic endeavor of investigating Pentecostalism's embodied doxological practices. Because persons are fundamentally oriented by their hearts, the proper method of investigation cannot chiefly involve the examination of doctrines. Following Naugle, if humans are *homo adorans*, the search for a worldview must, in the end, involve the investigation of embodied worship.[52] Thus, from investigating Pentecostal doxological practices, Smith identifies five elements of Pentecostal worldview: (1) a radical openness to God; (2) an enchanted theology of creation; (3) a nondualistic affirmation of embodiment and materiality; (4) an affective, narrative epistemology; and (5) an eschatological orientation to mission and justice.[53]

Lest one retorts that these elements are cognitive and not affective, Smith states that these five elements are pretheoretical intuitions or tacit, affective understanding. It is only by making explicit the implicit that one can propositionally identify these elements, and one should not confuse these intuitions with their propositionalized forms. Thus, he makes clear that their articulation "is *not* a requirement for absorbing the understanding."[54]

Immediately relevant to this work is the fourth element of Pentecostal worldview, affective, narrative epistemology (henceforth, narrative, affective knowledge, or NAK), according to which the primary and irreducible mode of knowledge is not cognitive but affectively and narratively pretheoretical. Pentecostal spirituality points to the primacy of tacit, embodied knowledge over against cognitive, propositional belief that traffics in terms of justification or warrant. Besides highlighting this alternative epistemology for consideration, NAK acts as a performative example of the worldview itself since the five elements of a Pentecostal worldview in their unarticulated forms are themselves narrative, affective understandings. The five elements point to the reality of NAK and are themselves NAK. For example, Pentecostalism's radical openness to God is not primarily a doctrinal belief but more fundamentally a posture or lived, imaginative possibility—pneumatological imagination to use Yong's terminology—that one understands "in her bones."

The reason why Smith considers his epistemology as Pentecostal is because he sees it rooted in the embodied doxological practices of Pentecostalism. However, before expositing and examining Smith's Pentecostal epistemology, the exposition of modernity and postmodernity is needed. This exposition is required to understand why Smith's Pentecostal epistemology is considered postmodern, and postmodernism cannot be understood apart from modernity. The next section thus describes modernity and postmodernity in ways that are consistent with Smith's understanding.

POSTMODERNISM

Postmodernism is a notoriously difficult and slippery concept.[55] It is characterized by the denial of characterization because any essentialist and universal definition is self-defeating.[56] Postmodernism lacks unified doctrines, and some of its major representative figures "indignantly deny membership."[57] J. Wentzel van Huyssteen considers postmodernism as "more of a cultural attitude and a point of view . . . [that escapes] any and all linear characterizations," lacking any "doctrinal platform that might lend itself to some kind of systematic survey."[58] Kevin Vanhoozer and Myron Penner recognize postmodernism's theoretical dimensions but describe it chiefly as a "condition," "mood," "world-and-life view," "ethos," intellectual "attitude," and a *Zeitgeist*.[59] One can also distinguish between postmodernism as a philosophical outlook and postmodernity as a cultural phenomenon.[60]

According to Lloyd Spencer, the question of meaning is at the heart of the debate of postmodernism and judges the attempts at defining postmodernism as a red herring. The combative deployment of terms and definitions by many of its adherents contributes to the seemingly impossible task of defining postmodernism.[61] However, if simple definition is an impossibility, this project seems destined to fail.

Given these constraints, utilizing Wittgenstein's notion of family resembles is once again helpful because it avoids essentialist definitions.[62] The strength of this notion is that it allows for generalization of both modernity and postmodernity and makes understanding possible, and such a generalization is necessary in order to avoid radical nominalism that would make speaking about postmodernism impossible.[63] Importantly, it recognizes differences within postmodernism. Like Pentecostalisms, it is more appropriate to speak about postmodernisms. One member does not make a family, and the relativistic ontological and epistemological anti-realism does not get to represent all postmodernisms even if all the boys in the playground wants to pick him first. With resemblances, the need for skillful know-how is evident for the discernment of these resemblances in order to recognize similarities without conflating each particularity into a uniform whole. There is thus an aesthetics to identifying similarities and differences.

My presentation of postmodernism is this attempt to describe one member that represents the situated, hermeneutic, and pragmatic features of Smith's postmodern epistemology. Importantly, Smith's own professed postliberalization must be taken seriously. Postliberalism's influence was not a later development but one that existed as early as his first monograph. The pragmatics of knowledge and language also appear in his first monograph on Radical Orthodoxy, *Speech and Theology*, that some consider belonging under the postliberal umbrella.[64] While the exposition of postliberalism will come later, I have chosen Jean-François Lyotard and Michael Polanyi as representatives to describe Smith's postmodernism because their epistemologies are consonant with the linguistic pragmatism of postliberalism. Other prominent figures of postmodernism, such as Jacques Derrida and Michel Foucault, are represented in chapter 4 in the exposition of Smith's appropriation of their thoughts.

Postmodernism in Relation to Modernism

Postmodernism and modernism are two peas in a pod. That is, postmodernism is codependent on modernism.[65] Peter Leithart similarly argues that postmodernism is an intensification, inversion, and unmasking of modernity, arising as a protest against modernity's mythic claim to control, liberation, and progress.[66] Likewise, Lloyd Spencer describes postmodernism as a "variant of modernism which has given up hope of freeing itself from the ravages of modernity or of mastering the forces unleashed by modernity."[67] In this way, a postmodern person is one who has experienced modernity and is passing through it, even living in tension with it in factical experience.

David Tracy argues that modernity exists in multiple forms and that early modernity shares with postmodernity a culture of plurality and fragmentation. Not until the onset of Enlightenment modernity did totality come to repress difference in the name of neutrality and universality. Postmodern plurality existed within early modernism, and

> most forms of postmodernity are explosions of once-forgotten, marginalized, and repressed realities in Enlightenment modernity: the other, the different . . . , the fragments that disallow any totality system by demanding attention to the other, especially the different and the marginal other.[68]

The next section exposits the forms of modernism and postmodernism that are relevant to Smith's epistemology. The first section exposits Enlightenment rationalism since Smith's postmodernism is a reaction against it. The representatives of postmodernism in the next section, Non-Nihilistic Postmodernism, are chosen for their emphasis on the situated hermeneutical nature of know-how and, especially for Polanyi, the realism that undergirds such hermeneutic, personal, pragmatic knowledge.

Enlightenment Modernism

According to Albert Borgmann, modernism burst onto the scene against the horizon of the Middle Age's fading glory. Premodernity ended at the hands of Christopher Columbus, Nicholas Copernicus, and Martin Luther, as they upturned its "locally bounded, cosmically centered, and divinely constituted world" through discovering the "new" world, the cosmic decentering of geocentrism, and the usurping of the authority of the Catholic Church for the authority of Scripture and its reader.[69]

At the heels of these three undertakers were the three progenitors of modernism, Francis Bacon, René Descartes, and John Locke, who proclaimed a new "solid fundament."[70] Bacon preached the domination of nature for human progress, Descartes's radical doubt led to individual thought as the only certain epistemic foundation, and Locke uplifted individual autonomy. For Borgmann, modernism is the reification of their message, "The fusion of the domination of nature with the primacy of method and the sovereignty of the individual."[71]

Borgmann warns of the consequences of this seemingly liberating message of human autonomy. With the Enlightenment celebration of reason's liberation against the stifling control of authority and tradition came modernism's relentless thirst for conquest. Three features characterize modernism's project of conquest, each corresponding with the project of the three men: (1) aggressive realism with its disregard for anything or anyone that gets in its way; (2) methodical universalism and its ordering of the Baconian conquest through the rules of abstraction, dissection, reconstruction, and control; and (3) individualism with the dissolution of communal ties in the creation of public and private realms.[72] However, modernism is fading away in the present as people are questioning the social, intellectual, and economic consequences that arise from such conquest, universalism, and autonomy.[73]

For Merold Westphal, modernism is more than a certain system or framework. It is a philosophical attitude and faith in scientific, objective reason and method.[74] This faith in foundational reason marks the fundamental characteristic of Enlightenment modernism.[75] The legitimacy of inquiry rests on the indubitable epistemic foundation that guarantees epistemic neutrality. Both empiricism and rationalism—two philosophical camps many view as rivals—share a common Cartesian root. John Thiel remarks,

> Both empiricists and idealists assumed that philosophy is largely an exercise in epistemology. Both assumed that epistemological explanation involves naming the foundations of knowing as a requisite, first step in the philosophical task. Both assumed that the foundations of knowing, however chthonic or ethereal, are located in the human mind, thus establishing the mind's authority for evaluating or even constituting the noetic world. With regard to these shared assumptions, the empiricists and idealists comprise a single epistemological tradition which, in one way or another, remains committed to the orientations of philosophical method and inquiry proposed by Descartes.[76]

This Cartesian foundation transcends all situated contexts. Descartes's revolutionary method transferred authority from traditional institutions, including Scripture, to the individual knowing subject. This epistemology reimagined human beings as *res cogitans*, subsuming all knowledge and metaphysics under the certainty guaranteed by the *cogito*, the Archimedean point of all knowledge.[77] Neutral, objective reason eschews the particular and subjective as prejudiced and considers the "unenlightened" past with smugness.[78] "From Descartes's time, the ideal of human knowledge focused on the general, the universal, the timeless, the theoretical—in contrast to the local, the particular, the timely, the practical."[79] Unsurprisingly, many consider the natural sciences, with their Baconian-Cartesian heritage, as the pristine methodological conduit for achieving objective knowledge.

The modern person is *homo autonomous*, whose unbound rational capabilities allow for progress and mastery over the world.[80] Individual autonomy is thus a prominent thesis.[81] Smith agrees with this picture, describing the modern "persons as 'thinking things,' autonomous rational agent, transcendental logical egos, disembodied centers of cognitive perception."[82] Calvin Schrag describes this reductionistic, modern subject as

> an abstracted, insular knowing subject, severed from the context and contingencies out of which knowledge of self and knowledge of the world arise. The subject as abstracted epistemological pivot, as atemporal zero-point origin of cognition, is wrested from the lived-experiences of a speaking and narrating self that always already understands itself in its speech and in its narration.[83]

Because it assumes the actuality and authority of context-less, objective reason, modernity views religious belief as ignorant and irrational and seeks to liberate people from religion.[84] Enlightenment epistemology plays the role of emancipator of reason from other authorities. Christian authority, stemming from God, Scripture, and the church, gave way to the deistic God, which acted as mere ground and explanation of nature for the newly emancipated humanity of secularism.[85]

Modernism's "epistemological turn" prioritizes epistemology over ontology.[86] Unlike premodernity's metaphysical turn from Greek *mythos* to rational *logos* that maintained reason's relationship with external reality, modernity's epistemological turn detached from this mutually informing relationship between ontology and epistemology. The priority and limits of epistemology dictate the metaphysical enterprise. Reason plays arbiter for the limits of knowledge, while, at the same time, accepting the Herculean ability of the mind to make pronouncements of universal validity.[87] Succinctly put, Enlightenment modernism is a totalizing system and a faith in a disembodied, individual, autonomous, universal, objective, atemporal, rational subject as "the final arbiter of truth."[88]

Non-nihilistic Postmodernism

If modernism places faith in the possibility of pure objective reason to grasp truth, then postmodernism names the loss of this faith.[89] Westphal clarifies what this loss of faith entails by describing the generic postmodern thesis that "the truth is that there is no Truth."[90] "Truth," as opposed to truth, is the perfectly known. "Truth" is the attainment of knowledge from God's perspective.[91] "Truth" is univocal with divine knowledge that overcomes human fallibility and situatedness. Postmoderns, on the other hand, accept the inaccessibility of any putative "view from nowhere." "Postmodernity is the triumph of situatedness."[92] Such situated perspectivism is neither relativist nor skeptical; truth without Truth is still attainable.[93]

A postmodernism that replaces (objective, absolute) Truth for (creaturely, perspectival) truth is cautious of the limits of alethic claims due to the situated and finite conditions of human existence without dispensing of truth. Situatedness in given cultural and linguistic contexts dictates the impossibility of achieving total or pure objective knowledge. This loss of transcendent knowledge renders the neutrality thesis null and void, refuting the Platonic confidence of reason's ability to arrive at absolute truth. Human knowledge is always already committed and interpretive, and its perspectives are inherited from and passed down through traditions. As William Placher argues, even particular sense-data are organized through conceptual schemes that one learns from at a very early age.[94] This situatedness thus motivates postmodernism's hermeneutics of finitude and suspicion against claims to absolute truth.[95] The next section exposits the thoughts of Lyotard and Polanyi as representatives of this non-nihilistic postmodernism.

Jean-François Lyotard: Against Metanarratives

Lyotard contends famously that the understanding of knowledge itself is altered as societies transition into the postmodern age. Taking scientific knowledge as the object of his investigation and arguing against neutral reason, Lyotard argues that postmodernism unveils science as just another form of discourse that traffics in language games, dethroning its privileged claims as the highest form of discourse.[96] The postmodern condition—which he describes in extreme simplicity as "incredulity toward metanarratives"—is a crisis of narratives that is changing the rules for vast areas of study, encompassing the humanities and the sciences.[97] Against the belief in one neutral, overarching story, there exist multiple, competing stories. The postmodern condition is the story of intellectual tribalism that reveals the modern notion of global community as a myth.

For Lyotard, language is the "minimum relation required for society to exist."[98] At the moment of naming, a newborn enters the language game of her particular society. Language is not only the medium of a social bond; it is the social bond.[99] Lyotard appropriates Wittgenstein's notion of language games to describe the variegated phenomena of these vast communities of knowledge: "There are many language games—a heterogeneity of elements. They only give rise to institutions in patches—local determinism."[100] Scientific knowledge cannot bring unity to these various language games, for it is not an overarching, neutral language game that transcends and adjudicates all other language games. Scientific knowledge is itself a particular language game with its own particular rules. Lyotard reduces the supposed universality and neutrality of scientific knowledge to particularity and reveals the metanarrativity of scientific discourse as a myth. "The grand narrative has lost its credibility."[101] Science can no longer claim to be the grand arbiter of all truth because it, too, has lost its claim to neutrality.

Legitimation is central to Lyotard's understanding of metanarrative, and its misunderstanding often leads to an incredulity against postmodernism's incredulity toward metanarratives, as if the rejection of metanarratives is the rejection of ultimate and cosmic narratives or worldviews about reality.[102] The equating of metanarrative with ultimate narrative, an overarching story, is a misunderstanding of Lyotard's terminology.[103] Many local stories contain overarching stories that make universal and ultimate claims. Such stories are not metanarratives according to Lyotard's definition. The difference between a metanarrative and an overarching narrative is the latter's acknowledgment of its own narrative, *pistic* nature; the issue is not the scope, but epistemic neutrality. The misunderstanding of this definition of metanarrative is a reason why postmodernism is identified with relativism or radical locality.

How does metanarrative commit itself to epistemic neutrality? The answer is legitimation. Expounding on the features of language games, Lyotard writes, "[Language game's] rules do not carry within themselves their own legitimation, but are the object of a contract, explicit or not, between players (which is not to say that the players invent the rules)."[104] A metanarrative claims legitimation through neutral proofs and argumentation. Lyotard contrasts this type of legitimation from the auto-legitimation of oral traditions. In oral traditions, a narrator's authority resides in the narrator's previous position as hearer; faithful hearing transfers legitimate authority for faithful transmission. Within storytelling there is the self-legitimating "pragmatics of its own transmission."[105] Scientific knowledge denies such authority to narrative knowledge and self-legitimation, classifying any claims to knowledge without proof or argumentation as "savage, primitive, underdeveloped, backward, alienated, composed of opinions, customs, authority, prejudice, ignorance, [and] ideology."[106] Scientific knowledge claims for itself the ability to "*legitimate* [its] story and its claims *by an appeal to universal Reason.*" (edited by Myron B. Penner)[107] Postmodernism unmasks scientific knowledge as another narratival language game with its own pragmatic rules of legitimation.[108]

Commenting on the pragmatics of narrative knowledge, Lyotard argues that narrative knowledge is irreducible to denotative statements. Narrative knowledge is know-how. Know-how highlights the pragmatics of narrative knowledge, pointing to competence as an epistemological category.[109] Judgment of know-how requires inhabitation or familiarity with the narrative's cultural-linguistic community. There is a certain circularity to the pragmatics of narrative knowledge: "The narratives allow the society in which they are told, on the one hand, to define its criteria of competence and, on the other, to evaluate according to those criteria what is performed or can be performed within it."[110] Scientific knowledge, Lyotard suggests, partakes in this circularity.

The pragmatics of scientific knowledge carry its own rules of legitimation for what counts as scientific. First, any scientific claim must provide proofs and arguments for its position. Second, unlike the authority of the narrator of an oral tradition, there is equality between the sender and the addressee. Whereas the listener in an oral tradition submits to the authority of the narrator, the addressee (scientist B) in the scientific community can refute the sender (scientist A). Third, science must be realist. Scientific utterances involve ostensible referents, which are subject to proofs. A proof determines that the belief is objectively true.[111] As one satisfies the rules through the crucible of researched proofs and argumentations, the results of science gain the status of "indisputable truths."[112] However, these truth claims are the products of a language game with its own distinct set of rules. Lyotard writes,

> Scientific knowledge requires that one language game, denotation, be retained and all others excluded. A statement's truth-value is the criterion determining its acceptability. Of course, we find other classes of statements, such as interrogatives ("How can we explain that . . . ?") and prescriptives ("Take a finite series of elements . . ."). But they are only present as turning points in the dialectical argumentation which must end in a denotative statement. In this context, then, one is "learned" if one can produce a true statement about a referent, and one is a scientist if one can produce verifiable or falsifiable statements about referents accessible to the experts.[113]

The hubris and illegitimacy of metanarrative are unmasked in its claim "as a universal discourse of legitimation" even as it hides behind, but denies its own narrative particularity.[114] Postmodernism is an incredulity against modernism's denial of its own cultural-linguistic perspectivity and is a turn toward situatedness, narrativity, traditionality, and perspectivism.

Michael Polanyi: Personal, Tacit Knowledge

According to Mark Mitchell, Michael Polanyi offers "the tantalizing possibility of something that is truly postmodern."[115] For Jerry Gill, Polanyi's postcritical philosophy represents a reconstructive postmodernism that critiques modernist epistemological objectivism without totally deconstructing its positive values.[116] Although not a self-proclaimed postmodern, Polanyi's ideas are rightfully set in the stream of postmodern epistemology, and he argued against modernism's epistemological objectivism. For example, George Lindbeck credits Polanyi as one who had awoken several scholars from their Enlightenment slumbers.[117] Mitchell further argues that Polanyi follows the Augustinian dictum *fides quaerens intellectum*, to which Smith is also committed.[118] Like postliberalism, tradition's cultural-linguistic realities play a central role in the rational endeavor of interpreting the world, acting as the "the intellectual resources [and limitations]" for knowing.[119] In this way, Polanyi inadvertently represents a postmodernism that is congenial with Smith.

Central to Polanyi's thought is that knowledge contains a personal, tacit element that guides thinking. Personal knowledge applies even to science, which is an exercise of skills that scientists perform by following a set of rules.[120] Even the most seemingly objective science contains "an essential personal participation of the scientist" in which what is considered valid is determined by personal judgment.[121] While it may seem that science consists of only factual, propositional knowledge, scientific knowledge is accomplished through practical knowledge. Without this know-how, performance in any field of knowledge suffers.

Polanyi differentiates know-how and know-that with subsidiary awareness and focal awareness. With hammering, focal awareness is the explicit awareness of hitting a nail with the hammer. Subsidiary awareness is the feeling of holding the handle. This subconscious awareness is imperative because its absence renders effective hammering impossible.[122] Subsidiary awareness is like another instrument that one wields subconsciously to accomplish a task in conjunction with focal awareness, indicating that theoretical knowledge without underlying tacit knowledge is impossible. Tacit knowledge makes theorizing possible.[123] Tacit, subsidiary awareness makes tools essentially part of a person; one embodies and indwells one's tools, which one wields with tacit know-how.[124]

Tradition plays an important role in the passing on of practical knowledge. Language is tradition-dependent, that is, received from tradition. This dependent relation exposes the authority structure of tradition-dependent language and its rules. One gains knowledge only by submitting to its rules. Tradition is thus reason's condition of possibility.[125] Moreover, traditioned transmission of knowledge is more akin to apprenticeship than ostensive learning. An apprentice not only gleans theoretical knowledge from her master, but she participates in and indwells the process of knowing. This indwelling not only consists of learning the explicit skills required for mastering the craft but also of assimilating the unarticulated rules.[126] Through skillful observation, which is honed through this very process, she comes to see what was previously unnoticeable.[127] Polanyi argues that most knowledge that is passed down like this is "predominantly tacit" because tacit judgments are made and transmitted in the apprentice's imitation of the master.[128] A student's journey from neophyte to established practitioner includes the assimilation of not only theoretical ideas and information but also attitudes, affections, and kinesthetic judgments. This assimilation is a submission to tradition and is an important reminder of the situatedness of knowledge.[129] For postmoderns, one is always a native.[130]

The rules of science and its interpretative framework are the intellectual equivalent of tools that the scientist wields through the personal, practical knowledge of subsidiary awareness. The rules of science are unarticulated presuppositions she indwells and identifies with, just like concrete tools. She is committed to and practices these foundational presuppositions. Establishing rules to articulate these presuppositions is possible due to personal judgments that are made prior to this work. Thus, a fundamental circularity exists within personal knowledge;[131] any inquiry into this ultimate foundation "must be intentionally circular."[132]

This foundational circularity is a central concept of personal knowledge. Situated context, the "fiduciary framework," shapes personal knowledge.[133] This framework "can claim no self-evidence."[134] Polanyi thereby declares this postmodern ethos:

> This then is our liberation from objectivism: to realize that we can voice our ultimate convictions only from within our convictions—from within the whole system of acceptances that are logically prior to any particular assertion of our own, prior to the holding of any particular piece of knowledge. If an ultimate logical level is to be attained and made explicit, this must be a declaration of my personal beliefs. . . . The process of examining any topic is both an exploration of the topic, and an exegesis of our fundamental beliefs in the light of which we approach it; a dialectical combination of exploration and exegesis. Our fundamental beliefs are continuously reconsidered in the course of such a process, but only within the scope of their own basic premisses [sic].[135]

For Polanyi, "all fundamental beliefs are irrefutable as well as unprovable."[136] This foundational circularity is an inescapable human condition.[137]

Personal knowledge is present beyond fundamental beliefs. At every point "of knowing there enters a tacit and passionate contribution of the person knowing what is being known."[138] Tacit knowledge is inarticulate understanding, a sensibility that accompanies every knowledge and one that registers at the pretheoretical level; thus, Polanyi's famous words, *"We can know more than we can tell."*[139] Tacit knowledge is always at work in ratiocination, guiding further discoveries and reshaping the interpretative framework. When discovery is made, one gains tacit foreknowledge of yet unknown future discoveries and consequences. Each discovery creates an indeterminate range for future discovery and commits one "to a belief in all these as yet undisclosed, perhaps as yet unthinkable, consequences."[140] This tacit commitment determines the possible and impossible. For example, according to van Huyssteen, scientists are committed to the intelligibility of the universe and the possibility of rational investigation.[141] This tacit commitment determines the range of possibilities of discovery.

This epistemic personal indwelling propels Polanyi to deny complete objectivity as a "delusion and . . . a false ideal."[142] Since tacit, personal knowledge is an indispensable and necessary component of knowing, "the ideal of eliminating all personal elements of knowledge would, in effect, aim at the destruction of all knowledge. The ideal of exact science would turn out to be fundamentally misleading and possibly a source of devastating fallacies."[143]

The Polanyian subject is personally committed to the truth of inescapable interpretative frameworks of tacit knowledge. Tacit knowledge is pretheoretical, situated, and contingent, and it aligns well with the postmodern prioritizing of the practical over the theoretical.[144] The Polanyian subject is a postmodern self that is situated, historical, tradition-bound, perspectival, pragmatic, contingent, *pistic*, and embodied. Importantly, it is realist.[145]

The postmodern characterization of fallibilistic, perspectival knowledge rooted in situated and embodied humanity is a critique directed against the totalizing system of Enlightenment modernity that seeks to unite all diversity under the uniformity of the transcendental ego. The modernist quest for universal objectivity is unmasked as "a self-deceived conceit of some self-divinizing intellectuals inebriated with their belief of having finally thrown God out of the universe."[146] Calvin Schrag remarks that this difference is one of the chief marks of postmodernism and the object of celebration.[147] Paul Sheehan agrees: the impossibility of defining postmodernism is itself an indication of the centrality of difference, its own paradoxical description.[148]

Postmodernism relativizes reason with situated perspectivism. With its suspicion of universal foundationalism, postmodernism turns to language and hermeneutics and rejects the modernist notion of absolute truth.[149] First,

Stuart Sims argues that some common features of postmodernism are "scepticism, an antifoundational bias, and an almost reflex dislike of authority."[150] Postmodernism rejects classical or strong foundationalism and its indubitable, foundational beliefs. Second, postmodernism is a turn to language and hermeneutics. If the modern self is a *homo autonomous*, Middleton and Walsh state that the postmodern self is a *homo linguisticus* because the self is constructed by language.[151] Language, knowledge, and reality are intrinsically related and inseparable, bound together by interpretation.[152] Thus, Westphal states in a pithy way, "We are all Gadamerians now."[153] Third, Penner identifies the concept of truth as "the crux of the debate over Christianity and the postmodern turn."[154] How can postmodernism secure a nonrelativistic truth? While this question will be addressed in a later chapter, the exposition of postmodernism reveals the central features of postliberal postmodernism: finitude, contingency, embodiment, perspectivism, and pretheoricity. The next chapter exposits Smith's Pentecostal epistemology and begins to form a picture of Smith's broader postmodern epistemology.

CONCLUSION

Smith's Pentecostal epistemology is the product of a phenomenological examination of the embodied doxological practices of Pentecostalism. This method itself concurs with Pentecostalism that defines itself not as a doctrinal movement, but as an embodied spirituality. Pentecostal spirituality does not prioritize the cognitive and theoretical. This priority of the affective is highlighted by the five elements of a Pentecostal worldview in which NAK is contained in the worldview while also characterizing it. The chapter then described the relationship between non-nihilistic postmodernism and Enlightenment modernism, represented by Lyotard and Polanyi whose epistemologies set the scene for understanding Smith's postmodernism and his epistemology.

NOTES

1. See Robert M. Anderson, *Vision of the Disinherited: The Making of American Pentecostalism* (New York: Oxford University Press, 1979), 4.
2. D. William Faupel, "Whither Pentecostalism?," *Pneuma* 15, no. 1 (1993): 9–27 (19).
3. Amos Yong, *Renewing Christian Theology: Systematics for a Global Christianity* (Waco: Baylor University Press, 2014), 14; Keith Warrington, *Pentecostal Theology: A Theology of Encounter* (New York: T&T Clark International, 2008), 20; Byron Klaus, "The Holy Spirit and Mission in Eschatological Perspective: A

Pentecostal Viewpoint," *Pneuma* 27, no. 2 (2005): 322–42 (335); and Wolfgang Vondey, *Pentecostal Theology: Living the Full Gospel* (New York: T&T Clark, 2018), 18–20.

4. Vondey, *Pentecostalism*, 88. Also, see Veli-Matti Kärkkäinen, *Toward a Pneumatological Theology: Pentecostal and Ecumenical Perspectives on Ecclesiology, Soteriology, and Theology of Mission*, ed. Amos Yong (New York: University Press of America, 2002), 6.

5. William Kay, *Pentecostalism* (London: SCM Press, 2009), 13. For an example of the privileging of North American classical Pentecostalism as the definitional norm, see Robert P. Menzies, *Pentecost: This Story Is Our Story* (Springfield: Gospel Publishing House, 2013).

6. Cecil M. Robeck and Amos Yong, "Global Pentecostalism: An Introduction to an Introduction," in *The Cambridge Companion to Pentecostalism*, ed. Cecil M. Robeck and Amos Yong (New York: Cambridge University Press, 2014), 1–10 (1–2).

7. Harvey Cox, *Fire from Heaven: The Rise of Pentecostal Spirituality and the Reshaping of Religion in the Twenty-First Century* (Reading: Addison-Wesley Publishing Company, 1995), 102. Also, see Allan Anderson, *An Introduction to Pentecostalism: Global Charismatic Christianity* (New York: Cambridge University Press, 2004), 175.

8. Birgit Meyer, "Pentecostalism and Globalization," in *Studying Global Pentecostalism: Theories and Methods* (Berkeley and Los Angeles: University of California Press, 2010), 113–30 (121).

9. Michael J. McClymond, "Charismatic Renewal and Neo-Pentecostalism: From North American Origins to Global Permutations," in *The Cambridge Companion to Pentecostalism*, ed. Cecil M. Robeck and Amos Yong (New York: Cambridge University Press, 2014), 31–51 (34).

10. Allan Anderson, "Varieties, Taxonomies, and Definitions," in *Studying Global Pentecostalism: Theories and Methods*, ed. Allan Anderson et al. (Berkeley and Los Angeles: University of California Press, 2010), 13–29 (15). Also, see Cecil M. Robeck, "Taking Stock of Pentecostalism: The Personal Reflections of a Retiring Editor," *Pneuma* 15, no. 1 (1993): 35–60 (45).

11. Ludwig Wittgenstein, *Philosophical Investigations*, ed. P. M. S. Hacker and Joachim Schulte, trans. G. E. M. Anscombe, P. M. S. Hacker, and Joachim Schulte, 4th ed. (Malden: Wiley-Blackwell, 2009), 36 (§66–67).

12. Anderson, "Varieties, Taxonomies, and Definitions," 15.

13. See Peter D. Neumann, *Pentecostal Experience: An Ecumenical Encounter* (Eugene: Pickwick Publications, 2012), 122–61.

14. Steven J. Land, *Pentecostal Spirituality: A Passion for the Kingdom* (Cleveland: CPT Press, 2010); Daniel E. Albrecht and Evan B. Howard, "Pentecostal Spirituality," in *The Cambridge Companion to Pentecostalism*, ed. Cecil M. Robeck and Amos Yong (New York: Cambridge University Press, 2014), 235–53 (235); Veli-Matti Kärkkäinen, "Pentecostalism and Pentecostal Theology in the Third Millennium: Taking Stock of the Contemporary Global Situation," in *The Spirit in the World: Emerging Pentecostal Theologies in Global Contexts*, ed. Veli-Matti Kärkkäinen (Grand Rapids: Eerdmans Publishing Company, 2009),

xiii–xxiv (xvi–xvii); Peter D. Neumann, "Spirituality," in *Handbook of Pentecostal Christianity*, ed. Adam Stewart (DeKalb: Northern Illinois University Press, 2012), 195–201; Margaret M. Poloma, "The Future of American Pentecostal Identity: The Assemblies of God at a Crossroad," in *The Work of the Spirit: Pneumatology and Pentecostalism*, ed. Michael Welker (Grand Rapids: Eerdmans Publishing Company, 2006), 147–65 (155); and Daniel Castelo, "Pentecostal Theology as Spirituality: Explorations in Theological Method," in *The Routledge Handbook of Pentecostal Theology*, ed. Wolfgang Vondey (New York: Routledge, 2020), 29–39.

15. Russell P. Spittler, "Pentecostal and Charismatic Spirituality," in *Dictionary of Pentecostal and Charismatic Movements*, ed. Stanley M. Burgess, Gary B. McGee, and Patrick H. Alexander (Grand Rapids: Zondervan, 1988), 804–9 (804).

16. Daniel Albrecht, *Rites in the Spirit: A Ritual Approach to Pentecostal Charismatic Spirituality* (Sheffield: Sheffield Academic Press, 1999), 179.

17. Alister E. McGrath, *Christian Spirituality: An Introduction* (Malden: Blackwell Publishing, 1999), 1–4.

18. Don Baker, *Korean Spirituality* (Honolulu: University of Hawai'i Press, 2008), 5.

19. David B. Perrin, *Studying Christian Spirituality* (New York: Routledge, 2007), 18.

20. Perrin, 19.

21. Perrin, 18.

22. Land, *Pentecostal Spirituality*, 31.

23. John M. Frame, *The Doctrine of the Knowledge of God* (Phillipsburg: P&R Publishing Company, 1987), 163.

24. Similarity with postliberalism should not be missed here.

25. Land, *Pentecostal Spirituality*, 24.

26. Kevin Mathers Ranaghan, "Rites of Initiation in Representative Pentecostal Churches in the United States, 1901-1972" (PhD Diss., University of Notre Dame, 1974), 654–55.

27. Land, *Pentecostal Spirituality*, 12.

28. Land, 26.

29. Hannah R. K. Mather, "Affect, Ethics, and Cognition: A Renewal Perspective on the Spirit's Role in the Interpretation of Scripture," *Journal of Pentecostal Theology* 29, no. 2 (2020): 179–93 (181).

30. Smith, *Thinking in Tongues*, xviii.

31. Smith, xx.

32. Smith.

33. Neumann, "Spirituality," 199.

34. Smith, *Thinking in Tongues*, xxi.

35. Roger E. Olson, "Pietism: Myths and Realities," in *Pietist Impulse in Christianity*, ed. Christian T. Collins Winn et al. (Cambridge: James Clarke and Company, 2012), 3–16 (5-7). Olson also highlights orthopathos and orthopraxis as "the common spiritual ground shared by Pietism and Postmodernism." Roger E. Olson, "Pietism and Postmodernism: Points of Congeniality," *Christian Scholar's Review* 41, no. 4 (2012): 367–80 (375).

36. Daniel Castelo, *Pentecostalism as a Christian Mystical Tradition* (Grand Rapids: William B. Eerdmans Publishing Company, 2017), xv–xvi. Smith also acknowledges Pentecostalism's catholicity, but views Pentecostalism as "a kind of theoretical provocateur" to Christianity. Smith, *Thinking in Tongues*, xxi.

37. Cox, *Fire from Heaven*, 83.

38. Peter Althouse, "Toward a Theological Understanding of the Pentecostal Appeal to Experience," *Journal of Ecumenical Studies* 38, no. 4 (2001): 399–411 (402). George Schner argues that experience is irreducibly diverse due to "the constructive, intentional, derivative, and dialectical character of experience." George P. Schner, "The Appeal to Experience," *Theological Studies* 53, no. 1 (1992): 40–59 (50).

39. Smith, *Thinking in Tongues*, 27.

40. James H. Olthuis, "On Worldviews," *Christian Scholar's Review* 14, no. 2 (1985): 153–64 (155), cited in Smith, *Thinking in Tongues*, 27.

41. Smith, *Thinking in Tongues*, 28–29.

42. Smith stresses that he is merely clarifying the concept of worldview without rejecting it, even strengthening it by introducing an affective, embodied component. See James K. A. Smith, "Worldview, Sphere Sovereignty, and Desiring the Kingdom: A Guide for (Perplexed) Reformed Folk," *Pro Rege* 39, no. 4 (2011): 15–24.

43. James K. A. Smith, *Desiring the Kingdom: Worship, Worldview, and Cultural Formation* (Grand Rapids: Baker Academic, 2009), 45. Gregory Clark concludes similarly in his survey of evangelical worldview philosophers. Although pretheoretical, the contents of worldview are understood as beliefs and judgments. See Gregory A. Clark, "The Nature of Conversion: How the Rhetoric of Worldview Philosophy Can Betray Evangelicals," in *The Nature of Confession: Evangelicals & Postliberals in Conversation*, ed. Timothy R. Phillips and Dennis L. Okholm (Downers Grove: InterVarsity Press, 1996), 201–18 (205).

44. Smith, *Desiring the Kingdom*, 46.

45. Smith, 47.

46. David K. Naugle, *Worldview: The History of a Concept* (Grand Rapids: Eerdmans Publishing Company, 2002), 268.

47. Naugle, 270.

48. On this Reformed thought, see Herman Dooyeweerd, *In the Twilight of Western Thought*, ed. James K. A. Smith, Studies in the Pretended Autonomy of Philosophical Thought (Grand Rapids: Paideia Press, 2012); and Roy A. Clouser, *The Myth of Religious Neutrality: An Essay on the Hidden Role of Religious Belief in Theories* (Notre Dame: University of Notre Dame Press, 2005).

49. James W. Sire, *Naming the Elephant: Worldview as a Concept*, 2nd ed. (Downers Grove: IVP Academic, 2015), 141.

50. Sire, 98.

51. Sire, 143. John Frame acknowledges the intellectualism in some Reformed circles but argues against the "primacy of the intellect." He views the faculties of reason, emotion, and will to be interdependent and their distinctions artificial. See John M. Frame, *Cornelius Van Til: An Analysis of His Thought* (Phillipsburg: P&R Publishing Company, 1995), 141–49. Hans Boersma argues that worldview is not

overly cognitive because it operates in a nontheoretical manner and lists embodiment as a necessary component of theology. See Hans Boersma, "Introduction: The Relevance of Theology and Worldview in a Postmodern Context," in *Living in the Lamblight: Christianity and Contemporary Challenges to the Gospel*, ed. Hans Boersma (Vancouver: Regent College Publishing, 2001), 1–13.

52. In highlighting the religious dimension of all worldviews and lived existence, the Reformed tradition argues that the object of ultimate significance in a worldview need not necessarily involve a supernatural agent. For example, Roy Clouser argues that all worldviews are rooted in divinity beliefs. A divinity belief is a belief in an ultimate that has nondependent existence. The object of this belief can be a supernatural agent, but anything that has independent existence qualifies as a divinity, such as the Platonic Forms, numbers, the Void, and Nothingness. While Smith may criticize this view as overly cognitive, Clouser argues that divinity beliefs are not necessarily the products of ratiocination. They can be tacitly held. Importantly, this definition of divinity beliefs is just one part of Clouser's definition of religious belief. Religious belief also includes how the non-divine stands in relation to the divine, and those beliefs necessarily arise from religious experience. See Clouser, *The Myth of Religious Neutrality*, 9–24. Similarly, Smith demonstrates how embodied doxological practices do not require the worship of a supernatural agent with an illuminating example of desire at work in the doxological practice of shopping. See Smith, *Desiring the Kingdom*, 19–23.

53. Smith, *Thinking in Tongues*, 11–12.

54. Smith, 27.

55. Nancey Murphy, *Beyond Liberalism and Fundamentalism: How Modern and Postmodern Philosophy Set the Theological Agenda* (Valley Forge: Trinity Press International, 1996), 5. Also, see Bruce Ellis Benson, *Graven Ideologies: Nietzsche, Derrida & Marion on Modern Idolatry* (Downers Grove: InterVarsity Press, 2002), 41; and Mathew S. Clark, "Pentecostal Hermeneutics: The Challenge of Relating to (Post)-Modern Literary Theory," *Africa Journal of Pentecostal Studies* 1, no. 1 (2002): 67–92 (69).

56. Todd A. Salzman, "Experience and Natural Law: A Universal Method for Approaching Particular Values," in *Encountering Transcendence: Contributions to a Theology of Christian Religious Experience*, ed. Lieven Boeve, Hans Geybels, and Stijn Van den Bossche (Leuven: Peeters, 2005), 185–200 (187).

57. Christopher Butler, *Postmodernism: A Very Short Introduction* (New York: Oxford University Press, 2002), 2. Also, see David W. Tracy, "Fragments: The Spiritual Situation of Our Times," in *God, the Gift, and Postmodernism*, ed. John D. Caputo and Michael J. Scanlon (Bloomington: Indiana University Press, 1999), 170–84 (181–82).

58. J. Wentzel van Huyssteen, *The Shaping of Rationality: Toward Interdisciplinarity in Theology and Science* (Grand Rapids: William B. Eerdmans Publishing Company, 1999), 29.

59. Kevin J. Vanhoozer, "Pilgrim's Digress: Christian Thinking on and about the Post/Modern Way," in *Christianity and the Postmodern Turn: Six Views*, ed. Myron B. Penner (Grand Rapids: Brazos Press, 2005), 71–103 (77); and Myron B.

Penner, "Introduction: Christianity and the Postmodern Turn: Some Preliminary Considerations," in *Christianity and the Postmodern Turn: Six Views*, ed. Myron B. Penner (Grand Rapids: Brazos Press, 2005), 13–34 (17). Also, see Lloyd Spencer, "Postmodernism, Modernism, and the Tradition of Dissent," in *The Routledge Companion to Postmodernism*, ed. Stuart Sim (New York: Routledge, 2001), 125–34 (127).

60. See James K. A. Smith, *Who's Afraid of Postmodernism?: Taking Derrida, Lyotard, and Foucault to Church* (Grand Rapids: Baker Academic, 2006), 20n8; and Roger E. Olson, *Reformed and Always Reforming: The Postconservative Approach to Evangelical Theology* (Grand Rapids: Baker Academic, 2007), 125–26. Because this study is a philosophical and theological evaluation of Smith and does not evaluate the cultural aspects, it will utilize both terms interchangeably unless noted otherwise. The same usage will apply to modernism and modernity.

61. Spencer, "Postmodernism, Modernism, and the Tradition of Dissent," 126–28.

62. Ludwig Wittgenstein, *Philosophical Investigations*, ed. P. M. S. Hacker and Joachim Schulte, trans. G. E. M. Anscombe, P. M. S. Hacker, and Joachim Schulte, 4th ed. (Malden: Wiley-Blackwell, 2009), 36e (§67). Also, see Benson, *Graven Ideologies*, 41.

63. Peter J. Leithart, *Solomon Among the Postmoderns* (Grand Rapids: Brazos Press, 2008), 16–18.

64. See James K. A. Smith, *The Fall of Interpretation: Philosophical Foundations for a Creational Hermeneutic*, 2nd ed. (Grand Rapids: Baker Academic, 2012), 9–10; and James K. A. Smith, *Speech and Theology: Language and the Logic of Incarnation* (New York: Routledge, 2002), 81, 87. James Fodor includes Radical Orthodoxy under the umbrella of postliberalism. See James Fodor, "Postliberal Theology," in *The Modern Theologians: An Introduction to Christian Theology since 1918*, ed. David F. Ford and Rachel Muers, 3rd ed. (Malden: Blackwell Publishing, 2005), 229–48 (229).

65. Vanhoozer, "Pilgrim's Digress," 77

66. Leithart, *Solomon Among the Postmoderns*, 35–58.

67. Spencer, "Postmodernism, Modernism, and the Tradition of Dissent," 125.

68. Tracy, "Fragments: The Spiritual Situation of Our Times," 171. Romanticism, which was contemporary to Enlightenment modernism, opposed the Enlightenment's cold rationalism. Romanticism was a break from the positivistic objectivism of the Age of Reason and represented a turn toward subjectivism and historicism. See Keith W. Clements, *Friedrich Schleiermacher: Pioneer of Modern Theology* (San Francisco: Collins Liturgical, 1987), 12–13. For arguments about the complexity of modernity, see J. Richard Middleton and Brian J. Walsh, *Truth Is Stranger than It Used to Be: Biblical Faith in a Postmodern Age* (Downers Grove: InterVarsity Press, 1995), 14; and Peter L. Berger, *The Many Altars of Modernity: Toward a Paradigm for Religion in a Pluralist Age* (Boston: De Gruyter, 2014), 68.

69. Albert Borgmann, *Crossing the Postmodern Divide* (Chicago: University of Chicago Press, 1992), 22.

70. Borgmann, 23.

71. Borgmann, 25.
72. Borgmann, 27–47.
73. See Borgmann, 48–77. For Margaret Poloma, postmodernism uncovers modern culture as "fragmented, devoid of deep emotions, and superficial." Margaret M. Poloma, "The 'Toronto Blessing' in Postmodern Society: Manifestations, Metaphor and Myth," in *The Globalization of Pentecostalism: A Religion Made to Travel*, ed. Murray W. Dempster, Byron D. Klaus, and Douglas Petersen (Eugene: Regnum Books International, 1999), 363–85 (366).
74. Merold Westphal, *Overcoming Onto-Theology: Toward a Postmodern Christian Faith* (New York: Fordham University Press, 2001), 78.
75. Nancey Murphy and James Wm. McClendon, Jr., "Distinguishing Modern and Postmodern Theologies," *Modern Theology* 5, no. 3 (1989): 191–214 (192).
76. John Thiel, *Nonfoundationalism* (Minneapolis: Fortress Press, 1994), 6.
77. René Descartes, *Discourse on Method and Meditations on First Philosophy*, trans. Donald A. Cress, 4th ed. (Indianapolis: Hackett Publishing Company, 1998), 63–65 (§24-27).
78. Robert C. Solomon and Kathleen M. Higgins, *A Short History of Philosophy* (New York: Oxford University Press, 1996), 175–78.
79. Nancey Murphy, "Introduction," in *Theology without Foundations: Religious Practice and the Future of Theological Truth*, ed. Stanley Hauerwas, Nancey Murphy, and Mark Nation (Nashville: Abingdon Press, 1994), 9–31 (11).
80. Middleton and Walsh, *Truth Is Stranger than It Used to Be*, 20, 47–49.
81. Thomas C. Oden, *After Modernity... What?: Agenda for Theology* (Grand Rapids: Zondervan, 1992), 47–51.
82. Smith, *Thinking in Tongues*, 54.
83. Calvin O. Schrag, *The Self after Postmodernity* (New Haven: Yale University Press, 1997), 25–26.
84. Van Huyssteen, *The Shaping of Rationality*, 22.
85. Bernard M. G. Reardon, *Religion in the Age of Romanticism* (New York: Cambridge University Press, 1985), 33. Both Smith and van Huyssteen view Enlightenment epistemology as the progenitor of secularism and its withering, privatizing impact on religious belief, rooted in the disparagement of religious belief as fundamentally irrational. See Smith, *Thinking in Tongues*, 56; and van Huyssteen, *The Shaping of Rationality*, 23. The secularization thesis that religious commitment declines as secularization increases seems almost commonsensical. However, Charles Taylor contends that the secularization thesis is a narrative with its own presuppositions that validates its own thesis. He offers a counternarrative, showing how the current secular age is not one of decline of religious belief but of multiple options of belief. For a concise exposition of Taylor's *Secular Age*, see James K. A. Smith, *How (Not) to Be Secular: Reading Charles Taylor* (Grand Rapids: Eerdmans Publishing Company, 2014).
86. Craig G. Bartholomew, *Contours of the Kuyperian Tradition: A Systematic Introduction* (Downers Grove: IVP Academic, 2017), 103.
87. John D. Caputo and Michael J. Scanlon, "Introduction: Apology for the Impossible: Religion and Postmodernism," in *God, the Gift, and Postmodernism*,

ed. John D. Caputo and Michael J. Scanlon (Bloomington: Indiana University Press, 1999), 1–19 (2).

88. Penner, "Introduction," 23.

89. Peter Augustine Lawler, *Postmodernism Rightly Understood: The Return to Realism in American Thought* (Lanham: Rowman & Littlefield Publishers, 1999), 1.

90. Westphal, *Overcoming Onto-Theology*, 81.

91. Westphal, 79.

92. Kevin J. Vanhoozer, "Lost in Interpretation?: Truth, Scripture, and Hermeneutics," *Journal of the Evangelical Theological Society* 48, no. 1 (2005): 89–114 (92).

93. Westphal, *Overcoming Onto-Theology*, 79–80.

94. William C. Placher, *Unapologetic Theology: A Christian Voice in a Pluralistic Conversation* (Louisville: Westminster John Knox Press, 1989), 28–29.

95. See Merold Westphal, "Appropriating Postmodernism," in *Postmodern Philosophy and Christian Thought*, ed. Merold Westphal (Bloomington: Indiana University Press, 1999), 1–10 (3).

96. Jean-François Lyotard, *The Postmodern Condition: A Report on Knowledge* (Minneapolis: University of Minnesota Press, 1984), 3, 40.

97. Lyotard, xxiv.

98. Lyotard, 15.

99. Lyotard.

100. Lyotard, xxiv.

101. Lyotard, 37.

102. The synonyms "metadiscourse" and "grand narrative" also pertain to legitimation.

103. For such misunderstandings, see Craig G. Bartholomew and Michael W. Goheen, *Christian Philosophy: A Systematic and Narrative Introduction* (Grand Rapids: Baker Academic, 2013), 16; and Stewart E. Kelly and James K. Dew Jr., *Understanding Postmodernism: A Christian Perspective* (Downers Grove: IVP Academic, 2017), 166–67 . This misunderstanding leads Kelly and Dew to argue that autonomous reason does not mark metanarratives since the metanarratives of Buddhism and Hinduism reject autonomous reason. However, they are not metanarratives precisely because they reject autonomous reason. This response may limit metanarratives to the West, as they argue, but Lyotard's report on the postmodern condition is contextualized to the West. See Kelly and Dew Jr., 196.

104. Lyotard, *The Postmodern Condition*, 10.

105. Lyotard, 27.

106. Lyotard.

107. James K. A. Smith, "A Little Story about Metanarratives: Lyotard, Religion, and Postmodernism Revisited," in *Christianity and the Postmodern Turn: Six Views* (Grand Rapids: Brazos Press, 2005), 123–40 (125).

108. Smith, *Who's Afraid of Postmodernism?*, 66–67.

109. Lyotard, *The Postmodern Condition*, 18.

110. Lyotard, 20.

111. Lyotard, 23–24.

112. Lyotard, 25.
113. Lyotard.
114. Smith, "A Little Story about Metanarratives," 131. Like modernist science, correlational theology and classical apologetics also assume neutral reason and qualify as metanarratives that legitimate themselves through neutral reason. See Smith, 138n48; and Smith, *Introducing Radical Orthodoxy*, 35–37, 157–58.
115. Mark T. Mitchell, "Michael Polanyi, Alasdair MacIntyre, and the Role of Tradition," *Humanitas* 19, no. 1 (2006): 97–125 (98).
116. Jerry H. Gill, *The Tacit Mode: Michael Polanyi's Postmodern Philosophy* (Albany: State University of New York Press, 2000), 71–72.
117. George A. Lindbeck, "Atonement & the Hermeneutics of Intratextual Social Embodiment," in *The Nature of Confession: Evangelicals & Postliberals in Conversation*, ed. Timothy R. Phillips and Dennis L. Okholm (Downers Grove: InterVarsity Press, 1996), 221–40 (225).
118. Mitchell, "Michael Polanyi, Alasdair MacIntyre, and the Role of Tradition," 108.
119. Mitchell, 109.
120. Michael Polanyi, *Personal Knowledge: Towards a Post-Critical Philosophy* (Chicago: University of Chicago Press, 1974), 49.
121. Polanyi, 20.
122. Polanyi argues that becoming focally aware of what should remain subsidiary leads to the ineffectiveness of one's task. Stage-fright is an example of the result when one becomes focally aware of each word and gesture. Polanyi, 56.
123. Michael Polanyi, *The Tacit Dimension* (Chicago: University of Chicago Press, 2009), 21.
124. Polanyi, 17–18. Also, Polanyi, *Personal Knowledge*, 55–59.
125. Mitchell, "Michael Polanyi, Alasdair MacIntyre, and the Role of Tradition," 102–3.
126. Polanyi, *Personal Knowledge*, 53.
127. Johnson, *Biblical Knowing*, 126.
128. Polanyi, *The Tacit Dimension*, 61; and Polanyi, *Personal Knowledge*, 206.
129. Even the submission to authority bases itself on personal judgment. Polanyi, 208–9. The traditions of Pentecostal spirituality pass down know-how through its practices. See Smith, *Thinking in Tongues*, 27.
130. The postmodern self is "fully aware of one's situatedness." Vanhoozer, "Pilgrim's Digress," 77.
131. Polanyi recognizes the danger of being mistaken for making an objective statement here. Thus, he carefully articulates that all of his statements arise from his own personal commitments. See Polanyi, *Personal Knowledge*, 256. Gill argues that deconstructive postmodernists also argue from their own system of thought. No critique is possible in a vacuum. Gill, *The Tacit Mode*, 86–87.
132. Polanyi, *Personal Knowledge*, 299.
133. Polanyi, 266.
134. Polanyi, 267.
135. Polanyi.

136. Polanyi.
137. Polanyi, 312.
138. Polanyi.
139. Polanyi, *The Tacit Dimension*, 4.
140. Polanyi, 23.
141. J. Wentzel van Huyssteen, *Essays in Postfoundationalist Theology* (Grand Rapids: Eerdmans Publishing Company, 1997), 219.
142. Polanyi, *The Tacit Dimension*, 18.
143. Polanyi, 20.
144. Madison, *The Politics of Postmodernity*, 137.
145. Mitchell, "Michael Polanyi, Alasdair MacIntyre, and the Role of Tradition," 119–20; and Jon Fennell, "On Authority and Political Destination: Michael Polanyi and the Threshold of Postmodernism," *Perspectives on Political Science* 42, no. 3 (2013): 154–61 (159).
146. Smith, *Moral, Believing Animals*, 29.
147. Schrag, *The Self after Postmodernity*, 27.
148. Paul Sheehan, "Postmodernism and Philosophy," in *The Cambridge Companion to Postmodernism*, ed. Steven Connor (New York: Cambridge University Press, 2004), 20–42 (21).
149. See Salzman, "Experience and Natural Law," 187. Also, Mathew Clark highlights the different ranges of postmodernism and argues that the question of foundations and absolutes is directly tied to the question of the nature of truth in the modernist/postmodernist debate. See Clark, "Pentecostal Hermeneutics," 72.
150. Stuart Sim, "Postmodernism and Philosophy," in *The Routledge Companion to Postmodernism* (New York: Routledge, 2001), 3–11 (4).
151. Middleton and Walsh, *Truth Is Stranger than It Used to Be*, 51. Myron Penner argues that the linguistic turn away from modernism is a fundamental shift about knowledge without certainty. See Penner, "Introduction," 25.
152. Penner, 24.
153. Merold Westphal, "Taking Plantinga Seriously: Advice to Christian Philosophers," *Faith and Philosophy* 16, no. 2 (1999): 173–81 (175). For Westphal, this acknowledgment is synonymous with the confession that "'we are all postmodernists now.'" Westphal, "Must Phenomenology and Theology Make Two?," 711.
154. Penner, "Introduction," 29.

Chapter 2

Pentecostal Epistemology

INTRODUCTION

Having a clearer grasp of Pentecostal spirituality and postmodernism, the reader is now better prepared to understand why Smith's epistemology is Pentecostal and postmodern. This chapter exposits Smith's claim that Pentecostal epistemology is narrative and affective, explaining how these features, which are not traditionally the targets of analytic epistemology, are forms of understanding that are prior and more fundamental to propositional, cognitive knowledge. Given that Smith's first presentation and his later reiteration are but outlines ready to be filled, the chapter quickly moves from exposition to critique, investigating the relationship between narrative, affective knowledge (NAK) and truth and Smith's claim about its primacy to cognitive knowledge.

PENTECOSTAL EPISTEMOLOGY

According to Smith, contained within Pentecostalism's embodied doxological practices is a postmodern embodied anthropology that acts as the basis for his Pentecostal epistemology. As postmodern, this anthropology rejects the Cartesian anthropology that motivates the propositional and ratiocinative rationalism of Enlightenment modernity. Enlightenment modernism's overvaluation of ratiocination devalues the body, reducing persons to "thinking things." Like Platonism, modern epistemology values the abstract and universal above the perspectival and material. Objective reason and logic unify the many tongues of global society.[1] Just like the Platonic soul's escape to the pristine realm of the rational forms, the modern epistemic dream is to shed the burdens of embodied particularity to attain rational homogeneity. Even Christian theology participates in this reductive epistemology when it assumes that theology can only begin after the construction of a rational prolegomenon that sets the framework for rational deliberation of revelation.[2]

Postmodern sensibilities counter this reductive anthropology and rationalism with its embodied anthropology. Rather than a hindrance, situated particularity is a human condition that colors thinking and knowledge. The resulting panoply of different epistemic contexts "is not a regrettable state of affairs to be lamented, but rather an essential aspect of being human that is to be affirmed."[3] Not only does situated particularity deny the dream of neutral reason, it inverts cognitive reason's primacy, granting authority to the affective heart, the center-point of the body.

Embedded within Pentecostal spirituality is this postmodern anthropology that "honors our primarily affective, precognitive, communal, and 'practiced' mode of being-in-the-world."[4] This is because Pentecostalism is a "quintessentially incarnational faith and practice."[5] Pentecostalism is a worldly expression of a holistic faith, despite its seeming otherworldliness.[6] Early Pentecostals rejected rationalism and replaced it with the authority of experience that was couched in a communal Pentecostal narrative.[7] This rejection of rationalism was not rejection of propositional knowledge as such, but the inclusion of different forms of knowledge that were embedded within their practices. Their experientially driven doxological practices, such as dancing, speaking in tongues, laying on of hands, testifying, and being "slain" in the Spirit, involved the whole person, not just the mind. These practices engaged the affections and elicited a tacit knowledge about God, themselves, and their mission in the world. They did not need to prove their knowledge through discursive means. Yet, the refrain they often recited upon encountering the Lord through worship was, "I know that I know that I know." Thus, they devalued ratiocination in order to revalue it properly.

With the rejection of modern rationalism and the high value placed on embodiment and its contingency, Smith proclaims that Pentecostal anthropology is postmodern. Indeed, postmodernism's characteristics identified in the previous chapter aligns with the emphasis Pentecostalism places on the material body. The body, unlike universal reason, is finite and contingent. It is always already located in particular places and times, and its experiences, including knowing, occur from particular locations.[8]

Observing the almost bewildering liturgy of Pentecostalism reveals how tacit knowledge is passed down. Such activities as being "coached" to speak in tongues or watching fellow worshippers fall prostrate on the floor (to be caught by the expectant arms of the deacons who are also readily armed with light blankets to cover the ladies) form worshippers into Polanyian subjects who begin to take on the attitudes, affections, and kinesthetic judgments of the tradition.

This situatedness reveals that knowledge is perspectival, interpretive, and tacit. The anthropology of Pentecostal spirituality reflects the postmodern features of finitude, contingency, embodiment, perspectivism, and pretheoricity. In fact, Smith is so confident in the postmodern characteristics of Pentecostalism that he boldly proclaims that the Azusa Street Revival was a "postmodern revival!"[9]

Smith identifies within postmodern Pentecostal anthropology a narrative, affective epistemology, and he argues that this epistemology can contribute toward contemporary epistemology, which he views as preoccupied with cognitive, propositional knowledge. Smith sees this preoccupation at work in contemporary philosophy of religion where conversations primarily revolve around beliefs rather than persons, reducing religion to mere doctrines.[10] Against this dominant strain, Smith proposes a different form of knowledge called NAK. Whereas contemporary epistemology considers propositional and theoretical knowledge as primary, Smith argues that NAK is actually primary and irreducible. These attributes are not only epistemological but ethical. For conceptualizing the pretheoretical life via cognition is objectifying insofar as the things themselves are pre- or noncognitive. Such act is an (Levinisian) ethical issue for Smith because theoretical description and conceptualization of pretheoretical life violates the alterity and transcendence of the noncognitive and pretheoretical.[11] There exists a seeming incommensurability between pretheoretical facticity and theoretical understanding of this facticity through its own conceptual categories. Contemporary epistemology's prioritization of theoretical knowledge must be seen through this ethical lens, and the retrieval of NAK's irreducibility and primacy is one step toward undoing the violence of theoretical thought.

Narrative, Affective Knowledge

What, then, is NAK, and why is it irreducible and primary? Narrative and affect are pretheoretical modes of understanding that act as the basis for theoretical thought. Smith utilizes Heidegger's distinction between theoretical knowledge (*wissen*) and pretheoretical understanding (*verstehen*) to describe their differences. Whereas *wissen* refers to the types of propositional belief, such as justified true belief, that takes center stage in contemporary epistemology, *verstehen* is a precognitive knowledge that acts more like a worldview than propositional belief due to its hermeneutical role. NAK is tacit knowledge that is "a more primordial, affective 'attunement' to the world that constitutes the matrix for knowledge."[12] One makes her way in the world through NAK even in the absence of propositional beliefs. Let us now examine the epistemological nature of narrative and affect.

Narrative organizes actions and events into coherent wholes that provide meaning to those actions and events by indicating how they fit into the wholes.[13] Narrative should not be understood merely as chronological listing of events. The epistemological feature of narrative is the conveying of significance and meaning to various events and forming them into a single coherent and interrelated account. The narratives that one embodies and tells are significant and meaningful. One does not tell all accounts of one's life, only those that are meaningful.[14] Smith thus states, "Narratives . . . always have a point, are always about the explanation and meaning of events and actions in human life, however simple these may be."[15] This is noticeable in personal lives. Not all truths are interesting; one primarily recalls and pursues truths that are pertinent to one's biography.[16] Narrative determines what is important, sacred, and meaningful, providing cosmic and existential meaning to life. In this way, narrative is inherently interpretive and perspectival.[17]

Consequently, narrative is a hermeneutic mode of imagining and experiencing the world.[18] Gabriela Spector-Mersel argues that narrative is an interpretive paradigm, a worldview that opposes positivist and post-positivist views of reality as objective and uniform. Narrative indicates reality as multifaceted and contextually constructed from one's perspective.[19] Every story is perspectival and is but a selection from "a range of alternatives lying within our life history."[20] Therefore, narrative is hermeneutic knowledge that forms both the narrator and the hearer in dialectical fashion as they partake in telling, listening, and participating in countless narratives. Narrative knowledge is thus ubiquitous, countering the myth of the priority of propositional knowledge. Lyotard writes, "Scientific knowledge does not represent the totality of knowledge; it has always existed in addition to, and in competition and conflict with, another kind of knowledge, which I . . . call narrative."[21] For Christian Smith, the moral nature of social existence shows that not only are all social institutions rooted in "narratives, traditions, and worldviews," but they express these epistemic contents.[22]

Unlike propositional knowledge, narrative is pretheoretical because it registers at the level of imagination. For example, Christian Smith argues that people mark significant time by narratives. The significance of national holidays or religious holy days does not derive from propositional arguments but from their stories that fuel imaginations and meanings. The stories behind these days "define who we as a people are, what we are here for, how we ought to live, what we ought to feel, what is good and bad, right and wrong, just and unjust, worthy and unworthy, sacred and profane."[23] Narrative drives one's meaning and imagination, one's very identity.

> Narrative is our most elemental human genre of communication and meaning-making, an essential way of framing the order and purpose of reality, that we moderns need and use every bit as much as our primitive ancestors. Most other forms of abstract, rational, analytic discourse are always rooted in,

contextualized by, and significant because of the underlying stories that narrate our lives.[24]

Worldview is narratival because narrative shapes the imagination. Narrative is also irreducible in that its affective and imaginative elements become lost when reduced to a propositional point. Often, narrative *is* the point and need not be reduced into one.[25] "The truth *is* the story; the narrative *is* the knowledge."[26]

To be human is to be a "story-telling animal."[27] One tells and participates in stories to make sense of the world. Narrative is not an option for narrative animals because every speech and act find their coherence and intelligibility in narrative.[28] One's search for meaning and identity occurs in one's "inhabiting characters embedded within socially shared roles and by creatively appropriating those roles, even to the point of coauthoring new ones."[29] At the moment of conception, one is thrust into a narrative. For one's reception of a name or identification with a gender already immerses oneself into a language game as a referent.[30] The roles one receives or takes on place constraints and possibilities on one's identity. Making sense of one's life and identity is not achievable without involvement in narratives.[31]

Perspectivally integrated with narrative is its affective component.[32] First, within narrative is an emotional import that is both internal and external to the narrative. Internal emotional responses are the emotions within the narrative itself, what those in the narrative feel. The emotional response from encountering the narrative is external. This response can vary, which raises the question of appropriateness.[33] Appropriateness of emotion presupposes evaluation or judgment. Narrative and affect are not value neutral. Like theoretical evaluation, one can evaluate affections.[34]

Second, drawing on David Velleman, Smith argues that narrative construes the world into a coherent structure according to an affective, rather than inductive or deductive, logic. Although efficient causality is important, narrative logic does not necessarily follow efficient causality in its reasoning. "Story makes sense of our world, our experience, and events on a register different from the deductive logic of efficient causality."[35] Stanley Hauerwas has argued similarly about the logic of narrative. Narratival connections are not necessarily logical or sequential. Narrative logic is "designed to move our understanding of a situation forward by developing or unfolding it."[36] Narrative logic provides the connections between contingent events to move the story forward non-arbitrarily. In other words, while narrative connects *contingent* events, it provides coherence and intelligibility in the form of a plot.

Third, affect is itself a construal, a hermeneutical filter that aids and is aided by narrative knowledge.[37] Affect provides meaning to reality and provides reasons for one's actions. The scriptural, testimonial, and experiential narratives one embodies form the affective dispositions in such a way that one sees the world in particular ways. As Steven Land argues, those who have been shaped by the teachings of Jesus and the Spirit will have the disposition of care and concern for the world so that it would be irrational to pass by a homeless person without desiring to help the person.[38] Hence, there exists "a kind of 'fit' or proportionality between narrative and our affective register."[39] Affections reflect their intended narratives.

Narrative is epistemic due in part to the affect's role in making the narrative coherent and intelligible. Lack of affect makes the adjudication of narrative's meaningfulness impossible. Even when causal connections are missing, a narrative can be meaningful due to the accompaniment of affections.[40] Illustrating the power of affect, Velleman argues that the conclusory affection, "the emotion that resolves a narrative cadence," impacts how one understands an entire saga.[41] For example, the climaxing affections of hope and deliverance at the end of a testimony can wrap up how one understands the entire testimony. Important to note, however, is one's involvement in many narratives. One does not inhabit just one narrative with one conclusory affection. The complexity of life is partly due to the many narratives and their affections of which one is part. There are also different levels of narratival importance. Smaller narratives shape the overarching narrative while the overarching narrative gives coherence to the other narratives.

Narrative, affective anthropology undergirds narrative, affective epistemology's irreducibility and primacy. In Smith's words, "We *feel* our way around the world more than we *think* about it, *before* we think about it."[42] Similarly, Velleman states that the affective patterning of events into a narrative is stored "in experiential, proprioceptive, and kinesthetic memory—as we might say, in the muscle-memory of the heart."[43] NAK is prior to theoretical reflection because it is precognitive and pretheoretical. Because humans are fundamentally precognitive, pretheoretical, affective beings, the primary mode of epistemic construal is pretheoretical and embodied.

Shelly Rambo powerfully demonstrates this embodied knowledge in her theology of trauma. Trauma leaves its victims with gaps of understanding. They become enmeshed in a narrative that they cannot fully or clearly narrate with cognitive understanding. They are effectively left speechless; they must witness to the unwitnessable for they must "stand in a place where [they] cannot see clearly and where the evidence of what took place is not fully available to [them]."[44] Rambo thus states that trauma studies have shifted its language from comprehension to witness and testimony, signaling the shift from theoretical knowledge to NAK.[45] Even more, Rambo's findings demonstrate that embodied and narrative knowledge is more than linguistic. That is, inculcation in narrative does not necessitate verbal or written language since trauma often renders victims speechless. Although recovery of narrative is essential to healing, the narrative of trauma can be more than linguistic. Even without words, trauma can be communicated.[46] While knowledge of trauma can be unclear and nonlinguistic, it is knowledge nonetheless, an inchoate, embodied understanding. In the haze of trauma, between life and the death of the life once known, the victim feels her way around the world more than think it. Hence, recovery from trauma does not primarily proceed from cognitive reassurance but from the senses and the imagination. Because the senses become sensitive to triggers that hearken one back to the traumatic event, Rambo argues that existence after trauma must begin with the body, to imagine that unimaginable[47]: "it is essential to first reconnect a person to the movement of her body, enabling her to reestablish and navigate her physical connection to the world."[48] Rambo thus advises that trauma studies reveal the need for an epistemology after trauma, a knowledge beyond words and theoretical comprehension. NAK, as an inchoate, pretheoretical knowledge is an example of this fitting epistemology.

For Pentecostals, their practices and experiences seize the affections and draw them to view the world differently, securing a paradigm that sets the boundaries of credibility and possibilities for reflection. The Pentecostal heartbeat of experiential encounter leads its narratives and affections to drive its theology. For Pentecostals, testimony is the propagation of a communal affect that shapes identities and frames the hermeneutic filter to interpret the world through a passional orientation. Pentecostal worship illustrates this passional perspectivalism as an "affective, tactile, and emotive" experience.[49] Pentecostal worship is passional because it is experiential in its quest for encounter with God. The worshipper seeks to be "moved by the Spirit," to be "slain in the Spirit," or to speak in tongues as the Spirit gives utterance (Acts 2:4). She also testifies to and shares God's intimate involvement in her life, further concretizing the affect directed toward the divine. Encountering and testifying of God elicits participation in the hearers. NAK is an embodied, practical knowledge, a know-how. Narrative is not merely a telling, but a participation. To know a narrative is to know how to live and enact it, to be part of it; narrative is pragmatic knowledge.

NAK as Schematic Knowledge

The concept of schema clarifies the pragmatics of NAK. Like a paradigm, schema sets the context for understanding and organizing incoming data, and it varies from person to person.[50] Developed through experiences, schema sets certain expectations for future interpretations. Schema is a form of stereotyping that imposes "expectations about the nature of the incoming information, reducing our openness to novelty and surprise."[51] As such, schema is not epistemologically objective, but is a skillful know-how that takes in the raw data of sense experience and shapes them for comprehension. Schema takes the dizzying amount of information that perception provides and actively selects and interprets relevant information.[52]

Schema is a perceptive and interpretive skill, an intentional activity requiring both the physiological and the psychological.[53] Without the physiological, there can be no reception of sense data. Without the psychological, there cannot be selection of information. According to David Heywood, "a schema is therefore a feedback mechanism whereby physical experience is assimilated, stored and made available in psychological form for future use."[54] Schema is not rigid, but continually adapts as it encounters new information, displaying its "highly flexible bodily memory."[55] Schema can either assimilate new information into the existing schema or accommodate the itself to new information. New information can even lead one to choose one schema over another. Either way, past experiences of involvement in the world shape one's interpretation of it.[56]

Because schema develops through past experiences, schematic knowledge is personal knowledge that is honed through interactions with the world. What Heywood calls "explicit knowledge," knowledge that "involves formal rules and definitions," aids in understanding and sharing concepts.[57] Understanding and internalizing concepts also require making connections within one's total experience. Heywood makes the Polanyian statement that in various areas of life, people learn to "see as" the objects of experience through the lens of previous experiences. Experiences form together as one recognizes similarities, and these experiences inculcate one to see patterns for meaning-making.[58] Seeing these similarities is not possible without a history of narrative and affective experiences. Noticing and connecting these similarities takes skill. One sees these similarities in the first place through value or salience, and one's experiences are intimately connected to one's affective values.[59] Schematic knowledge is thus skillful, hermeneutical know-how, one tightly integrated with experiences and values.

Heywood's depiction of schema helps with understanding Smith's Pentecostal epistemology. NAK is inseparable from embodiment; it is a participatory knowledge that is pragmatic, perspectival, and situated. As pretheoretical, this knowledge is irreducible and primary. Not only countering the primacy of theoretical, propositional knowledge, it acts as the basis for theoretical knowledge. For Smith, this differentiation marks the division between modernism and postmodernism. The former is committed to "dispassionate, disinterested objectivism" whereas the latter views knowledge as passional and perspectival.[60]

Smith's portrayal of Pentecostalism as an implicit, performative rejection of Enlightenment rationalism is shared by Margaret Poloma, who argues that Pentecostalism is an "anthropological protest against modernity."[61] Pentecostal spirituality carries fundamental commitments or *affective sensibilities*, which inhabit and express themselves in rituals. These doxological practices reveal "that human being-in-the-world is oriented more fundamentally by desire than thinking, and manifests itself more in what we do than in what we think."[62] Contra reductive rationalism's priority of theory over practice, pretheoretical affection arise from and are embedded in practice, acting as guides for beliefs. *Res cogitans* thinks its way to practice, but Pentecostalism's "affective (nonrationalist) philosophical anthropology" reverses this direction.[63] Pentecostal epistemology begins with praxis that always already carries an affective understanding of the world that acts as the basis for ratiocination. NAK is thus a knowing otherwise, a primary and irreducible understanding that acts more like a worldview as a tacit hermeneutical filter.

CRITIQUE OF PENTECOSTAL EPISTEMOLOGY

Pentecostal epistemology sets a hierarchy between the primacy of pretheoretical understanding and its derivative theoretical belief. In Pentecostal spirituality, embodied practices and experiences elicit pretheoretical understanding and doctrinal beliefs arise from this pretheoretical understanding. In this way, Smith opposes the view that practice follows theory. Second-order reflection is "always already informed by pretheoretical faith commitments."[64] Smith elaborates on this relationship by distinguishing theology[1] from theology[2]. Theology[1] represents the prereflective doxological confessions of the church that act as the boundary for the church's theoretical reflections on its confessions.[65] Theology[1]'s primacy expresses itself in its function "as the root of Christian theoretical reflection across the disciplines."[66] Theology[2] represents second-order reflection. Pretheoretical understanding and theoretical knowledge reflect the two levels respectively, and the embedded epistemology within Pentecostal praxis reflects the contents of theology[1].

Smith's distinction between theology[1] and theology[2] is helpful, and there is much to commend. However, this unidirectional, foundationalist relationship between pretheory and theory violates Steven Land's definition of Pentecostal spirituality as the integration of orthopraxis and orthodoxy in orthopathos by neglecting orthodoxy. It is insufficiently triperspectival. *Nous* lacks integrity in itself and requires the foundational support from praxis and pathos without influencing them. By neglecting the orthodoxy of Pentecostal theology, Smith's epistemology is insufficiently Pentecostal. Even if theology is secondary to orthopathos and orthopraxis, it should play an important role in the design of its epistemology. Instead, the relationship between cognitive belief and affect-praxis is foundationalist and unidirectional in Smith's methodology and epistemology. Noetic belief is like nonbasic belief that is based on basic NAK. Smith is an affective foundationalist even if he rejects the neutrality and epistemic certainty of classical foundationalism. If belief is merely the product of praxis, then it seems possible to construct a similar epistemology from other traditions. Smith's faulty methodology negates the uniqueness of *Pentecostal* epistemology. Smith's epistemology may be congenial with and appropriate for Pentecostalism and illustrate Pentecostalism's contribution to epistemology, but it disqualifies as a uniquely Pentecostal epistemology.

Klaas Bom and Simo Frestadius also critique this tension between pretheoretical and theoretical knowledge. Bom provides a sympathetic critique of Smith and seeks to bolster Smith's epistemology by clarifying the role of reason and its relationship to the heart. Smith's enthusiastic endorsement of the heart is understandable, given his resistance against the dominance of reductive and propositionally driven rationalism. However, this enthusiasm clouds ratiocination with ambiguity.[67] First, Bom grants that reason still plays a role in Smith's epistemology. However, due to the overemphasis on the heart, reason functions covertly. The danger with this overemphasis is that reason "can easily dominate experience" in the guise of the heart, using it to pass off unjustified claims.[68] In this way, Smith kicks rationalism out the front door only to let it in through the back, except in disguise. Smith's claim that narrative knowledge makes an "*exclusive* claim of truth" makes this danger is even more acute.[69]

Relatedly, Bom's second critique that affective knowledge seems insulated from critical evaluation by reason exacerbates the danger mentioned earlier.[70] If an unjustified narrative, affective claim passes off as a truth claim while insulated from rational evaluation, then breakdown of discourse might result because people can retreat into their narratives. Particularity then leads to an inflexible exclusivism and fideism, the mark of hypermodernism. Smith is not ignorant of this issue. He sets prescription for affective truth: right ordering of desire.[71] This prescription is needed due to the affective effects of sin, an important reminder for any Christian epistemology.[72] According to Beáta Tóth, a Christian account of emotion must acknowledge that both reason and emotion are directed toward God, but also recognize that they are both fallen. "[Both] can be the source of self-delusion and fallacy."[73]

For Frestadius, a one-sided relationship exists between beliefs and practices in Smith. The same applies to the relationship between beliefs and affections. Smith's affective foundationalism places pretheoretical knowledge in the foundations, which provides the norms and rules for second-order reflection. Smith overlooks "the role theology plays in influencing religious practices."[74] Since integrative Pentecostal spirituality involves beliefs, Frestadius judges Smith's epistemology as deficient due to its ignoring of the rich tradition of Pentecostal theology and history, especially given that they have shaped and are continually shaping Pentecostal spirituality and practices.[75] For Bom and Frestadius, the issues of truth and justification and the tension between pretheoretical understanding and theoretical knowledge raise questions about Smith's Pentecostal epistemology. I will address these two issues in turn.

NAK and Truth

Highlighting the prescriptive elements for NAK raises two observations about Smith's epistemology. First, Smith's epistemology is mostly descriptive: knowledge is primarily narrative and affective. Second, Smith offers right ordering of desire as the lone prescriptive criterion for affective knowledge. Epistemically responsible NAK cannot arise from any pathos and praxis, but must arise from *ortho*pathos and *ortho*praxis, just as it should be informed by *ortho*doxy.

Central to achieving the status "ortho-" must be some condition of appropriateness. It has been long presupposed that knowledge requires truth. Is there a role for truth in NAK? Is the nature of NAK so discontinuous from noetic knowledge that truth is unnecessary? Before this question can be addressed, a difficulty in language must be addressed. For propositional epistemology, knowledge must include a connection to truth. For nonpropositional epistemologists like Smith, knowledge is used to describe meaning-making activity. A linguistic issue is present here. Is it appropriate to use "knowledge" to describe meaningful understanding that may not be tied correctly or appropriately to mind-independent reality? Smith would answer affirmatively. This mode is how humans normally know the world. This is a descriptive statement.

However, this statement falls afoul of the is/ought fallacy. Mere construal, however meaningful and ubiquitous, is insufficient for (right) knowledge. Pretheoretical understanding must strive for that vaunted positive epistemic status called "knowledge," which is not possible without robust prescriptive criteria that includes truth, and Smith's lone prescriptive criterion of orthopathos is reductive and impotent to secure knowledge, let alone is it consistent with Pentecostal spirituality as triperspectival integration. While narrative-affect, practice, and belief are epistemic on their own, a robust Christian epistemology should integrate orthopathos, orthopraxis, and orthodoxy. Not only does Smith fail in this integration, his inconsistent utilization of Pentecostal spirituality leads to an insufficient Pentecostal epistemology. In fact, inasmuch as false or fictional narrative and its affections still qualify as NAK because they are meaning-making activities that act as hermeneutical filters for understanding and imagining reality, ambiguity arises about how these construals are right or appropriate construals. Smith's epistemology seems to run afoul of "knowledge" arising merely out of pathos and praxis rather than orthopathos and orthopraxis. However, meaning and knowledge do not make one.

More precise language is required to eliminate this ambiguity. Smith rightfully presents NAK as *sui generis* and neglected by modernist epistemology. NAK is hermeneutic construal of reality that differs from the standard alethically aimed propositional knowledge. Smith is correct that construal should be considered knowledge of a particular kind, a knowing otherwise. But calling this knowledge raises linguistic confusion since standard epistemological language differentiates mere belief, even basic belief, from knowledge. Like NAK, mere belief is ubiquitous, but meaningful belief is not knowledge. In order to differentiate between warranted NAK and unwarranted "NAK," I propose distinguishing narrative, affective *construal* (NAC) from NAK. This differentiation affirms narrative and affect as meaning-making understanding apart from narrative and affect that have achieved the vaunted status of warrant, that is, knowledge. While I will continually use NAK for stylistic purposes in this work, I will later demonstrate that Smith's pathic criterion for NAK requires modification, and that is provided by Reformed epistemology.

Egalitarian Primacy

Although Smith is adamant in his insistence on the irreducibility and primacy of NAK, he is aware of the irony in his theoretical explanation of pretheoretical concepts. He confesses that one should not confuse narrative theology with narrative knowledge because the former is still a "genre of propositional and theoretical analysis that makes the case for the importance of narrative in a nonnarratival mode."[76] Although he tackles this "methodological challenge" head-on, the answer remains theoretical. Noticing that philosophy of religion remains rationalist in assuming the primacy of theory over practice, Smith argues that such an assumption reduces religion to ideas; rationalistic philosophy of religion eliminates the fullness of religion as a lived experience and practice, a form of life.[77] His solution is to upturn the Cartesian anthropology assumed in current philosophy of religion by replacing it with an affective, nonrationalist anthropology, which appreciates the fullness and priority of human existence and practice over theory.[78] This solution is nevertheless theoretical. Even a phenomenological philosophy of religion that focuses on the practices of religion remains a theoretical work. Coming to understand the primacy of pretheoretical understanding occurs through theoretical means. Thus, the irony of Smith's claim to the *primacy* of NAK remains.

Smith's inability to communicate his epistemology—let alone his broader works on the pretheoretical—through pretheoretical means indicates a gap in Smith's sub-cognitivist epistemology that requires repair. Could there be a greater harmonious relationship between pretheory and theory than Smith indicates? Smith correctly argues that one's predominant mode of operation is pretheoretical. NAK is ubiquitous. One *predominantly* construes the world pretheoretically, and theoretical ideas are always already informed by know-how. One traffics in unavoidable affective narratives through participation in life as storytelling, embodied animals, even if some of these understandings are NAC, not NAK.

Smith's sub-cognitivism pictures a unilateral movement from pretheory to theory. Smith's rejection of foundationalism is thus ironic since he assumes an affective foundationalism. This foundationalism motivates the primacy of pretheory. Yet, coming to awareness of the formative power of practices through reflection and enacting changes in practices, narratives, and affections indicate that theory can greatly shape pretheoretical construal. Smith himself demonstrates this reality as he helpfully guides his readers to the formative power of pretheory through propositional and theoretical means. With Smith's theoretical tutelage, one can become conscious of the different "liturgies" that shape one's hermeneutic construal of reality. Therefore, the primacy of pretheory must be understood as *quantitative* primacy. That is, tacit know-how operates in all-knowing and meaning-making activities. In certain times, however, discursive reason has greater epistemological impact on knowledge and on the direction of the affections and narratives. This is *qualitative* primacy.

Insofar as social imaginary shapes theoretical thought, NAK has both quantitative and qualitative primacy. However, contra Smith, cognitive and theoretical knowledge influence pretheoretical knowledge in various ways, such that pretheoretical knowledge does not necessarily have absolute primacy.[79] Their relationship is integrated, perspectival, and reciprocal. Against Smith's unidirectional affective foundationalism, then, a hermeneutical spiral better captures the reciprocal relationship between pretheory and theory.

Others have proposed similar views. For Amos Yong, faith can never be merely pretheoretical because humans are "through and through thinking animals."[80] Faith is integrationist, marrying both pretheory and theory. John Milbank similarly states that no clear division between first-order discourse (theology[1]) and second-order discourse (theology[2]) exists. Symbols, rituals, and narratives of liturgy are "*somewhat* reflective" and discursive theology informs and qualifies "first order belief and practice."[81] Commenting on the relationship between liturgy and theology, Dennis Ockholm argues that they are mutually informing.[82] The Reformed presuppositionalist John Frame, who champions the primacy of the presuppositions over beliefs, questions the clear distinction between pretheoretical and theoretical thought.[83] Importantly, Steve Land, upon whose ideas Smith frames his epistemology, defines theology as reflective activity upon lived reality and a passion for

God. Not only is theology an affective work, such passions require ongoing reflection as part of its nature. For Land, affect and reflection are unified, and their merging defines true theology.[84]

Although Smith utilizes Charles Taylor's notion of social imaginary to differentiate between the Reformed tradition's all-too-noetic concept of worldview and NAK, Taylor views pretheory and theory as permeable. On the one hand, social imaginary is pretheoretical, "inarticulate understanding of our whole situation" and is "largely unstructured."[85] Even though social imaginary is unstructured, it is not incoherent. Imagination unifies parts into a whole. Imagination helps one "see as whole what those without imagination see only as unrelated parts."[86] Imagination helps make sense of one's place in and relation with the world. It provides images of how the world is and ought to be. Imagination is carried in narratives and practices, and, as such, understanding and inhabiting this imaginary requires skills rather than explicit instruction.[87] On the other hand, Taylor demonstrates that theory often penetrates social imaginary. Theory provides a new "outlook" to practices and allows one to see the world anew, which in turn becomes sedimented and taken for granted. Indicating the reciprocal relationship between theory and practice, Taylor argues that theory is shaped by practices even while shaping them. "The new practice, with the implicit understanding it generates, can be the basis for modifications of theory, which in turn can inflect practice, and so on."[88] This dialectical movement eschews the dominance of dispassionate logic. As arguments take on proponents and opponents, they become part of one's narratives and form of life. The arguments and the corresponding narratives create, renew, shape, and carry affective-valences. The relationship between pretheory and theory is thus perspectivally integrated. For Taylor, ideas and practices are "often inseparable."[89] Problem arises when one is overemphasized, such as in modernity's reductive rationalism or Smith's affective foundationalism. The language of primacy must be understood quantitatively and qualitatively. While the pretheoretical mode operates more ubiquitously, there is a mutual relationship between pretheory and theory, and one can more intensely impact the other at certain times.

CONCLUSION

This chapter explored Smith's Pentecostal epistemology and explained how narratives and affections are epistemic construals, a knowing-otherwise. It is worldview-like in that it is a schema to understand reality. Humans primarily operate in these pretheoretical modes of knowledge because they are rooted in human anthropology. While Smith is generally correct about this type of knowledge, I argued that two problematic areas require critique and clarification. First, I argued that the account of NAK is too general. A further division between meaning (NAC) and knowledge (NAK) is required. With this clarification in place, one can understand Smith's claim about the primacy of NAK as quantitative primacy. People predominantly understand the world through NAC and NAK. However, knowledge requires truth. There remains further explanation on how NAC can become NAK. Moreover, theory can have qualitative primacy over pretheory. In this way, I sought to repair Smith's affective foundationalism that neglects cognitive beliefs, which also disqualifies the Pentecostal distinctive of Smith's epistemology, and suggested a reciprocal relationship between pretheory and theory. This claim finds support in moral psychology and philosophy of emotions. In the next chapter, I turn to Jonathan Haidt's work in moral psychology, whose project has similarities with Smith in bringing the focus away from reductive rationalism and highlighting the roles of intuition and intersubjective reasoning, and Robert Solomon's cognitive theory of emotions to argue for the cognitive and conceptual features of affections.

NOTES

1. Smith, *Thinking in Tongues*, 55.
2. Paul D. Janz, *The Command of Grace: A New Theological Apologetics* (New York: T&T Clark, 2009), 4.
3. Smith, *Thinking in Tongues*, 58.
4. Smith, 113.
5. Smith, 61.
6. Pentecostal worship involves a kinesthetic dimension in which the worshipper's this-worldly movements are seen as related to the otherworldly movement of the Spirit. See Albrecht, *Rites in the Spirit*, 147–48.
7. Bradley Truman Noel, *Pentecostal and Postmodern Hermeneutics: Comparisons and Contemporary Impact* (Eugene: Wipf & Stock, 2010), 70.
8. Smith, *Thinking in Tongues*, 136.
9. Smith, 112.
10. Smith, 110–11.
11. See James K. A. Smith, "Taking Husserl at His Word: Towards a New Phenomenology with the Young Heidegger," *Symposium* 4, no. 1 (2000): 89–115. Also, see James K. A. Smith, "Alterity, Transcendence, and the Violence of the Concept: Kierkegaard and Heidegger," *International Philosophical Quarterly* 38, no. 4 (1998): 369–81 (376–81); and James K. A. Smith, "Between Predication and Silence: Augustine on How (Not) to Speak of God," *The Heythrop Journal* 41, no. 1 (2000): 66–86 (84).
12. Smith, *Thinking in Tongues*, 29. Also, see Smith, 64n35. As described earlier, NAK forms part of the Pentecostal worldview and describes the nature of the

worldview itself. It is thus unsurprising that Smith's description of social imaginary and NAK are similar.

13. Smith, *Moral, Believing Animals*, 65.
14. Peter Goldie, "Narrative and Perspective; Values and Appropriate Emotions," in *Philosophy and the Emotions*, ed. Anthony Hatzimoysis, Royal Institute of Philosophy Supplement: 52 (New York: Cambridge University Press, 2003), 201–20 (203).
15. Smith, *Moral, Believing Animals*, 65.
16. Calhoun, "Subjectivity and Emotion," 113–16.
17. Goldie, "Narrative and Perspective," 217–18.
18. See Mark Johnson, *Moral Imagination: Implications of Cognitive Science for Ethics* (Chicago: University of Chicago Press, 1993), 11; and Stanley Hauerwas, *The Peaceable Kingdom: A Primer in Christian Ethics* (Notre Dame: University of Notre Dame Press, 1983), 25.
19. Spector-Mersel, "Narrative Research," 209–12.
20. Spector-Mersel, 212.
21. Lyotard, *The Postmodern Condition*, 7.
22. Smith, *Moral, Believing Animals*, 22.
23. Smith, 79.
24. Smith, 81.
25. Hauerwas, *The Peaceable Kingdom*, 26.
26. Smith, *Thinking in Tongues*, 64.
27. Alasdair MacIntyre, *After Virtue: A Study in Moral Theory*, 3rd ed. (Notre Dame: University of Notre Dame Press, 2007), 216.
28. MacIntyre, 210–12.
29. Johnson, *Moral Imagination*, 151.
30. Lyotard, *The Postmodern Condition*, 15.
31. Johnson, *Moral Imagination*, 178.
32. Cornel W. du Toit, "Emotion and the Affective Turn: Towards an Integration of Cognition and Affect in Real Life Experience," *HTS Toelogiese Studies/ Theological Studies* 70, no. 1 (2014): 1–9 (7).
33. Goldie, "Narrative Thinking, Emotion, and Planning," 98–99.
34. Goldie, "Narrative and Perspective," 211–15.
35. Smith, *Thinking in Tongues*, 70.
36. Hauerwas, Bondi, and Burrell, *Truthfulness and Tragedy*, 28.
37. Adenekan Dedeke, "A Cognitive-Intuitionist Model of Moral Judgment," *Journal of Business Ethics* 126, no. 3 (2015): 437–57 (445).
38. Land, *Pentecostal Spirituality*, 132.
39. Smith, *Thinking in Tongues*, 66.
40. J. David Velleman, "Narrative Explanation," *The Philosophical Review* 112, no. 1 (2003): 1–25 (18–19).
41. Velleman, 19.
42. Smith, *Thinking in Tongues*, 72.
43. Velleman, "Narrative Explanation," 19.
44. Shelly Rambo, *Spirit and Trauma: A Theology of Remaining* (Louisville: Westminster John Knox Press, 2010), 23.

45. Rambo, 27.
46. Rambo, 21.
47. Rambo, 158.
48. Rambo, 153.
49. Smith, *Thinking in Tongues*, 72.
50. Heywood, *Divine Revelation and Human Learning*, 22.
51. Heywood, 27.
52. Heywood, 42.
53. Heywood, 21.
54. Heywood.
55. Heywood, 25.
56. Heywood, 33.
57. Heywood, 60.
58. Heywood, 61.
59. Heywood, 70.
60. Smith, *Thinking in Tongues*, 59.
61. Smith; and Poloma, *The Assemblies of God at the Crossroads*, 19. Like Smith, she argues that the worldview of rationalistic evangelicalism is at odds with the experiential worldview of Pentecostalism. See Poloma, "The Future of American Pentecostal Identity," 164.
62. Smith, *Thinking in Tongues*, 114.
63. Smith, 113.
64. Smith, 5.
65. Smith, *Introducing Radical Orthodoxy*, 177. The influence of Lindbeck's regulative theory is apparent here.
66. Smith, 173. This division between theology as reflection and pretheoretical worldview that broadens knowledge beyond the discursive has been part of the neo-Calvinist tradition. See Bartholomew, *Contours of the Kuyperian Tradition*, 126–27; and Hendrik Hart, "The Articulation of Belief: A Link between Rationality and Commitment," in *Rationality in the Calvinian Tradition*, ed. Hendrik Hart, Johan Hoeven, Van Der, and Nicholas Wolterstorff (Eugene: Wipf & Stock, 1983), 209–48 (210).
67. Klaas Bom, "Heart and Reason: Using Pascal to Clarify Smith's Ambiguity," *Pneuma* 34, no. 3 (2012): 345–64 (349).
68. Bom, 351.
69. Bom, 350.
70. Bom, 351.
71. Smith, *Desiring the Kingdom*, 52.
72. James K. A. Smith, "Questions About the Perception of 'Christian Truth': On the Affective Effects of Sin," *New Blackfriars* 88, no. 1017 (2007): 585–93 (592).
73. Beáta Tóth, *The Heart Has Its Reasons: Towards a Theological Anthropology of the Heart* (Cambridge: James Clarke and Company, 2016), 17.
74. Simo Frestadius, "In Search of a 'Pentecostal' Epistemology: Comparing the Contributions of Amos Yong and James K. A. Smith," *Pneuma* 38, no. 1 (2016): 93–114 (111).

75. Frestadius.

76. Smith, *Thinking in Tongues*, 65.

77. While agreeing with Smith's differentiation between pretheory and theory, Amos Yong argues that the overemphasis of pretheory can galvanize the anti-intellectual sectors within Pentecostalism. Amos Yong, "Whither Systematic Theology?: A Systematican Chimes in on a Scandalous Conversation," *Pneuma* 20, no. 1 (1998): 85–93 (87).

78. Smith, *Thinking in Tongues*s, 110–14.

79. Smith acknowledges the possibility of the theoretical impacting the pretheoretical. Yet, he continually argues for "the *autonomy* and *primacy* of [the] pretheoretical." Smith, "Taking Husserl at His Word" (96, 100).

80. Yong, "Whither Systematic Theology?," 87.

81. John Milbank, "Foreword," in *Introducing Radical Orthodoxy: Mapping a Post-Secular Theology* (Grand Rapids: Baker Academic, 2004), 11–20 (14).

82. Dennis L. Okholm, *Learning Theology through the Church's Worship: An Introduction to Christian Belief* (Grand Rapids: Baker Academic, 2018), 20–26.

83. Frame, *The Doctrine of the Knowledge of God*, 309–10.

84. Land, *Pentecostal Spirituality*, 191, 219.

85. Charles Taylor, *Modern Social Imaginaries* (Durham: Duke University Press, 2004), 25.

86. Vanhoozer, "Lost in Interpretation?," 109.

87. Taylor, *Modern Social Imaginaries*, 23–29.

88. Taylor, 30. Smith agree with Taylor on this point. See, Smith, *Desiring the Kingdom*, 69n56.

89. Taylor, 31.

Chapter 3

Pretheory, Theory, and Their Integrated Relationship

INTRODUCTION

The previous chapter critiqued Smith's sub-cognitivism and affective foundationalism to argue for an integrative, reciprocal relationship between pretheory and theory. This chapter recruits assistance from moral psychology and philosophy of emotion as cumulative evidence for this relationship. But rather than arguing for a reciprocal relationship that maintains the hard division between affect and cognition, I blur that line by identifying affect as a form of cognition. Moreover, I identify similar tendencies with Smith in Haidt and provide corrections. After establishing the perspectival relationship between affect and reason, I correct Smith's sub-cognitivism with the aid of Pentecostalism while recognizing Smith's nuanced view on the reciprocity between pretheory and theory. But because such nuanced view is missing in his Pentecostal epistemology, this chapter acts to pivot from Smith's Pentecostal epistemology to his postmodern epistemology in the next chapter.

INTUITION, REASON, AND COGNITION: PERSPECTIVES FROM MORAL PSYCHOLOGY

According to Jonathan Haidt's social intuitionist model for moral judgment (SIM), most moral judgments are intuitive rather than reflective. Intuition is like perception: pretheoretical and akin to basic beliefs. It is "defined as the sudden appearance in consciousness of a moral judgment, including an affective valence (good-bad, like-dislike), without any conscious awareness of having gone through steps of searching, weighing evidence, or inferring a conclusion."[1] Intuition contrasts with discursive reasoning, which "occurs more slowly, requires some effort, and involves at least some steps that are accessible to consciousness."[2] Reasoning is frequently a post hoc justification of an already-made intuitive judgment. Although he is quick to mention that he is not stating how moral judgments *ought* to be made, he argues that reason rarely produces moral judgments.[3] Similar to Smith, Haidt's SIM rejects the primacy of reason advocated by the rationalist model of moral judgment-making, according to which reason primarily directs moral judgments.

Rationalist Model

Eliciting Situation → Reasoning → Judgment

SIM's Six Links

Contrariwise, Haidt's SIM presents a complex interrelationship between intuition, judgment, and reason. There are six links or processes between intuition, judgment, and reason, and the SIM includes an intersubjective component.

Social Intuitionist Model

Eliciting Situation →
A's Intuition (Link 1) → A's Judgment (Link 2) → A's Reasoning
A's Reasoning (Link 3) → B's Intuition (Intersubjective)
A's Judgment (Link 4) → B's Intuition (Intersubjective)
A's Reasoning (Link 5) → A's Judgment (Rare)
A's Reasoning (Link 6) → A's Intuition (Rare)

Link 1, the intuitive judgment link, is an immediate move from moral intuition to moral judgment. Link 2 represents the post hoc reasoning link between moral judgment and moral reasoning. Unlike the rationalist model where moral reasoning precedes moral judgment, the SIM presents reason as a biased process that seeks to confirm intuition's already-made moral judgment. Reasoning is the rationalizing of one's judgment.[4] Reasoning thus carries an *illusion* of objectivity. Moral intuition, on the other hand, is trained by culturally formed moral norms.[5] Like Smith, Haidt is not an anti-rationalist; reason can play a significant role. However, private reasoning is mostly ineffective in changing one's own moral intuitions.

Link 3 represents an interpersonal link that moves from one's moral reasoning to another person's moral intuition. Haidt hypothesizes that this impact of reason on intuition occurs not so much by the logic of compelling arguments but by the arguments' triggering of new affective intuitions.[6] If

Haidt is correct, then affections are not merely integrated with narratives, but also with propositions. However, inasmuch as theory can influence affective intuition, it can have qualitative primacy.

Haidt further argues that reason is effective in non-defensive dialogue, which points to the importance of personal affective postures. When adversarial postures are present, such as in debates, one bears down on one's intuitions and post hoc justifications. This explains why debates rarely don't convince the debaters. Reason rarely persuades people in conflict situations.[7] This is not typically the case in non-adversarial situations. When no conflict exists, reason can influence intuition through the reasoned-persuasion link. Therefore, attempts at persuasion require attending to the mood of the interpersonal encounter. A listener's affective posture toward her interlocutor can influence how she affectively interprets and accepts her interlocutor's arguments and come to see an issue in a different way.[8]

Link 4 is another interpersonal link, but the impact moves from moral judgment to another person's moral intuition. This link reveals that moral judgments can influence others apart from arguments. When positive affections exist, persuasion can offer merely by sharing one's intuitions and judgments.[9] People are like chameleons and unconsciously mimic the behavior and mannerisms of others because they naturally seek to agree with others they like.[10] This is why a friend's moral judgment may be sufficient for others to adopt the same judgment. In such cases, the reasoning process is not involved. One is affectively drawn to the friend's moral judgment.

What about private moral reasoning? If reason is mostly a post hoc justification of an already-made judgment and its influence is mostly intersubjective, does private moral reasoning play any role in shaping one's moral intuitions and judgments? Can change in one's moral intuitions and judgments occur through private soliloquy? Haidt considers private moral reasoning in links 5 (reasoned judgment link) and 6 (private reflection link). Link 5 moves from reasoning to judgment, and link 6 moves from reasoning to intuition. In these reasoned moves, one can change one's intuitions and judgments by using the sheer force of logic, thereby activating new intuitions or providing multiple intuitions from which one can choose. One can choose an intuition out of multiple options by either choosing the strongest intuition or allowing reason to choose by following certain rules or principles.[11]

These links partly relieve the tension in Smith's affective foundationalism. However, Haidt is pessimistic about the success rate of these links. He points out that only one group has shown to be successful in using private reasoning to arrive at different intuitions or judgments: philosophers.[12] While this finding may look like a triumph for reason, celebration may not be in order. For those who can exercise such influence upon their intuitions "have been *extensively* trained and socialized to follow reasoning even to very disturbing conclusions."[13]

This evidence raises further questions because not all philosophers are alike. Those influenced by the Enlightenment ideal of objectivity and neutrality, such as the logical positivists, will rely heavily on objective logic, being careful to avoid subjectivity. However, postmodern philosophers value subjectivity's importance. Furthermore, the qualification of extensive training makes it difficult to set this link as the most important link. Even if all adequately trained philosophers can accomplish such a feat, the ratio of philosophers to world population makes it implausible that such ability should be the epistemic norm and ideal.

Importantly, a philosopher's work is rarely private. Even the most private reasoning often involves consultation with others' ideas. Books do not engage in verbal dialogue, but they are intersubjective.[14] Accompanying this intersubjectivity are embedded affections that one has toward the ideas. When Haidt argues against the efficacy of private moral reasoning, he has in mind those activities that lack discourse partners.[15] Although Haidt does not mention them, books and other similar objects count as discourse partners; they are written to inform and persuade. At root, language "is an essentially *relational* phenomenon and thus necessarily involves *others*."[16] This intersubjectivity was the critique of Husserl by Derrida. Husserl's attempt to find full presence and immediacy of the speaker in solitary mental life fails because even this soliloquy utilizes the social phenomenon of language. Even the supposed privacy of the isolated mental life is structured by intersubjectivity.[17] Sources used in private moral reasoning have intersubjective origins.

Absolutely private moral reason is rare.[18] Rarer is the success of changing one's intuition or judgment through absolutely private moral reasoning. Most people simply do not overcome their intuitions by the sheer force of logic. As an example, Haidt argues that formidable deductive proofs against the existence of God often cannot face up to the emotional power of religious experiences that change how one views the world.[19]

Because private moral reasoning is rarely successful in changing one's moral intuitions and judgments, Haidt considers the first four links as central.[20] Nevertheless, Haidt reiterates that reason impacts moral judgment.[21] The combination of various cultural intuitions and beliefs form through pretheoretical enculturation and theoretical reflection. "Cultural knowledge is a complex web of explicit and implicit, sensory and *propositional*, affective, cognitive, and motoric knowledge."[22] Like Smith, Haidt replaces a rationalist model with pretheoretical, affective model. He is unlike Smith in giving an important role to reason for shaping pretheoretical intuition and judgment. Therefore, Haidt looks favorably upon models of moral development that encourage not only praxis-oriented modeling and participation that fosters implicit understanding but also reflection, discussion, and persuasion.[23] This interplay between pretheory and theory leads to a mutual relationship of influence.

Haidt further reduces the gap between affective and theoretical knowledge by unifying cognition with intuition. While intuition is not ratiocinative, it is a form of cognition.[24] Cognition is just information-processing.[25] Intuition is lower, automatic cognition and reason is higher, controlled cognition.[26] Haidt emphasizes, "It must be stressed that the contrast of intuition and reasoning is not the contrast of emotion and cognition. Intuition, reasoning, and the appraisals contained in emotions . . . *are all forms of cognition.*"[27] If Haidt is right, affect is neither precognitive nor preconceptual. Joshua Greene also states that cognitive processes that distinguish from affections are nevertheless integrated with affections and that any real distinction between emotion and cognition is one of degree.[28] If so, then even reasoned arguments involve affect in some way, no matter how small. Although Smith acknowledges that the term "cognitivism" is an ambiguous term, he antithetically juxtaposes cognition with affect.[29] Haidt states that this mistaken contrast between affect and cognition led to his personal crusade to correct this mistake. The distinction to be made is between affective, cognitive knowledge and theoretical, cognitive knowledge.

Correcting Haidt

Cordelia Fine and others have challenged Haidt's two claims about the post hoc or intersubjective qualities of reason and the ineffectiveness of private reasoning. She admits that the number of occurrences in which people use private moral reasoning to override automatic intuitions and form accurate judgments is an empirical question.[30] However, her core claim is that Haidt has overstated his case; controlled cognitive processes can impact moral intuition and moral judgment.[31] Reason, not intuition, causes moral judgment; private reasoning is a separate link that runs parallel with link 1. Fine is not advocating for a return to a rationalist paradigm. Rather, she presents intuition and reason as having a greater integrative relationship than what Haidt claims.

Citing a study in which participants' brain activities were measured by functional magnetic resonance imaging (fMRI) as they were given either easy or difficult moral dilemmas, Fine argues that those who faced a difficult moral dilemma showed "significant activity in the anterior dorsolateral prefrontal cortex (anterior DLPFC), a region associated with abstract reasoning processes."[32] While acknowledging that this finding could be an imaging of post hoc justification, Fine argues that the more plausible explanation is that it is the occurrence of private moral reasoning in search for a moral judgment. She hypothesizes this because the participants were not asked to justify their judgments and there was greater neural activity when utilitarian judgment-making was more appropriate, indicating that reason was challenging moral intuitions.[33] Therefore, without denying that moral intuitions can lead to judgments, Fine concludes that this is not always the case.[34]

Joshua Greene and others have put forward the dual-process theory of moral judgment, according to which deontological judgments are tied to emotional responses and utilitarian judgments are tied to ratiocination that is not based on moral intuitions.[35] When one faces a difficult moral decision, especially one dealing with the possibility of actively causing harm to bring about a greater good, one engages in theoretical reasoning.[36] Greene argues that reason in such cases can change one's beliefs or judgments.[37] Moreover, those who were instructed to ponder an argument prior to making a judgment were able to overturn their initial intuition.[38] These findings indicate that reason can greatly influence pretheoretical intuition and judgment.

These challenges provide valuable correctives to Haidt without overthrowing the SIM. The main challenge revolves around reason's ability to challenge pretheoretical intuitions prior to judgment-making. This challenge weakens Haidt's claim that private moral reasoning is mostly ineffective. Fine's second challenge alludes to this claim that rapid and automatic moral judgments may be the product of automatized theoretical judgment.[39] However, purely private moral reasoning that is devoid of intersubjectivity and affectivity would have more difficulty overcoming strong affective intuitions. Perhaps such reasoning will have a better chance of overcoming affectively weak intuitions. However, any reasoning that is accompanied by strong affections will have a greater chance of influencing affectively strong intuitions through a dialectical process involving reasoning, intuitions, and judgments.[40]

The challengers' claim that prior reasoning can have input in moral intuitions, reason, and judgments does not overthrow the model.[41] Haidt agrees that reason can shape intuitions and judgments. However, reason may not always be post hoc. Not only can private reason causally direct moral judgments prior to intuition, reason can also become pretheoretical over time.[42] If "conscious reflection or reasoning . . . [took] place at an earlier point in the individual's history," then the conclusion of the reflection has become an intuition.[43] Such sedimentation of reasoning shows that a hard demarcation between pretheory and theory is false. Fine's critique must be seen as a corrective to the dominance of pretheoretical intuition in Haidt rather than a replacement. There is greater interplay between pretheory and theory than Haidt is willing to admit.

While my intention is not to defend any one psychological model of moral judgment, I agree with Haidt that intuitions play a large and frequent role in moral judgments.[44] But just as Smith overemphasized affect to the detriment of reason, Haidt overemphasizes the claim that private reason does not have greater causal role on intuitions and judgments. Haidt is correct about the quantitative and often qualitative primacy of moral intuition in moral judgment-making, but reason can have greater qualitative primacy on the direction of intuitions and judgments. Moreover, his nuanced distinction between different cognitions challenged Smith's dichotomization between affect and cognition. Affections are not devoid of cognition. They are information-processing, even though such processing may not always involve propositional information. Narratives and embodied actions are informative in nonpropositional ways. And such cognitive processes are automatic rather than controlled. Haidt's contribution, his "crusade," to this issue provides more nuance than Smith's simple distinction between affect and cognition. A better distinction is between affect-cognition and ratiocinative-cognition.[45]

EMOTION, REASON, AND COGNITION: PERSPECTIVES FROM PHILOSOPHY OF EMOTION

The philosopher of emotion Robert Solomon exhibits much similarity with Smith and can clarify Smith's deficiencies. His book *The Passions* laid the foundation for the cognitive theory of emotions, which he first called "Rational Romanticism."[46] Although Solomon bemoans the term "cognitivist" because it insinuates that emotion is essentially intellectual and informational, his theory best correlates with Smith because it views emotion as intelligent and rational. However, he differs from Smith by equating emotion with cognition, even including propositions and reflection in emotion.

Emotion is cognitive judgment. Judgment is not merely propositional, conscious, or reflective. Similar to Haidt, Solomon's project has been to overcome the reason-emotion dualism.[47] Reason and emotion are integrally related: "'Reason' is the passions enlightened, 'illuminated' by reflection and supported by a perspicacious deliberation that the emotions in their urgency normally exclude."[48] Passional reason is a knowing-otherwise. By broadening the categories of knowledge, Solomon escapes criticisms made against cognitive theories that view judgments as merely propositional attitudes or beliefs.[49]

For Solomon, the passions encompass emotions, moods, and desires.[50] Moods and desires are rooted in the emotions. Moods are generalized emotions with no particular objects, which leads some to argue that moods do not have intentionality.[51] Solomon argues that they do have a general object: the world. Moods tune persons to the world. In this sense, although moods can change, mood is never absent.[52] Emotions can also structure moods while moods can be expressed by emotions. Desires can be instinctual, but many can be based on the evaluative structures of emotions.[53] Due to the central role of the emotions, they form the core of Solomon's philosophy of passion.

Central to Solomon's cognitive theory is that emotion is evaluative and oftentimes a complex judgment.[54] "An emotion is a basic judgment about our Selves and our place in our world, the projection of the values and ideals, structures and mythologies, according to which we live and through which we experience our lives."[55] Emotion as judgment is akin to worldview and can be both episodic or long-term, articulate or inarticulate.[56] Emotion is thus a construal, although Solomon prefers the term "judgment" over "construal" because he considers the latter voluntaristic and biased toward reflection.[57] Nevertheless, Solomon views construal and others, such as perception, seeing as, and appraisal as consistent with judgment, albeit with some differences.[58]

Emotion is world-making in that it's a construal of the world and is made by the world. It is intentional and carries an essential logical connection with the world via a formal object. In Mark Wynn's terms, bodily feeling is "world-directed."[59] The object of this intentionality need not be real. According to Solomon, emotion straddles the real and the unreal. The object could be either nonexistent or imagined.[60] The intentionality of emotion indicates that an object is always subjectively experienced. Even if the object is illusory, subjectivity is intertwined with its object. There is no separation between emotion and object. "The emotion is determined by its object just as it is the emotion that constitutes its object."[61] Emotion is *my* experience in *my* world. There is no pure objective reality, no brute facts, for emotions. For example, the object of paranoia may not exist in reality. However, the fictional object is still an intentional object in the paranoid person's world. Without this intentionality, emotions and objects are unrelatable. Without emotions, there can be no world "for me."[62] Therefore, there is no purely objective reality, but only "surreality," a "reality plus."[63]

This does not mean that objective reality does not exist. However, objective reality is, at minimum, uninteresting and, at most, unknowable without emotions. The reality that one knows is not reality in itself, but surreality. Reality is an involvement. As an involvement of the whole person with reality, surreality is post-Kantian in rejecting the dualism between the noumena and phenomena. The subject is not severed from the object. Passion does not merely follow some brute fact. Emotion is a mode of judging the facts. Without emotion, the world is meaningless.[64] Passional reason's comingling with the world necessitates that reason is never purely objective.

Solomon considers pretheoretical thought as an aspect of emotion and argues that it can arise spontaneously, whether invited or uninvited. Unlike thoughts "conjured up," which he equates with active reflection, invited and uninvited thoughts are spontaneous. The difference between the two is that invited thought is the result of the mind having reflected on the topic sometime beforehand. This spontaneity indicates the passive nature of emotion, although emotion is active as a judgment.[65] Because emotion is judgment and judgment is value-laden, emotion is active and passive. Emotion actively colors the world but also arises in involuntary ways. However, even involuntary thoughts arise from one's participation in the world. That is, the active and passive aspects of emotion point to their intentionality with the world.

Cognitive Emotion

Like Haidt, Solomon argues that emotion is cognitive and sets out to clarify the nature of cognition.[66] Although he admits that there are precognitive or "preconceptual forms of cognition," emotion as judgment is still a form of cognition. Emotion as a response to something (e.g., listening to testimony or being healed) is a form of recognition, and "recognition is a form of cognition."[67] Recognition is not one of reflection "*that* one has an emotion . . . [but is] constitutive of the emotional response."[68] Perhaps Smith can argue that affect is a precognitive physiological response: for example, a toothache. The feeling of toothache would color the world. If the suffering is long-term, perhaps the world shows itself as bleak. Yet, do mere physiological responses qualify as precognitive or preconceptual? If mere feeling is recognizable, then it seems to qualify as a form of cognition. If the mere feeling of toothache colors one's world, feeling would qualify as a form of judgment, as a mood.[69] In fact, if feeling is cognitive, then feeling can be scrutinized for rationality. For example, if the feeling of toothache leads to the emotion of lust, then it's irrational.

Solomon does not demarcate emotion from reason. As forms of cognition, their differences are only "in scope and perspective."[70] Reason, or belief, is generally articulate, whereas emotion is generally unreflective.[71] However, just like reason, emotion has its reasons, which act as the basis for evaluation even if it's not necessarily reflective.[72] Therefore, although emotion is intentional and actively engages the world, this engagement is not always cognizant.[73] Emotion can be conscious, unconscious, and anything in-between.[74] Also, prereflective need not mean preconceptual.[75] Emotional judgment is rational because judgment requires "an advanced degree of *conceptual* sophistication, including a conception of Self and at least some ability in abstraction."[76] In other words, emotion is a value-laden conceptual structure.[77]

Viewing cognition as only reflective thought or belief, which has been the criticism laid at this theory, is a mistake. Emotional cognition need not be "necessarily conscious—and self-conscious—reflective, articulate judgments."[78] The "intelligence" of emotion is merely to state that it has its reasons; emotion's conceptuality is not necessarily ratiocinative. However, emotion can still be information-processing if this act is not understood as ratiocinative. According to Aaron Ben-Ze'ev, there are two forms of information-processing mechanisms: schematic and deliberative. The former is part of the emotional mode and is like tacit knowledge: prereflective and automatic. The latter is typical of the intellectual mode and is a slow, conscious process. They are interrelated and work together, but can also conflict with each other.[79]

For Solomon, reflective thinking can be an aspect of emotion.[80] Although such thinking is "an antecedent or consequence of emotion," Solomon is clear that it is still a part of emotion.[81] Thus, he continually holds in tension the unbroken relationship between affective cognition and theoretical cognition while differentiating the two and avoiding their collapse into each other. Because reason can be tied to emotion, reason is passional. Unlike Smith, Solomon avoids the sharp dichotomy between affect and reason, pretheory and theory, preconceptual and conceptual. By drawing attention to these different dimensions of cognition, Solomon provides a non-dualistic view of reason and affection.[82]

Mark Wynn argues that the distinction between concept and emotional construal is not clear. New conceptual information, besides emotional change, can modify perception and its salience. This new perception can infuse an object with the concept in sensory form.[83] One's perception changes so that one can "see" this theoretical idea in the object.[84] Even when theory does not structure one's perceptual gestalt, theory can aid one's understanding of a particular experience. Unlike animals that do not have God-concepts, humans, through their God-concepts, can grasp the truth and existence of a transcendent reality. Without this theoretical concept, the world remains a world, but not the world that pervades with the presence of God.[85]

Pretheoretical experience lacks the ability to construe the world rightly without the theoretical (nor can the theoretical exist without the pretheoretical). For Wynn, theoretical concepts can structure sensory appearances, even penetrating the experiences of the sensory world.[86] When ideas penetrate sensory objects, perception changes because one can "see" the idea in the object. Wynn's descriptions of the spiritual life can extend to existence in general. Life is not structured primarily affectively, theoretically, or perceptually. Instead, all three constitute one's views and participation in the world.[87] What I have been arguing for is this greater continuity between pretheory and theory.

Wynn argues that there is a two-way relationship between affect/kinesthetics and thinking. His description of this relationship is a hermeneutical spiral whose ideal state is equilibrium.[88] This description is not a quantitative statement about an equal engagement of the faculties. Smith is correct that humans mostly operate pretheoretically. Theoretical reflection cannot "completely undo the formative power of [the pretheoretical] . . . because of the sheer quantity of our immersion in them."[89] The issue of primacy lies on the qualitative impact of the various faculties on knowledge. In fact, the difficulty of measuring the impact one has over the other makes the term "primacy" unhelpful.

Regarding emotion's rationality, Solomon argues similarly with Smith that emotion contains its own distinct, objective, purposive logic. Emotion's logic, although prereflective and subjective, can be "explained by *reasons* or 'in-order-to' explanations."[90] Even if an emotion may seem irrational, it would be rational if it "fit into a person's overall purposive behavior."[91] Solomon does not solely equate rationality with theoretical thought. The logic of emotion as a purposive act renders it intelligent in ways that might differ from ratiocination. In fact, because "'rationality' signifies intelligent purposive activity," Solomon considers emotion to be paradigmatic rationality.[92]

Violation of this logic deems the emotion irrational.[93] Ben-Ze'ev, who disagrees that emotion represents paradigmatic rationality, nevertheless argues that the logic of emotion differs from the logic of intellect, although both are important and should be integrated. Rationality carries two different senses: descriptive and normative. Descriptive rationality is reflective activity. Normative rationality is an optimal and appropriate response to a given context. Emotion is rational in the normative sense.[94] Emotion's intentionality is critical to this normativity, for the rationality of emotion is dependent on the appropriate response to its object.

While Smith also views affective knowledge as intentional, it is an intentionality devoid of the cognitive. Affect is "*noncognitive* and prereflective."[95] While Smith likens affect to Heidegger's notion of mood, which is precognitive, Solomon also draws from Heidegger and argues that the distinction between emotion and mood is not sharp.[96] Their relationship is "one of mutual support and even identity."[97] Their difference is merely one of focus and generalization. Solomon departs from Heidegger in that he views mood as a form of cognition.

Smith's dichotomization arises from his imprecise understanding of cognition and thought. Cognition distinguishes ipso facto from "noncognitive" affection and thought *is* thinking. However, Solomon and others reveal cognition as encompassing both affect and belief because emotion as cognition accommodates both embodiment and mind.[98] Emotion may be prereflective, but it is not noncognitive. As a judgment arising from involvement with the world, emotion is a conceptual construal of the world. Because involvement with the world involves ratiocination, ratiocination can shape emotions and emotions can depend on ratiocination.[99]

Kinesthetic Emotion

Emotional judgments, including physiological feeling, are judgments of the body that yields know-how. Not only does know-that lack primacy, know-that cannot be independent of know-how.[100] Mark Wynn's description of emotional judgment is similar. Emotion can evaluate an object's significance, its salience recorded by perception and phenomenal "feel," with the latter being like kinesthetic judgment. Wynn not only finds the new salience of perception and phenomenal feel as integrated, but he argues that both color the world, so that the world takes on the quality of one's emotions.[101] This judgment is more phenomenological than propositional. Likewise, Solomon not only integrates affect and belief, pretheoretical and theoretical, he also broadens cognition to encompass the affective, noetic, and kinesthetic. He also distinguishes between pretheoretical thought and theoretical thinking and provides room for both know-that and know-how. To summarize Solomon's position so far, quoting Solomon at length is fitting:

> Thus the judgments that I claim are constitutive of emotion may be non-propositional and bodily as well as propositional and articulate, and they may further become reflective and self-conscious. What is cognition? I would still insist that it is basically judgment, both reflective and pre-reflective, both knowing how (as skills and practices) and knowing that (as propositional knowledge). A cognitive theory of emotion thus embodies what is often referred to as "affect" and "feeling" without dismissing these as unanalysable. But they are not analysable in the mode of conceptual analysis. . . . There are feelings, "affects" if you like, critical to emotion. But they are not distinct from cognition or judgment and they are not mere "read-outs" of processes going on in the body. They are judgments *of* the body, and this is the "missing" element in the cognitive theory of emotions.[102]

Solomon provides a more nuanced view of emotion than Smith. Like Smith, Solomon's account entails that emotion is hermeneutical. Emotion is mostly pretheoretical. But for Solomon, the line between pretheory and theory blurs. Emotion is a form of cognition, and cognition ranges from the pretheoretical to theoretical. Contra Smith, hermeneutical emotion is neither precognitive nor preconceptual. Emotion is both knowing-that and knowing-how. Discursive reasoning cannot be divorced from emotion. To do so is to divorce cognition itself.

Wayward Emotion and the Reason-Emotion Interface

Even if emotion is epistemic, it can mislead. Right judgments require right emotional dispositions and right attunement with the world. Without these, wrong judgment can ensue. For example, an emotional experience in one area can affect an unrelated area, such that a terrifying experience could make one nervous in unrelated circumstances.[103] Goldie is right that "if one is not properly disposed, or if there is some undue interference with one's emotional response, then there is a significant risk of getting things wrong. Not only that; one's emotions can also *distort* perception and reason."[104] The distinction between NAC and NAK explains how meaningful emotion can be an incorrect judgment.

Emotion can mislead with wrong dispositions. Emotion can distort perception and reason by skewing them in its favor through misinterpretation or dismissal of evidence, either knowingly or unknowingly.[105] However, although Goldie may be correct that "one's epistemic landscape is liable to be skewed by one's emotional feelings," this case is not necessary.[106] His solution is that one should be aware of one's emotional dispositions and reflect on their reasons, a solution that is unduly cognitive in the rationalist sense and which values the primacy of reason.[107] First, since people most often operate pretheoretically, his solution is an unobtainable ideal. Second, the non-neutrality of reason means that reason cannot be the sole adjudicator of other forms of knowledge. One's total epistemic package is liable to be skewed by one's rational commitments. The particular commitments of reason highlight reason's placement in a wider worldview, which consists of big and small narratives that are affectively valenced. While Goldie acknowledges that one is not always cognizant of one's emotions and thus criticizes reason's ability to adjudicate emotions as "unduly *optimistic*," he is unduly pessimistic about emotion's ability to judge the world rightly.

Instead of being pessimistic about this (in)ability, I offer two proposals.[108] First, emotion and reason are integrative rather than hierarchical. By eliminating the undue pressure of adjudication on reason, reason becomes freed to act as an integrative partner with emotion (and action). Both reason and emotion can adjudicate judgment together or separately, depending on particular circumstances. Second, emotion is rational judgment. Although emotion can be irrational and inaccurate, it often provides accurate pictures, even correcting reason at times. It accompanies reason and helps adjudicate between reasons.

Solomon is right that emotion is a form of judgment. Goldie rightfully raises the issue of normativity. While he is correct that reason can rightly adjudicate a flawed emotional disposition or judgment, I have argued that emotion can also rightly adjudicate reason. My argument is fundamentally a Solomonic rendition of cognitive theory, which views emotion and reason holistically. Emotion is rational because it is logical and intentional. Because of its internal logic, reflection is not always required as long as it does not violate emotion's logic. Irrationality can occur when emotion violates its own internal logic or when it is misdirected. However, even if irrationality is expected, it does not disprove Solomon's theory.

Solomon shores up Smith's brief sketch of a Pentecostal epistemology. He pictures the nonhierarchical and multifaceted relationship between pretheory and theory, affect and reason, and distinguishes the two as different forms of cognition and establishes the theoretical dimension of emotion. He accomplishes this integration while sharing the same concepts with Smith, especially the concepts of know-that and know-how, which Solomon demonstrates are both emotive. Solomon helpfully clarifies and corrects Smith's ambiguous relationship between reason and affect.

AN ASSIST TO SMITH

Smith's Pentecostal epistemology offers important critique to the reductive rationalism of Enlightenment epistemology. He rightly draws attention to pretheoretical knowledge, an irreducible, embodied, narrative, and affective know-how that counters the Enlightenment's supposed objectivity, neutrality, and primacy of reason. His overemphasis on the pretheoretical is understandable given the prevailing priority and attention given to propositional, theoretical thought and neglect of the formative power of practice, narrative, and affect. Yet, there is tension in the clear distinction between pretheory and theory. Developments in moral psychology and philosophy of emotion reveal that such clear distinction is illegitimate.

In his quest to counter the overreaches of reductive rationalism, Smith overreaches himself, constructing a sub-cognitive epistemology that is dangerously close to dichotomizing the integral relationship between affect and *nous*. The problem arises from his methodology that only considers the phenomenology of Pentecostal praxis while ignoring its theology. The resulting epistemology is an affective foundationalism that relegates noetic beliefs to infrequency and secondary role. But this sub-cognitivism should not be if the tradition of Pentecostalism is taken seriously. Daniel Castelo, who argues that Pentecostalism is a mystical tradition, depicts a perspectivally integrated relationship between spirituality and theology. He states,

> If spirituality has to do with the lives led by Christ-followers and theology has to do with the speech and concepts used by Christians to account for their lives as such, then it makes perfect sense how, at least formally, the two can and should be complementary and mutually constituting. Experience and imagination, consciousness and language—these are simply coinhering features of a sustained identity over time. They are connected aspects of Christian lives because at the center of theology and spirituality is the God of Christian witness

and confession, who in turn is contemplated and beheld by the totality of a creature's being. . . . One's embodied life—including one's practices, activities, and loves (spirituality), as well as one's ideas, concepts, and categories (theology)—is representative of the totality required in the beholding of this revealed mystery.[109]

The bifurcation between pretheory and theory manifests itself in the division between spirituality and theology in much of Pentecostal theology, according to Castelo. Instead, he argues for a spirituality-theology interface. To approach Pentecostal theology from spirituality as advocated by Steven Land, theology must not be merely theoretical, deductive, or conceptual. Neither is theology supposed to be anti-intellectual or merely experiential. Theology must be holistic, following the logic of *lex orandi, lex credendi*, in which the goal of theology is an encounter with the mysterious, self-disclosing God and holistic transformation of the person-in-community.[110]

Even though Pentecostals have been known to be anti-intellectual, they have always been doctrinal. The reason for this seeming inconsistency is due to the "direct concern of Pentecostals to keep theological reflection in check, lest it compromise the experience of genuine faith."[111] However, this (pretheoretical) experience of genuine faith, as stated by the early Pentecostal Myer Pearlman, is made possible by (theoretical) Christian doctrine.[112]

Smith's Nuanced View of Reason

Contrasted with the affective foundationalism of his Pentecostal epistemology, Smith's broader works acknowledge the dialectical relationship argued for thus far. In *Desiring the Kingdom*, Smith notes that "the 'fruit' of theological reflection (e.g., the Nicene Creed) trickles down and infiltrates the Christian social imaginary such that it has now become absorbed as a kind of noncognitive 'understanding.'"[113] Critical reflection can help one become aware of and minimize the effect of the misdirected and idolatrous formative power of cultural practices and institutions.[114] Smith also addresses this dialectical relationship in *Introducing Radical Orthodoxy*, considering the "creeds and the confessions of the church . . . [as] the fruit of theological^2 reflection," and argues that "theology^2 . . . will inform the church's confession articulated in theology^1."[115]

An example of this relationship is found in the reification of ideas. Recognizing the sedimentation of theoretical thought into factical world, Smith remarks that ideas become "reified parts of the shared physical environment, and consequently constrain future actions."[116] Commenting on Etienne Wenger's notion of communities of practice and how each group contains a limited range of acceptable "actions, interactions, and relationships,"

Smith states that reification of ideas occurs to put constraints on practices.[117] Reification and practices are thus dialectical for Smith.[118] Rebecca Konyndyk DeYoung agrees and highlights their individuality and inseparability. Drawing from Aristotle, Konyndyk DeYoung argues that development in virtue must include both practice and reflection. Practice aids and expands reflection while reflection gives meaning and sustains practice.[119]

The clearest acknowledgment of this dialectical relationship in Smith is found in *Imagining the Kingdom*. Responding to his critics, Smith argues that his emphasis on the pretheoretical is not to set up a dichotomy between pretheory and theory.[120] He states,

> My hope is to foster intentional reflection *on* practice in order to encourage reflective immersion *in* practice. . . . While ultimately we will close the gap between knowledge and action through rehabituation that operates on our cognitive unconscious . . ., there is a moment for reflection here that makes a crucial difference: becoming intellectually aware of what's at stake in my eating practice, and becoming cognizant of how other practices have recruited my habits, will *convince* me to seek new environments and new communities of practice. Being convinced of the importance of practice for "automating" my behavior, I will then *choose* to submit myself to different rhythms and habit-forming routines in order to rehabituate my wants and desires to a different *telos*.[121]

Smith encourages analyzing practices in order to discover its logic. Worship requires not only embodied participation but also conscious reflection. For example, Smith endorses mystagogical preaching, which explains the sacraments and rites of initiation to catechumens. Reflection on worship impacts how one conducts worship.[122] Smith even argues that reason is rooted in the affections and that reason can motivate affective practices: "[Our] affective immersion is never untethered from our intellectual being-in-the-world. So a truly holistic Christian education will be a formation of both heart and mind, both intellect and affect."[123] A careful reading of Smith reveals no dichotomy between reason and affect.

Back to Sub-cognitivism?

Yet, this dialectical view is missing in his Pentecostal epistemology. From its methodology to its product, NAK is presented in hierarchical form. Smith's wider works correct this affective foundationalism. However, there are hints of his continual favoring of pretheory in his admission of integration. In his comments on mystagogical preaching, Smith states that reflection was merely an explanation of worship practice.[124] Reflection seems to lack its own integrity. Reason's importance lies in its reflection on practice, lacking an importance in itself as its own practice. If so, the purer method for the practice of systematic theology is not the investigation of the church's confessions, but a meta-systematic theology, one which investigates the practice of systematic theology. If reflection is always rooted in affect, then should not reflection, even abstract system of doctrines, be affirmed for its importance as its own affective practice?[125] Must practical *ministry* lord over systematic theology? Is not systematic theology a form of practical *theology*, an interrelationship of praxis between reflection and practice? If one rejects modernist systematic theology as a timeless system of doctrines and understands it as always related triperspectivally with affect and praxis, then systematic theology should have its own integrity.

Smith's claim that the training of the heart, to some extent, is accomplished only through practices is an overstatement.[126] While his claim is true in part, discursive reasoning punctuates the predominant pretheoretical navigation of the world. Such punctuation is required to navigate the world correctly, and even makes this navigation perspectivally possible. If, as I have argued, Pentecostal spirituality is triperspectival, then it is better represented by the picture of knowledge forwarded by Haidt, Solomon, and others. A more appropriate Pentecostal epistemology should not centralize affect (orthopathos) or embodied acts (orthopraxis), but nonhierarchically integrate noetic beliefs and theoretical thought (orthodoxy) because triperspectival spirituality does not locate a center in any one perspective. Each perspective incorporates others, so that one cannot exist without the others.[127]

Qualitative primacy allows for emphasis or intensification of one aspect that nevertheless includes the others in Trinitarian manner. This comprehensive vision perspectivally integrates without opposing the propositional and the nonpropositional, knowing-that and knowing-how, pretheory and theory. Because all involved modes of knowledge are harmoniously integrated, the question of primacy becomes one of ad hoc need than necessity. Both pretheoretical and theoretical thought can have greater influence than the other at different times, all the while involving each other. Context will determine when one perspective is more prominent than the others. One is not essentially more primary than the other, but only in emphasis, even if pretheory is the default mode of being-in-the-world and thus quantitatively primary.

I have argued that Smith's Pentecostal epistemology is insufficiently Pentecostal due to its neglect of reason and beliefs. Theoretical beliefs are required to differentiate between Pentecostal spirituality and other spiritualities. Similarly, without Pentecostal theology, Pentecostal epistemology loses its distinctiveness, as can be seen in the similarities between Smith, Haidt, and Solomon.

CONCLUSION

The embodied praxis of Pentecostalism indicates a postmodern anthropology and epistemology. Pentecostal epistemology is narrative and affective, an irreducible, pragmatic, hermeneutic knowledge that has primacy over theoretical knowledge. Utilizing the works of Jonathan Haidt, Robert Solomon, and others, I argued that Smith's Pentecostal epistemology does not account for the integrative relationship between pretheoretical understanding and theoretical knowledge. Smith's dichotomization between cognition and affect was shown to be a generalization. Haidt and Solomon demonstrate that intuition and emotion are forms of cognition. Because Smith does not attend to the theoretical beliefs of Pentecostalism, his Pentecostal epistemology cannot remain uniquely Pentecostal. Rather, it is more specifically a postmodern hermeneutic epistemology. To that topic, I will now turn.

NOTES

1. Haidt, "The Emotional Dog and Its Rational Tail," 818.
2. Haidt.
3. Haidt, 815.
4. Haidt, 814–18.
5. Haidt, 822.
6. Haidt, 819.
7. Haidt, 823.
8. Haidt.
9. Haidt.
10. Haidt, 821.
11. Haidt, 819.
12. Haidt, 829. I will be limiting my comments to Haidt's argument and will not explore whether scholars of other fields can use reason in such a way. However, Haidt also includes in this group those with "a high need for cognition." Haidt, 820.
13. Haidt, 829. Emphasis mine.
14. In his famous book, Mortimer Adler states that "reading . . . should be a conversation between [the reader] and the author." Mortimer J. Adler and Charles Van Doren, *How to Read a Book: The Classic Guide to Intelligent Reading* (New York: Touchstone, 1972), 49.
15. Jonathan Haidt, "The Emotional Dog Gets Mistaken for a Possum," *Review of General Psychology* 8, no. 4 (2004): 283–90 (284).
16. James K. A. Smith, *Jacques Derrida: Live Theory* (New York: Continuum, 2005), 17.
17. Smith, 27–38.
18. Haidt, "The Emotional Dog Gets Mistaken for a Possum," 286.
19. Haidt, 287.

20. Haidt, "The Emotional Dog and Its Rational Tail," 819.

21. Haidt does not denigrate reasoning. He attributes formative power to intersubjective reasoning and gives some credence to private reasoning. Missing this nuance leads to a fundamental misunderstanding of an important part of Haidt's theory, which Herbert Saltzstein and Tziporah Kasachkoff have done. See Herbert D. Saltzstein and Tziporah Kasachkoff, "Haidt's Moral Intuitionist Theory: A Psychological and Philosophical Critique," *Review of General Psychology* 8, no. 4 (2004): 273–82. For Haidt's response, see Haidt, "The Emotional Dog Gets Mistaken for a Possum."

22. Haidt, "The Emotional Dog and Its Rational Tail," 827. Emphasis mine.

23. Haidt, 829.

24. Haidt, 814. Also, see Joshua D. Greene et al., "The Neural Bases of Cognitive Conflict and Control in Moral Judgment," *Neuron* 44, no. 2 (2004): 389–400 (397–98).

25. Haidt, *The Righteous Mind*, 52. Steven Land also makes this connection between affect and cognition. Affections are "complex, cognitive integrations . . . [and] also operate on and are expressions of different levels or dimensions of human consciousness." Land, *Pentecostal Spirituality*, 171.

26. Haidt, "The Emotional Dog Gets Mistaken for a Possum," 286.

27. Haidt, "The Emotional Dog and Its Rational Tail," 818. Emphasis mine.

28. Greene et al., "The Neural Bases of Cognitive Conflict and Control in Moral Judgment," 397–98.

29. Smith, *Thinking in Tongues*, 56n19.

30. Cordelia Fine, "Is the Emotional Dog Wagging Its Rational Tail, or Chasing It?: Reason in Moral Judgment," *Philosophical Explorations* 9, no. 1 (2006): 83–98 (97); and Jeanette Kennett and Cordelia Fine, "Will the Real Moral Judgment Please Stand Up?: The Implications of Social Intuitionist Models of Cognition for Meta-Ethics and Moral Psychology," *Ethical Theory & Moral Practice* 12, no. 1 (2009): 77–96 (91). Also, see Greene et al., "The Neural Bases of Cognitive Conflict and Control in Moral Judgment."

31. Kennett and Fine, "Will the Real Moral Judgment Please Stand Up?," 88.

32. Fine, "Is the Emotional Dog Wagging Its Rational Tail, or Chasing It?," 89. Also, see Greene et al., "The Neural Bases of Cognitive Conflict and Control in Moral Judgment," 397.

33. Fine, "Is the Emotional Dog Wagging Its Rational Tail, or Chasing It?," 89.

34. Fine, 86–87.

35. Joshua D Greene, "Dual-Process Morality and the Personal/Impersonal Distinction: A Reply to McGuire, Langdon, Coltheart, and Mackenzie," *Journal of Experimental Social Psychology* 45, no. 3 (2009): 581–84 (581).

36. Joseph M. Paxton and Joshua D. Greene, "Moral Reasoning: Hints and Allegations," *Topics in Cognitive Science* 2, no. 3 (2010): 511–27 (521–23). Also, see Joshua D. Greene et al., "An FMRI Investigation of Emotional Engagement in Moral Judgment," *Science* 293 (2001): 2105–8.

37. Paxton and Greene, "Moral Reasoning: Hints and Allegations," 513–15.

38. Paxton and Greene, 517–18.

39. Fine, "Is the Emotional Dog Wagging Its Rational Tail, or Chasing It?," 85.

40. Haidt also describes how such a reasoning process may occur. See Haidt, "The Emotional Dog and Its Rational Tail," 329.

41. Haidt agrees that reasoning can play an important role in moral judgments, even when reason and intuition conflict. See Joshua D. Greene and Jonathan Haidt, "How (and Where) Does Moral Judgment Work?," *TRENDS in Cognitive Sciences* 6, no. 12 (2002): 517–23 (522).

42. Kennett and Fine, "Will the Real Moral Judgment Please Stand Up?," 92–93.

43. Fine, "Is the Emotional Dog Wagging Its Rational Tail, or Chasing It?," 93.

44. The question whether such corrections replace the SIM is a different topic. For example, other models have been presented by Joshua Greene (Dual-Process Theory) and Adenekan Dedeke (Cognitive-Intuitionist Model). See Greene et al., "The Neural Bases of Cognitive Conflict and Control in Moral Judgment"; and Dedeke, "A Cognitive-Intuitionist Model of Moral Judgment." However, my aim is normative, even though it utilizes descriptive, empirical findings. Therefore, even if reason is used infrequently (a descriptive claim), my aim is to discover whether reason ought to be given a more critical role in knowledge (a prescriptive claim).

45. There is also noetic-(basic belief)cognition and ratiocinative-cognition.

46. Robert C. Solomon, *The Passions: Emotions and the Meaning of Life*, 2nd ed. (Indianapolis: Hackett Publishing Company, 1993), 58–64. Solomon also calls it judgmentalism. See Robert C. Solomon, "Emotions, Thoughts, and Feelings: Emotions as Engagements with the World," in *Thinking about Feeling: Contemporary Philosophers on Emotions*, ed. Robert C. Solomon (New York: Oxford University Press, 2004), 76–78. Henceforth, ETFEEW.

47. Solomon, "ETFEEW," 76. Beáta Tóth states that reflections on cognitive emotion have shown "the essential interrelatedness of reason and emotionality." Tóth, *The Heart Has Its Reasons*, 18.

48. Solomon, *The Passions*, 15.

49. For examples of such critiques, see Justin D'Arms and Daniel Jacobson, "The Significance of Recalcitrant Emotion (or, Anti-Quasijudgmentalism)," in *Philosophy and the Emotions*, ed. Anthony Hatzimoysis, Royal Institute of Philosophy Supplement: 52 (New York: Cambridge University Press, 2003), 127–45; and Cheshire Calhoun, "Cognitive Emotions?," in *What Is an Emotion?: Classic and Contemporary Readings*, ed. Robert C. Solomon, 2nd ed. (New York: Oxford University Press, 2003), 236–47. Both accounts raise the problem of differing emotion and belief. Calhoun especially distinguishes between emotion and fully conceptualized belief. Yet, her critique is consonant with Solomon's view.

50. Solomon distinguishes between emotion and feeling, the former being able to exist without the latter. For Solomon, feeling can be a form of judgment, but is episodic, and, unlike emotion, is not intentional. Solomon equates feeling with affect, so Smith's understanding of affect is akin to emotion for Solomon. See Robert C. Solomon, "Emotions and Choice," in *What Is an Emotion?: Classic and Contemporary Readings*, ed. Robert C. Solomon, 2nd ed. (New York: Oxford University Press, 2003), 224–35 (225); Solomon, *The Passions*, 96–102; and Robert C. Solomon, "Emotions, Thoughts and Feelings: What Is a 'Cognitive Theory' of

the Emotions and Does It Neglect Affectivity?," in *Philosophy and the Emotions*, ed. Anthony Hatzimoysis, Royal Institute of Philosophy Supplement: 52 (New York: Cambridge University Press, 2003), 1–18 (16). Henceforth, ETFCTE. The line of argument I will be presenting does not engage the vigorous debate on the nature of emotion. I have chosen Solomon for his affinity with NAK. While I believe that Solomon's theory of emotion is correct, there are multiple views on the nature of emotion. For a good survey, see Julien A. Deonna and Fabrice Teroni, *The Emotions: A Philosophical Introduction* (New York: Routledge, 2008); and Aaron Ben-Ze'ev, "Emotion as a Subtle Mental Mode," in *Thinking about Feeling: Contemporary Philosophers on Emotions*, ed. Robert C. Solomon (New York: Oxford University Press, 2004), 250–68.

51. Deonna and Teroni, *The Emotions*, 4.

52. Charles B. Guignon, "Moods in Heidegger's Being and Time," in *What Is an Emotion?: Classic and Contemporary Readings*, ed. Robert C. Solomon, 2nd ed. (New York: Oxford University Press, 2003), 180–90 (184–86).

53. Solomon, *The Passions*, 71–72, 112.

54. Solomon, 125.

55. Solomon, 126.

56. Solomon, 61; and Solomon, "ETFCTE," 10–11.

57. Patricia Greenspan resists the term "construal" because it seems to deny the necessity of the propositional in affective evaluation. Because the thesis of her article is that affect has propositional content for rational evaluation, this resistance is understandable. However, Solomon's article in the same edited volume argues that his cognitive theory allows for the propositional, even if judgment is not always propositional. See Greenspan, "Emotions, Rationality, and Mind/Body," 122n22; and Solomon, "ETFCTE," 16.

58. Solomon, 8–9; Robert C. Solomon, "The Philosophy of Emotions," in *Handbook of Emotions*, ed. Michael Lewis, Jeannette M. Haviland-Jones, and Lisa Feldman Barrett, 3rd ed. (New York: The Guilford Press, 2008), 3–16 (12); and Solomon, "ETFEEW," 79–80. While judgment is the best heuristic to understand emotion, Solomon later admits that even judgment cannot truly capture all of the different manners that emotion engages the world and advises that the real work of analysis lies with particular emotions rather than a general theory. See Solomon, "ETFEEW," 83–84.

59. Mark R. Wynn, *Renewing the Senses: A Study of the Philosophy and Theology of the Spiritual Life* (Oxford: Oxford University Press, 2013), 32.

60. Solomon, "The Philosophy of Emotions," 10–13; and Solomon, "ETFEEW," 77.

61. Solomon, *The Passions*, 117.

62. However, Solomon is careful to articulate that emotional subjectivity is essentially intersubjective. My world is our world. See Solomon, 19–20.

63. Solomon, 19.

64. Solomon, 135.

65. Solomon, "ETFCTE," 7. Desiree Berendsen incorrectly charges Solomon that he does not adequately address the passive nature of emotions. See Desiree

Berendsen, "Religious Passions and Emotions: Towards a Stratified Concept of Religious Passions: Robert Solomon Versus Thomas Dixon," in *Encountering Transcendence: Contributions to a Theology of Christian Religious Experience*, ed. Lieven Boeve, Hans Geybels, and Stijn Van den Bossche (Dudley: Peeters, 2005), 201–12 (210–12).

66. Although he views emotion as a mental mode, Ben-Ze'ev argues that it still consists of cognition and evaluation. Ben-Ze'ev, "Emotion as a Subtle Mental Mode," 259–60. For David Heywood, cognition includes "facts and concepts but also such things as beliefs, hopes, attitudes, likes and dislikes." Heywood, *Divine Revelation and Human Learning*, 67.

67. Solomon, "ETFEEW," 79

68. Robert C. Solomon, "Emotions, Cognition, Affect: On Jerry Neu's A Tear Is An Intellectual Thing," *Philosophical Studies* 108, no. 1 (2002): 133–42 (138).

69. Solomon admits that feeling had been discounted as a judgment in the past. He has since reconsidered his earlier view. See Solomon, "ETFCTE," 16.

70. Solomon, *The Passions*, 58.

71. Solomon, "The Philosophy of Emotions," 12. Solomon differs here with the way Alvin Plantinga understands basic belief. Solomon's usage of belief is similar to ratiocination. Plantinga finds basic belief to be similar to perception. See Alvin Plantinga, *Warrant and Proper Function* (New York: Oxford University Press, 1993), 89–101.

72. Solomon, "The Philosophy of Emotions," 14.

73. Solomon, 11. Total unawareness, as opposed to being consciously unaware, of an emotion would nullify it as an emotion. For Solomon, totally unaware emotion cannot be a judgment. See Solomon, 12.

74. Solomon, "ETFEEW," 82; and Deonna and Teroni, *The Emotions*, 16–18.

75. Solomon, *The Passions*, 61.

76. Solomon, 181. Emphasis mine.

77. Solomon, 60. Also, Solomon, "The Philosophy of Emotions," 11.

78. Solomon, "ETFCTE," 2.

79. Ben-Ze'ev, "Emotion as a Subtle Mental Mode," 260–61.

80. Solomon, *The Passions*, 60–61. According to Patricia Greenspan, who is not a cognitivist, affect is evaluative, and its evaluation can be put into propositions. See Greenspan, "Emotions, Rationality, and Mind/Body," 118–25. Likewise, Ben-Ze'ev argues that thinking and emotion are not dichotomous. The former can occur in the latter. Thus, the logic of emotion does not necessarily eliminate intellection. See Ben-Ze'ev, "Emotion as a Subtle Mental Mode," 267; and Aaron Ben-Ze'ev, "The Logic of Emotions," in *Philosophy and the Emotions*, ed. Anthony Hatzimoysis, Royal Institute of Philosophy Supplement: 52 (New York: Cambridge University Press, 2003), 147–62 (162).

81. Solomon, "ETFCTE," 7.

82. This differentiation is important to answer the charge against cognitive theory from recalcitrant emotion. Recalcitrant emotion conflicts with one's judgment. For example, the recalcitrant emotion of fear of flying involves the judgment that it's an irrational fear. This critique involves recognizing the conflict between construal and

judgment: "Recalcitrance . . . arises when an agent emotionally construes the circumstances as being one way, despite judging otherwise." D'Arms and Jacobson, "The Significance of Recalcitrant Emotion (or, Anti-Quasijudgmentalism)," 131. However, construal *is* judgment. The fear itself *is* a form of knowledge or appraisal even if it conflicts with its rational assessment. With recalcitrant emotion, one's rational assessment is necessarily ratiocinative. Therefore, recalcitrance does not involve a conflict between construal and judgment. Rather, recalcitrant emotion involves a conflict between affective, cognitive construal and ratiocinative, cognitive appraisal. They are judgments of different kinds. Insofar as they relate to (sur)reality, these appraisals can be further divided between NAC and NAK.

83. Wynn, *Renewing the Senses*, 46–47.
84. Wynn, 54–57.
85. Wynn, 143.
86. Wynn, 47–49.
87. Wynn, 128.
88. Wynn, 65.
89. Smith, *Desiring the Kingdom*, 209, 56–57n34.
90. Solomon, "Emotions and Choice," 233.
91. Solomon, 234.
92. Solomon, *The Passions*, 183.
93. Solomon, 186.
94. Ben-Ze'ev, "The Logic of Emotions," 150–52. Ben-Ze'ev distinguishes between the logic of ratiocination and emotion by utilizing the Kantian differentiation between analytic rules and synthetic principles of reasoning. While they share the analytic rules of formal logic, they differ synthetically in assigning meaning to particular events. Whereas the logic of intellect is broader and more general, emotion is more immediate and personal. Where his explanation lacks, however, is their lack of integration, although he encourages such integration. For example, he states that reflection "typically eliminates the emotional experience." See Ben-Ze'ev, 152–62.
95. Smith, *Desiring the Kingdom*, 50. Emphasis mine.
96. Guignon, "Moods in Heidegger's Being and Time," 181.
97. Solomon. *The Passions*, 112.
98. Solomon, "ETFCTE," 13.
99. Solomon, *The Passions*, 126.
100. Solomon, "ETFCTE," 14–15.
101. Wynn, *Renewing the Senses*, 35–36. For Ronald De Sousa, emotion manages the salience of the objects of attention. See Ronald De Sousa, "The Rationality of Emotion," in *What Is an Emotion?: Classic and Contemporary Readings*, ed. Robert C. Solomon, 2nd ed. (New York: Oxford University Press, 2003), 248–57 (249).
102. Solomon, "ETFCTE," 16.
103. Peter Goldie, "Emotion, Feeling, and Knowledge of the World," in *Thinking about Feeling: Contemporary Philosophers on Emotions*, ed. Robert C. Solomon (New York: Oxford University Press, 2004), 91–106 (91–99).
104. Goldie, 99.
105. Goldie, 99–102.

106. Goldie, 102.
107. Goldie.
108. Goldie, 103.
109. Castelo, *Pentecostalism as a Christian Mystical Tradition*, 56–57.
110. Castelo, 1–36. Castelo finds testimony and narrative qualifying as expanded forms of systematic theology in the holistic vein of Irenaeus that privileges the spirituality-theology interface because they operate on the theo-logic of encounter and transformation, not merely of conceptual knowledge. Castelo, 28–36. Therefore, knowledge of God that arises from this spirituality-theology interface is participatory and embodied. Daniel Castelo, *Revisioning Pentecostal Ethics: The Epiclectic Community* (Cleveland: CPT Press, 2012), 24.
111. Castelo, *Pentecostalism as a Christian Mystical Tradition*, 31.
112. Douglas Jacobsen, *Thinking in the Spirit: Theologies of the Early Pentecostal Movement* (Bloomington: Indiana University Press, 2003), 5.
113. Smith, *Desiring the Kingdom*, 69n56.
114. Smith, 209. Therefore, he advocates for an ethnographic role for the pastorate, arguing that unveiling the implicit theology embedded in everyday rituals helps the church identify the misdirected theologies that shape its practitioners. See James K. A. Smith, *Awaiting the King: Reforming Public Theology* (Grand Rapids: Baker Academic, 2017), 194–97, 205. A lack of attending to critical reflection can encourage an opposite effect. Cf., James K. A. Smith, "Keeping Time in the Social Sciences: An Experiment with Fixed-Hour Prayer and the Liturgical Calendar," in *Teaching and Christian Practices: Reshaping Faith & Learning*, ed. David I. Smith and James K. A. Smith (Grand Rapids: Eerdmans Publishing Company, 2011), 140–56 (155–56).
115. Smith, *Introducing Radical Orthodoxy*, 178. In an email exchange with the publisher, the publisher confirmed with Smith of a misprint, correcting that theology^2 informed the creeds. Yoon Shin, email message to the publisher, November 9, 2016.
116. David I. Smith and James K. A. Smith, "Introduction: Practices, Faith, and Pedagogy," in *Teaching and Christian Practices: Reshaping Faith & Learning*, ed. David I. Smith and James K. A. Smith (Grand Rapids: Eerdmans Publishing Company, 2011), 1–23 (13).
117. Smith and Smith, 12–13.
118. Smith and Smith, 13.
119. Rebecca Konyndyk DeYoung, "Pedagogical Rhythms: Practices and Reflections on Practice," in *Teaching and Christian Practices: Reshaping Faith & Learning*, ed. David I. Smith and James K. A. Smith (Grand Rapids: Eerdmans Publishing Company, 2011), 24–42 (39–42).
120. Smith, *Imagining the Kingdom*, 186.
121. Smith.
122. Smith, 187–88.
123. Smith, 189–90.
124. Smith, 188. Smith's latest iteration of Pentecostal epistemology also does not acknowledge the hints of integration in his wider works but maintains the hierarchy between pretheory and theory. In fact, this latest iteration remains virtually

unchanged. See James K. A. Smith, "Pentecostalism," in *The Oxford Handbook of the Epistemology of Theology*, ed. William J. Abraham and Frederick D. Aquino (New York: Oxford University Press, 2017), 606–18.

125. Smith, *Imagining the Kingdom*, 190.

126. Smith, 13.

127. An epistemic perichoresis may be a fitting term.

Part 2

SMITH'S POSTMODERN EPISTEMOLOGY

Chapter 4

Postmodern Hermeneutic Epistemology

INTRODUCTION

The chapters in this part act as a pivot, moving away from Pentecostal epistemology to a fuller postmodern epistemology and preparing the conversation with Reformed epistemology. The overall aim is to present Smith's epistemology as hermeneutic, postliberal, and realist, while building on his embodied epistemology.

Although Smith believes that Pentecostal philosophy can contribute to Christian philosophy, the movement of his epistemology is rather the reverse. His Pentecostal epistemology is merely an instantiation of his postmodern epistemology. This chapter exposits this lineage in a thematic way, drawing out the themes of his Pentecostal epistemology from his wider corpus. What becomes evident is his fully formed embodied epistemology by the time of *Thinking in Tongues*. His latter works also show consistency with his earlier writings, especially with the themes of anthropology, hermeneutics, and epistemology. Specifically, the postliberal themes of situatedness and hermeneutics of language games that are based on the goodness of embodied, situated, and hermeneutical creation appear consistently throughout Smith's corpus.[1]

Important to note in this exposition is the chosen methodology of attending to Smith's interpretation and appropriation of his various sources rather than the sources themselves. Not only are his works voluminous, but so are those with whom he interacts due to his wide interdisciplinary interests.[2] An investigation into Smith's correct interpretation of his interlocutors would enlarge the scope of this book beyond practicality. Furthermore, as a constructive synthesizer, Smith is not so much concerned with mere exposition, but with creatively constructing and synthesizing ideas for his own purposes.[3] My method is similar. The concern of this chapter is ultimately to understand *his* ideas rather than investigating the orthodoxy of his interpretations. Nevertheless, where Smith's misinterpretation poses a danger to my constructive project, I critique and repair Smith's interpretations. Moreover, because Smith's epistemological themes appear in many of his works, my method can be seen as that of a funnel, gathering the scattered themes into a coherent whole. This systematization is required because Smith has not written an extended work on epistemology.

POSTMODERN HERMENEUTIC EPISTEMOLOGY: ITS THEMES

In *Who's Afraid of Postmodernism*, Smith presents French philosophy as a major intellectual influence on postmodernism and extricates three hermeneutic themes—themes that occur frequently in his other writings[4]: the ubiquity of interpretation, the ultimate narrativity of all beliefs and language games, and the formative power of discipline. While some have criticized postmodernism as relativist and anti-Christian, Smith argues that postmodernism is misunderstood and connects it to the ancient faith: "The best way to be postmodern is to be premodern."[5] Both eras affirm the goodness of finite, embodied, situated, and contingent creaturehood.[6] The repudiation of modernism's desire to transcend contingency is a return to acknowledging the Creator-creature distinction, that no aspect of creation is autonomous.

The Ubiquity of Interpretation as Human Structure

Humans are structurally hermeneutic. The impossibility of an unmediated reading of reality is a confession of creatureliness. Appropriating Derrida's claim that "there is nothing outside the text," Smith argues that to be human is to interpret. Experience of reality is interpretive.[7] This claim challenges the view of prelapsarian hermeneutic immediacy that attributes the mediation of interpretation to the Fall, one to be overcome in the eschaton. This "eschatological immediacy model" is a rejection of finitude and contingency.[8] For others, the "present immediacy model" represents the fallenness of interpretation that is presently redeemable. Unlike the previous model in which finitude is overcome in the eschaton, this model disavows present finitude and embraces the possibility of present objectivity, not realizing that any claims to an unadulterated reading are already a traditioned reading. Even an appeal to *sola scriptura* is an interpretive act of an interpreted principle.[9] Immediacy is an impossibility for finite, situated creatures. Yet, both models consider the medium of interpretation as fallen and long for its overcoming. For Martin Heidegger and Jacques Derrida, interpretation is an inevitable condition of being-in-the-world, of being finite, situated, and contingent; interpretation is structural to one's being because being is social. For the condition of possibility even for the soliloquy of a solitary mental life is the social phenomenon of language. Being-in-the-world is being-with. Even the retreat into the solitary mind to avoid the Other is made possible by the Other, the alterity of language.[10]

Yet, their "violent mediation model" considers the inevitability of interpretation as violent. For Heidegger, the interpretive fore-structures condition one to become immersed in the everydayness of the public, "the they." Related to the they is "the they-self" who is conditioned to consider only the superficiality of everydayness, losing one's authentic existence. The danger of becoming the they-self is the result of *Dasein's* thrownness into fallen intersubjectivity.[11] For Derrida, language marks the structural fallenness of interpretation because the full presence of the author is missing. Speech is not pure and writing fallen, as thought by Ferdinand Saussure, due to the respective proximity and absence of the speaker. Writing is originary violence because language, as an infinite interplay of meaning, does not contain full presence.[12] Without this pure presence that allows for full comprehension, any interpretation of the Other is always violent. This violence points to the fallenness of intersubjectivity because intersubjectivity marks the condition of possibility for interpretation of the Other.[13]

Contrary to these models, Smith's creational hermeneutic maintains the structural goodness of interpretation. Creational hermeneutic agrees with the violent mediation model that interpretation is original to creation, but it does not cast aside the goodness of mediation as originally fallen. Interpretation goes all the way down, having received the benediction of God in creation. While the interpretive faculties are damaged by sin, interpretation itself is not structurally fallen. "The effects of the Fall is not the appearance of interpretation but rather the distortion or corruption of interpretation."[14] Denying the inherent goodness of interpretation entails that to be human, as interpretive beings, is to be necessarily violent in being. In this model, the eschaton indeed fulfills and completes, but fulfillment is not a consummation from lack. The eschaton is the completion of what was nascent in creation and the healing of the damage to mediation.[15] Humans will continue to be finite and situated as they were in Eden, but in consummated form.[16]

Human finitude, which marks the necessity of interpretation, is composed of perspectivally integrated features of intersubjectivity, situationality, traditionality, and undecidability. First, interpretation is necessary due to the lack of immediate access to another mind. Such access would eradicate the need for communication.[17] Instead, "every act of reading or listening is an act of translation: a negotiation between two (or more) universes of discourse, two (or more) traditionalities, two (or more) ways of understanding the world."[18]

Second, embodied intersubjectivity indicates the situationality of spatiotemporal location.[19] Embodied intersubjectivity requires interpretation but is not relegated merely to communication. Smith equates intersubjectivity with worldview.[20] It is a hermeneutic filter for knowledge. Intersubjectivity, which is a situated traditioned way of understanding, delivers the world as a particular something.[21] Without this grounding in situationality, the impossible dream of *sub specie aeternitatis*, the transcending of human embodiment to attain God's view of the world, would be one step away from becoming possible. Situationality is the acceptance of the ubiquity of interpretation. Hermeneutics is the erasure of that dream of all dreams that seeks to reduce all differences to the same, to commensurability.[22]

Third, spatiotemporal intersubjectivity indicates traditionality. Tradition conditions not only the possibilities and parameters of the sources one engage (e.g., language, sociocultural context, geography, religion, etc.) but also one's worldview. Worldview is the gift of tradition. Tradition plays a normative role in shaping one's imagination of the world, drawing the boundaries of "acceptable" interpretations and acting as a launchpad for new possibilities of interpretations.[23] Even creative imagination is not wholly new, but arises from the possibilities and impossibilities afforded by one's multiple traditions. To be human is to be traditioned: "Traditionality is a *heritage* that one both receives and shapes."[24] Traditionality implies situationality and intersubjectivity, since to be traditioned is to be part of human culture.

Finally, the plurality of interpretive options necessitates hermeneutic undecidability. Undecidability is the loss of the metaphysics of presence, the pure determination of meaning. Undecidability, which is not indecision, arises from facing multiple interpretive options. Given this plurality of interpretations, misunderstanding is also a possibility. But this undecidability is an inescapable human condition that is not structurally and originally violent.[25] Without using the term, Shelly Rambo provides a compelling reminder about undecidability by arguing that victims of trauma lose the ability to understand the trauma clearly. Trauma alters the linear conception of time, as the traumatic past invades the present and makes the future bleak. It physically alters the body's limbic system so that the prefrontal cortex that regulates experience and meaning becomes inhibited. Moreover, inasmuch as there is nothing outside the text, trauma negates epistemic certainty by altering the human ability to understand reality through spoken or written language, especially due to the breaking down of one's social world through the loss of trust. In this way, trauma reveals that full cognitive awareness is impossible.[26] What remains are multiplicity of interpretations.[27]

What are the implications of undecidability? First, the ubiquity and multiple options of interpretation mean that interpretation is "at root a commitment of faith."[28] Faith is not Cartesian certainty; doubt and uncertainty always accompany faith. Second, multiplicity of interpretive options and limits of perspectival worldview necessitate epistemic humility because misunderstanding and misinterpretation are possible.[29] Truth becomes perspectival but is not abandoned. The criterion for truth is not objectivity but is sectarian. Intersubjective tradition determines "good" interpretation and certain interpretations become privileged and normative.[30] In fact, the goodness of creation is itself a *mythos*.[31] Stripped of epistemic objectivity, situated beings face multiple interpretive options and are mired in undecidability. They must choose and each choosing is an act of faith. Interpretation governs human existence: "There is no uninterpreted reality."[32]

Worldview as Myth

Structural hermeneutic of human be-ing burrows down to the level of worldview. Interpretation goes all the way down: "All knowledge is rooted in *some* narrative or myth."[33] The foundational and mythic picture of worldview reveals that worldview is a commitment to an ultimately unprovable narrative. Worldview is *pistic*. This view does not abandon truth. Rather, confession of *pistic* worldview is "the retrieval of a fundamentally Augustinian epistemology that is attentive to the structural necessity of faith preceding reason, believing in order to understand—trusting in order to interpret."[34]

Smith appropriates mythic worldview with Herman Dooyeweerd's philosophy of modal aspects and argues that pretheoretical commitments reveal human structural religiosity. That is, one takes in the world pretheoretically as a concrete whole. Reflection on one or more modal aspects of reality (e.g., the economic sphere, the physical sphere, the psychic sphere, etc.) is an artificial mode of knowing. Absolutizing a modal aspect confuses a part for the whole.[35] Theoretical reflection is an abstraction of a sphere or a combination of spheres and is based on the "nontheoretical or natural attitude" of worldview, what Dooyeweerd calls ground-motive, and it is with this ground-motive that one predominantly operates. Moreover, ground-motive reveals the ultimately religious or confessional motivation of existence. Because interpretation of reality is ultimately confessional, humans are ultimately religious, confessional beings. The modernist is correct; religion is biased. However, if worldview is mythic, then everyone is religious; everyone is biased.

Affective, Kinesthetic Formation

That Smith's epistemology arises from an Augustinian anthropology is clear, centrally represented by the importance of embodiment and the *ordo amoris*. He views "humans as most fundamentally oriented and identified by [pretheoretical, embodied] love."[36] In an extended reflection on Augustine for his own affective epistemology, Smith argues that humans are primarily lovers, rather than thinkers or believers.[37] The direction of love is guided by formative practices which Smith calls liturgies.[38] The centralization of human be-ing in the heart designates humans as ultimately loving, desiring animals whose knowledge of the world is primarily affective and pretheoretical. It is primarily the affective faculties that are fed by aesthetic mediums, such as narratives and images, that constitute one's world and give one meaning and significance.[39]

Not all loves are of equal value. Ultimate loves are what form one's vision of the good life and fundamentally orients and shapes her beliefs, affections, and behavior.[40] There are five characteristics about this love. First, love is teleologically *intentional*. This intentionality, according to Augustine, is an unavoidable structural condition of humanity, even if the direction of the structure can be iconic or idolatrous: "What distinguishes us . . . is not *whether* we love, but *what* we love."[41] Participation in the world is directed by desire's intentionality, especially by one's ultimate love.[42]

Second, love is *teleologically* intentional. As structurally loving beings, persons are erotically intentioned toward some ultimate love. While the structure (of love) is always the same, the direction/aim of love can differ.[43] Love always has an end: a vision of human flourishing. This *telos* is the vision of the kingdom, the desirable life, even if it is not the Kingdom of God. Ultimate desire captures human affections and pulls one toward the vision of the good life, shaping her interpretations of the world in the process. Hermeneutic vision is determined by one's ultimate desires, and this vision shapes her everyday decisions and habits, constituting her very identity in the process. Smith writes,

> Thus we become certain kinds of people; we begin to emulate, mimic, and mirror the particular vision that we desire. Attracted by it and moved toward it, we begin to live into this vision of the good life and start to look like citizens who inhabit the world that we picture as the good life. . . . So many of the penultimate decisions, actions, and paths we undertake are implicitly and ultimately aimed at trying to live out the vision of the good life that we love and thus *want* to pursue.[44]

This attention to the decisions, actions, and habits leads to the third feature of love; ultimate love is shaped by habits. Habits are dispositions that "incline us to act in certain ways without having to kick into a mode of reflection" and are products "of long development and formation."[45] Habits direct the aim of love, while love is embedded in habits.[46] A perspectival spiral exists. The human-being-in-the-world is not a mere passive animal that is moved here and there by the affections. Her desires shape her imagination while her habits (and beliefs) shape her desires. "What we do (practices) is intimately linked to what we desire (love), so what we do determines whether, how, and what we can know."[47] Love and practice are intricately related. What one does shapes what one loves, and what one loves shapes what one does.

Fourth, habits direct love by training the heart toward its *telos*. Repetitive practices tend to shape one's dispositions because the heart is closely tied to the practices of the body. Integrated with "aesthetic phenomena like pictures and stories . . . [these practices] mold and shape our precognitive disposition to the world by training our desires."[48] The most formative of these practices is what Smith calls liturgy. Liturgies are identity-forming practices that accomplish their function by shaping one's desires and visions of the kingdom.[49] Daily practices shape one into a particular person by directing one's desires, necessitating that she pay attention to her formative practices.[50] Because practice directs desire, Smith confesses to the power of practice, stating that practice is prior to understanding.[51] This hierarchy is consistent with his axiomatic claim that "behind every pedagogy is a philosophical anthropology."[52] Knowledge is based on loves and habits.

Finally, practices are communal; they are social products addressing human needs and desires that constitute culture.[53] Desires are primarily shaped by cultural institutions that are formed through communal practices. Institutions and their practices carry their own *teloi*, and participation in these practices trains hearts toward their ends. This easily explains how the marketing machine of capitalism produces persons-as-consumer. To aim for the *telos* of the Kingdom, then, one must be aware of the competing *teloi* that seek to capture one's heart through foreign liturgies. Therefore, Smith calls for counter-liturgies that will sanctify one's heart and aim her life toward the Kingdom of God.

Postmodern Critical Augustinianism

These three themes of postmodernism—hermeneutic structure of human be-ing, the *pistic* nature of worldview, and the primacy of theological affections and habits—are nicely encapsulated by Smith's summary of the five themes of Radical Orthodoxy (RO).[54] First, RO critiques the supposed universality and neutrality of modernistic reason that created the sacred/secular dichotomy.[55]

Second, after exposing modernity's mythic ground, RO eradicates the dichotomy. The supposed "religious" voices can now gain an equal hearing in the marketplace of ideas in this post-secular realm. For Christians, this leveling of the field amounts not just to an equal hearing; Smith claims that Christianity has greater and more consistent explanatory power of reality.[56]

Third, RO rejects the "flattened" ontology of secularism that reduces all reality to immanence and replaces it with a participatory ontology in which the immanent and material world participates in the transcendent Creator. Significantly, participation negates the nihilism that accompanies ontological autonomy. If reality is detached from a transcendent Creator, then reality is relegated to radical immanence and nihilism because it is grounded in nothing. Participation, however, allows for meaning and value as endowed by the Creator.[57] Because materiality and embodiment, alongside the noetic and spiritual, also participate, they too become meaningful and important.

Fourth and consequently, affirmation of embodiment leads to the material as an icon toward worship and the knowledge of God. Embodiment becomes epistemic. Moreover, if immanence participates in transcendence, then materiality's iconic role must participate in transcendence for meaning and value.[58] Relatedly, RO's affirmation of embodiment leads to an affective, aesthetic epistemology. The iconic role reaffirms the goodness of aesthetics and the eliciting of the passions. This affectivity of embodied aesthetics views itself as more fundamental and primordial than ratiocination.[59] Smith considers this epistemic embodiment as reflecting "the centrality of an experiential aspect in postmodernity."[60]

This claim is made six years prior to *Thinking in Tongues* and his Pentecostal epistemology. My claim that Smith's postmodern epistemology is fully formed prior to *Thinking in Tongues* is solidified in this passage by Smith in *Introducing Radical Orthodoxy*:

> [A] Christian epistemology in the Augustinian and Pascalian tradition affirms the priority of "reasons of the heart of which reason knows nothing".... Christian aesthetic is part of a Christian epistemology and ontology that, epistemologically, challenge the hegemony of cognitive knowing that dominates the Western tradition and, thus, ontologically, question the devaluation of images.... Given a Christian anthropology that affirms the integrity of the embodied self (in contrast to a Platonic privileging of the soul), a Christian epistemology must resist the Western temptation to reduce knowing to only one of its modes—the cognitive—and rather appreciate the multiple modes of knowing (affective, tactile, sensible, etc.). Or to put it in terms of classic discussions of the faculties, rather than privileging the intellect, a Christian epistemology accords equal status, if not primacy, to the senses and imagination.... The result is the revaluing of images and aesthetic media as perhaps the most fundamental and effective means for the communication of truth.[61]

This passage could've been redacted into *Thinking in Tongues* without any inconsistency. Pentecostal epistemology is really an extraction from Smith's postmodern epistemology.

Fifth, this distinctively Christian approach untethered from the oppressive hegemony of secularism can offer a genealogy of other perspectives for the purpose of culture-critique and transformation. Moreover, this culture-critique flows from participatory ontology due to God's concern for the immanent, material world.[62] RO affirms neither secularism's radical immanence nor certain Christian strains of radical spiritualism. Instead, "transcendence is affirmed in immanence . . . as 'enfolded transcendence,'" which creates the motivation to critique the immanent for its transformation.[63]

THE TRANSCENDENTAL CONDITION: LITURGICAL ANTHROPOLOGY

Smith states that "behind the politics . . . lies an epistemology . . . which is in turn undergirded by an ontology."[64] More specifically, between epistemology and ontology lies an anthropology. These relationships can be understood transcendentally. A transcendental condition is "a necessary condition for the possibility of something else," such that X acts as the necessary condition for Y.[65] Just as ontology is the transcendental condition for epistemology, anthropology, more specifically, a postmodern Augustinian anthropology, is the transcendental condition for Smith's epistemology.

The priority of affective know-how is based on a philosophical anthropology that Smith calls "liturgical anthropology," which represents the central core of his work on cultural liturgies.[66] Central to liturgical anthropology is a philosophy of action. Liturgies are repeated, formative practices and habits that inculcate persons in narratives over time.[67] Humans are liturgical, kinesthetic animals that participate in various liturgies. Pretheoretical knowledge inhabits action, is shaped by it, and gives meaning to action. Liturgical anthropology reveals the dynamic nature of this action-knowledge. Anthropology is not merely about the ontology of human be-ing but determines the qualities and forms of knowledge.

Liturgies are not modes of explicit knowledge. As *embodied* meaning-making activities, they orient the imagination by inculcating one in their narratives. In Smith's words, kinesthetics (embodied meaning) primes one for poetics (imagination and narratives).[68] Through action, with its attendant narratives, affections, and *teloi*, one experiences and construes the world. Thought occurs because of action. Action is the basis for meaning-making. As such, humans are primarily actors, not thinkers. In the vein of Polanyi, Smith argues that thinking arises from doing and serves it.[69] Practice and knowledge are inseparable.

Smith clarifies this relationship through the exposition of Pierre Bourdieu's concept of *habitus*, which is the embodied dispositions or habitual ways one construe the world.[70] As habitual, this know-how is impossible without action. Even narrative is part of action. For hearing, reading, telling, and watching are all different modes of action.

Habitus thus indicates the central role the body plays in constituting one's world. Following Maurice Merleau-Ponty, Smith argues that the body is the condition of possibility for experience. As one encounters the world, one's body perceives the world as something, so that one takes in the world without deliberating over every encounter with the objects of the world. Such bodily perception points to the pragmatics of knowledge. The objects of experience are encountered primarily as something to use in one's navigation of the world, not as things to observe primarily for intellectual consumption. This mode is primary and tacit. It works at a pretheoretical, perceptual level such that *habitus* makes sense of the world without continually alerting one to its "contents." *Habitus* is always operative without one's knowing.[71] Hence, Smith argues that perception is an evaluation based on the background of one's multidimensional be-ing.[72] What the body encounters as information only counts as information because the body has already evaluated through perception.

As actions of the body, perception and evaluation integrate synergistically with affect and narrative.[73] They are bodily habits. Because the body has a history, a particular involvement with the world, its evaluative construal of reality is not neutral. The intertwining of subject and object creates "embedded, embodied actors [who are] at home in an environment that [they] navigate with a kind of intentionality that precedes knowledge and whose locus is in the body."[74] This immersion in the world is critical to Smith's understanding of human be-ing, which he draws from Martin Heidegger's concept of *Dasein*.

As a "*unified* phenomenon," *Dasein* reintegrates the subject and object that Descartes sundered.[75] The subject is "absorbed in the world."[76] There exists an inseparable relationship between being and the world:

> In factical experience, we do not find the encounter between a subject and an object—which is a derivative experience found in theoretical consciousness. Rather, factical experience is characterized by a certain immediacy such that the subject is not yet rigidly distinguished from the object, but rather finds itself imbedded in its world, its environment. "I" am imbedded in "life," and any distillation of "I" or the "world" as distinct components is always already a derivative mode of being-in-the-world.[77]

As an integrated phenomenon, *Dasein* rejects the priority of epistemology above ontology, of subject over object.[78] Being-in-the-world unifies knowledge with embodiment and points to the condition of *pragmata*, an involvement with the world as participator rather than spectator.[79]

Smith's liturgical anthropology is the key to understanding his epistemology. Embodiment implies situatedness, finitude, perspectivism, affectivity, and pretheoreticity. The center of embodiment is not the head, but the heart, and the heart and action are intricately intertwined. Embodied kinesthetic know-how is affectively, narratively, and imaginatively motivated and directed. As such, Smith describes this knowledge as "kinaesthetic." The performative and aesthetics of knowledge is akin more to a "'poetics' than an epistemology."[80]

CONCLUSION

This chapter identified the epistemological themes that are present in Smith without the aid of Pentecostalism. Centrally, Smith's postmodern epistemology is embodied and hermeneutic. Knowledge, even worldview, is interpretative due to situated embodiment. While some believe in the actuality of pure seeing, Smith argues that God intended embodied creatures to be structurally interpretive. Although marred by sin, interpretation as such is not originally fallen. Even the consummation of the eschaton will not erase interpretation. Like all things, interpretation will be healed and redeemed. Like Pentecostal epistemology, the primacy of know-how is maintained through affective, narrative, and kinesthetic elements of embodied anthropology. Embodiment necessitates interpretation and perspectives. These "Pentecostal" characteristics are also present in RO. Given these features in Smith's wider corpus, it is questionable how distinct Pentecostal epistemology is in Smith's mind. In fact, Smith's Pentecostal epistemology really seems to be the product of his postmodern epistemology. Similar to the view of Pentecostalism as merely an Evangelicalism "plus" the doctrine and experience of Spirit baptism, Smith's Pentecostal epistemology seems to be a postmodern epistemology "plus" the articulation of particular Pentecostal doxological practices. Therefore, it seems more appropriate to drop the Pentecostal moniker and concentrate on further identifying the features of Smith's postmodern hermeneutic epistemology. The next chapter continues this investigation, moving from continental philosophical theology to linguistic pragmatism and Lindbeckian postliberalism, which raises the inevitable question that postmodernism faces: relativism.

NOTES

1. Against this view, Mark Bowald incisively argues that tension in Smith's earlier and later writings exists. Specifically, Smith denigrates the particularities of traditioned theology in *Speech and Theology* while affirming particularity in *Who's*

Afraid of Postmodernism. See Mark Alan Bowald, "Who's Afraid of Theology: A Conversation with James K. A. Smith on Dogmatics as the Grammar of Christian Particularity," in *The Logic of Incarnation: James K. A. Smith's Critique of Postmodern Religion*, ed. Neal DeRoo and Brian Lightbody (Eugene: Pickwick Publications, 2009), 168–81. Smith admits of this tension, which he attributes to a personally trying time with his former denomination and an insufficient understanding of the implications of his creational hermeneutic. Smith desires his readers to view this matter as a progression rather than tension. Embedded within his earlier writings was an intuition that was implicitly and "insufficiently post-liberal." The emergence of postliberalism in his later writings is evidence of "an outworking of earlier intuitions whose implications were inadequately grasped," rather than representing an eventual turn. James K. A. Smith, "Continuing the Conversation," in *The Logic of Incarnation: James K. A. Smith's Critique of Postmodern Religion*, ed. Neal DeRoo and Brian Lightbody (Eugene: Wipf & Stock, 2009), 203–23 (216–17). Commenting elsewhere on his postliberalization, Smith states that this postliberal seed was already present in his first monograph, the first edition of *The Fall of Interpretation*. See Smith, *The Fall of Interpretation*, 9–10. The pragmatics of knowledge and language is also evident in *Speech and Theology*. See Smith, *Speech and Theology*, 81, 87.

2. Between the years of 1999 and 2010, which represents the completion of his PhD and his promotion to full professorship, Smith had published a combination of eighteen monographs, edited volumes, a coauthored volume, and the translation of Jean-Luc Marion's *The Crossing of the Visible*, besides numerous peer-reviewed articles and article contributions to various edited projects. I want to thank Smith for graciously providing his curriculum vitae.

3. Nevertheless, Smith is concerned with correct interpretation of his sources, illustrated in his attempts to clarify the widespread misunderstandings of Lyotard's and Derrida's respective claims that "postmodernism is an incredulity toward metanarratives" and that "there is nothing outside the text."

4. Smith, *Who's Afraid of Postmodernism?*, 19.
5. Smith, 137.
6. Smith, 129.
7. Smith, 38, 39.
8. See Smith, *The Fall of Interpretation*, 63–79.
9. Smith, 35–61.
10. Smith, *Jacques Derrida*, 36–37.
11. Smith, 97–102. Also, see Martin Heidegger, *Being and Time*, trans. Joan Stambaugh (Albany: State University of New York Press, 2010), 123–25. John Milbank also finds an inherent fall in Heidegger's philosophy. See Milbank, *Theology & Social Theory*, 302.
12. Jacques Derrida, *Of Grammatology*, trans. Gayatri Chakravorty Spivak (Baltimore: Johns Hopkins University Press, 1997), 37.
13. Smith, *The Fall of Interpretation*, 122–27.
14. Smith, 24–25.
15. Smith, 70n16.

16. In his critique of Wolfhart Pannenberg, Smith argues that Pannenberg cannot maintain his defense of eschatological finitude while, at the same time, maintaining that such eschatological human beings will experience time as God experiences time, which is not sequential experience, and will overcome the provisionality of knowledge of God. If so, such atemporal, aperspectival finitude cannot be finite in the end since even eschatological speech and spatiality will be sequential and perspectival. See Smith, 71–78.

17. Smith, 159–61.

18. Smith, 160.

19. Smith, 161.

20. Smith, 160n2.

21. Smith, 175. Anthony Thiselton makes a similar point. Agreeing with Schleiermacher, Thiselton argues that hermeneutics and epistemology overlap because hermeneutics necessarily involves "the problem of understanding." See Anthony C. Thiselton, *Hermeneutics: An Introduction* (Grand Rapids: William B. Eerdmans Publishing Company, 2009), 158.

22. Smith, *Who's Afraid of Relativism?*, 93.

23. Smith, *The Fall of Interpretation*, 164–65.

24. Smith, 164.

25. According to Smith, original creation was good but not perfect. Because creation was not perfect, misunderstanding was a possibility. However, misunderstanding is not necessarily sinful, but merely the possibility of finitude. See Smith, *The Fall of Interpretation*, 168. To acknowledge the possibility of misunderstanding reveals that Smith is not a relativist.

26. Rambo, *Spirit and Trauma*, 18–21.

27. Rambo participates in this multiplicity of interpretations by reinterpreting the biblical witness from the perspective of trauma. See Rambo, 81–110.

28. Smith, *The Fall of Interpretation*, 169.

29. Smith, 168–70.

30. Smith, 175.

31. Smith, 171, 173.

32. Smith, *Who's Afraid of Postmodernism?*, 54.

33. Smith, 69.

34. Smith, 72.

35. Smith, *Introducing Radical Orthodoxy*, 171.

36. Smith, *Desiring the Kingdom*, 46.

37. Smith, 47.

38. Smith, 25.

39. Smith, 66.

40. Smith, 51.

41. Smith, 52. Cf., Smith, *Introducing Radical Orthodoxy*, 114–15, 227.

42. Smith, *Desiring the Kingdom*, 47–52.

43. Smith attributes this structure/direction schema, which occur in several of his works, to Albert Wolters. See Smith, 52n22. Smith also uses this schema with

interpretation. See Smith, *The Fall of Interpretation*, 174–75; and Smith, *Who's Afraid of Postmodernism?*, 99–103.

44. Smith, *Desiring the Kingdom*, 54.
45. Smith, 56.
46. Smith. Cf., James K. A. Smith, *You Are What You Love: The Spiritual Power of Habit* (Grand Rapids: Brazos Press, 2016), 187.
47. Smith, *Desiring the Kingdom*, 70.
48. Smith, 59.
49. Smith, 86–87.
50. Smith, 85.
51. Smith, 67n53.
52. Smith, 27.
53. Smith.
54. That Smith identifies as Radically Orthodox is easy to see given Milbank's identification of Radical Orthodoxy as *postmodern* critical *Augustinianism*.
55. Smith, *Introducing Radical Orthodoxy*, 70–72.
56. Smith, 73–74. Smith claims that this view is consonant with Kuyper and Dooyeweerd. Smith, 72n33.
57. Smith, 74–77. Smith critiques the Platonic elements of participatory ontology, arguing that Plato is ultimately against the goodness of materiality. Instead, he offers a creational/incarnational ontology that affirms the goodness of materiality. Smith, 197–204, 218–23.
58. Smith, 77–78.
59. Smith, 224.
60. Smith, 78.
61. Smith, 224–25.
62. Smith, 78–79.
63. Smith, 220.
64. Smith, 143.
65. Robert Stern, "Introduction," in *Transcendental Arguments: Problems and Prospects*, ed. Robert Stern (Oxford: Oxford University Press, 1999), 1–11 (3).
66. Smith, *Awaiting the King*, 6.
67. Smith, *Imagining the Kingdom*, 109.
68. Smith, 101.
69. Smith, 113.
70. Smith, 81.
71. Smith.
72. Smith, 34–35.
73. Smith, 38–39.
74. Smith, 44.
75. Heidegger, *Being and Time*, 2010, 53.
76. Heidegger, 55.
77. Smith, *Speech and Theology*, 76.
78. This subject/object problem was one that Kant believed must be given philosophical treatment. The Enlightenment question, "Is there such thing as an external

world outside of our minds, and how could we know it?" needed rational proof. However, Heidegger turned this epistemological problem upside down. The problem was not that this question had not received its proof, but that it required such a proof in the first place. This Cartesian skepticism of the external world revealed the "unquestioned and sovereignty of epistemology." Charles B. Guignon, *Heidegger and the Problem of Knowledge* (Indianapolis: Hackett Publishing Company, 1983), 53.

79. Smith, *Speech and Theology*, 25.

80. Smith, *Imagining the Kingdom*, 117n24.

Chapter 5

Smith the Relativist?

INTRODUCTION

Smith's philosophy bears the marks of non-nihilistic postmodernism: finitude, contingency, embodiment, perspectivism, and pretheoricity. They are present in his creational hermeneutic that is represented by the contingencies of intersubjectivity, situationality, traditionality, and undecidability. While these marks seem constructed predominantly from continental philosophical theology, another tradition has greatly influenced Smith: postliberalism. This chapter exposits *Who's Afraid of Relativism*, a controversial book that seems to confirm conservative Evangelicalism's suspicion of postmodernism as the bearer of insidious relativism. In the book, Smith makes the case for relativism through the exposition of linguistic pragmatism and represents Lindbeckian postliberalism as its Christian instantiation due to their shared commitments to contingency in meaning, social justification, and communal rationality. While this book may seem to be just one among many in Smith's corpus, its ideas must be taken seriously because Smith states that the trajectory of his thought from beginning to the present has always been consistently postliberal. Therefore, Smith's postmodern epistemology is a postliberal epistemology.[1] However, despite Smith's presentation of postliberalism as relativistic, I argue that Smith has misunderstood postliberalism. I provide a rereading of Lindbeck and read Smith against Smith to demonstrate that they are both ontologically and epistemologically realist.

LINGUISTIC PRAGMATISM

When epistemology is made hermeneutic and perspectival, a natural question about relativism arises. Is every construal objectively true? Interestingly, Smith advocates Christians to adopt a qualified relativism, which he argues is represented by linguistic pragmatism and its theological cousin, postliberalism. Smith argues that pragmatism represents a "serious articulation of 'relativism'" that consistently affirms the (Christian) claim to contingency.[2] Meaning is relative because it is *relative to* situated, communal perspectives. Being human is to be a relativist; the conditions of creaturehood require that "meaning and knowledge [be] ineluctably *social* and communal."[3] Denial of this contingency is tantamount to denying creaturely dependence. It is the assumption of the possibility of objective, neutral knowledge through which religious knowledge is dismissed as unenlightened.[4] The stakes are high for Smith. This denial is a return to Enlightenment modernity.

In *Who's Afraid of Relativism*, Smith provides the clearest interaction with pragmatism and postliberalism through expositions of Ludwig Wittgenstein, Richard Rorty, and Robert Brandom. The three philosophers are introduced in that order to build a "conceptual snowball" to establish Smith's argument for relativism.[5] Wittgenstein sets the pragmatist agenda that "meaning is use." Rorty furthers the claim that truth claims are ineluctably social. Brandom provides pragmatic normativity for beliefs within linguistic communities. Broadly, the central tenets of pragmatism are meaning as use, meaning as constituted by contingent communities, anti-referentialism, and the normative rationality of contingent conceptual practices. Importantly, Smith stresses that his argument for relativism is foremost concerned with meaning, not truth. However, as I argue later, claim to knowledge must address truth since meaningful construal (i.e., narrative, affective construal [NAC]) can be false.[6]

Wittgenstein

The main point Smith exegetes from the later Wittgenstein is that meaning is primarily used rather than ostensive. Wittgenstein is reacting against the view that ostensive naming, in which words refer to their corresponding objects, is the primary function of language. For Smith, this referentialist theory of meaning is static by not taking into account the dynamics at work in speech.[7] Without denying that reference occurs, Smith demonstrates that ostensive learning is possible due to the prior framework that acts as the condition for such learning, a framework that is more kinesthetic than noetic.[8] This kinesthetic background makes even the teaching by pointing possible; behind the pointing is a host of non-pointings that was inculcated through participation in a community of practice. Participation in community allows one to absorb the *telos* and meaning embedded in practice apart from explicit ostensive training.[9]

Action is basic, not words. Ostensive meaning is dependent on understanding in practice whose aim is to accomplish a contextual end. Reference, therefore, is an embedded event in contextual practices that is neither neutral nor objective. If meaning is use, dependent on teleological know-how, then meaning is *relative* to context. Practice constructs meaning within the various usages of language. Mere words do not provide meaning because "meaning is wider than words."[10] Words and meaning follow the conventions of a language game. Without this practical context, words don't make sense.

Learning a language game primarily involves learning to navigate its rules more than learning to explain them. To give a personal example, I missed the critical grammar lessons from third to sixth grade as those years were primarily spent learning the language of my newly adopted country. For many years, and even now at times, I navigated through the difficulties of the English grammar more through how it feels than applying explicit rules. I gained this know-how more through osmosis than formal instruction.

Becoming a competent practitioner of language games, knowing how to navigate their conventions, makes possible the lineaments of know-that, such as ostensive meaning and analysis.[11] Smith calls this emphasis on social conventions "the turning point in Wittgenstein's alternative account of language and meaning. And it's why we're all relativists."[12]

Does this claim still leave open the possibility of nihilistic relativism? Not so for Smith. Pragmatic meaning is "game-relative . . ., always *conventional*."[13] Because pragmatic meaning is game-relative, meaning is *socially* conventional. The relativism that Smith espouses is not an individualistic, anything-goes relativism. Moreover, Smith does not negate reference in favor of pragmatic meaning. Reference occurs through language use. Naming is communally conventional and justified and is not dependent on an object's essence. Correspondence may be a social construction, but it is still correspondence. Correspondence is secondary to use, but not eliminated. Once a community has ratified certain names, they have become justified. Naming, therefore, isn't individualistically subjective.[14]

Objects and signs are not disparate things. It may seem that signs, but not objects, signify. Yet, an object can be a sign based on how it is used. How an object acts as a sign is not dependent on its being, but on its contextual function, when it is used or taken as a sign by persons.[15] The primary function of word-signs isn't to refer to object-realities. Such reductive correspondence is secondary to how object-realities act as signs in the various ways they are employed. Importantly, the correctness of their employment is primarily dependent on social conventions. Meaning is primarily pragmatic, and function is based on the conventions of a social community. With this idea of social convention, Smith turns to Rorty.

Rorty

Smith presents Rorty as continuing Wittgenstein's anti-referentialism. Knowledge is not mere correspondence of words to objective reality. What is understood as objective reality is merely a social understanding that has become so commonsensical that its reality as a language game has been forgotten. This amnesia causes one to think that knowledge is an individual mirroring of the world "out there." Rorty furthers the idea that knowledge and its justification are the products of social convention, resisting the myth that objective knowledge is obtained through pure "seeing."[16]

If knowledge isn't dependent on correspondence to objective reality, how is nihilistic relativism avoided? Rorty doesn't reject reality as such. The world impresses itself on people and does not allow any interpretation. Some interpretations are unsustainable because the world does not allow it.[17] However, there is no "extralinguistic" reality available for knowledge. The world is social, and one can only know it through social conventions. Epistemic justification is a social convention based on the efficacy of a belief's ability to help one cope with the world. That which copes best is taken to be true.[18] For Smith, the interplay between social conventions and the world provides normative standards that avoid nihilistic relativism. In fact, Smith is affirming a type of realism, albeit not referentialism, if understood as the mirroring of words to reality.[19]

Smith portrays correspondence and objectivity as individualist and neutral. The hubris of representationalism, that "we could 'know' *on our own*," is rejected by Smith.[20] He is continually motivated by the creational condition of contingency. He does not reject the ontological objectivity of mind-independent reality.[21] What he rejects as impossible is the possibility of an individualist representationalism of such reality. Because knowledge is socially justified, it cannot be individualistically referential. Instead, knowledge is pragmatic know-how, a product of society's interactions with the world.[22] Because Smith seeks to maintain objective reality while couching its knowledge and justification in social contingency, Smith seeks a middle ground between nihilistic relativism and individualistic, neutral objectivism. To illustrate his position, Smith claims that his position is akin to nominalist Platonism: it accounts for what is real (Platonism), while the knowledge of the real is based on the community's naming (Nominalism).[23]

The reason for Smith's position is theological. He views referentialism as an epistemology that denies creaturely dependence and screams of autonomy. Pragmatism's social contingency maintains the Creator-creature distinction and creaturely dependence.[24] Smith's positive regard for interpretation is entirely based on God's proclamation of the goodness of finitude and communal perspectives. Efforts to overcome this creaturely dependence on God and others commit the sin of the Enlightenment: creaturely autonomy.

Smith contends that pragmatism demonstrates the inculcation of Christian beliefs through participation in Christian communities as one interacts with God's revelation. Because God's self-revelation is an act of incarnational condescension occurring at the level of human finitude and contingency, even revelation takes into account both (communally shaped) interpretation and the mind-independent reality of divine self-revelation.[25] Since epistemic justification hinges on pragmatic efficacy, Smith is confident in the ability of the Christian narrative to "out-narrate" other construals, thus staking its place as the true take on the world. However, the Christian communities with which one interacts with shape one's knowledge, so that the Christian narrative is "true" only to Christians, even if it is claimed to be universal in scope. Smith is being consistent with Lyotard's claim that local narratives have replaced metanarratives, even while they can remain universal in scope.

Brandom

Smith uses Wittgenstein and Rorty as the conceptual framework to present pragmatism's concept that meaning as use is made possible by the know-how engendered by social communities in its interactions with the world. Smith then introduces Robert Brandom as one who builds on the social nature of pragmatic meaning by introducing rational normativity to concept usage in linguistic communities. Smith seeks to show that meaning is socially relative, but such relativity is constrained by the rules of linguistic communities of practice and the world.

For Brandom, humans are distinct from animals because they are rational, and rationality is tied to language, not communication. Animals can communicate, but humans can give and take arguments through language. Language is a social and conceptual practice that partakes in rationality.

Rationality plays a central role in practice. Unlike Wittgenstein's view that language is like an ancient city with no central downtown, Brandom pictures linguistic practices as having a central downtown of conceptual inference. Brandom claims that certain linguistic practices depend on *conceptual* contents within other, more central, linguistic practices.[26] Concepts are inherently normative within the rules of a linguistic community. Concepts carry inferential implications; holding a concept commits one to other concepts based on the language game of one's community within the confines of objective reality. For example, to state that a bottle is blue implies the inferential implication that it is not green, which the linguistic community of practice that determined the bottle to be blue binds one responsible to hold. Claiming a different color would be irrational insofar as the community deemed it blue. The rationality of concepts and their inferential implications are relative to the community, and their justification is dependent on other concepts. One must answer to the community, giving and taking reasons for concepts and their inferential implications.

A concept is know-how that helps distinguish between correct and incorrect inferences. A concept is "practical mastery" of inferences, the ability to navigate through life without always making explicit the implicit contents of practice.[27] Linguistic concept is still in practice, but it is a central practice that carries inferential implications within the bounds of the linguistic community of concept users who hold each other responsible and who have mastered the know-how of inference.

With these three representatives, Smith highlights the central features of pragmatism: meaning as use, meaning as constituted by contingent communities, anti-referentialism, and the normative rationality of contingent conceptual practices. Pragmatic relativism is non-nihilistic due to the presence of social justification. The attractiveness of pragmatism to Smith is evident in its sociality. Justification arises out of the situated context of particular language games, culture, and social rationality. Due to his commitment to creaturely finitude, Smith views linguistic pragmatism as broadly representing the important facets of his creational hermeneutic. Humans are relativists because all knowledge is *relative to* context. While this view leads to a benign relativism, social justification of meaning detached from referential truth invites charges of cultural relativism. There must be a stronger sense of ontological and epistemological correspondence if Smith is to avoid the latter charge. Because question remains whether Smith's deflationary account of reference and conceptual normativity can escape this charge, the next section investigates Smith's (mis)reading of postliberalism and argues that postliberalism can answer this charge.

POSTLIBERALISM

For Lindbeck, doctrines function as regulative rules for governing how religious communities of practice can rightly speak about religious matters.[28] His cultural-linguistic model contends that doctrines are second-order claims that make explicit what are implicit in first-order religious practices, which in turn makes one responsible for holding a doctrine within the communal "space of reasons."[29] Therefore, "To confess that Jesus is 'God from God, Light from Light, true God from true God' is to *articulate* what was already implicit in our prayers, a worship way of life nourished by the Scriptures."[30]

Because doctrines are based on religious practice, the priority of know-how over know-that is maintained.

This model contrasts with cognitive-propositionalism, which considers doctrines as timeless propositional truth claims about objective reality, and experiential-expressivism that reduces doctrines to "noninformative and nondiscursive symbols of [universal] inner feelings, attitudes, or existential orientations," in which the universality of experience and feeling absorbs the particularities of religion.[31]

In the cultural-linguistic model, doctrines are meaningful claims that are neither true nor false.[32] The relationship between doctrines and practices is inferential rather than referential, functioning like rules of grammar with each other that regulate religious speech. That is, doctrines are not referential descriptions about God and reality.[33] They are based on particular practices and do not stand as neutral, universal truths that are detached from religious life. Wrong doctrine violates what is implicit in religious practice. A crusader crying "Christ is Lord" while wielding his cleaver is unjustified:

> The crusader's assertion is not "true"—it's not justified or authorized as "rational," given the canons of the ecclesial community of practice. Its falsity and irrationality is a matter of (bad) inferences that cannot be "licensed" by the relevant community of practice.[34]

"Christ is Lord," while seemingly accurate propositionally, is deemed inaccurate in the practice of the violent act because the claim and the act are inconsistent with the practices and narratives of the peaceable Kingdom displayed in Scripture; the statement is meaningless (but neither true nor false) because it has violated the grammar of practice. The practices and the doxological utterances within the practices constitute first-order truth claims, and these practices act as the determinate setting that makes truth claims possible.[35]

The cultural-linguistic model presents religion as a form of life that acts as a hermeneutical filter for beliefs, emotions, and experiences that emphasizes the embodied realities of formation, socialization, and acculturation.[36] Religion is a pragmatic, contingent a priori, consisting of a set of acquired skills gained through practice and training.[37] Applied especially to the sacred texts that are communally authoritative, those who inhabit the world of such texts, with its rituals, skills, symbols, and practices, "absorb the universe" through the text.[38] Form of life is all-encompassing, interpreting the world rather than being interpreted by the world. This hermeneutic framework is the antithesis of experiential-expressivism in which experience provides the nondiscursive symbols of religion.[39] Neither does the cultural-linguistic model place beliefs as the central hermeneutic medium, as does cognitive-propositionalism. Instead, beliefs receive their validity and possibility through "the conceptual vocabulary and the syntax or inner logic" of a given form of life.⁴⁰ Thus, postliberalism puts forth a missional strategy of immersion rather than demonstration. This missional strategy is an invitation "to immigrate to a different world, to become citizens of a different culture,"⁴¹ thereby enacting and producing particular beliefs, affective experiences, and liturgical practices.⁴²

However true this theory of formation may be, its agnosticism about the truth of doctrines seems troubling. If doctrines are neither objectively true nor false but only regulate *speech* about first-order beliefs and practices, can they regulate first-order beliefs and practices? Like Smith's unidirectional affective foundationalism, it seems to suffer from performative foundationalism. Moreover, if the justification of doctrines is socially determined, then can it avoid cultural relativism? If postmodernism is at minimum ontologically realist, then it cannot be committed to nihilistic or cultural relativism; more so for postliberalism. Is postliberalism ontologically and epistemologically realist?

Correspondence and Intratextual Meaning

According to Smith, both Rorty and Lindbeck accept referentialism or correspondence, but not representationalism.⁴³ Representationalism is the type of correspondence that is devoid of social justification. Ostensive description of reality is sufficient for truth. Knowledge is "an assemblage of accurate representations" in which the foundation of knowledge is constituted by "a special privileged class of representations so compelling that their accuracy cannot be doubted."⁴⁴ By differentiating referentialism and correspondence from representationalism, Smith seeks to retain realist truth claims.

Smith correctly claims that Rorty is not committed to an anti-realist idealism, for Rorty explicitly rejects such idealism.⁴⁵ Rorty's epistemological behaviorism sought to move modernist epistemology to hermeneutics in order to leave behind the metaphysical realism and idealism debate.⁴⁶ However, even if he is not a metaphysical realist, he is at minimum a post-metaphysical, ontological realist. Rorty aligns his position with Hilary Putnam's internal realism, which is, in Rorty's words, the minimalist, uncontroversial view that humans (pragmatically) cope with the world.⁴⁷ Rorty is not what Plantinga calls an existentialist anti-realist who denies mind-independent reality.⁴⁸ However, coping is not accomplished through referential claims that pristinely describe objective reality. Current state of knowledge is merely the claim that one view has won out for the moment in history. The "common sense" view of the world at the current moment is merely the view that one has inherited at a point in time, "but to proclaim our loyalty to these distinctions is not to say that there are 'objective' and 'rational' standards for adopting them."⁴⁹

For Rorty, objectivity is not correspondence to outer reality. An objective view is the "property of theories, which, having been thoroughly discussed, are chosen by a consensus of rational discussants."[50] Smith interprets Rorty as stating that the "antics" of the world are ontological, which eliminates an anything-goes relativism.[51] Communities interpret the world in many ways, but the range of these interpretations is finite, for communities will limit the conversations to those that make most sense.[52] This social justification is objective without being correspondent.

For Smith, postliberalism tracks with Rorty by redescribing objectivity.[53] The intratextual semiotic system guards tradition's meaning from "external and alien frame of reference," such as modernism's neutral objectivity, especially for postliberalism that view meaning as found within Scripture and the faithful practices of the church from the text.[54] However, guarding against alien frames does not reject reference as such. An act that authentically utilizes Christian narratives corresponds with God's being and will; this is a realist claim. Thus, Smith connects Lindbeck's "extratextuality" with ontological truth. "This addresses the realist's worries: the claims that 'Jesus is Lord' is a claim *about* the world we inhabit, and is in some sense accountable *to* that environment as part of the context in which 'Jesus is Lord' is uttered."[55]

It is important to understand Lindbeck's notions of intratextuality and extratextuality. Lindbeck, like Smith, is primarily interested in meaning, not truth, which is another reason to distinguish between NAC and narrative, affective knowledge (NAK).[56] Intratextuality locates meaning in the way language is used in a community, which then generates the community's interpretation of extratextual reality. Meaning in extratextuality, on the other hand, is located outside semiotic systems, either in objective reality (such as in the cognitive-propositional model) or in universal experience (such as in the experiential-expressive model) and is incompatible with the cultural-linguistic model. In the cultural-linguistic model, meaning is immanent to language and culture, not external to independent reality.[57]

However, this view again raises the worries about anti-realism and relativism.[58] By rejecting neutral rationality, intratextuality seems to leave the judgment between different religious and nonreligious traditions to irrationality, arbitrariness, and fideism.[59] As Robert Cathey stresses, "Issues of realism call upon us to follow the path in our thinking from the issue of meaningfulness to the issue of truthfulness in our God-talk."[60] Determining the validity of such charges requires moving beyond Lindbeck's theory of meaning to his theory of truth.[61]

Three Theories of Truth and the Question of Realism

Lindbeck offers three types of truth in *The Nature of Doctrine*. First, categorial truth is truth based on pragmatic adequacy.[62] Addressing the question on the possibility of one form of life being superior over another, Lindbeck argues for investigating the adequacy of the categories. Categories are the pragmatic conditions that a form of life must have in order to describe what is taken to be real. They provide the conceptual framework to make meaningful statements possible, which can in turn make propositional truth and falsity possible, although they "do not guarantee, propositional, practical, and symbolic truth."[63] If a language game lacks a particular category, any claim made without such a category would be false within that language game. Because categories neither share nor make up a common framework, forms of life are incommensurable.

What is true beyond categories is that which corresponds to reality, such as God's being and will. When language and practices within the adequate categories correspond to ultimate reality, the form of life can be considered propositionally true. In this sense, Lindbeck argues that a religion could qualify as a gigantic proposition. Lindbeck, however, distinguishes his cultural-linguistic model from cognitive-propositionalism. Lindbeck emphasizes that categorial truth is a necessary condition for correspondence. Right performance, not mere ostension, utilizing a tradition's categories is required for the achievement of ontological truth.[64] In other words, the achievement of ontological truth requires *participation* in the form of life that contains adequate categories. Ontological truth is performative and participatory, not merely ostensive. Therefore, categorial truth is a necessary condition for ontological truth.

Intrasystematic truth, or truth of coherence, forms the second type of truth. An utterance is coherent, and thus intrasystematically true, if it coheres with the rest of the form of life. Intrasystematic truth is also a necessary condition for ontological correspondence. A statement can be intrasystematically true, but ontologically false and meaningless when its system lacks adequate categories. Conversely, a claim can be ontologically true when it is categorially and intrasystematically true.[65]

The third type, ontological truth, is correspondent truth. Lindbeck clearly identifies this as epistemologically realist.[66] However, such correspondence is not merely ostensive, but participatory and performative. A proposition is not true in itself. It becomes true if the proposition is accompanied by a performance that creates the ontological correspondence.[67]

Performative Correspondence

Lindbeck utilizes Aquinas to explain how such correspondence occurs. Arguing that while the *modus significandi* cannot correspond to God, Lindbeck argues that the *significatum* does correspond in a way that is beyond human knowledge. Despite this informational vacuity, language allows one to understand at the creaturely level how such knowledge applies and provides the concepts and contexts to perform the truth of those utterances.[68] Bruce Marshall also presents Aquinas as marking coherence of linguistic contexts and appropriate practices as conditions for linguistic correspondence to divine reality.[69] As Smith stressed, context is necessary for achieving propositional truth. Lindbeck writes,

> The sentence "This car is red," as it occurs on this page, for example, cannot be a proposition, for it specifies no particular auto and no particular time before or after which the vehicle might be of a different color: it can be neither true nor false. The same point holds *mutatis mutandis* for religious sentences: they acquire enough referential specificity to have first-order or ontological truth or falsity only in determinate settings, and this rarely if ever happens on the pages of theological treatises or in the course of doctrinal discussions. The theological and doctrinal uses of, e.g., "Christ is Lord" are important . . . , but they are not propositional. For Christian theological purposes, that sentence becomes a first-order proposition capable . . . of making ontological truth claims only as it is used in the activities of adoration, proclamation, obedience, promise-hearing, and promise-keeping which shape individuals and communities into conformity to the mind of Christ. . . . One must be, so to speak, inside the relevant context; and in the case of a religion, this means that one must have some skill in *how* to use its language and practice its way of life before the propositional meaning of its affirmations becomes determinate enough to be rejected.[70]

Religious statements, including doctrine, can be neither true nor false unless one is proficiently skilled in the language and practices of the religion. This proficiency represents the relevant context that can turn an utterance into a true proposition. This account provides a richer account of agency, whose speech is part of an involvement in a form of life. For Lindbeck, expecting correspondence by merely stating a proposition is meaningless because propositions can only become true or false within the right categorial and intrasystematic context. For example, uttering "Christ is Lord" by a crusader, a pious worshipper, and an atheist without context would be neither true nor false, for they all mean something different.[71] The performative context born out of doxological practices of the community of worship is what achieves the statement to correspond to God's being and will.[72] Bruce Marshall thus rightly highlights Lindbeck's project as giving "an account . . . of the *conditions* under which true propositions can be uttered."[73]

This view is consistent with Dru Johnson's important claim that the biblical concept of truth is not primarily about propositional correspondence between words and external reality but about the process of determining the reliability of a claim to actualize what ought to be, that is, fidelity with God; truth imagined this way pertains to relationality and participation. Truth is diachronic. It is not ultimately about knowing whether something is true or false. Instead, truth dictates the knower to be enmeshed in an epistemic process that requires one to attend to the reliability of a claim to be faithful to what ought to be. This process is neither merely subjective nor noetic. It is a communal process that requires one to be open to another's interpretation in determining the fidelity of a claim.[74] Essentially, participating in a diachronic path toward truth occurs through participating in a cultural-linguistic community. Thus, the statement, "Christ is Lord," becomes true when it is faithfully interpreted and practiced in a categorically adequate community of practice. Knowledge is ultimately obedient knowledge. Truth, in the end, arrives with performative obedience.

Against cognitive-propositionalism, Robert Cathey argues that mere ostension reduces persons to concepts. In this sense, the traditional view of ostension is more reductionist than Smith claims. The concern that Smith has regarding ostension is the reduction of social justification to the individual. For Cathey, on the other hand, ostension separates concepts from the speaker, eliminating the need of the speaker altogether. He explains,

> The standard Augustinian account of meaning strips away our agency in the use of language. We assume that words and concepts mean in-and-of-themselves apart from our deployment of them in the tasks of our lives. We assume that meaningful and truthful language refers to objects apart from our engagement as the agents of reference. We tend to think that concepts refer themselves to reality rather than speakers.[75]

Lindbeck's "'performative-propositional' theological theory of religious truth" preserves correspondence and propositional truth without resorting to one-to-one identification between concepts and external reality, preserving the speaker and the form of life.[76] Against the ostensive position of cognitive-propositionalism, Lindbeck's *via media* secures correspondence between knowledge and reality in God, but justifies this correspondence at the human realm through coherence and performance in light of the gap between knowledge and reality existent in limited, finite, perspectival human knowledge.[77]

This performative correspondence explains how non-propositional, perspectival NAK can refer to reality. This is especially important in light of trauma when victims are ostensively detached from the traumatic event through loss of speech and understanding. The forgetting and the eclipsing of clear boundary between life and the death of the life once known, what Rambo calls eliding, invited by trauma demonstrate that "certain truths are suppressed, omitted, ignored, or passed over."[78] How can a victim's understanding be considered to correspond to reality when she is left without full access to truth and comprehension? This performative correspondence that witnesses to the existence in the middle between life and death better accommodates the victim's reality of remaining after survival. This life of remaining is uncertain and often speechless. But it is performative. Linking the biblical word "remain" (e.g., Jn 15:4-5) with survival, Rambo argues that the command to remain in Jesus cannot be understood in terms of belief because belief does not align with the context and urgency of Jesus's final hours. Rambo states, "They are being asked to do more than maintain belief in him. They are, instead, placed on the other side of his death and asked to witness love there."[79] In this way, correspondence with God's reality is performative. Inasmuch as ostensive correspondence negates the necessity of performance, it is inadequate by negating a vast population of people who are victims of trauma. Correspondential remaining, on the other hand, points to an epistemology that does not require propositional clarity or theoretical understanding. Victims of trauma remain and witness to the life after trauma without clear ostensive language.

Lindbeck emphasizes the pragmatic aspect of knowledge. While his regulative theory does not dismiss propositional and ontological truth, the practices and categories of a cultural-linguistic community contextualize the alethic status. Their importance is also relativized. If knowledge is analogical, then speculating on whether second-order doctrine achieves ontological reference is less important, since certainty of attainment of such knowledge is only an eschatological possibility. The important point is whether a doctrine has achieved normative status as a rule, and the best doctrine is that which has achieved the necessary conditions of categorial and intrasystematic truths and has achieved performative correspondence.[80] Rather than focusing on endless speculations, rule theory is interested in a community's life and language since they provide the context through which ontological reference is achieved.[81]

Jeffrey Hensley's differentiation between conceptual and alethic anti-realism provides clarity to the question of postliberalism's alleged anti-realism and rejection of correspondence. Conceptual anti-realism is the thesis that understanding of entities is dependent on conceptual schemes. Alethic anti-realism is a subset of conceptual anti-realism in which diverse conceptual schemes determine the truth of the understandings of entities. Alethic anti-realism weakens truth, such that truth is merely warranted assertability.[82] These two anti-realisms are epistemic anti-realisms. Even though they are ontologically realist, they are epistemically anti-realist in that understanding, meaning, and truth are dependent only on conceptual schemes, negating the need for correspondence. Without correspondence, epistemic anti-realism reduces ontological realism to Kantian idealism.[83] Because Lindbeck gives a role to correspondence, he is neither a conceptual nor an alethic anti-realist. Hensley thus concludes that truth for Lindbeck is "ultimately . . . a relation between statements and the reality to which they refer," in which truth "is thought of as an internal coherence of propositions which *as a whole* relate to particular states of affairs."[84] If so, postliberalism is clearly ontologically and epistemologically realist, even if it takes seriously the reality of conceptual schemes.

Postliberalism is committed to correspondent, ontological truth; objective reality grounds hermeneutic, situated knowledge, but participation is necessary for achieving correspondence.[85] It differs from cognitive-propositionalism with its performative/contextual criterion for correspondence. Yet, Lindbeck has admitted that his language on truth was confusing and provides further clarifications on the primacy of correspondence theory of truth. First, Lindbeck clarifies that categorial and intrasystematic truths are necessary, but insufficient conditions for ontological truth.[86] He regrets using the term "truth" to describe these *conditions* and affirms the primacy of ontological truth.[87] Due to the repeated charges of relativism and anti-realism against postliberalism, it is important to quote Lindbeck in length:

> Categorical adequacy and intrasystematic coherence are "truth" only equivocally. Properly speaking, they are necessary though not sufficient conditions for truth in the third (but primary) sense of correspondence. My original discussion of the matter refers in passing to the distinction between conditions for truth and truth itself, and is thus technically free of error. But the references are tangential and fail entirely to advert to the related and decisive distinction between the justification of belief (for which categorical and intrasystematic "truth" are conditions) and the truth of belief (which is a matter of correspondence). Because of these deficiencies, it has been easy to suppose that the second, intrasystematic kind of "truth" is an alternative to rather than a condition for propositional or ontological truth. . . . A corrected formulation, in contrast, simply notes that special attention to the intrasystematic (and categorical) *conditions* for affirming ontological *truth* is inseparable from a cultural-linguistic perspective on a religion such as Christianity. It most emphatically does not imply that the realities which faith affirms and trusts are in the slightest degree intrasystematic. They are not dependent on the performative faith of believers (as if, for example, Christ rose from the dead only in the faith of the Church), but are objectively independent.[88]

What is clear in this statement is the differentiation between ontological truth and the epistemological attempts at justifying and knowing that truth. Mind-independent truth exists, but access to that truth is categorically and intrasystematically performative. Postliberalism is realist through and through with this modified correspondence.[89] Reference is the consequence of correct performance within adequate and coherent categories of a form of life. Individualist ostension is rejected, but correspondence and realism remain.[90] C. C. Pecknold agrees, stating that Lindbeck makes "ultimately realistic claims. His pragmatism has a realist texture to it that, however modestly, holds out . . . for ultimate truth in the long-run."[91] In common parlance, ostensive correspondence equates to "cheap talk" or "cheap grace."

This performative correspondence acts as a buffer against fideism and relativism. Amid the myriad of different conceptual schemes, or cultural-linguistic communities, truth can be rationally discovered, even if the fullness of truth is unrealizable until the eschaton.[92] The lack of neutral criteria does not render the choice between different schemes arbitrary. Rational norms exist, but they are too complex to outline with specificity without becoming reductionist. They have an aesthetic character and their reasonableness is detectable by conceptual analysis but also by know-how that is more akin to skillful competency. "[I]ntelligibility comes from skill, not theory, and credibility comes from good performance, not adherence to independently formulated criteria."[93] *Phronesis* is important to rational adjudication as much as nuanced arguments. Adjudication is itself a performative aesthetics. Thus, Lindbeck states that theological positions are like Thomas Kuhn's scientific paradigms that cannot be definitively refuted or confirmed. Nevertheless, various parties can utilize rational ways to test them. Reason's importance cannot be discounted because they place constraints against relativism. These arguments and dialogues will make a difference over time as successful or unsuccessful arguments are considered and the seemingly more rational claims are upheld while others become disreputable. Hence, the rational work of theologians, especially when coupled with correspondent practice, is important to the vitality of their traditions.[94]

The rational progress is not linear since multiple cultural-linguistic communities exist with different rationalities. Progress occurs within and with other cultural-linguistic frameworks as they march unevenly toward the eschaton, some having achieved more adequate correspondence with reality. Those that have achieved better correspondence are those that have provided more "intelligible interpretation in [their] own terms of the varied situations and realities adherents encounter."[95] Claims that correspond to reality are those that seem to explain the world adequately, that correspond with the reality of lived existence.

Smith is also a realist. He advocates for a "realism without representation . . . [or] correspondence."[96] His rejection of critical realism is necessitated by its representationalism, the mirroring of nature.[97] For Smith, representationalist or correspondent realism assumes that knowledge is individualist, neutral, and devoid of context. His realism deflates reference and correspondence, locating them in the contingencies of communities of practice.[98] Within his sacramental ontology, the Creator-creature distinction is maintained. God is an independent reality in whom all creation, as dependent on God's being for existence, participates.[99]

By confessing God's existence, Smith affirms the independent existence of at least one objective reality.[100] This confession is a contingent confession of the way things are because God's free act of revelation occurs in contingent history. Smith argues that this confession is the most rational account because God's revelation represents the world as it is, and the Christian narrative best copes with the world. This confession is learned through participation in Christian cultural-linguistic communities of practice.[101] Knowledge thus requires the objective existence of God (and God's creation) and the contingent cultural-linguistic communities of practice.

Smith's rejection of correspondence truth *tout court* is too hasty. Correspondence does not necessitate the acceptance of individual, neutral mirroring of words to external reality. Smith himself agrees with Derrida that reference is necessary for deconstruction inasmuch as it requires the Other (reference).[102] That is, language as alterity, an absence of the full presence of meaning, requires the Other if it is to avoid reduction into the isolated mind. His portrayal of postliberalism as rejecting correspondence and realism thus indicates his misunderstanding of Lindbeck. Lindbeck, like Smith, is referentialist. But their referentialism is a more robust account of performative correspondence rather than mere ostensive correspondence. Lindbeck's correspondent realism disqualifies it as an anti-realist Wittgensteinian fideism, which is anti-realist regarding religious language games by rejecting referential claims about God. God-talk is understood merely as immanent speech-acts.[103] Postliberalism may be inspired by Wittgenstein but is not wholly Wittgensteinian. Postliberalism is firmly entrenched in the metaphysics of Christianity and intensifies correspondence by requiring a performative condition to participating in truth.

Postliberal Pentecostalism

Smith's own Pentecostal heritage affirms this participatory understanding of truth and knowledge. Although Land does not engage postliberalism, his description of knowledge of God is consistent with the regulative theory. Land writes,

> For Pentecostals, to know God is to be in a right relation, to walk in the light and in the Spirit. To know and not to do the truth is a lie, to exist in contradiction. In that case even the light one has will become darkness. For example, to say 'God is with us' without being with God is to lie or merely to speculate. Christian theology as spirituality must be consistent with, appropriate to, and responsive to its source and object, the living God.[104]

Similarity with Lindbeck's commentary on *"Christus est Dominus"* is clear. While "God is with us" seems objectively true to cognitive-propositionalism, it does not become contextually true to the postliberal unless one's form of life witnesses to the reality of God's presence. For Pentecostals, this witness may be exemplified as a narrative, affective testimony of experiencing God's presence through a doxological life, of pursuing the sanctified life in the power and presence of the Spirit who leads into all truth.[105]

Land's meta-theology also bears resemblance with postliberalism. As noted, Land considers theology in less rationalistic terms in favor of embodied terms. Theology is spirituality. As such, theology is not mere cognitive activity pursuing ostension of propositions to reality. It is second-order reflection on living reality of divine-human relations; it is "a commentary on the worship which has always been the central reality [for Pentecostals]."[106] And such commentary cannot occur without participation in the divine life. For Land, theology is "the engagement of the whole person within the communion of charisms."[107] Principally, this engagement in theological reflection occurs as prayerful response. Apart from this context, theological speeches become darkness. If all truth is God's truth, then not just the knowledge of God but the knowledge of reality as God's creation ultimately requires participation in the divine life. In other words, knowledge of reality outside theology is realizable through performative correspondence. However, ultimately, without acknowledging the Creator through participation in the divine life, even that knowledge becomes foolishness. Hence, Proverbs 1:7 states, "The fear of the Lord is the beginning of knowledge" (NIV). Without the fear that animates a certain form of life in the worshipper, knowledge is ultimately unobtainable due to misdirected participation with reality. Knowledge is obedient knowledge exemplified in the relational knowledge denoted in the Hebrew term *yada*. For Pentecostals, knowledge obtains by situating oneself in the story of God, narrowly in the story of redemption, but also broadly in the story of human history.[108] Without finding oneself in this divine story, one cannot truly participate with reality.

CONCLUSION

Smith is primarily viewed as a continental philosopher specializing in deconstruction and phenomenology. Yet, he confesses that his philosophy has always consistently followed a postliberal trajectory. After identifying the central features of linguistic pragmatism, I argued that a stronger acceptance of ontological and epistemological realism is needed if Smith is to avoid the charge of anti-realist cultural relativism. However, he promotes relativism that is motivated by linguistic pragmatism and postliberalism.

A careful reading of Smith revealed that Smith is a realist and that he promotes a benign relativism, the mere position that knowledge and meaning are relative *to* context. The benign nature of this relativism is exposed by Smith's realistic sacramental ontology that rejects thin ostensive correspondence, which tracks postliberalism's participatory correspondence. However, due to the combination of Lindbeck's confusing language about three theories of truth and Smith's misreading of postliberalism, Smith argues for a situated epistemology that is antifoundationalist, anti-realist, and relativist. Therefore, I undertook the task of presenting postliberalism as ontologically and epistemologically realist with a more rigorous, performative requirement for achieving correspondence truth in order to situate Smith's postliberalism in line with Lindbeck. The next chapter will test the ontological and epistemological commitments of my developing "Smithian" epistemology by answering the charges of relativism and arbitrariness that Richard Davis and Paul Franks direct toward Smith's Pentecostal (postmodern) epistemology.

NOTES

1. For Lindbeck's identification of postliberalism with postmodernism, see George A. Lindbeck, *The Nature of Doctrine: Religion and Theology in a Postliberal Age* (Louisville: Westminster John Knox Press, 1984), 135n1. Cf., Smith, *Who's Afraid of Relativism?*, 152n2. Some have distinguished between postmodernism and postliberalism despite Lindbeck's own identification. See Richard Lints, "The Postpositivist Choice: Tracy or Lindbeck?," *Journal of the American Academy of Religion* 61, no. 4 (1993): 655–77; and Tasi Perkins, "Beyond Jacques Derrida and George Lindbeck: Toward a Particularity-Based Approach to Interreligious Communication," *Journal of Ecumenical Studies* 48, no. 3 (2013): 343–58.
2. Smith, *Who's Afraid of Relativism?*, 18.
3. Smith, 60.
4. Smith, 35.
5. Smith, 37.
6. Recall my distinction between NAC and NAK.
7. Smith, 41.
8. Smith, 48–50.
9. Smith, 45.
10. Smith, 46.
11. Smith, 57.
12. Smith, 44.
13. Smith, 48.
14. Smith, 50–53.
15. Smith, 66–68.
16. Smith, 81–83.
17. Smith, 92.

18. Smith, 100.
19. Smith, 85–88, 94.
20. Smith, 105.
21. For the political features of the Kingdom of God to be true, the Christ-event must be historically true, argues Smith. See Smith, *Awaiting the King*, 78–79. His acceptance of ontological universality is evident in other places. For example, he considers the gospel as transcultural. Since space is always accompanied by time, a transcultural gospel is also transtemporal. The gospel is ontologically universal. The gospel unveils the truth of creation and human nature, and thus is an apocalyptic instrument of the common or universal good. What becomes apparent is Smith's ontological objectivism and epistemological perspectivism. Even though the gospel is universal, its manifestations are particular. See Smith, 124, 158. Similarly, approving of Oliver O'Donovan's affirmation of objective morality, Smith argues that such moral reality is knowable through the flawed filter of human perspectives. See Smith, 154–55.
22. Smith, *Who's Afraid of Relativism?*, 97, 106. For Smith's critique of Rorty on this point, see Smith, 82n8.
23. Smith, 108–13.
24. Smith, 108–109.
25. Smith argues that God's revelation is contingent and given within the contingencies of space-time. God is not compelled to reveal God's self. Smith, 110–11.
26. Smith contends that this "concept-centrism" is not essential to Brandom's rationalist pragmatism. While he does not offer reasons for this contention in this book, one can infer that it is based on Smith's prioritization of pretheory over theory. See Smith, 125.
27. Smith, 123–33. Smith highlights Brandom's non-referentialism by showing that inference is, for Brandom, not referential but based on the language game of the community of practice. See Smith, 130.
28. Lindbeck, *The Nature of Doctrine*, 18–19.
29. Smith, *Who's Afraid of Relativism?*, 167.
30. Smith, 162.
31. Lindbeck, *The Nature of Doctrine*, 16. David Tracy challenges this description, arguing that liberal theologians have been rethinking the dialectical relationship between experience and hermeneutics. See Tracy, "Lindbeck's New Program for Theology," 460–67.
32. Lindbeck, *The Nature of Doctrine*, 69.
33. Smith, *Who's Afraid of Relativism?*, 164.
34. Smith, 168.
35. Lindbeck, *The Nature of Doctrine*, 68.
36. Smith, *Who's Afraid of Relativism?*, 160.
37. Smith; and Lindbeck, *The Nature of Doctrine*, 33.
38. Lindbeck, 117. This statement has been controversial for Lindbeck. For Terrence Tilley, Lindbeck's statement assumes a monolithic Christianity, which betrays the diversity of Christianity throughout the ages. See Terrence W. Tilley,

"Incommensurability, Intratextuality, and Fideism," *Modern Theology* 5, no. 2 (1989): 87–111.

39. Lindbeck, *The Nature of Doctrine*, 21. Lindbeck clarifies that interpretation can be bidirectional; experience and form of life mutually shape one another, even if the latter is primary. See Lindbeck, 33–34.

40. Lindbeck, 35.

41. Smith, *Who's Afraid of Relativism?*, 175. A Polaynian insight, knowledge is tradition-dependent and submissive to authority. Changing traditions requires submitting to another authority, partaking in the form of life of another. Mitchell, "Michael Polanyi, Alasdair MacIntyre, and the Role of Tradition," 118.

42. See Lindbeck, *The Nature of Doctrine*, 32–41.

43. The trouble with this language is that Smith is too loose with his words. He uses representationalism and referentialism at times as synonyms in the book. At other times, he equates representationalism, correspondence, and referentialism. Still more, he offers "deflationary" and "situated" accounts that make these three terms incompatible. Even after qualifying these terms, he argues that representation and correspondence, even a correspondence that has dispensed with representationalism, are incompatible with pragmatism. For examples, see Smith, *Who's Afraid of Relativism?*, 24–25, 41, 49–53, 101–07, and 128.

44. Rorty, *Philosophy and the Mirror of Nature*, 163.

45. Rorty, 345.

46. Smith, *Who's Afraid of Relativism?*, 86; see Rorty, *Philosophy and the Mirror of Nature*, 325.

47. Rorty, 298.

48. Alvin Plantinga, "How to Be an Anti-Realist," *Proceedings and Addresses of the American Philosophical Association* 56, no. 1 (1982): 47–70 (48). Cf., Paul D. Murray, *Reason, Truth and Theology in Pragmatist Perspective* (Leuven: Peeters, 2004), 45. He is also not an epistemological anti-realist, as he is not a skeptic concerning knowledge. See Kelly and Dew Jr., *Understanding Postmodernism*, 143.

49. Rorty, *Philosophy and the Mirror of Nature*, 331.

50. Rorty, 338. For Rorty, subjectivity is the conversation that is irrelevant to the topic at hand. See Rorty.

51. Smith, *Who's Afraid of Relativism?*, 92. However, even given an ontological basis, Rorty can escape neither epistemological relativism nor skepticism. The question of relativism hinges on how one can know truly. William Placher argues that both Foucault and Rorty are relativists due to their lack of criteria that can adjudicate between different values. With those whom they disagree, their philosophy cannot accommodate further conversation. Against Rorty's own argument of the purpose of philosophy as one of continual conversation, his philosophy is in the end a conversation stopper. See Placher, *Unapologetic Theology*, 92–102. Amos Yong arrives at a similar conclusion. See Yong, *The Dialogical Spirit*, 4. For Paul Murray, Rorty's negation of true knowledge of reality results in skepticism. Murray, *Reason, Truth and Theology in Pragmatist Perspective*, 71.

52. Lindbeck's differentiation between *intra*textuality of postliberalism and *inter*textuality of deconstructionism clarifies this point. Intertextuality democratizes

all interpretation, whereas intratextuality privileges interpretation toward the sacred. Lindbeck, *The Nature of Doctrine*, 136n5.

53. Smith, *Who's Afraid of Relativism?*, 168.

54. Timothy R. Phillips and Dennis L. Okholm, "The Nature of Confession: Evangelicals & Postliberals," in *The Nature of Confession: Evangelicals & Postliberals in Conversation*, ed. Timothy R. Phillips and Dennis L. Okholm (Downers Grove: InterVarsity Press, 1996), 7–20 (13).

55. Smith, *Who's Afraid of Relativism?*, 168–69.

56. Smith, 151n1.

57. Lindbeck, *The Nature of Doctrine*, 113–14.

58. For example, see Phillips and Okholm, "The Nature of Confession," 15; Alister E. McGrath, "An Evangelical Evaluation of Postliberalism," in *The Nature of Confession: Evangelicals & Postliberals in Conversation*, ed. Timothy R. Phillips and Dennis L. Okholm (Downers Grove: InterVarsity Press, 1996), 23–44 (35–39); Miroslav Volf, "Theology, Meaning & Power: A Conversation with George Lindbeck on Theology & the Nature of Christian Difference," in *The Nature of Confession: Evangelicals & Postliberals in Conversation*, ed. Timothy R. Phillips and Dennis L. Okholm (Downers Grove: InterVarsity Press, 1996), 45–66 (55–60, 70–72); Pecknold, *Transforming Postliberal Theology*, 7; and Robert A. Cathey, *God in Postliberal Perspective: Between Realism and Non-Realism*, Trascending Boundaries in Philosophy and Theology (Burlington: Ashgate, 2009), 10–11. David Trenery argues that Lindbeck's criteria of intrasystematic and categorial truths cannot provide the basis for claiming religious superiority, which leaves Lindbeck open to the charge of fideism and relativism. He turns to MacIntyre's traditioned rationality, which provides pragmatic and empirical justification based on warranted assertability, the ability to withstand internal and external challenges and the ability to survive epistemological crises that do not rely on neutral justification. See David Trenery, *Alasdair MacIntyre, George Lindbeck, and the Nature of Tradition* (Eugene: Pickwick Publications, 2014), 207–47.

59. Lindbeck, *The Nature of Doctrine*, 130.

60. Cathey, *God in Postliberal Perspective*, 72. Kevin Vanhoozer's statement on biblical interpretation, that interpretation and truth are intertwined, can be extended to apply to interpretation of reality. See Vanhoozer, "Lost in Interpretation?," 89–90.

61. While Lindbeck's theory of truth is ascertainable in his work, it was never his intention to construct a theory of truth. Lindbeck did not even consider his work to be novel, acknowledging that Alasdair MacIntyre and Stanley Hauerwas had already produced similar works on traditioned knowledge. The aim of his work was to construct a pretheological theory that would aid ecumenism. Due to the aim of his book, Lindbeck admits that he inadequately addressed antifoundationalism and the relation between truth and justified belief. See George A. Lindbeck, "Foreword to the German Edition of The Nature of Doctrine," in *The Church in a Postliberal Age*, ed. James J. Buckley (Grand Rapids: Eerdmans Publishing Company, 2002), 196–200 (197–99). Also, see Lindbeck, *The Nature of Doctrine*, 7–8; George A. Lindbeck, "I Pray That They Might Be One as We Are One," in *Postliberal Theology and the Church Catholic: Conversations with George Lindbeck, David Burrell, and Stanley*

Hauerwas, ed. John Wright (Grand Rapids: Baker Academic, 2012), 55–75 (70); and George A. Lindbeck, "Confession and Community: An Israel-like View of the Church," in *The Church in a Postliberal Age*, ed. James J. Buckley (Grand Rapids: Eerdmans Publishing Company, 2002), 1–9 (4). Mike Higton also demonstrates that Lindbeck's purpose for regulative theory of doctrine was to aid in ecumenical reasoning. See Mike Higton, "Reconstructing The Nature of Doctrine," *Modern Theology* 30, no. 1 (2014): 1–31 (15–27).

62. Sometimes, Lindbeck call this categorical truth.
63. Lindbeck, *The Nature of Doctrine*, 48.
64. Lindbeck, 47–52.
65. Lindbeck, 64–65. Also, see Bruce D. Marshall, "Aquinas as Postliberal Theologian," *The Thomist: A Speculative Quarterly Review* 53, no. 3 (1989): 353–402 (366).
66. Lindbeck, *The Nature of Doctrine*, 66. Also, see Marshall, "Aquinas as Postliberal Theologian," 358–59. James Fodor states that postliberal theology does not require, but makes room for, a modest cognitive realism. See Fodor, "Postliberal Theology," 233.
67. Lindbeck, *The Nature of Doctrine*, 65. Hunsinger is thus incorrect in his portrayal of Lindbeck as a neoliberal. He argues that Lindbeck's theory of doctrine and truth are "significantly non-cognitive" and continues "the modern liberal aversion to propositional content." See Hunsinger, "Postliberal Theology," 44. Lindbeck's reply to Avery Cardinal Dulles also applies to Hunsinger, that his regulative theory is compatible with Aquinas's modest cognitivism or propositionalism. See George A. Lindbeck, "George Lindbeck Replies to Avery Cardinal Dulles," *First Things*, no. 139 (2004): 13–15 (14); and Lindbeck, *The Nature of Doctrine*, 66. Proposing a view of doctrinal truth beyond the reductionistic propositionalist view, Vanhoozer argues that truth occurs through theodramatic correspondence. Truth corresponds with God's reality when one's words and deeds participate in the redemptive drama of God. See Vanhoozer, "Lost in Interpretation?," 101–2.
68. Lindbeck, *The Nature of Doctrine*, 66–67.
69. See Marshall, "Aquinas as Postliberal Theologian," 370–402.
70. Lindbeck, *The Nature of Doctrine*, 68.
71. Cf., Marshall, "Aquinas as Postliberal Theologian," 379–82. Even statements about abstract objects would be understood differently between a realist and a fictionalist, so such statements need not be confined only to religious matters.
72. Cf., Pecknold, *Transforming Postliberal Theology*, 24–26.
73. Marshall, "Aquinas as Postliberal Theologian," 367.
74. Dru Johnson, *Knowledge by Ritual: A Biblical Prolegomenon to Sacramental Theology* (Winona Lake: Eisenbrauns, 2016), 72–78.
75. Cathey, *God in Postliberal Perspective*, 77.
76. Lindbeck, *The Nature of Doctrine*, 67. Lindbeck and Rorty differ in that Rorty redefines truth as communally warranted assertability and Lindbeck affirms correspondence. Therefore, Smith's connecting of Rorty and Lindbeck is unwarranted. Cf., Murray, *Reason, Truth and Theology in Pragmatist Perspective*, 10.

77. George A. Lindbeck, "Response to Bruce Marshall," *The Thomist: A Speculative Quarterly Review* 53, no. 3 (1989): 403–6 (404). Also, see Pecknold, *Transforming Postliberal Theology*, 6–7.

78. Rambo, *Spirit and Trauma*, 41.

79. Rambo, 104.

80. Lindbeck, *The Nature of Doctrine*, 105–7.

81. Lindbeck, 107.

82. Jeffrey Hensley, "Are Postliberals Necessarily Antirealists? Reexamining the Metaphysics of Lindbeck's Postliberal Theology," in *The Nature of Confession: Evangelicals & Postliberals in Conversation*, ed. Timothy R. Phillips and Dennis L. Okholm (Downers Grove: InterVarsity Press, 1996), 69–80 (74). In this taxonomy, Rorty represents conceptual and alethic anti-realism.

83. Westphal, "Taking Plantinga Seriously," 178.

84. Hensley, 'Are Postliberals Necessarily Antirealists?,'" 79. Emphasis mine.

85. George A. Lindbeck, "Scripture, Consensus and Community," in *The Church in a Postliberal Age*, ed. James J. Buckley (Grand Rapids: Eerdmans Publishing Company, 2002), 201–22 (283n8).

86. Lindbeck, *The Nature of Doctrine*, 65.

87. Lindbeck, "George Lindbeck Replies to Avery Cardinal Dulles,"14–15. Lindbeck's identification of these two truths as conditions is similar to Nicholas Rescher's identification of pragmatics as a methodological medium for obtainment of truth rather than identifying pragmatics with truth. See Murray, *Reason, Truth and Theology in Pragmatist Perspective*, 112.

88. Lindbeck, "George Lindbeck Replies to Avery Cardinal Dulles," 15. This "original discussion" still makes clear that intrasystematic truth is a truth of coherence that is secondary to ontological truth. See Lindbeck, *The Nature of Doctrine*, 64-65. Bruce Marshall argues that the failure on the reader's part in distinguishing between truth and its justification is the source of the confusion. See Marshall, "Aquinas as Postliberal Theologian," 367. For such a misreading, see McGrath, "An Evangelical Evaluation of Postliberalism," 38.

89. Therefore, I am puzzled as to why Ronald Michener describes Lindbeck's position as a coherentist, pragmatic epistemology, considering he acknowledges that statements can be referential. See Michener, *Postliberal Theology*, 98.

90. Postliberalism acts as a counterexample to Westphal's claim that the rejection of God's view of the world commits one to epistemic anti-realism. See Westphal, "Taking Plantinga Seriously," 178–80. Epistemic realism does not necessitate a universal perspective. See Plantinga, "On Heresy, Mind, and Truth," 190–91.

91. Pecknold, *Transforming Postliberal Theology*, 35.

92. According to Daniel Castelo, humble eschatological apophaticism assumes a doxological realism. See Castelo, *Pentecostalism as a Christian Mystical Tradition*, 129.

93. Lindbeck, *The Nature of Doctrine*, 131.

94. Lindbeck, 130–31.

95. Lindbeck.

96. Smith, *Who's Afraid of Relativism?*, 107.

97. Smith, 40. For Smith, critical realism still allows for neutral access to reality, apart from any determinate perspective. Thus, he criticizes Christian Smith's critical realism as a "nontheistic natural theology." See Smith, "The (Re)Turn to the Person in Contemporary Theory," 86–87; and James K. A. Smith, "Natural Law's Secularism?—A Response to Christian Smith," *Christian Scholar's Review* 40, no. 2 (2011): 211–15 (214).

98. Smith, *Who's Afraid of Relativism?*, 106.

99. Smith, 106. Another term for Smith's sacramental ontology is Radical Orthodoxy's Platonic participatory ontology, which Smith reworks as a creational/incarnational ontology after exorcizing it of its Platonism. See Smith, *Introducing Radical Orthodoxy*, 186–229.

100. Smith, *Who's Afraid of Relativism?*, 36. Within a non-idealist Christian narrative, God's objective existence guarantees the existence of the objective world.

101. Smith, 108–11

102. Smith, *Jacques Derrida: Live Theory*, 61–62.

103. Nicholas Wolterstorff, "Are Religious Believers Committed to the Existence of God?," in *Practices of Belief: Selected Essays*, ed. Terence Cuneo, vol. 2 (New York: Cambridge University Press, 2010), 350–71 (364–71).

104. Land, *Pentecostal Spirituality*, 26.

105. Cf., Land, 81.

106. Ranaghan, "Rites of Initiation in Representative Pentecostal Churches in the United States, 1901-1972," 654.

107. Land, *Pentecostal Spirituality*, 23.

108. Land, 67–68.

Chapter 6

Against Narrative, Affective Knowledge

INTRODUCTION

Although I argued that Smith's postmodern epistemology is realist, Richard Davis and Paul Franks (henceforth, DF) argue that narrative, affective knowledge (NAK) is relativistic and cannot non-arbitrarily adjudicate between different narrative, affective truth claims. In this chapter, I answer DF's critiques through three phases. First, I exposit their claims, locate incongruence and misunderstandings in their claims, and expose their internalist and modernist assumptions. Second, I further comment on Smith's ontological and epistemological realism that ultimately terminates in the being of God and the obtainment of affective truth through the Augustinian criterion of *ordo amoris* (right ordering of desire). Third, I present categorial adequacy, intrasystematic coherence, immanent critique, transcendental argument, and *phronesis* as means to rationally adjudicate different claims without accepting neutral rationality. In the second half of the chapter, I continue to defend Smith's realism, showing that reference properly understood terminates in God without achieving conceptual totality, while further healing the relationship between pretheory and theory by correcting Smith's latent Platonism.

NEO-KANTIANISM, NARRATIVE RELATIVISM, AND ARBITRARINESS

Even without the repair of Smith's misunderstanding of postliberalism, I argued that Smith is a realist. The repair strengthened this claim by clarifying postliberalism's intrasystematic, categorial, performative correspondence theory of truth. Nevertheless, DF is convinced that hermeneutic NAK is nihilistically relativist and arbitrary even if it's referentially realist. Although DF's criticisms are laid against Smith's postmodern Pentecostal epistemology (PPE), insofar as PPE is just an instantiation of his broader postmodern hermeneutic epistemology, their criticisms apply to the rest of his epistemology.

Specifically, DF argues that Smith is mired in Kantianism: knowledge of reality is an impossible feat. Only a myriad of differing and arbitrary interpretations of phenomenal claims to knowledge are left. The impetus for Smith's alleged Kantianism is what they call Derrida's Axiom (DA), "the claim that *everything is an interpretation*."[1] DA nullifies the possibility of knowing "*the* fact of the matter," including the gospel as an objective truth.[2]

DF levels two charges against Smith for his alleged Kantianism. First, if all knowledge is interpretation, then PPE results in self-refuting story-relativism. Second, it results in fideistic story-ism, an arbitrary favoring of one story over another.[3] When knowledge is reduced to narrative interpretations and communal discernment that only an appropriate affective fit can verify, judging competing truth claims of diverse narrative-affective traditions becomes impossible. To avoid devastating consequences to the truth of the gospel, objective rules with which to measure these competing claims are needed.[4]

To understand DF's charge of story-relativism and story-ism more clearly, I will provide three points that pertain to their critique. First, responding to Joshua Harris' defense of Smith, DF argues that their objection does not depend on assuming a correspondence theory of truth.[5] DF's charge of Kantianism is primarily an epistemological critique.[6] Even if empirical transcendentals limit interpretation, one can never know whether one's interpretation has obtained the "fact of the matter." One needs to meet some internalist awareness criterion to secure epistemic justification.

Second, DF understands Smith as arguing that rightly interpreted narratives have right fit with their attendant affections. DF seems to be inputting a prescriptive criterion to which Smith's descriptive NAK is not necessarily committed. Smith's position is merely that narratives contain affections. They also elicit affections, but they both combine to form a particular interpretive knowledge.

Third, DF is clearly committed to an epistemological objectivism that assumes the possibility of neutral reason's ability to grasp mind-independent state of affairs. Knowing objective truth and avoiding story-relativism and story-ism require obtaining the uninterpreted fact of the matter, which occurs when stories end and understanding corresponds with uninterpreted reality.[7] One obtains objective truth if one's statement *p* corresponds with the objective world, when the speech is "a blunt factual statement about *the way the world really is*."[8] This is not a mere appeal to ontological correspondence; it is an epistemological appeal for unmediated grasp of reality. Admittance of mind-independent reality is inadequate (ontological realism). The noumena must be accessible through the pure seeing of objective facts.[9] Without the ability to appeal to uninterpreted facts, there cannot be objective adjudication between different narratives.[10] For DF, then, there is no need for the noumena/phenomena distinction; one can objectively know the thing-in-itself.[11]

Analysis of DF's Critique

Let's examine these three points. First, DF claims that their critique is primarily epistemological. They charge Joshua Harris of simply assuming "that [their] critique *depends upon* the idea that truth is correspondence."[12] However, this is no simple assumption, for their argument is intricately tied to correspondence. Moreover, they charge Smith of rejecting correspondence. Is correspondence truly unimportant for DF? The answer is a clear no.

First, DF views the central impetus behind Smith's commitment to DA as motivated by his rejection of correspondence truth. Again, grounding story in "extramental, extralinguistic reality" is critical for DF.[13] For DF, Smith's rejection of correspondence means that any story can be true. This is nihilistic, anything-goes relativism. But the situation is worse. For DF, one can't even know the truth of a story.[14] DA is the bogeyman of postmodernism, the harbinger of relativism and skepticism. Second, and relatedly, DF criticizes Smith for understanding the fit between narrative and affect as interpretive, not correspondent, fit.[15] Commenting that the Apostle Peter's narrative explanation of Pentecostal tongues corresponds to objective fact, DF states that "the Apostle Peter can appeal to the facts; Smith cannot."[16] Ending the regress of interpretive stories requires grounding stories in objective fact. Third, DF charges Smith of inadequate understanding of objective truth as correspondence. Obtainment of objective truth occurs merely by words representing objective reality (ostensive correspondence).[17]

Clearly, correspondence is central to DF's critique, which is baffling since they charge Smith of rejecting correspondence to mind-independent reality and yet acknowledge Smith's acceptance of what he calls empirical transcendentals. For Smith, empirical transcendentals are objective reality. *The Fall of Interpretation* highlights this ontological commitment. Against the charge that the rejection of neutral reason leads to the denial of interpretive norms, Smith argues that reality acts as the normative criterion for interpretations. Reality as empirical transcendentals acts as an interpretive norm, constituting "the *phenomenological criterion* of every construal . . . that are binding upon interpretation."[18] It represents the "something or someone who stands *before* all of our interpretations . . . [which] is binding upon every construal."[19] They are transcendent in limiting interpretation: "As such it imposes upon me limits for its interpretations; bad interpretations will be precisely those construals that transgress those limits."[20]

DF is correct that empirical transcendentals aren't a sufficient condition for true interpretation.[21] However, since Smith affirms correspondence in the ways that DF suggests that he does not, they either need to explain why he is wrong about his own commitments or explain why they are willfully misreading his claims.[22] While ontological realism as such does not relieve Smith of all forms of epistemological relativism, acknowledging Smith's referentialism negates "anything-goes" relativism and should dispel DF's worries about story-relativism.

Second, DF understands right NAK as having appropriate fit between a narrative and its affection, and appropriateness is judged by either proportion or coherence. However, the "fact of the matter" is that fallen humanity won't find such affective fit with the gospel story.[23] One will take the gospel as the right story with the right affective fit only if one already assumes that the gospel is the right story, eliciting the right fit with Spirit-inspired emotion. While much of this is true, this critique cannot be applied to Smith because PPE does not assume such a prescription of fit.[24] As an Augustinian, Smith understands orthopathos not in terms of its fit with a story, but ultimately on its proper aiming toward the ontologically ultimate empirical transcendental: God. This epistemic criterion ultimately grounds knowledge claims on objective reality, the personal God. While this criterion is incomplete, its incompleteness neither necessitates relativism nor arbitrariness.

Third, DF's epistemological objectivism presupposes a subject/object dualism that assigns relativism to subjectivity and truth to objectivity. Subjectivity guarantees truth to mere opinions.[25] However, obtainment of mind-independent truth requires the perspective-less truth of epistemological objectivism.[26] DF finds story-relativism necessarily resulting from hermeneutic epistemology due to their epistemological objectivism. But why think that is true? Why must the difficulty of adjudication necessitate the rejection of interpretedness of human being-in-the-world?

For Richard Bernstein, the specter of relativism haunts epistemological objectivism due to the Either/Or dichotomy of Cartesian Anxiety: "*Either* there is some support for our being, a fixed foundation for our knowledge, *or* we cannot escape the forces of darkness that envelop us with madness, with intellectual and moral chaos."[27] Just because no neutral interpretive adjudication exists does not entail that rational adjudication is impossible. Rational adjudication need not be merely noetic. For Bernstein, theory-choice is affective and pragmatic, a rational judgmental activity that requires "imagination, interpretation, the weighing of alternatives, and application of criteria that are essentially open."[28] Like Lindbeck, Bernstein points to the know-how of *phronesis* as such rational adjudication.[29] DF's critiques miss the mark because they beg the question. Their epistemological objectivism cannot but see relativism because their Cartesian Anxiety can only accommodate the false dichotomy of either objectivism or relativism.

Smith rejects this dualism by following Heidegger's idea of *Dasein* that integrates the subject in the object. Factical experience reveals that one's involvement in the world carries such an immediacy in the pretheoretical mode that it is difficult to distinguish the subject from the object. "[A]ny distillation of 'I' or the 'world' as distinct components is always already a derivative mode of being-in-the-world."[30] Even the realization of subjectivity is the product of theoretical consciousness. To use Dooyeweerd's terminology, it arises from the function of the analytical modal aspect. Without such reflection, this realization of subjectivity does not occur as one operates in the concrete pretheoretical mode.

Dasein fundamentally rejects the Cartesian priority of subjective reason and the priority of epistemology over ontology. The embeddedness of existence in facticity contextualizes understanding. One always already carries pretheoretical understanding of the world in virtue of one's inhabitation. Presuppositionless knowledge is an impossibility.[31] But in assuming epistemological objectivism, DF requires "objective reason" to justify subjective claims to knowledge. Without such reason, what is left is the "mere reshuffling of . . . presuppositions, one for which there is no justification."[32] Must one give into this demand? Must one accept the (in)human demands of epistemological objectivism?

Smith's Realism Revisited

Smith gives the impression that reality seems to be dependent, in some sense, on our (social) knowledge. For example, Smith states that "if pragmatism is right—that representation and correspondence and even 'realism' are games that we learn to play from a community of social practice—then our realisms (and attendant claims to correspondence) are *dependent upon* communities of practice."[33] Again, Smith states, "The point is that a sacramental ontology is itself a social and cultural *accomplishment*, dependent upon and relative to environmental conditions and a community of practice."[34] However, understanding Smith correctly requires filtering such statements through his emphasis on hermeneutics and rejection of neutral reason. Perspectivism and interpretation play central roles in Smith's philosophy. When Smith claims that realism is a social accomplishment, he means that *knowledge* of reality is a social accomplishment. Smith is making an epistemological claim rather than an ontological claim. Therefore, Smith's socially contingent epistemology clouds, but does not deny, his realism.

Although Smith painstakingly avoids the term "realism," he uses realist terms such as "obduracy' of reality,"[35] "antics of things,"[36] "material conditions,"[37] "state of affairs,"[38] and "environmental conditions"[39] to describe the ontological reality with which one must cope. Successful coping with the world requires right concepts (and desires, will, and acts). Objective reality acts as the ontologically universal criterion for epistemic claims: "What is at stake is not the *ontological* universality . . . but rather the epistemological particularity of its disclosure."[40] Objective reality opens up a range of warranted (and unwarranted) interpretations. Perspectives are the only means to know and gain access to reality, but "interpretation is not itself the state of affairs."[41] Not all postmodernisms are committed to an absolute open-endedness and randomness of meaning.[42] Smith thus claims the priority of the order of being over the order of knowing. The former restricts claims made by the latter. Ontology is universal, whereas its understanding is particular. The misreading of Smith occurs when the reader reverses this hierarchy.

Even if Smith is an ontological realist, could he be an epistemological anti-realist? The charge seems plausible given Hensley's taxonomy of conceptual and alethic anti-realism and Smith's anti-correspondence rhetoric. Yet, as I have shown, Smith does not reject all forms of correspondence, merely those he equates with neutrality and mere ostension.[43] Smith is not an existential anti-realist in this regard.

Is he, however, to be grouped with Rorty and Putnam, whom Plantinga labels as creative anti-realists?[44] Creative anti-realism posits that mind-independent entities exist, but are significantly structured by the mind, such that they would be empty of their properties unless furnished by the mind.[45] Smith's hermeneutic epistemology seems to be a form of creative anti-realism since the only way to know and understand the world is through one's hermeneutical filters, such that what is real seems dependent on the communal subjectivity of the hermeneut.

Is this admission fatal to Smith's postliberal epistemological realism? No. First, Smith does not give hint that knowledge furnishes properties to its object. Second, the question is inappropriate since it assumes subject/object dualism. Third, Plantinga argues that theism is compatible with sensible anti-realism. Using Hegel's dialectic as a heuristic, he presents the thesis that truth cannot be mind-independent. Truth seems inextricably linked to *knowing* persons. Without persons, speaking about truth seems impossible. Antithetically, truth is mind-independent. Their synthesis leads that truth is ultimately dependent on God's mind. Plantinga argues that the truth of propositions is independent of God's belief, and God believes them because they are true. However, they exist because God conceives them. True propositions are necessary because God necessarily conceives them in all possible worlds.[46] With these theses, Plantinga concludes that "the fundamental anti-realist intuition—that truth is not independent of mind—is indeed correct" while qualifying the claim with divine noetic activity.[47]

Smith is compatible with Plantinga's sensible anti-realism. While knowledge, meaning, and truth claims are dependent on human noetic activity, truth ultimately participates in God, the ultimate empirical transcendental. The mind structures epistemological reality, but this structuring activity must rightly participate in God. Analogously, what is affectively and performatively "true" is that which is rightly ordered toward God. This view of truth better aligns with the biblical concept of truth than ostensive correspondence, as Dru Johnson has argued. The grammar of cultural-linguistic community can be misdirected. Human activity that generates hermeneutic truth claims sits under the judgment of the universality of the truth of God.[48] Since truth ultimately depends on a divine mind, sensible anti-realism is really a form of realism. Because Smith grounds normativity in the reality of God, in the right ordering of desire, he is an ontological and epistemological realist regarding truth. The question that remains is one of justification. Smith can argue for the right ordering of desire as a criterion for truth, but his criterion will be foreign to different cultural-linguistic communities. To judge competing truth claims, Smith's epistemology requires a non-neutral modes of justification.

Non-neutral Rational Adjudication

DF charges Smith of lacking justificatory conditions for adjudicating between different narratives and forms of life. They acknowledge that Smith provides justification within a Christian worldview, that God is the objective reality to which one's affections must ultimately point. Smith utilizes this affective Augustinian criterion as a measure to gauge the rightness of pretheoretical affective understanding. DF finds this justification unsatisfactory since such immanent criterion or presupposition cannot judge the rationality and truth of other narratives.[49] The only way forward is to confess the possibility of obtaining brute, uninterpreted facts through neutral reason.

However, the holistic elements of hermeneutic knowledge explain why disagreements occur even in supposedly objective science. Data-facts are always already understood through interpretive tacit knowledge. Traditioned worldviews, imagination, prejudices, and reason judge their relevance and validity through the use of *phronesis* that is gained through a long period of apprenticeship and participation. These interpretive acts do not necessitate relativism, but merely point to "human fallibility and the finitude of human rationality," the conditions of human be-ing.[50]

Given the pervading ethos of the Enlightenment, that Smith's perspectivism raises the charge of relativism is unsurprising. Lindbeck's statement that language games are incommensurable does not help the matter.[51] However, Terrence Tilley has argued that incommensurability does not negate the ability to compare concepts. Even though concepts and practices may have different meanings, one can compare and even adapt them for one's own contexts and meanings even if no neutral or a priori standards for comparison exist due to incommensurability.[52] Hence, apologetics for Lindbeck must be ad hoc, that is, contextually based. In fact, postliberalism's ad hoc comparison of incommensurable language games aids in understanding Smith's non-neutral apologetic method of immanent critique.

Immanent critique is a form of rational critique that operates from postliberalism's notion of categorial adequacy. By attending to the properties of the other language game, immanent critique aligns with Tilley's point that incommensurable language games can be compared. Such analysis is possible because immanent critique only utilizes the terms provided by the Other. It is the act of seeing from the other side (from the inside), inhabiting the Other's rules, and analyzing the Other's categorial adequacy.[53] By questioning the internal categorial adequacy of the foreign language game, immanent critique can non-neutrally adjudicate different interpretive communities. Postliberal apologetics is ad hoc because its method requires this contextual flexibility.

Moreover, insofar as two traditions share similar concepts for comparison, they can use transcendental arguments to determine which tradition has the categorial adequacy to account for the concepts. Recall that a transcendental condition X is a necessary condition for Y. A transcendental argument examines whether a position that accepts the reality of Y has the categorial adequacy to account for the existence of Y. If Y is a shared concept as an empirical transcendental, then two traditions can have meaningful arguments testing the categorial adequacy through transcendental arguments.[54]

For these reasons, DF's charge of relativism is unsuccessful. Hermeneutic epistemology that eschews brute facts does not succumb to story-relativism nor story-ism. It is grounded in a non-story, an objective reality that is opened up through a performative correspondence. Performative correspondence accommodates the integrated subject-object of being-in-the-world better than the ostensive referentialism that dualistically divides the subject from the object. Moreover, empirical transcendentals limit interpretive ranges so that all interpretive meaning is not equally valid. Moreover, non-neutral means of adjudication—categorial adequacy, intrasystematic coherence, immanent critique, transcendental argument, and *phronesis*—can compare incommensurable language games that avoid arbitrarity.

Postliberalism thus makes room for (non-neutral) justification. Importantly, with NAK, I must stress again that Smith's epistemology is broadly about the descriptive activity of narrative, affective construal (NAC). Our embodied mode of "knowledge" is a meaningful and often rational construal of the world, but it can be misdirected or performatively inadequate. As I argue later, Smith's epistemology needs to be supplemented with a theory of warrant rather than justification, so that one can better understand how NAC can achieve that vaunted status of NAK.

REFERENCE AND THE ETHICS OF KNOWLEDGE

This section further demonstrates Smith's realism and referentialism while addressing Smith's latent Platonism that assumes the original fallenness of theoretical knowledge. Utilizing Smith's own creational hermeneutic, I repair the division between theoretical knowledge and pretheoretical experience, an issue Smith calls the problem of incommensurability. Once one views the pretheoretical-theoretical relationship through the lens of original integrity, the problem of incommensurability becomes a pseudo-problem.

For Smith, phenomenology is a "pretheoretical originary science."[55] Against the Husserlian tendency to reduce phenomenology to noetic perception, Smith argues that Heidegger relocates phenomenology to the investigation of pretheoretical experience. However, this relocation creates a problem for phenomenology, insofar as it is a theoretical enterprise that seeks to conceptualize that which is pretheoretical and prethematic.[56] For Heidegger, the mode of being-in-the-world is not perceptually noetic, but embodied, intending the world not "as a collection of objects to be perceived, but as things (*pragmata*) to be used within an environment."[57] On the other hand, philosophy is theoretical by nature, which Smith considers an unnatural abstraction of everyday experience in its attempt to grasp the "excessiveness" of pretheoretical experience.[58] Pretheoretical experience is radically different than theoretical conceptuality. The problem of incommensurability arises due to this difference. Phenomenology's theoretical description of that which is other than theoretical violates the integrity of pretheoretical experiences' otherness by transforming concrete factual experience into abstract conceptuality.[59]

Formal Indication

Can one traverse this supposed incommensurable gap? Smith argues that the young Heidegger's idea of formal indication heals the "concept" of concept. Conceptualization, the theoretical comprehension of an object defined as the achievement of final meaning, has been an instrument of violence against the alterity of pretheoretical experience.[60] Comprehension denies alterity, reducing the (transcendence of the) Other to the (immanent) concepts of the ego.[61] Formal indication is a new kind of conceptual language that does not comprehend and objectivize, but merely "point to" the transcendence of pretheoretical experience.[62] Formal indication is not a concept that makes the object "present within a concept," a mode of assimilating the Other to the same.[63] Because it indicates or alludes to the object, formal indication does not violate the object. Not all conceptualization or predication are necessarily violent. The issue is not conceptualization per se but objectification: How to speak without violating alterity?[64]

The problem of incommensurability is thus a problem of language: How can one speak justly about transcendence without violating that transcendence by grasping it through immanent means, turning the Other into the same?[65] Explicating Augustine's philosophy of language, Smith argues that affirming the necessary but insufficient nature of signs protects the alterity of transcendence. On the one hand, signs are necessary for learning; conceptualizing the Other requires signs. On the other hand, signs are insufficient: they neither present the thing nor are the thing.[66] Furthermore, no knowledge occurs without the knowledge and meaning of the thing. For example, without prior knowledge of walking, one's (sign of) pacing cannot be understood. Knowledge of the thing (walking) precedes the sign.[67] Nevertheless, signs can "'point' to things, direct our attention and *refer* us to the thing itself," to experience the Other for ourselves, thereby preserving the transcendence of the Other by not equating itself with the Other.[68] According to Smith, "This movement of reference marks the *completion* of the sign."[69]

In this referential and iconic role of formal indication, Smith discovers at play the logic of incarnation: "The Incarnation is precisely an immanent sign *of* transcendence."[70] In the incarnation, transcendence is housed in the immanent without the loss of either transcendence (Arianism) or immanence (Docetism). Against these metaphysics of full presence, the logic of incarnation offers real presence, the "immanent sign *of* transcendence . . . [retaining] the structural incompleteness of the sign which is constitutive of language."[71] Whereas full presence denies the alterity of transcendence, real presence protects transcendence by leaving room for excess. Real presence contains both presence and absence.[72] This real presence is indicated in the incarnation, in which Christ's presence is "attended by inadequation, indicating a reference to a transcendence which exceeds the appearance, but is also embodied in the appearance."[73] Formally indicative conceptualization of facticity thus allows for knowledge of the pretheoretical without the violation of comprehension by manifesting the (pretheoretical) Other in "a mediated, incarnational manner."[74]

Ethical Reference

Noticing that Smith's semiotic presentation of the problem and solution of incommensurability revolves around the issue of reference is important. Smith ultimately redeems reference. Formal indication is intentional, and correct or incorrect semiotic reference can be made. Illuminating Augustine, Smith writes,

> The conceptual idol represents a kind of semiotic sin, a failure of reference which is a failure to recognize the (in)completion of the sign, but rather treats it as an end in itself. On the other hand, an icon, as a sign, shares the same structure of incompleteness... and this structural incompleteness is precisely that which marks the structure of reference. It is precisely when the sign (world or word) is taken to be complete in and of itself that we fall into idolatry, since we fail to be referred beyond it. The idol represents the forgetting of transcendence, the reduction of immanence, and the denial of alterity; the icon presents respect for transcendence, the rupture of immanence, and reference to an alterity.[75]

The problem is not reference but the immanent completion of reference. The conceptual idol no longer refers, having satisfied itself in the meaning found in the theoretical abstraction of the transcendent Other. However, through (incarnational) formal indication, correct (and just) reference can occur by indicating, rather than grasping for full meaning. In the end, reference is to an ultimate reality, namely God; all signs are to point to God; the world is a *sacramentum* that is to be used in order to refer the soul to the enjoyment of God and not to itself.[76]

In one sense, reference does not end with God. For the end of reference indicates the totalization of conceptualization. Reference does not suddenly make God present-at-hand as an object for theoretical molestation. Semiotic reference is always structurally inadequate: achieving the thing itself is impossible. Referential totality is still "a web of meaning, a significant whole."[77] Because "*reference* is a purpose or meaning that helps us make sense of an entity," it cannot deliver the end of reference, the entity itself.[78] In another sense, however, reference ends with God, for there is nothing beyond God. If there is something to be enjoyed more ultimately, then by definition that something is God, and any other thing is something to be used as a reference to that ultimate enjoyment. This sense of final reference does not present the thing as immanent since all creaturely signs of God are analogical.

Unlike the totalizing epistemological sense of the former, the latter is an ontological (and ethical) claim. God as the final ontological referent provides an affective criterion, the *ordo amoris*, through which one can judge right reference, with epistemological consequences.[79] However, linguistic communities of practice operate language games to justify their epistemic claims, their claims are ultimately judged by reference to the reality of God. The non-disciple does not follow the ways of the Master and has not learned to use the world as a reference to love the Master. As a result, the referential life of the non-disciple plunges into semiotic idolatry. Such is the sin of epistemological objectivism.

Moreover, even if one understands all reference to be formally indicative, incorrect reference can occur since reference may not ultimately refer to God.

Pretheoretical Primacy and Smith's Latent Platonism

The logic of incarnation operative in formal indication can bridge the seemingly incommensurable gap between pretheoretical experience and theoretical conceptualization. However, similar to Smith's claim that the realism/anti-realism debate is a pseudo-problem, the problem of incommensurability is a pseudo-problem created by Smith's latent Platonism. Smith assumes that conceptualization of pretheoretical experience via theoretical means is necessarily violent. Smith judges not only theory as objectifying, but nontheoretical cognitive perception as well, since the gaze of cognitive perception does injustice to the precognitive dimension of facticity.[80] Given this violent incommensurability, Smith (correctly) offers the logic of incarnation to prevent the silence of total apophatics. In a postlapsarian context, the (logic of) incarnation is a necessary redemptive event. However, by prioritizing the incarnation, Smith presupposes the Fall. Moreover, by emphasizing the incarnation, Smith seems to prioritize one part of God's whole redemptive act, ignoring that incarnation, life, death, resurrection, ascension, and glorification are all critical elements of the whole redemptive event.[81]

More importantly, latent in Smith's problem of incommensurability is a Platonic heresy, as evidenced in his ascription of fallenness to the theoretical: "There is . . . a sense in which I would say that the theoretical attitude is in a way *un*natural, a modification of and abstraction from everyday naïve experience."[82] Likewise, "There is a qualitative difference—*an abyss*—between the order of thought and that of experience. . . . In other words, as incommensurate, they have nothing in common, no common point of overlap; it is radical difference of order."[83] Given his continual emphasis on the primacy and autonomy of pretheoretical experience and the attendant incommensurability that necessarily accompanies this emphasis, Smith assumes the logic of fallenness. Such incommensurability seems structural to creation, an inherent fissure and disharmony prior to the Fall and the incarnation. This logic of fallenness is not necessary to Smith's thought, however. Good creation creates a harmonious relationship between pretheory and theory that exists from the very beginning; the disharmony of incommensurability is replaced by the harmony of creational (and now, eschatological) *shalom*.

Reading Smith against Smith: Creation to the Rescue

Smith is correct that God cannot remain epistemologically wholly Other, for the alterity of the wholly Other would render the wholly Other unknowable.

Smith rightly argues that the wholly Other must reveal the self through the free act of self-condescension, a gift of revelation, which is not conditioned by the will of the receiver.[84] Such movement of condescension "privileges the intentional direction *from* the Other *to* the Same."[85] However, is the incarnation the supreme model or metaphor of God's self-condescending act of revelation, the act by which the creature can speak of the Creator? Just as the incarnation is the condition for Jesus's death and resurrection, is not creation the condition for the incarnation? The incarnation is impossible without creation. Even the unbroken communion between God and humans in prelapsarian creation required divine condescension to the epistemic capabilities of Adam and Eve. The incarnation is but one of the more intense moments of God's condescension.[86] God's self-condescension begins from creation, for revelatory communion with creation must occur through the conditions of finite creatures.

If communion was actual with the wholly other God prior to the incarnation in prelapsarian creation, then the logic of incarnation is embedded in the logic of creation; the former must apply to the latter, and without the disharmony of incommensurability.[87] The logic of incarnation is at work in the logic of creation; they are two sides of the same coin. Incommensurability, on the other hand, is the result of the Fall. In a moment of *kenosis*, God creates persons in God's image, creating an eternal analogical identification with humanity, so that the wholly Other is both structurally similar and other, God's transcendence both present and absent.[88] Incommensurability is absent in the original *shalom*, nullified by the image of God, only rearing its head after the Fall. If incommensurability is the absence of a "common point of overlap," then God's revelational and Trinitarian gift of the *imago Dei* as the structure and activity of humanity nullifies incommensurability, the implication being that humans can know transcendence *like* God.[89] Knowledge of transcendence is not an incommensurate impossibility inherent to creation, but an analogical possibility as the result of God's self-condescending gift.

The image of God is the creational condition of possibility for revelation and is itself revelation, an inherent condition of the immanent recipient made possible by the transcendent (and self-condescending) God. The otherness of God is not nullified, however. The image is a gift that neither sacrifices transcendence nor transforms immanence into transcendence, as if Adam and Eve became gods in their creation. The image is a Trinitarian gift that preserves both the presence and absence of transcendence. As God's self-revelation, this gift does not identify with Emil Brunner's understanding "of an enduring *formal* image of God . . . [that] fatally smuggles in a *material* content abstracted from revelation."[90] The image acts as an inherent link that binds the creature to the Creator *as a condition of possibility*—a necessary, but insufficient condition. To admit of sufficiency reopens the door to natural theology, as if this image that is wrecked by sin can naturally know God without other revelational conditions. Even this revelational condition requires the gracious Christological and pneumatological redemptive acts of God, which "grants the ability to participate actively in the revelation of God by way of human thought and speech."[91] In this way, Smith's argument for an equality that does not destroy the difference between two "incommensurable" subjects, which is found in the *"incarnational appearance* in which God [appears] in terms that the finite knower can understand," is affirmed, but modified.[92] The incarnational appearance is indeed a divine descent, but it is preceded by the *creational appearance* of the Trinitarian God in the *imago Dei*. In other words, the incarnation is not the only condition of possibility for knowing.[93] Creation and the *imago Dei* are also part, one that precedes the logic of incarnation.[94]

Because a focus on the image is in danger of descending into natural theology, highlighting the full spectrum of God's redemptive activity—the divine incarnation through glorification—is important because the *missio Dei* is a reminder of the need for the image's rehabilitation and perfection. For without redemption, the defaced image cannot produce right belief, desire, or will. For the image to function properly as the condition of epistemic possibility, it must be conditioned by redemption.

This creational-redemptive model is consistent with Smith's incarnational account of language, but understands the pretheory-theory relationship as one of commensurable qualitative difference. Difference, even excessiveness and irreducibility, need not denote the disharmony of incommensurability. Incommensurability is the product of the Fall, necessitating the incarnation. The logic of creation in its postlapsarian condition leaves room for the possibility of objectivizing conceptualization, understood as objective knowledge, just as Smith's creational hermeneutic accounts for the potentiality and actuality of wrong interpretation in postlapsarian creation.[95] Nevertheless, creation remains the basis for the incarnation. Although the image is damaged, it is not destroyed and is on the way toward redemption. The revelational link remains, and creaturely knowledge of transcendence as an answer to loving invitation remains possible and good.

This invitation to be known is the gift of communion present in prelapsarian creation, which is ongoing today. Knowledge of transcendence, whether pretheoretical experience, the subjectivity of the Other, or God, is not something to be achieved through an overcoming, but through the inbuilt structure of possibility for God's creatures. As an inbuilt *gift*, it is not, consistent with Smith,

> a positive capacity of human beings to rise up to the Infinite, but . . . a movement of the [W̶h̶o̶l̶l̶y̶] Other toward human beings, condescending to appear under the conditions of perception which alone would make the revelation revelatory.[96]

Understanding the image of God as a revelational gift is critical. (Neutral) Natural theology would result without this understanding. The gift of revelational creation maintains the Creator/creature distinction and preserves analogical knowledge, the "incarnational account of knowledge."[97] Because the logic of incarnation is embedded in the logic of creation, of which the image of God is part, analogical knowledge is a creational account of knowledge.

If the logic of creation and the image of God eliminate the wholly otherness of God, then the incommensurable relationship between pretheoretical experience and theoretical conceptualization is eliminated. In good creation, just as the transcendence of God invites loving communion, of which theoretical understanding is part, could it not be that pretheoretical experience in its prelapsarian condition was also designed for theoretical understanding? If so, then the occasional shaping of pretheoretical experience through the theory or the sedimentation of theory is a glimpse of this original design. Rather than Smith's call for the autonomy and primacy of pretheoretical experience that creates the disharmony of incommensurability, the logic of creation operates under the hermeneutics of mutuality and *shalom*.[98]

CONCLUSION

The goal of this chapter was to answer DF's charge of story-relativism and arbitrary story-ism. I argued that internalism, modernist epistemological objectivism, and misunderstanding of Smith motivate their criticisms. In response, I demonstrated Smith's ontological and epistemological realism and provided non-neutral modes of justification. I then reexamined correspondence through Smith's semiotic referentialism and augmented his logic of incarnation with the logic of creation (and redemption). Both logics demonstrate the importance of correspondence for right knowledge. The logic of creation goes one step further by healing the broken relationship between pretheory and theory and reimagines their relationship as one of commensurable qualitative difference, establishing theoretical knowledge of pretheoretical experience as a creational possibility.

The next part of the book pivots to Reformed epistemology. Reformed epistemology is valuable due to its extensive work on the criteria for knowledge. Although Smith's *ordo amoris* is one such criterion, Reformed epistemology can provide the language, concepts, and epistemic criteria that can strengthen postmodern epistemology through augmentation. Through this conversation, Reformed epistemology, especially in Wolterstorff's rendition, is shown to be compatible with postmodernism.

NOTES

1. Davis and Franks, "Against a Postmodern Pentecostal Epistemology," 131.
2. Davis and Franks, 133.
3. Davis and Franks, 130.
4. Davis and Franks, 141–43.
5. Richard B. Davis and Paul Franks, "On Jesus, Derrida, and Dawkins: Rejoinder to Joshua Harris," *Philosophia Christi* 16, no. 1 (2014): 188.
6. Davis and Franks, 186.
7. Davis and Franks, "Against a Postmodern Pentecostal Epistemology," 136.
8. Davis and Franks, 136. They fail to realize that they also face the problem of knowing how their claims correspond to reality.
9. For a sense of their acceptance of R. Scott Smith's argument for the possibility of "simple seeing," see Davis and Franks, 132n23.
10. Davis and Franks, 140.
11. On Smith's schema, DF represents the present immediacy model that purports that interpretation is a postlapsarian condition that can be overcome in the present. See Smith, *The Fall of Interpretation*, 35–61.
12. Davis and Franks, "On Jesus, Derrida, and Dawkins," 188.
13. Davis and Franks, "Against a Postmodern Pentecostal Epistemology," 131.
14. Davis and Franks.
15. Davis and Franks, 135.
16. Davis and Franks, 136.
17. Davis and Franks, 133.
18. Smith, *The Fall of Interpretation*, 181.
19. Smith. For Pentecostals, this someone is the God of their encounter. Daniel Castelo writes, "For Pentecostals, the theme of encounter involves an implicit theological realism. Rather than going deeper within, Pentecostals typically urge seekers to 'get more of God' by pressing deeper into *God's* reality." See Castelo, *Pentecostalism as a Christian Mystical Tradition*, 81. As a Pentecostal, Smith should accept the implicit realism at work in the Pentecostal practice of seeking encounter.
20. Smith, *The Fall of Interpretation*, 181. With Smith appropriating Derrida's dictum, "There is nothing outside the text," it is important to note that even Derrida does not deny referentialism of the Other, specifically for ethical reasons. See Smith, *Jacques Derrida: Live Theory*, 13–14.
21. Davis and Franks, "Against a Postmodern Pentecostal Epistemology," 137.
22. For examples of Smith's realism, see Smith, *Introducing Radical Orthodoxy*, 206–23; and Smith, *Who's Afraid of Relativism?*, 101–109. Granted, Smith is frustratingly loose with his verbiage about correspondence in *Who's Afraid of Relativism* in ways that would drive analytic philosophers away from continental philosophy forever. However, upon scrutiny, it becomes clear that Smith accepts truth as a form of correspondence to ultimate reality.
23. Davis and Franks, "Against a Postmodern Pentecostal Epistemology," 142–43.
24. For Smith, the fit between narrative and affection represents the integrative way narrative draws from the affective faculties even while affections themselves are

interpretive construals. This fit is a descriptive account, not a prescriptive criterion for adjudicating correct NAK. Again, my distinction between NAC and NAK should help distinguish between the descriptive, meaningful construal of NAC and NAK that has achieved the more vaunted status of knowledge. See Smith, "Pentecostalism," 612.

25. Davis and Franks, "Against a Postmodern Pentecostal Epistemology," 133.

26. Their allegiance to objectivism is exemplified in their literalistic and elementary prooftexting of 2 Peter 1:20. See Davis and Franks, 134.

27. Richard J. Bernstein, *Beyond Objectivism and Relativism: Science, Hermeneutics, and Praxis* (Philadelphia: University of Pennsylvania Press, 1988), 18.

28. Bernstein, 56.

29. Bernstein, 54.

30. Smith, *Speech and Theology*, 76.

31. Heidegger, *Being and Time*, 146. While DF dismisses this idea as presuppositionalist, this idea is shared by Heidegger, Polanyi, Lyotard, and Lindbeck.

32. Davis and Franks, "Against a Postmodern Pentecostal Epistemology," 140.

33. Smith, *Who's Afraid of Relativism?*, 107.

34. Smith, 108.

35. Smith, 111.

36. Smith.

37. Smith, 132

38. Smith, 142

39. Smith, 148

40. James K. A. Smith, "Re-Kanting Postmodernism?: Derrida's Religion within the Limits of Reason Alone," *Faith and Philosophy* 17, no. 4 (2000): 558–71 (567). Also, see Smith, "The (Re)Turn to the Person in Contemporary Theory," 88n44; and Smith, "Natural Law's Secularism?," 214n8. Smith argues that Derrida commits the poststructuralist *faux pas* by arguing for a pure transcendental religion that is without any determinate content and thus falls into modernism. See James K. A. Smith, "Determined Violence: Derrida's Structural Religion," *The Journal of Religion* 78, no. 2 (1998): 197–212; and Smith, "Between Predication and Silence," 81–84.

41. Smith, *The Fall of Interpretation*, 185. Smith's view can thus be seen as compatible with William Alston's argument that conceptual schemes shape phenomenal appearing without determining the ontological reality of the object. See William P. Alston, *Perceiving God: The Epistemology of Religious Experience* (Ithaca: Cornell University Press, 1991), 35–43.

42. Gill, *Deep Postmodernism*, 61. Maurizio Ferraris wrongly describes postmodernism as essentially antirealist and idealist. See Maurizio Ferraris, "Transcendental Realism," *The Monist* 98, no. 2 (2015): 215–32.

43. For example, see Smith, *Who's Afraid of Relativism?*, 106.

44. Plantinga, "How to Be an Anti-Realist," 50–59. This charge has merit since Plantinga links Kant with creative anti-realism and DF charge Smith with Kantianism. Wolterstorff argues that Rorty and Putnam are not creative anti-realists, but conceptual relativists. Conceptual relativism is metaphysically anti-realist but accepts extramental entities. However, conceptual relativism makes the further argument that truth is dyadic, not monadic. That is, truth is not objective, but always relative to a

conceptual scheme. However, Wolterstorff argues that this view is itself monadic and self-defeating. See Nicholas Wolterstorff, "The World Ready-Made," in *Practices of Belief: Selected Essays*, ed. Terence Cuneo, vol. 2 (New York: Cambridge University Press, 2010), 12–40 (22–23).

45. Plantinga, "How to Be an Anti-Realist," 48–50. Plantinga seems to argue that Kant's creative anti-realism logically ends in existential anti-realism. If the properties of entities depend on a creative mind and since the existence of property-less entities is impossible, no mind-independent entities can exist. See Plantinga., 48.

46. Plantinga, "How to Be an Anti-Realist," 67–70.

47. Plantinga, 70.

48. Due to this universality, Smith is neither a conceptual relativist. Joshua Harris agrees that Smith's postmodernism, what Harris calls comprehensive hermeneuticism, accounts for non-neutral universal claims to truth because the divine *Logos* is the ontological condition of possibility for all knowledge. See Joshua Lee Harris, "Who's Truth? A Response to Davis and Franks's 'Against a Postmodern Pentecostal Epistemology,'" *Philosophia Christi* 16, no. 1 (2014): 175–84 (181–83).

49. Smith's presuppositionalism is not lost on DF, which they acknowledge, but does not adequately address. However, they understand presuppositionalism as the arbitrary acceptance of presuppositions. See Davis and Franks, "Against a Postmodern Pentecostal Epistemology," 132n23, 136n32, 139n45, 140.

50. Bernstein, *Beyond Objectivism and Relativism*, 69.

51. Lindbeck, *The Nature of Doctrine*, 49. While in agreement with Lindbeck, Jeannine Hill Fletcher states that Lindbeck makes interreligious dialogue practically impossible since genuine understanding of a foreign cultural-linguistic community requires one's full immersion in it. See Jeannine Hill Fletcher, "As Long as We Wonder: Possibilities in the Impossibility of Interreligious Dialogue," *Theological Studies* 68, no. 3 (2007): 531–54 (539). For Marianne Moyaert, postliberalism represents an exclusivism that shuts down interreligious dialogue. See Marianne Moyaert, "Postliberalism, Religious Diversity, and Interreligious Dialogue: A Critical Analysis of George Lindbeck's Fiduciary Interests," *Journal Of Ecumenical Studies* 47, no. 1 (2012): 64–86. While agreeing with Lindbeck, Tasi Perkins states that postliberalism in its "rawest form" makes interreligious dialogue difficult but also argues that intermixing of cultural-linguistic communities do occur. See Perkins, "Beyond Jacques Derrida and George Lindbeck," 343–58. David Trenery states that Lindbeck is open to charges of fideism and relativism. However, just because Lindbeck has not developed the epistemological conditions for cross-traditional dialogue does not render postliberalism as either fideistic or relativistic. See Trenery, *Alasdair MacIntyre, George Lindbeck, and the Nature of Tradition*, 215.

52. Tilley, "Incommensurability, Intratextuality, and Fideism," 90–94.

53. James K. A. Smith, "The Spirit, Religions, and the World as Sacrament: A Response to Amos Yong's Pneumatological Assist," *Journal of Pentecostal Theology* 15, no. 2 (2007): 251–61 (258–59).

54. This explanation reveals the flaw of DF's (mis)representation of presuppositionalism. Presuppositionalism does not allow rational authority to any

presuppositions. Instead, presuppositionalism argues for the rationality of Christianity by seeking to show how Christian presuppositions can account for such empirical transcendentals as laws of logic and objective morality, which is akin to an argument for categorial adequacy. Insofar as a language game assumes their reality, transcendental argument can be utilized. For a critical presentation of presuppositionalism, see Frame, *Cornelius Van Til*, 311–17.

55. See James K. A. Smith, "Liberating Religion from Theology: Marion and Heidegger on the Possibility of a Phenomenology of Religion," *International Journal for Philosophy of Religion* 46, no. 1 (1999): 17–33 (25); and Smith, "Alterity, Transcendence, and the Violence of the Concept," 377.

56. Smith, *Speech and Theology*, 9, 42, 67–78.

57. Smith, 81.

58. Smith, 81–83.

59. Smith, "Taking Husserl at His Word," 91–92. For Smith's extended commentary on this problem, see Smith, *Speech and Theology*, 26–63.

60. Smith, 132.

61. The problem of incommensurability is an ethical matter. See Smith, "Alterity, Transcendence, and the Violence of the Concept," 369–70. For Smith's exposition of Emmanuel Levinas on this matter, see Smith, *Speech and Theology*, 27–32.

62. Smith, *Speech and Theology*, 69.

63. Smith, 10.

64. Smith, 78–79, 84–86, 131–133.

65. Smith, 43.

66. Smith, 120.

67. Smith, 119.

68. Smith, "Between Predication and Silence," 119.

69. Smith, *Speech and Theology*, 120.

70. Smith, 123. Smith's usage of the logic of incarnation is metaphorical and brackets Christology. See Smith, 10.

71. Smith, "Between Predication and Silence," 75.

72. James K. A. Smith, "A Principle of Incarnation in Derrida's (Theologische?) Jugendschriften: Towards a Confessional Theology," *Modern Theology* 18, no. 2 (2002): 217–30 (225–27).

73. Smith, 227.

74. Smith, *Speech and Theology*, 56.

75. Smith, "Between Predication and Silence," 74.

76. Smith, 72–74.

77. Richard F. H. Polt, *Heidegger: An Introduction* (Ithaca: Cornell University Press, 1999), 52.

78. Polt, 53.

79. Smith, *Speech and Theology*, 121–22.

80. Smith, "Taking Husserl at His Word," 93–97.

81. These redemptive acts of Christ are represented as his twofold state of humiliation and exaltation. See J. van Genderen and W. H. Velema, *Concise Reformed*

Dogmatics, trans. Gerrit Bilkes and Ed M. van der Maas (Phillipsburg: P&R Publishing Company, 2008), 468–511. Van Genderen and Velema also warn that isolating and emphasizing a single facet of Christ's work, such as the incarnation, often lead to erroneous understandings of Christ's work. van Genderen and Velema, 462.

82. Smith, "Taking Husserl at His Word," 106.

83. Smith, *Speech and Theology*, 9. Emphasis mine.

84. Smith, 158–61.

85. Smith, 160.

86. Here I borrow Smith's utilization of degree, which opposes binary logic. See Smith, *Thinking in Tongues*, 103–5.

87. According to Jason Sexton, the image is Christocentric because Christ is the goal of the image. But as "anthropology and theology (proper) together have yielded in the incarnation," anthropology presupposes creation, such that the incarnation and (Christocentric) creation are inextricably interrelated. Thus, the divine goal for the image was always to enjoin God and humanity in the true image of Christ through the work of the Spirit. Jason S. Sexton, "The Imago Dei Once Again: Stanley Grenz's Journey toward a Theological Interpretation of Genesis 1:26–27," *Journal of Theological Interpretation* 4, no. 2 (2010): 187–206 (196–99). Because the Spirit is at work in creating the bond of commensurability, the Spirit is central to the dissolution of incommensurability in creation.

88. Richard Hess argues that the Ancient Near Eastern practice of erecting divine images that represented the kings' dominion over his empire must be the lens to understand the image. Humanity's imaging God thus creates an analogical extension of God's self to humans, marking God's presence, while also accounting for God's absence, hence, the image. See Richard S. Hess, "Equality with and without Innocence: Genesis 1-3," in *Discovering Biblical Equality: Complementarity without Hierarchy*, ed. Rebecca Merrill Groothuis and Ronald W. Pierce (Downers Grove: InterVarsity Press, 2005), 79–95 (81). Cf., Phyllis A. Bird, "'Male and Female He Created Them': Gen 1:27b in the Context of the Priestly Account of Creation," *Harvard Theological Review* 74, no. 2 (1981): 129–59 (141–44). C. L. Crouch dissents against this view. See C. L. Crouch, "Genesis 1:26-7 as a Statement of Humanity's Divine Parentage," *Journal of Theological Studies* 61, no. 1 (2010): 1–15 (9). Furthermore, Crouch argues that the image describes God's parentage. If humanity is God's children, then incommensurability is an impossibility since parentage necessitates likeness. See Crouch, 10–15. Richard Briggs argues that the purpose of the image is to set up humanity's significant role in Scripture's narratives and what entails from the image. In this way, Genesis may not provide a clear picture of the nature of the image, but the reader can get glimpses of the image throughout Scripture. Examples such as Abraham and Moses arguing with God (Gen 18:23-25; Num 14:13-19) show "how a human being can stand before God and aspire to God's justice and compassion, attempting even to argue before God by *grasping God's own perspective on human affairs*. Moments such as these suggest all manner of characteristics of humans at their best, as they image God." Richard S. Briggs, "Humans in the Image of God and Other Things Genesis Does Not Make Clear," *Journal of Theological Interpretation* 4, no. 1 (2010): 111–26 (123). Emphasis mine. This view

further solidifies the argument that the *imago Dei* is a divine gift that creates a (gifted) commensurability through creation between God and humanity. Incommensurability, then, must be seen for what it is: a result of the Fall.

89. Smith, *Speech and Theology*, 9. Later in the book, Smith sides with Emile Brunner. "Even if we want a theology that begins from revelation, that revelation must first be *received*, and there are conditions for that reception: all reception is according to the mode of the perceiver." Smith., 167. Besides the image's structural dimension, a teleology exists, the goal of "mediating the Creator's immanence in the world." Sexton, 'The Imago Dei Once Again," 193.

90. Paul T. Nimmo, "Karl Barth," in *The Oxford Handbook of the Epistemology of Theology*, ed William J. Abraham and Frederick D. Aquino (Oxford: Oxford University Press, 2017), 523–34 (526). Because the *imago Dei* is a gift, it can act as the means and act of perpetual revelation without becoming something humans can control. This understanding still frees God to be God, the divine initiator of revelation, and is not inconsistent with Barth's theology of revelation. For a clear elucidation of Barth's theology of revelation that reveals its complementarity with my argument, see Kevin Diller, *Theology's Epistemological Dilemma: How Karl Barth and Alvin Plantinga Provide a Unified Response* (Downers Grove: InterVarsity Press, 2014), 54–60.

91. Nimmo, "Karl Barth," 527.

92. Smith, *Speech and Theology*, 162.

93. Smith, 163.

94. According to Cornelius Van Til, the *imago Dei* is the point of contact between the Christian and the non-Christian. Van Til, "Introduction," 6.

95. See Smith, *Speech and Theology*, 165.

96. Smith, 168.

97. Smith, 164.

98. Smith, "Taking Husserl at His Word," 100. My previous distinction between quantitative and qualitative primacy is applicable here. My proposal is an attempt to clarify Smith by identifying his logic of fallenness and the necessary relationship between the logic of creation and incarnation, the former eliminating Smith's sense of fallenness between pretheory and theory. In this way, this section has been an attempt to read Smith against Smith.

Part 3

REFORMED AND POSTMODERN EPISTEMOLOGY

Chapter 7

Plantinga's Reformed Epistemology

INTRODUCTION

Alvin Plantinga has extensively explored the questions about justification, rationality, and warrant. Like Smith, Plantinga rejects epistemic neutrality and focuses on pretheoretical basic beliefs. He is ontologically and epistemologically realist and shares Smith's Reformed view on the *pistic* nature of metaphysical beliefs. Other Reformed epistemologists also make similar claims to Smith. For example, Nicholas Wolterstorff demonstrates the situatedness of rationality and argues for contextual entitlement of beliefs. Kelly James Clark argues that affect guides reason.[1] Similarities abound between Smith and Reformed epistemology. Even though Smith does not rely on Reformed epistemology for his epistemology, he acknowledges the congeniality between Reformed epistemology, postmodernism, and postliberalism in various places.[2]

The three chapters of this part exposit the principal representative of Reformed epistemology, Alvin Plantinga, along with Nicholas Wolterstorff, for his clearer congeniality with postmodernism, in order to identify areas of convergence, assist, and critique of Smith for the purpose of modifying and constructing a robust postmodern Christian epistemology. The importance of Reformed epistemology lies in its extensive work on the prescriptive criteria for knowledge.

This chapter presents Plantinga's theory of warrant and the relevant issues of justification, internalism, and externalism. The next chapter presents his Aquinas/Calvin and extended Aquinas/Calvin models. These two chapters provide the materials necessary for constructing a more robust prescriptive epistemic criteria for Smith through augmentation. I will specifically argue that Plantinga's externalism, realism, prescriptive criteria for warrant, and

152   Chapter 7

foundationalism can repair Smith and provide valuable contribution toward my proposal.

The chapter on Wolterstorff's Reformed epistemology highlights a more dynamic picture of the knower than is presented by Plantinga. The usefulness of this section was inspired by Nathan Shannon's argument that Plantinga's warrant model portrays a modernistic static knower.[3] Although I disagree with Shannon, Wolterstorff's situated rationality is a more dynamic, postmodern epistemic model that remains consistent with Plantinga's warrant project. Wolterstorff's situated rationality, when juxtaposed with Plantinga, provides another picture of Reformed epistemology that illumines its consistency with Smith. Because there is no principal contradiction between Plantinga and Wolterstorff, Wolterstorff aids in presenting Reformed epistemology's compatibility with the type of postmodernism presented in this book.

DEONTOLOGICAL JUSTIFICATION

Four questions drive Plantinga's epistemological project. First, is undefeated evidence or argument necessary for the rationality of theistic belief? Second, what properties transform belief into knowledge? After using various terms, such as positive epistemic status and epistemic aptness, Plantinga settled on warrant because it does not carry as strong an association with epistemic deontology as does justification.[4] Warrant is a quality or quantity that comes in degrees. With sufficient strength, warrant turns mere true belief into knowledge.[5] Third, is there a viable de jure objection independent from the de facto question of the truth of Christianity? Fourth, is Christian belief warranted, and does it qualify as knowledge? Plantinga addresses these questions chronologically throughout his career, beginning with *God and Other Minds* and "Reason and Belief in God" and developing his ideas of warrant in his warrant trilogy.

God and Other Minds marks the genesis of Reformed epistemology, a work that tentatively concludes that belief in God can be rational without possessing undefeated proof. This conclusion is the result of Plantinga's analysis of several important theological and atheological arguments about God's existence and the analogical argument for other minds. Concluding that they all fail to accomplish their intended goals, Plantinga reasons that belief in God may be like belief in other minds: rational to believe without possessing undefeated proof.[6] Reformed epistemology took its decisive step with *Faith and Rationality*, the product of a yearlong inquiry by the Calvin Center for Christian Scholarship into the Reformed view on faith and reason.[7] Plantinga's contribution, "Reason and Belief in God," develops his earlier tentative conclusion, and its central claims have remained stable throughout the maturation of Plantinga's thought. Most important is the claim that theistic belief does not need inferential justification through evidence or arguments, rejecting what Plantinga calls the evidentialist objection to theistic belief.[8] The evidentialist objection purports that "belief in God is irrational or unreasonable or not rationally acceptable or intellectually irresponsible or somehow noetically below par because . . . there is *insufficient evidence* for it."[9] The evidentialist objection is a normative objection that presupposes epistemic deontology; one must discharge one's epistemic duty to be justified.[10]

For the evidentialist objector, epistemic obligation is ubiquitous. Even epistemic non-voluntarism, the view that belief-formation is involuntary, does not excuse one from this obligation. Plantinga identifies three reasons why epistemic obligation can still apply. First, that some beliefs are unjustified despite one's sincerity in holding them seems intuitive. For example, one may involuntarily believe through one's social location that human sacrifice appeases the gods. However sincere the belief, it is probably unjustified, and one ought to investigate its appropriateness. Second, one could voluntarily accept or reject involuntary beliefs. For example, one's inability to refrain from believing in God does not preclude one from rejecting the belief. This control over acceptance retains the validity of epistemic deontology over involuntary beliefs. Third, one can enact an epistemic regimen that directs involuntary belief-formation over time. For example, one can reject involuntary theistic belief and immerse herself only in atheistic literature and culture, leading to possible suppression of her theistic belief over time.[11] Thus, some volitional control over belief-formation is possible. For these reasons, the evidentialist objector promotes the exercise of epistemic duty for justification.

However, the evidentialist objector does not hold that all beliefs must have evidence. Basic, immediate beliefs are not accepted on the basis of other beliefs.[12] They are pretheoretical and non-inferential. Nonbasic, mediate beliefs require inferential support from each other until this support finally terminates on some basic belief. With this basic and nonbasic differentiation, Plantinga argues that the evidentialist objector presupposes classical foundationalism, a normative noetic structure that governs the rationality of beliefs.[13]

Classical foundationalism is a normative deontological noetic structure that sets epistemic standards and rational duties. The structure of classical foundationalism, like all forms of foundationalism, consists of a foundation of properly basic beliefs that support nonbasic beliefs. For ancient and medieval (classical) foundationalists, properly basic beliefs consisted of self-evident beliefs and beliefs that are evident to the senses. Modern (classical) foundationalists consider both self-evident and incorrigible beliefs as properly basic.[14] Put more succinctly, classical foundationalism's conditions for proper basicality dictates that a "proposition p is properly basic for a person

S if and only if *p* is either self-evident to *S* or incorrigible for *S* or evident to the senses for *S*."[15] For the classical foundationalist (and the evidentialist objector), belief in God is neither self-evident, evident to the senses, nor incorrigible.

Plantinga sees classical foundationalism as self-referentially incoherent because it neither meets its own conditions for proper basicality, nor is it supported by properly basic premises. Classical foundationalism's criteria are overly stringent and negate many beliefs that seem properly basic, such as belief in other minds, memory beliefs, and perceptual beliefs.[16] For these reasons, the deontological requirements of classical foundationalism collapse along with its evidentialist objection, opening the door for the proper basicality of theistic beliefs. However, the jump from classical foundationalism's collapse to the proper basicality of theistic belief is not guaranteed. For deontology may remain in another form. Plantinga traces this remaining deontology to internalism.

INTERNALISM AND EXTERNALISM

From the time of the *Theaetetus* and until Edmund Gettier, the components of knowledge comprised of justified true belief (JTB). Knowledge requires true belief. Because belief may result from accident or ignorance, a belief must be deontologically justified, which avoids epistemic irresponsibility. Plantinga traces this deontology to René Descartes and John Locke. Both promote the deontological obligation to regulate beliefs with reason. For Plantinga, "justification *is* deontological" and regulates epistemic duty and permission.[17]

This long-established JTB view was dismantled by Edmund Gettier, whose central argument was that JTB may be accidentally true.[18] Plantinga cites Bertrand Russell's pre-Gettier example that illustrates this argument well. Imagine that a clock stopped at midnight. At 12 p.m. the next day, a person takes a brief glance at the clock and sees the clock pointing to 12, forming the belief that it is noon. Unbeknownst to her, it is 12 p.m. She justifiably holds a true belief. However, her belief is accidental and does not qualify as knowledge.[19]

Internalists have traditionally accepted the JTB conditions. For internalists, justification requires epistemic access to the justificatory elements that are internal to the person.[20] Epistemic access, what Michael Bergmann calls the awareness requirement, defines internalism. The motivation behind the awareness requirement is what Bergmann calls the "Subject's Perspective Objection" (SPO). According to the SPO, ignorance of the justificatory elements renders the belief unjustified because its truth could be accidental.[21] Such belief is no different from "a stray hunch or an arbitrary conviction."[22]

Two broad forms of internalism exist that correspond with the quality of awareness. Strong internalism requires the awareness of justificatory elements for justification. Weak internalism merely requires the capability to become aware of those elements.[23] However, internalism's identification with JTB is its fatal flaw. JTB can arise from accident or cognitive malfunction.[24]

According to James Beilby, two broad responses emerged following Gettier. The "Post-Gettier Optimists" are internalists who view Gettier problems as exposing a mere incompleteness of JTB, thus requiring a fourth condition for knowledge. "Post-Gettier Pessimists" are externalists who have abandoned the requirements for JTB and internal access.[25] In this way, externalism is the negation of internalism. Externalism does not reject all instances of internal access, however, but only its necessity.

For Plantinga, externalism represents a turn away from justification to warrant.[26] Rejecting the access requirement, externalism ties warrant with properties external to the mind's reflective activity, such as reliable epistemic mechanisms.[27] Warrant is obtained if the belief connects with those relevant external conditions and reality without any need for epistemic awareness. Externalism thus represents a break with the JTB tradition.[28]

Internalists find this lack of epistemic access troubling. Assuming the truth of the SPO, internalists argue that internal access is necessary to examine whether a belief has met external conditions.[29] Only this internal awareness can overcome the threat of skepticism. Yet, for Plantinga, internalism is more troubling because deontology severs connection with the world. If "contingent factors external to the mind cannot make an epistemic difference," one could be justified even if misled.[30] For example, a person residing in the Matrix can be internally justified but lack knowledge.

Some have questioned Plantinga's portrayal of internalism as necessarily deontological. As internalists, Earl Conee and Richard Feldman agree with Plantinga that deontological internalism is flawed. They view the best of internalism as represented by evidentialism. The availability and accessibility of evidence justify belief.[31] However, evidentialism also faces difficulties. First, a classical Plantinga response is that cognitive malfunction could render an evidence-based belief as lacking warrant. A belief can seem highly probable with respect to other beliefs and evidence, but it will not qualify as knowledge if it results from psychosis.

Second, evidentialism faces a dilemma regarding doxastic experience, the affective aura that accompanies beliefs (e.g., the positive feeling one experiences when seeing $2 + 2 = 4$ compared to the negative feeling when seeing $2 + 2 = 5$). If evidence is taken narrowly to include propositional and sensuous phenomenal (e.g., perceptual) evidence, but not doxastic experience, then justification is unnecessary for warrant since doxastic experience accompanies all beliefs. That is, there are warranted beliefs that are neither propositional nor sensuous, such as memory beliefs. Therefore, propositional nor sensuous evidence is neither necessary nor sufficient for warrant. If evidence is taken broadly to include doxastic experience, then justification becomes tautological since to have a belief is to have such evidential justification. Evidence construed broadly cannot function as a condition for warrant; the evidence of doxastic experience is merely an account of a necessary condition of belief.[32] Moreover, cognitive malfunction could lead to an erroneous doxastic experience. In this way, whether internalism is deontological or evidential, it is insufficient for warrant.[33]

Feldman does not wholly disagree. In fact, he argues that contemporary internalists include an externalist clause for warrant.[34] As post-Gettier optimists, they remain internalists regarding justification. With warrant, a fourth, external condition is required beyond JTB.[35] Plantinga disagrees that internal justification is necessary, however construed. Beilby's comment on this point is insightful:

> While the internalist is acquainted with the features that contribute to justification, because (in a post-Gettier world) the "fourth condition" is invariably externalist, he must remain an externalist with respect to knowledge. Moreover, if the internalist in question is a realist, he must remain an externalist with respect to the truth of his belief. He will hold that truth is not determined by justification or even ideal justification. So my question is this: What doth it benefit an epistemologist if he gains internalism with respect to justification, but fails to gain internalism with respect to those things that justification is aiming at, knowledge and truth? In terms of decision-making, the truth and knowledge status of one's beliefs seem at least as (if not more) relevant to the decision-making process as the "justification-status" of one's beliefs.[36]

For Plantinga, externalist proper function does not require internalist justification, and no fourth condition for warrant is necessary. If externalism is right, then one is loosed from the awareness requirement and the evidentialist objection.

This foray into internalism and externalism illumines Smith as an externalist. Narrative, affective construal (NAC) becomes narrative, affective knowledge (NAK) not through theoretical awareness of some justificatory element, but through right ordering of desire toward the empirical transcendentals, and the *ordo amoris* can be easily understood as a term describing proper function. The problem with DF's critique of Smith is that they impose an internalist requirement on Smith. Their appeal to "the facts" assumes the truth of evidentialism; some internal access to these brute facts is necessary to rise above narrative relativism. Yet, if hermeneutic knowledge results from proper function, then hermeneutic knowledge can be warranted without further justification. To explain why, the next section exposits Plantinga's concept of warrant.

WARRANT

While his warrant criteria include propitious environment, a good design plan successfully aimed at truth, and degrees of warrant, Plantinga calls proper function as "the rock on which the canvassed accounts of warrant founder."[37] Officially, Plantinga's warrant criteria states,

> A belief has warrant for a person S only if that belief is produced in S by cognitive faculties functioning properly (subject to no dysfunction) in a cognitive environment that is appropriate for S's kind of cognitive faculties, according to a design plan that is successfully aimed at truth. We must add, furthermore, that when a belief meets these conditions and does enjoy warrant, the *degree* of warrant it enjoys depends on the strength of the belief, the firmness with which S holds it.[38]

Proper Function

Proper function is not normal function, as if epistemic privilege is rooted in statistical majority. Statistical abnormality can be consistent with proper function, as exemplified by the abnormal abilities of an Olympic athlete compared to the average person.[39] Statistical normality can also be consistent with improper function. For example, sin's deleterious effect on the cognitive faculties explains why vast number of people reject God's revelation. However, this rejection by the statistical majority is foolishness to Christians (Ps 14:1-3).

Proper function, for Plantinga, is a commonsensical notion, one that all humans have.[40] People recognize when something is not working rightly. Proper function does not entail that all faculties must function properly at the same time for a belief to achieve warrant. Only those involved with a particular belief-formation require proper function.[41] They need not necessarily function properly during the entire belief-producing duration. Nor is warrant prohibited by the use of outside aids, such as glasses. This point demonstrates that proper function need not be ideal function.[42]

The crux of the matter is that cognitive faculties must function properly for warrant. Proper function is a necessary condition. Neither faithfulness to epistemic duty nor coherence can achieve warrant with the presence of cognitive malfunction.[43] Both internalist and externalist accounts of warrant require proper function in order to avoid accidentally true beliefs.

Propitious Environment

Although necessary, proper function is insufficient for warrant. Proper function in one environment does not guarantee proper function in another environment for which it was not designed. By way of example, Plantinga invites the reader to imagine someone whose cognitive faculties are working swimmingly on earth who is suddenly and unknowingly transported to a radically different epistemic environment where invisible elephants reside. These elephants emit an unknown radiation that causes earth-beings to form the belief that a large gray object is nearby. An elephant walks by, triggering the corresponding belief. After investigating the area, no large gray object is found. This example demonstrates that properly functioning cognitive faculties can produce unwarranted beliefs in epistemologically inappropriate environments.[44]

Examples need not seem so far-fetched. Gettier cases show that neither JTB nor proper function is sufficient for knowledge because belief can be the result of an accident. Consider Gettier's first case. Smith and Jones apply for the same job. Smith believes that Jones will get the job and that Jones has ten coins in his pocket. Smith has good evidence for both, and his cognitive faculties are functioning properly. Smith believes that the man who will get the job has ten coins in his pocket. Unbeknownst to Smith, he himself has ten coins in his pocket, and he, not Jones, will get the job.[45] His belief is JTB and results from proper function, but he does not have knowledge. His belief is accidentally true, the product of something amiss in his cognitive environment. These examples show that proper function requires a propitious environment designed for human cognitive faculties.[46]

The two examples highlight the need for precision. The first exemplifies what Plantinga calls the "maxi-environment," the global environment for which human cognitive faculties were designed. The second case exemplifies a "mini-environment," "a much more specific and detailed state of affairs . . . [that] includes all the relevant epistemic circumstances obtaining when that belief is formed."[47] Mini-environments are particular circumstances. Some mini-environments will be favorable and others unfavorable for the exercise of cognitive powers even when those powers are functioning properly. The abovementioned example of Smith and Jones exemplify a misleading mini-environment, even though the exercise of Jones's cognitive powers is in accord with the appropriate design for his maxi-environment. Both the maxi- and mini-environments must be propitious in order to avoid accidental beliefs.[48] Therefore, Plantinga adds a Resolution Condition to the environment clause, according to which "belief B produced by an exercise of cognitive powers has warrant sufficient for knowledge only if MBE (the mini-environment with respect to B and E) is favorable for E."[49] What does it mean for a mini-environment to be favorable? It is when the exercise of cognitive powers, E, is competent to recognize the relevant state of affairs, which Plantinga calls DMBE. More technically, "MBE is favorable just if for every state of affairs, S, such that S is taken for granted by E in the issuing of B, there is no state of affairs S* such that S* is included in MBE but not in DMBE and such that S* precludes S."[50]

Future defeaters may arise to challenge the environmental clause, but such a possibility is no problem for proper functionalism. First, Plantinga makes clear that the complexity of epistemology renders impossible neat and tidy relevant conditions for warrant outside central paradigm cases. All that can be said is that a favorable mini-environment is required.[51] Second, every epistemology suffers from the Gettier problem. However, proper functionalism provides the best account for warrant since any account that seeks to circumvent accidental beliefs requires proper function.[52]

Good Design Plan Successfully Aimed at Truth

For cognitive faculties to be reliable, they must have a good epistemic design plan.[53] Without this clause, proper function can still produce unwarranted beliefs. They could be designed to produce beliefs conducive for survival, not truth.[54] While survival beliefs may be beneficial, they would be unwarranted. For example, a properly functioning cognitive faculty could be designed to produce overly optimistic beliefs in the face of a deadly illness in order to aid survival.[55] As much as this optimistic belief may aid in survival, its primary aim is not truth. And without alethic aiming, a belief cannot be warranted. Moreover, the design plan governing the aiming toward truth must be a good one, so that there is high objective probability that it will be successfully aimed at truth. Plantinga calls this the reliability clause.[56]

Degrees of Warrant

Finally, warrant comes in degrees. If a belief meets the abovementioned conditions of warrant and is held with sufficient firmness and confidence, then it is warranted.[57] The degree of warrant depends on the firmness with which one holds a belief.[58] Even if all warrant conditions are met, holding a belief with insufficient firmness lacks warrant.

PROPER BASICALITY

Warrant is continuous with Plantinga's earlier idea that theistic belief is properly basic. Warrant does not require inference. However, Plantinga does not offer clear necessary and sufficient conditions for proper basicality, although this does not entail that any belief can be properly basic. Rather than constructing these conditions, Plantinga campaigns for an inductive method for investigating the conditions for proper basicality after having gathered obvious examples of beliefs that are properly basic and not properly basic.[59] Because the nature of epistemology is multifaceted, such an inductive method will not provide clear necessary and sufficient conditions. The clearest instances apply to paradigmatic cases, but even they lack "stylishly sparse set of necessary and sufficient conditions . . . [and require] various qualifications, additions and subtractions [as] necessary."[60] Outside the central cases are

> penumbral belt of analogically related concepts . . . and a more shadowy area of borderline possible cases, cases where it isn't really clear whether what we have is a case of warrant in the central sense, or a case of one of the analogically extended concepts, or neither above.[61]

Due to the dynamic reality of ever-shifting epistemic contexts, Plantinga even argues that proper basicality is dependent on circumstances, such that a belief may be properly basic in one, but not in another circumstance.[62] Rather than offering conditions for proper basicality, he addresses proper basicality in respect to justification, rationality, and warrant. After having inspected Christian beliefs, he argues that they are properly basic in respect to all three.[63]

The question of proper basicality is circumstance-specific; there is no generic case of a universally warranted belief. The proper basicality of Christian belief is tied contextually to the truth of Christianity, such that theistic belief would be unwarranted if Christianity is false. The conditions for proper basicality are thus up for debate. However, since what matters for knowledge is proper basicality in terms of warrant, the more important condition is warrant, not proper basicality.[64]

The warrant of Christian belief does not eliminate the possibility of defeaters. Warrant only provides *"prima facie*, not *ultima facie*, justification."[65] Even if warranted belief does not require evidence or argument, contrary evidence or argument can defeat this warrant.[66] This is why Plantinga addresses potential defeaters to Christian belief in *Warranted Christian Belief*. Nothing in the conditions of warrant eliminates the logical possibility of warrant defeaters. In fact, Plantinga's externalist warrant model contains one negative internalist condition called the "no-defeater condition," which stipulates that *S*'s belief is not defeated if "*S* does not believe (and would not upon reflection) that her belief that *p* is defeated."[67]

Moreover, Plantinga is more open to inference in his general epistemology. Although inference can, at most, provide an insufficient degree of warrant toward theistic belief, inference can provide enough warrant for nonreligious knowledge.[68] For example, Plantinga states that the belief in the existence of "electrons isn't (originally) warrant basic for us."[69] "Originally" is important. Electron belief cannot be warrant basic for humans with their current design plan because it originally arose through inductive, scientific investigation. Yet, belief in electrons can have warrant through inference that meets the warrant criteria. Nonscientists can also have warrant-basic beliefs about electrons through testimonial chains that passed down the original warrant.

Unlike internalism that requires inferential justification, Plantinga's warrant conditions act as necessary and sufficient conditions for inferential knowledge. If inductive beliefs meet the warrant criteria, they are warranted.[70] For example, Plantinga counts deduction along with intuition as part of the deliverances of reason that produce a priori knowledge.[71] Thus, Plantinga allows inferential knowledge in his general epistemology. But Plantinga is adamant that religious knowledge is only properly basic.[72]

Dependence Relations

Even if inferential knowledge is possible for general epistemology, another question remains. If properly basic beliefs do not depend on any other beliefs, whether basic or nonbasic, for their warrant, then how is it that some basic beliefs seem to rely on other beliefs? According to Evan Fales, the basic/nonbasic distinction does not explain "the phenomenology of ordinary belief-formation."[73] Plantinga purports that experience causes or occasions belief. However, many present perceptual beliefs are not occasioned by present experiences, but past ones, and are produced by subconscious mechanisms. Fales argues that this subconscious recalling is inferential and critiques Plantinga's assumption that inference is necessarily conscious. Fales entertains the belief, "It is very probable that most crows are black," to examine subconscious inference in detail. For Fales, foundationalists would take this belief as inductive, relying on the memory of perceiving many crows throughout time and concluding that most crows are black. However, one doesn't make such inductive recollections in forming the belief. Neither does one form the conscious belief, "the crow is black," upon seeing one nor add the belief to the storehouse of beliefs for future inductive purposes. The belief that most crows are probably black does not rely on "any conscious belief-forming process."[74] Even properly basic beliefs rely on background beliefs and experiences, and they form subconsciously, without conscious inference, whether complex or quick. This relationship, he argues, better represents the psychology of belief-formation: "The actual process of belief formation . . . is certainly a complex mixture of presentation of evidence, reasoning, memory, and unconscious processing and summarizing of information."[75] If this complex process is correct, Fales argues that the basic/nonbasic distinction dissolves. If one redefines proper basicality such that the only difference between basic and nonbasic beliefs is that the former allows unconscious inference and the latter conscious inference, then the differences are not wide enough to allow such distinction.[76]

This complex relationship is no problem for proper basicality, according to Plantinga. First, there are beliefs that seem clearly properly basic, such as belief in other minds. Second, no other possibilities between basic and nonbasic/inferential belief exist. Plantinga is doubtful of other categories beyond the basic/nonbasic categories.[77] Third, a clear distinction between properly basic and nonbasic belief is not critical to Plantinga's epistemology. The central point is that Christian belief can have warrant without arguments. Plantinga states,

> This is a challenge to foundationalism. . . . As far as that central thesis [of warrant] goes, it doesn't really matter whether or not there is a clear, important and precise distinction between basic and nonbasic belief. It doesn't really matter whether attempts to make such a distinction are deconstructible.[78]

Once again, warrant, not proper basicality, is the more important condition.

Furthermore, Plantinga responds to the crow argument by showing that the belief is properly basic in respect to justification—one doesn't flout any epistemic or rational duty accepting it, and there is no cognitive malfunction involved. The belief is also "warrant basic" by way of testimony and memory.[79] According to Fales, a properly basic belief is not derived from other beliefs. Yet, a belief can be based on testimony and be properly basic in respect to warrant if the testifier's belief also has warrant. Same applies to memory, which can act "as a special case of testimony."[80] Furthermore, prior to Fales's essay, Plantinga maintained that basic beliefs often depend on background beliefs even if they are the starting points for belief. That is, one can't have a basic belief about a truck without having some knowledge about trucks.[81] Yet, these beliefs are interrelated and working together without any quick inferential activity.

Inferential belief can also become properly basic over time. For example, after gaining inferential knowledge in the past, one can forget the inferential connection while maintaining the belief. The memory of the originally inferential nature of the belief can be forgotten, thus severing the inferential connection from the belief.[82] This leveling down of prior inferential knowledge can be understood as the transformation of know-that to know-how, such that background belief does not carry propositional content, but acts as an epistemic skill. William Alston gives an example of learning to drive a car. In the beginning, one follows inferential and propositional instructions. Once the knowledge is mastered as a skill, one bypasses the background information to perform the knowledge.[83]

This belief-formation aligns with Plantinga's understanding of induction in a broad sense. Induction taken narrowly is inferential, but induction taken broadly can be both reflective and unreflective, inferential or non-inferential. Plantinga writes,

> Broadly taken . . . the term denotes our whole nondeductive procedure of acquiring, maintaining, and discarding beliefs about what is so far unobserved or undetected or unknown. It is a complicated, multitudinous process involving inherited ideas about the ways of the world, interlocking chains of inductions in the narrow sense, views about what is essential and what [is] accidental and about which differences are important and which not, and judgments of initial plausibility. This process of considering, examining, and evaluating hypotheses may go on unreflectively and unselfconsciously, or by way of explicit, self-conscious reflective attention; it is guided by simplicity and in other ways by what we human beings find natural and familiar.[84]

Induction broadly understood is not necessarily inferential even though it is a "complicated, multitudinous process." Complexity need not necessarily denote nonbasicality. For example, know-how is complex pretheoretical knowledge. Arrival at a destination without remembering the drive occurs through practical knowledge that is unreflectively and non-inferentially inductive. Thus, basic beliefs can depend or be based on other beliefs without that relationship being inferential. When those beliefs meet the warrant conditions, they qualify as knowledge. Dependence or basing relations between beliefs do not negate the basicality of such a relationship.

Michael Bergmann agrees with this portrayal of proper basicality. Using the language of "seemings," Bergmann argues that theistic seemings are like Robert Audi's "'conclusions of reflection,' which are not based on inferences from premises but instead emerge noninferentially from awareness of a variety of observations, experiences, and considerations."[85] This awareness involves background experiences and beliefs to which the origins of their reflective conclusions are sometimes impossible to trace.[86] Against Fales's objection, Reformed epistemology does not discount background experiences and beliefs as part of proper basicality. These background experiences and beliefs need not act as subconscious inferences. Instead, they play basing relations; they can occasion or base properly basic beliefs.[87]

This investigation clarified the basing relations between background experiences, inductive beliefs, and properly basic beliefs, revealing that proper basicality need not be atomistic but can be dependent on other beliefs and experiences. Highlighting background experiences and beliefs draw attention to the hermeneutic nature of belief-formation. While people have countless experiences and beliefs, certain ones rise above others to play more prominent role in belief-formation. This selection, like belief-formation, is often involuntary. Because properly basic beliefs often have as their ground a host of situated background beliefs and experiences, they are not epistemically neutral. Beliefs are always already at the mercy of situated experiences. One also plays some active hermeneutic role in belief-formation through accepting or rejecting beliefs. Thus, both subconscious and conscious epistemic actions are hermeneutic and perspectival.

CONCLUSION

Plantinga's Reformed epistemology developed out of his early thesis that theistic belief could be rational without undefeated proof. His mature epistemology continued this insight through the development of the externalist version of warrant that revolves around the centrality of proper function. His rejection of internalism stemmed from this point, that a belief could be justified but lack knowledge due to cognitive malfunction. Whether belief is deontologically or evidentially justified, justification is unnecessary for knowledge. Insofar as belief meets the warrant conditions, then the belief will be warranted. Even the notion of proper basicality is not central for Plantinga. For his central thesis is that knowledge is only dependent on the warrant conditions. However, proper basicality is important for the conversation between Plantinga and Smith because it accords with pretheoretical understanding. Plantinga's argument that background beliefs and experiences shape pretheoretical beliefs demonstrates the reciprocal relationship between pretheory and theory. The next chapter exposits Plantinga's Aquinas/Calvin models that further demonstrate the hermeneutic nature of Reformed epistemology and utilizes Plantinga's affective analog for warrant to augment Smith's epistemology.

NOTES

1. Kelly James Clark, "A Reformed Epistemologist's Closing Remarks," in *Five Views on Apologetics*, ed. Steven B. Cowan (Grand Rapids: Zondervan, 2000), 364–73 (365).

2. Smith connects Reformed epistemology with postmodernism by associating Reformed epistemology with non-, anti-, and postfoundationalism, terms that he uses interchangeably. See Smith, *Thinking in Tongues*, 108, 109n7; Smith, *Who's Afraid of Relativism?*, 174; and Smith, *Introducing Radical Orthodoxy*, 43n45. Smith views the epistemology of the wider Reformed tradition as (postmodern) postfoundationalist. See, Smith, 80–85, 152n30.

3. Nathan D. Shannon, *Shalom and the Ethics of Belief: Nicholas Wolterstorff's Theory of Situated Rationality* (Cambridge: James Clarke and Company, 2015), 53–54.

4. Alvin Plantinga, *Warrant: The Current Debate* (New York: Oxford University Press, 1993), 5.

5. Plantinga, *Warranted Christian Belief*, 153.

6. See Alvin Plantinga, *God and Other Minds: A Study of the Rational Justification of Belief in God* (Ithaca: Cornell University Press, 1967), 271.

7. Nicholas Wolterstorff, "Reformed Epistemology," in *Practices of Belief: Selected Essays*, ed. Terence Cuneo, vol. 2 (New York: Cambridge University Press, 2010), 334–49 (334–35).

8. Alvin Plantinga, "Reason and Belief in God," in *Faith and Rationality*, ed. Alvin Plantinga and Nicholas Wolterstorff (Notre Dame: University of Notre Dame Press, 1983), 16–93 (52).

9. Plantinga, 17.

10. This intellectual duty is *prima facie* and "can be overridden by circumstances." Plantinga, 34.

11. Plantinga, 34–38. Cf., Nicholas Wolterstorff, "Can Belief in God Be Rational If It Has No Foundations?," in *Faith and Rationality*, ed. Alvin Plantinga and Nicholas Wolterstorff (Notre Dame: University of Notre Dame Press, 1983), 135–86 (153). This view illumines how volitional ratiocinative activity can affect pretheoretical and non-voluntarist affections.

12. Plantinga, "Reason and Belief in God," 52.

13. Plantinga, 48.

14. Plantinga, 58–59. Plantinga describes two components of self-evidence. First, self-evidence is epistemologically immediate. Second, self-evidence has a phenomenological "aura," a doxastic experience that prompts an experiential "tendency to accept or believe" the belief. Beliefs that are evident to the senses are perceptual propositions "whose truth or falsehood we can determine by looking or employing some other sense." Incorrigible beliefs are more cautious than sensorially evident beliefs. Incorrigible beliefs are about one's mental life. While one's sensorial beliefs can be mistaken, incorrigible beliefs carry a particular certainty. Being mistaken about one's seemings, about one's being appeared to, is difficult. Plantinga, 57–58. This "seeming" language traces back to Rodrick Chisholm who argued that being appeared to is not an adjectival claim about an entity, but a phenomenological account of describing what seems directly evident. See Roderick M. Chisholm, *Theory of Knowledge* (Englewood Cliffs: Prentice Hall, Inc., 1966), 30–34.

15. Plantinga, 'Reason and Belief in God," 59.

16. Plantinga, 59–61.

17. Plantinga, 14. For Locke, this duty of regulating belief by reason is based on its probability with respect to certainty. See Plantinga, *Warranted Christian Belief*, 87. Also, see Nicholas Wolterstorff, "Thomas Reid on Rationality," in *Rationality in the Calvinian Tradition*, ed. Hendrik Hart, Johan Van Der Hoeven, and Nicholas P. Wolterstorff (Eugene: Wipf & Stock, 1983), 43–69 (46–47). Wolterstorff provides an externalist account of justification that can complement

Plantinga's epistemology. He agrees that justification as intentional epistemic action that accrues accountability is inaccurate. However, he acknowledges that there is epistemic "ought" language that is neither intentional nor accountable for blame. As an example, "A person with considerable accomplishments to her credit should not believe that she is without talent." What explains this usage is a proper functionalist concept of ought. If we are functioning properly, we ought to hold, reject, or withhold certain beliefs. This externalist deontological justification is necessary for warrant. See Nicholas Wolterstorff, "Ought to Believe-Two Concepts," in *Practices of Belief: Selected Essays*, ed. Terence Cuneo, vol. 2 (New York: Cambridge University Press, 2010), 62–85 (77–83). For other externalist, non-deontological accounts of justification, see Alston, *Perceiving God*, 70–77; and Michael Bergmann, *Justification without Awareness* (New York: Oxford University Press, 2006), 3–9.

18. See Edmund L. Gettier, "Is Justified True Belief Knowledge?," *Analysis* 23, no. 6 (1963): 121–23.

19. Plantinga, *Warranted Christian Belief*, 157.

20. Non-epistemic access, such as access to one's internal organs, are irrelevant to a belief's epistemic status.

21. Bergmann, *Justification without Awareness*, 7, 12.

22. Bergmann, 12.

23. Laurence BonJour, "Externalism/Internalism," in *A Companion to Epistemology*, ed. Jonathan Dancy, Ernest Sosa, and Matthias Steup, 2nd ed. (Malden: Wiley-Blackwell, 2010), 364–68 (364).

24. Kenneth Boyce and Alvin Plantinga, "Proper Functionalism," in *The Bloomsbury Companion to Epistemology*, ed. Andrew Cullison (New York: Bloomsbury Academic, 2015), 143–61 (144–45).

25. James Beilby, "Externalism, Skepticism, and Knowledge: An Argument against Internalism," *Philosophia Christi* 10, no. 1 (2008): 75–86 (75–76).

26. Michael Bergmann helpfully remarks that some define internalism with respect to warrant. See Michael Bergmann, "Internalism, Externalism and the No-Defeater Condition," *Synthese* 110, no. 3 (1997): 399–417 (402).

27. George Pappas, "Stanford Encyclopedia of Philosophy," ed. Edward N. Zalta, Internalist vs. Externalist Conceptions of Epistemic Justification (The Stanford Encyclopedia of Philosophy, 2017), https://plato.stanford.edu/archives/fall2017/entries/justep-intext/.

28. Alvin Goldman offers a reliabilist account of externalism that "identifies justified belief with reliably produced belief." Hilary Kornblith, "Internalism and Externalism: A Brief Historical Introduction," in *Epistemology: Internalism and Externalism*, ed. Hilary Kornblith (Malden: Blackwell Publishing, 2001), 1–9 (2).

29. Beilby, "Externalism, Skepticism, and Knowledge," 77.

30. Earl Conee and Richard Feldman, "Internalism Defended," in *Epistemology: Internalism and Externalism*, ed. Hilary Kornblith (Malden: Blackwell Publishing, 2001), 231–60 (234).

31. Conee and Feldman, "Internalism Defended," 238. Plantinga acknowledges that the internalism of Conee and Feldman are not deontological. Plantinga, *Warrant*,

26. However, the stress on evidence still traces back to the Lockean *duty* of proportioning belief to evidence. Plantinga, *Warrant and Proper Function*, vi.

32. Alvin Plantinga, "Respondeo," in *Warrant in Contemporary Epistemology: Essays in Honor of Plantinga's Theory of Knowledge*, ed. Jonathan L. Kvanvig (Lanham: Rowman & Littlefield Publishers, 1996), 307–78 (359–61).

33. Plantinga, 339–40.

34. Michael Bergmann includes Laurence BonJour, Roderick Chisholm, and Keith Lehrer as internalists who include at least one necessary external condition for warrant. See Bergmann, "Internalism, Externalism and the No-Defeater Condition," 406.

35. Richard Feldman, "Plantinga, Gettier, and Warrant," in *Warrant in Contemporary Epistemology: Essays in Honor of Plantinga's Theory of Knowledge*, ed. Jonathan L. Kvanvig (Lanham: Rowman & Littlefield Publishers, 1996), 199–220 (200).

36. Beilby, "Externalism, Skepticism, and Knowledge," 83.

37. Plantinga, *Warrant and Proper Function*, 4. Plantinga views design plan aimed at truth and good design plan successfully aimed at truth as two central but separate aspects of warrant. See Plantinga, *Warranted Christian Belief*, 154–56. My division is for stylistic purposes only and does not affect Plantinga's theory of warrant.

38. Plantinga, 156. This account of warrant represents the central core of warrant. While the central core represents necessary and sufficient conditions for warrant, such clear conditions may not be available for analogical extensions and borderline cases due to the complexity of the epistemic situation. See Plantinga.

39. Plantinga, *Warrant and Proper Function*, 9.

40. Plantinga, 5. Plantinga attributes the influence of Thomas Reid on his epistemology. Plantinga, x.

41. Plantinga, *Warrant and Proper Function*, 10. This way, proper function does not succumb to the generality problem. Furthermore, such cases substantiate Plantinga's argument that epistemology is too complex to produce clear necessary and sufficient conditions for warrant. Hence, Plantinga's account is of central paradigm cases of warrant and of the ideal epistemic agent. See Plantinga, ix. Eleonore Stump's statement on epistemology is perceptive here: "Not everything can be made precise." Stump, "Orthodoxy and Heresy," 163n32.

42. Plantinga, *Warrant and Proper Function*, 10–11.

43. For Plantinga, proper functionalism represents the best externalism. He critiques reliabilism for failing to provide warrant since a reliable process can still produce accidentally true beliefs. Take, for example, the case of the epistemologically serendipitous lesion. Sam has a brain lesion that causes him to hold mostly false beliefs. However, part of the lesion's processes is causing the belief that its victim suffers from a brain lesion. Sam's belief is thus the result of a highly reliable process, but it lacks warrant due to cognitive malfunction. See Boyce and Plantinga, "Proper Functionalism," 146. Max Baker-Hytch critiques reliabilism for succumbing to the generality problem, a problem of identifying the respective repeatedly reliable cognitive process. In a personal conversation, Baker-Hytch stated that proper function does not seem to succumb to this problem because proper function need not

require repeatable processes. See Max Baker-Hytch, "Epistemic Externalism in the Philosophy of Religion," *Philosophy Compass* 12, no. 4 (2017): 1–12.

44. Plantinga, *Warrant and Proper Function*, 6–7.

45. Gettier, "Is Justified True Belief Knowledge?," 122.

46. Environment can also suffer from complexity and vagueness. However, "uncorrected and uncompensated" malfunctions cannot produce warrant. Plantinga, *Warrant and Proper Function*, 11.

47. Plantinga, "Respondeo," 314.

48. Plantinga, *Warranted Christian Belief*, 158.

49. Boyce and Plantinga, "Proper Functionalism," 152.

50. Boyce and Plantinga, 154.

51. Plantinga, *Warranted Christian Belief*, 160.

52. Boyce and Plantinga, "Proper Functionalism," 154.

53. Design does not necessarily connote supernaturalist design. In central and paradigm cases, design involves conscious design. Plantinga, *Warrant and Proper Function*, 21. However, the supernatural addendum is not an epistemological claim. Thus, his warrant conditions can be analyzed apart from metaphysical claims. See Plantinga, "Respondeo," 347; and Plantinga, *Warrant and Proper Function*, 13–14. For three possible options that could wed naturalism with proper function, see Bergmann, *Justification without Awareness*, 144–46.

54. This teleological point is central to Plantinga's Evolutionary Argument against Naturalism (EAAN) that any belief arising from the union between naturalism (N) and unguided evolution (E) has a defeater because N&E produces beliefs aimed at survival, not truth. See Alvin Plantinga, *Where the Conflict Really Lies: Science, Religion, and Naturalism* (New York: Oxford University Press, 2011), 307–50.

55. Plantinga, *Warrant and Proper Function*, 16.

56. Plantinga, 17–18. Plantinga is open to the possibilities that persons may have slightly different design plans. However, at least for the obtainment of knowledge, Plantinga seems clear that design plans must still be aimed toward true beliefs. See Alvin Plantinga, "Why We Need Proper Function," *Noûs* 27, no. 1 (1993): 66–82 (75).

57. Plantinga, *Warranted Christian Belief*, 206.

58. Joel Pust and Andrew Moon have argued that neither warrant nor belief come in degrees, respectively. See Joel Pust, "Warrant and Analysis," *Analysis* 60, no. 1 (2000): 51–57; and Andrew Moon, "Beliefs Do Not Come in Degrees," *Canadian Journal of Philosophy* 47, no. 6 (2017): 760–78. Also, see Feldman, "Plantinga, Gettier, and Warrant," 202. However, the issue of degree is not central to the dialogue between Plantinga and Smith. Neither critiques affect the conditions for warrant that turns belief into knowledge. For Moon, belief may not come in degrees, but firmness and confidence in belief do.

59. Plantinga, "Reason and Belief in God," 74–76.

60. Plantinga, *Warrant*, ix.

61. Plantinga.

62. Plantinga, "Reason and Belief in God," 74. This admission of Plantinga guards against Dru Johnson's critique that Reformed epistemology only captures the

existentially unreal epistemic situation: "singular reasoning upon singular propositional beliefs within a singular knower's mind at a single moment in time." However, Johnson is correct that the methodological delimitations of Reformed epistemology do not capture the epistemological picture of Scripture as a habit-body process that follows epistemic authorities. Johnson, *Biblical Knowing*, 175, 180.

63. Alvin Plantinga, "On 'Proper Basicality,'" *Philosophy and Phenomenological Research* 75, no. 3 (2007): 612–21 (615–16).

64. Warrant is more important than justification and internal rationality because the latter are not necessarily tied to truth. Wolterstorff also argues that basic/nonbasic distinction is secondary to the primary question of warrant and its conditions. See Wolterstorff, "Reformed Epistemology," 347.

65. Plantinga, "Reason and Belief in God," 77. Because Plantinga had not adopted the term "warrant" at this time, he still assumed the validity of justification. See Plantinga, *Warranted Christian Belief*, 259n34.

66. Andrew Moon, "Recent Work in Reformed Epistemology," *Philosophy Compass* 11, no. 12 (2016): 879–91 (882).

67. Bergmann, "Internalism, Externalism and the No-Defeater Condition," 407. According to Bergmann, this internal condition divides externalists, although they are united in that there are no other internal requirements. Bergmann suggests that moderate externalists could include some form of deontology and inference as internal sub-conditions under the no-defeater condition. Bergmann, 408–12. For Plantinga's delineation on the nature of defeaters, see Plantinga, *Warranted Christian Belief*, 359–66.

68. Kevin Diller argues that inferential arguments can boost warrant. See Kevin Diller, "Can Arguments Boost Warrant for Christian Belief?: Warrant Boosting and the Primacy of Divine Revelation," *Religious Studies* 47, no. 2 (2011): 185–200. Plantinga does not eliminate the possibility of theistic belief arising from inference, but admits that this possibility is not part of his model. Plantinga, *Warranted Christian Belief*, 250. Michael Sudduth provides helpful clarification on the role of positive theistic arguments for Reformed epistemology. See Michael C. Sudduth, "Reformed Epistemology and Christian Apologetics," *Religious Studies* 39, no. 3 (2011): 299–321 (311–17).

69. Plantinga, "On 'Proper Basicality,'" 619.

70. Plantinga, *Warrant and Proper Function*, 136.

71. Plantinga, 107–8.

72. Hence, Graham Oppy's critique that Plantinga has shifted his view on natural theology is unimportant. First, Plantinga's view seems clearly continuous from his earlier to later works. For example, see Plantinga, "Reason and Belief in God," 67–68; Plantinga, *Warranted Christian Belief*, 170, 499; Alvin Plantinga, "Internalism, Externalism, Defeaters, and Arguments for Christian Belief," *Philosophia Christi* 3, no. 2 (2001): 379–400 (384–86, 398); and Alvin Plantinga, "Replies to My Commentators," in *Plantinga's Warranted Christian Belief: Critical Essays with a Reply by Alvin Plantinga*, ed. Dieter Schönecker (Dordrecht: De Gruyter, 2015), 238–62 (240). Plantinga maintains that natural theology can boost warrant but cannot provide warranted knowledge, whereas defeaters can negatively affect knowledge.

Defeater-defeaters are aimed at the warrant of defeaters, not at basic beliefs. See Alvin Plantinga, "Reply," *Philosophical Books* 43, no. 2 (2002): 124–35 (127–28); Plantinga, "Reason and Belief in God," 84; and James Beilby, "Plantinga's Model of Warranted Christian Belief," in *Alvin Plantinga*, ed. Deane-Peter Baker (New York: Cambridge University Press, 2007), 125–65 (135–36). For Oppy's comments, see Graham Oppy, "Natural Theology," in *Alvin Plantinga*, ed. Deane-Peter Baker (New York: Cambridge University Press, 2007), 15–47.

73. Evan Fales, "Proper Basicality," *Philosophy and Phenomenological Research* 68, no. 2 (2004): 373–83 (376).

74. Fales, 377.

75. Fales, 379.

76. Fales, 379–83. For similar accounts, see Jeremy Randel Koons, "Plantinga on Properly Basic Belief in God: Lessons from the Epistemology of Perception," *Philosophical Quarterly* 61, no. 245 (2011): 839–50; and Winfried Löffler, "An Underrated Merit of Plantinga's Philosophy," in *Plantinga's Warranted Christian Belief: Critical Essays with a Reply by Alvin Plantinga*, ed. Dieter Schönecker (Dordrecht: De Gruyter, 2015), 65–81.

77. Plantinga, "Replies to My Commentators," 243.

78. Plantinga, "On 'Proper Basicality,'" 614.

79. Plantinga, 618. Plantinga follows Thomas Reid's principle of credulity, the inborn disposition to trust testimony. See Plantinga, *Warranted Christian Belief*, 147–48.

80. Plantinga, "On 'Proper Basicality,'" 614.

81. Plantinga, *Warranted Christian Belief*, 83.

82. Plantinga, "Reason and Belief in God," 50–51. Similarly, Plantinga states that theistic arguments can aid in one's journey toward gaining a properly basic belief in God. See Plantinga, 73.

83. Alston, *Perceiving God*, 91. Remember that know-how is still involved in know-that. Recall Polanyi's argument of the simultaneous presence of focal and subsidiary awareness.

84. Plantinga, *Warrant and Proper Function*, 123.

85. Seemings are not merely perceptual. For example, Bergmann identifies moral, mathematical, and logical intuitions as seemings. See Michael Bergmann, "Religious Disagreement and Rational Demotion," in *Oxford Studies in Philosophy of Religion*, ed. Jonathan L. Kvanvig, vol. 6 (New York: Oxford University Press, 2015), 21–57 (35, 36).

86. Bergmann, 36.

87. Jeremy Koons has not recognized the basing relation. He argues that supposedly basic beliefs receive their warrant from background *theories*. One wonders how belief in other minds is based on the theory of other minds. See Koons, "Plantinga on Properly Basic Belief in God," 848.

Chapter 8

Warranted Christian Belief

INTRODUCTION

Reformed epistemology is sometimes understood as an apologetics methodology. Although it is more accurately an epistemology, it has apologetics value. However, it is unlike the apologetics methodologies that are modernistic due to its view of hermeneutical knowledge. Ultimately, it does not aim to prove the truth of Christianity because ultimate beliefs are *pistic*. This postmodern posture of hermeneutic humility is leveraged by a humble confidence toward its rationality. Even if ultimate commitments are *pistic*, one can be confident in their warranted status. Moreover, Plantinga's Christian commitments lead him to value the important role of the affections in the life of the believer. Although he does not devote an equal amount of literature to the affections, his affective analog of warrant is invaluable for furnishing the warrant criteria for narrative, affective knowledge (NAK). This chapter explores these themes within Plantinga's Aquinas/Calvin (A/C) models for later augmentation with Smith.

THE AQUINAS/CALVIN MODEL

One of the central goals of *Warranted Christian Belief* is to identify a successful de jure objection that is independent of the de facto objection. The de facto objection is a straightforward objection against the truth of theism. The de jure objection, on the other hand, is less straightforward, arguing that theistic belief is somehow epistemically irrational or unjustified even if true.[1] Plantinga's search for a viable de jure objection leads him to what he terms the Freud and Marx (F&M) complaint. For Freud, religious belief is illusory, arising from wishful thinking. While illusion has its functions, it is not aimed at true beliefs. For Marx, religious belief results from cognitive malfunction due to social disorder.[2] The F&M complaint is a viable de jure objection targeting the warrant of Christian belief. However, the complaint merely presupposes the falsity of Christianity.[3] Thus, this de jure objection is dependent on the de facto question about Christian truth. Plantinga's project has been to show that the de facto objection is irrelevant. Not only are evidence or arguments unnecessary for theistic belief, in his estimation, there are no successful theological or atheological arguments about God's existence.[4]

Questions of rationality and warrant are intricately tied to truth. Hence, Plantinga argues that his model of warrant for Christian belief can only be true if Christianity is true. But he is pessimistic about the viability of demonstrating the truth or falsity of theism. Epistemology is at root a hermeneutic, *pistic* commitment to a metaphysical view, a view with which Smith concurs.[5] This point is made clear in Plantinga's arguments for the warrant of Christian beliefs through what he calls the A/C models.

In light of the F&M complaint against the warrant of Christian belief, Plantinga offers the A/C model and the extended A/C model to establish the possibility of warrant for Christian belief. They are aptly named the A/C model because Plantinga draws inspiration from their shared claim that a natural knowledge of God exists, although he modifies this view as a capacity for knowledge rather than inborn knowledge.

According to the A/C model, theistic beliefs are properly basic with respect to justification and warrant. First, if justification is tied to epistemic duty, then one can be deontologically justified if one studied atheological arguments and remained unconvinced. Second, humans are endowed with the *sensus divinitatis*, which is a divinely designed cognitive faculty that can be triggered in various ways to form theistic beliefs.[6] As divinely designed, it is successfully aimed toward true beliefs. When operating in a congenial environment, it will most likely produce true theistic belief. The A/C model thus makes way for warranted theistic belief.

If humans are endowed with the *sensus divinitatis*, why do they not all have theistic beliefs? According to the A/C model, sin damaged the *sensus divinitatis*. Sin is like a cognitive (and affective and volitional) disease. Defining sin this way, Plantinga integrates hamartiology with philosophical warrant in order to show that nonbelief is the result of cognitive malfunction. Against the F&M complaint, then, it is nonbelief that is actually unwarranted.[7] Moreover, by including this theological clause to his epistemology, Plantinga further demonstrates that epistemology is not neutral.

The A/C model provides an important link between Reformed epistemology and evidentialism. The *sensus divinitatis* is like other faculties that produce basic beliefs as a response to triggering events. These events act as the evidential ground or occasion for theistic belief. While some may think Reformed epistemology is anti-evidentialist, Plantinga makes clear that evidence can be important for Reformed epistemology, acknowledging his compatibility with a "sensible" or "moderate" evidentialism.[8] It is the role that evidence plays in the production of theistic belief that is controversial. Only if evidence is taken as a necessary and inferential condition for the justification of theistic belief does Plantinga depart from evidentialism because no quick inference from the evidential event to belief occurs. Theistic belief is still properly basic.

Truth and the A/C Model

Plantinga does not intend to demonstrate the truth of the A/C model. The truth of the A/C model is dependent on the truth of Christianity. If God does not exist, then theistic belief, as a false belief, lacks warrant. Although it is possible that false belief resulting from cognitive faculties working at their limits has warrant, such warrant is insufficient for knowledge. If God does not exist, then the highest status theistic belief can achieve is warrant that is insufficient for knowledge because human cognitive faculties would not have been designed to produce true beliefs. However, theistic belief does not seem to result from cognitive faculties working at their limits, evidenced by the firmness with which people often hold religious beliefs.

If Christianity is true, then theistic belief probably has warrant, and Plantinga's model or something similar is most likely true.[9] God probably placed humans in propitious environments with properly functioning cognitive faculties and a good design plan that is successfully aimed toward knowing truth. It is logically possible that divinely designed faculties that are aimed toward producing theistic belief don't produce it. Conversely, it is possible that a faculty that is not designed to produce theistic belief produces it due to some malfunction. Yet, proper function doesn't denote perfect function. Even if unwarranted beliefs are produced at times, if theism is true, it is more likely that divinely designed faculties that are aimed toward true theistic beliefs will reliably produce them.[10]

The A/C model and its warrant-basicality are contextualized within Plantinga's consideration of the de jure objection. The question about the warrant-basicality of the A/C model is not ultimately about its rationality, as the de jure objection seems to indicate. The question is ultimately about its truthfulness. However, Plantinga takes a similar line as Lindbeck. The answer is dependent on one's metaphysical or religious commitments, that is, one's language game. One's ultimate commitments inform one's anthropology, epistemology, and ontology. Ultimately, the answer to the warrant status of a theistic belief is a theological matter.[11]

174   Chapter 8

Ensconced in the question of metaphysical truth, the A/C model beckons the nonbeliever to reexamine her de jure objection by showing the inextricable relationship between the rationality of a belief and the status of its metaphysical truthfulness. Given that the A/C model meets the warrant conditions if Christianity is true, the more important question must be about metaphysical truth. The de jure objection cannot solely be about rationality or justification. No de jure objection is independent of the de facto objection.[12] If one presupposes metaphysical naturalism, then one will believe that theistic belief is irrational. If the atheist acknowledges her de facto assumptions, then her de jure objection fails because she is admitting to the circularity of her argument since she begins from the premise that theism is false.[13] This circularity is the fatal flaw of the F&M complaint.

Pistic Commitment

Ultimately, the warrant of theistic belief is a religious matter. Theistic belief is a *pistic* commitment that is not rationally demonstrable without circularity. One begin from faith and doesn't argue to it, just as one begins from perception instead of arguing to perception, which is impossible without question-begging.[14] Use of the cognitive faculties always involves trusting those very faculties to function reliably and properly.[15]

Plantinga is comfortable admitting that belief in God is unprovable. Stating what Smith takes to be an antifoundationalist claim of Reformed epistemology, Plantinga states that the warrant of only a minority of human beliefs is demonstrable.[16] Kevin Diller agrees with this statement. The movement of belief starts from ontological commitments. For theological knowledge, this starting point is "the givenness of the reality of the revelation of God."[17] Lest one is uncomfortable with this commitment to epistemic circularity, Michael Bergmann states that most epistemologists accept epistemic circularity at the most basic level because they believe some beliefs are non-inferentially justified.[18]

This epistemic circularity is benign circularity that must be accepted to avoid skepticism. It contrasts with malignant circularity, which disqualifies justification for belief.[19] If one rejects this view and seeks inferential justification for all levels of belief, then infinite regress of justification results. Externalists like Plantinga do not have this awareness requirement for justification and do not face the infinite regress problem. Bergmann notes that epistemic circularity only becomes a problem if one already doubts her sources of belief or the reliability of her cognitive faculties. Those who do not harbor such doubts are not infected with a problematic circularity.[20] Given that the choices are either accepting the reliability of one's cognitive faculties or facing infinite regress and skepticism, accepting the former is more reasonable.

This trust in the reliability of one's cognitive faculties is inspired by the common sense philosophy of Thomas Reid and is shared by Bergmann, Plantinga, and other Reformed epistemologists.[21]

Charges against the A/C Model

If the truth of metaphysics cannot be demonstrated, does this admission disallow any belief to be warrant-basic? Is Plantinga subject to Richard Davis and Paul Franks (DF)'s critique of arbitrariness? Plantinga has been heavily criticized on this point.[22] As Deane-Peter Baker points out, many do not critique Plantinga's A/C model, which attests to its internal consistency. The target of their critique is Plantinga's unwillingness to address the de facto question. This point is succinctly put by Baker as the "so what?" problem: even if Christian belief may have warrant, why should the de facto question merit attention from non-Christians?[23] If metaphysical truth is unprovable, are each epistemic communities left to their own claims, however outrageous they might seem to others? Does not this relativism eliminate rational dialogue? Could not other religions co-opt the model for their own claims to warrant?[24] Reformed epistemology answers negatively to these questions.

First, "outrageousness" of belief is a hermeneutical matter. Some atheists consider religious belief outrageous while theists believe otherwise. *Pistic* trust necessarily opens the door to epistemic uncertainty and undecidability. Yet, they do not necessitate relativism. Second, Plantinga addressed this worry by responding to the Great Pumpkin objection, according to which any belief can be properly basic, and the Son of Great Pumpkin objection, that any belief within particular epistemic communities can be properly basic. Against the first objection, Plantinga argues that not all beliefs can be properly basic. One can investigate the proper basicality of a belief through inductive research, and the Great Pumpkin belief as it is presented does not seem to meet the inductive test. There is no natural tendency, such as the *sensus divinitatis* or design plan, to believe in the Great Pumpkin. Great Pumpkin belief rather seems to result from cognitive malfunction. Furthermore, proper basicality does not entail groundless beliefs. Properly basic beliefs require relevant circumstances for their warrant, such as religious experiences that occasion theistic belief. Against the second objection, truth of one religion can negate the truth of another. If Christianity is true, then beliefs of a different community, such as a voodoo community, cannot have warrant since Christian beliefs negate the truth claims of voodoo. Moreover, some epistemic systems cannot account for warrant. If skepticism or evolutionary naturalism is true, beliefs will not be warranted. The same is true for the Great Pumpkin belief. If the A/C model is true, then the Great Pumpkinites lack the cognitive faculties and processes necessary for warranted belief.²⁵ Therefore, that the A/C model entails epistemic relativism is certainly untrue.²⁶

Of course, Plantinga's replies to the Great Pumpkin objections do not satisfy the "so what?" question. Does not Plantinga's inability to answer the de facto question indicate the uselessness of his model outside Christianity? The answer is a resounding no. First, Christianity is irreducible to a belief system. Even taken naturalistically, Christianity is a highly complex affective, moral, cultural, political, and ritual system. Christianity is not an intellectual puzzle for the enjoyment of a small group of bourgeois intellectual elite. As the largest global religion with a deep moral, cultural, political, and intellectual history, its influence reaches everywhere. Christianity's prominent place in human history and continual influence should be enough motivation for the nonbeliever, especially the sincere, to investigate its truth. The lack of desire to undertake such an investigation may reflect more of one's affective commitment to a host of personal priorities rather than a purely intellectual one.

Second, Plantinga does not eliminate the need of natural theology altogether. Even if natural theology cannot deliver convincing demonstration, it can provide plausible arguments for intellectual persuasion. Going further, James Beilby believes that inferential means must play a more prominent role in belief-formation, one that eliminates the claim to exclusive proper basicality of theistic belief, if Plantinga's epistemology is to account for the typical Christian's journey to faith. For most Christians, "Christian beliefs are not properly basic but are based on a complicated web of arguments, experiences, testimony, and pneumatological intervention."²⁷ Beilby's account of typical faith-formation seems to describe this phenomenon correctly.

With Plantinga's admission of the prima facie warrant of theistic belief and the internalist no-defeater condition, arguments and evidence play more prominent roles in the faith of the Christian than Plantinga's model alludes. Admittedly, Plantinga's adoption of Calvin's notion of faith as "firm and certain knowledge" applies to the paradigmatic believer.²⁸ Beilby convincingly argues that this approach weakens the applicability of the A/C model to the typical believer. Since most are not paradigmatic believers, they often lack such certainty, which raises questions about the warrant of their belief. Plantinga tries to explain that one with deficient faith may lack knowledge, but still have faith.²⁹ This answer seems impossible. If the definition of faith is firm and certain *knowledge*, then to lack knowledge is to lack faith.

Has Beilby demonstrated that Christian belief can be inferential? Perhaps an answer lies in pneumatology. Unlike other beliefs, faith is divine gift (Eph 2:8). Even if arguments are utilized in one's coming to faith, they should be understood as secondary causes. The pneumatological intervention that causes faith is the direct cause. Without this pneumatological intervention, faith would be mere belief, not knowledge, resulting from improper function of the *sensus divinitatis*. This pseudo-faith would be an epiphenomenon unintended in the design plan. In this way, epistemic faith is different than other knowledge, which can be inferentially warranted. Without this distinction, faith (and God) would be the product of human arguments, which violates the nature of faith (and God). While all knowledge may be pneumatologically inspired, only faith requires the enlivening of the human spirit. However, this solution leaves room for arguments to play a rational role in the journey toward faith.

Foundational Circularity

For the one who is still unsatisfied with the lack of independent reasons for its truth, Reformed epistemology cannot provide an answer. However, Reformed epistemology is not the only theory that is beset with this problem. This issue applies to externalism in general. Thus, the third answer to the "so what?" question is externalist. Just like the A/C model, externalism does not seek independent reason for the justification or warrant of the belief in question. Externalism contends that one's belief is justified or warranted if the external conditions are satisfied; no further inferential justification is required. Theistic belief has warrant insofar it satisfies the warrant conditions. Bergmann acknowledges that such an externalist view seems intellectually unsatisfying. People seem naturally to want good reasons for why one holds a certain belief, hence, the prominence of the "so what" question. Despite externalism's unsatisfactory stance, however, internalism fares worse. For the awareness, requirement leads to infinite regress and skepticism. If justification is required for properly basic beliefs, then skepticism results. Renouncement of internalism makes the achievement of warrant possible even without justificatory reasons if the warrant conditions are met. While Bergmann uses justification, his point remains[30]:

> For if there is noninferential justification, then the sensible thing to say—when someone ask for a reason to think that some allegedly noninferentially justified belief satisfies the condition C on which noninferential justification is supposed to supervene–is that you don't need to give such a reason in order for the belief to be justified; it's enough for justification that the belief does in fact satisfy C. This will, of course, be a conditional claim saying that a belief is justified if it satisfies C. But the reason this claim is given is to make it clear that the justification is noninferential in nature—that satisfying C is enough.[31]

Bergmann points out that this externalist explanation is *permissible* as a philosophical move because externalism is a philosophically robust position, one that escapes internalism's infinite regress. Given such options, externalism is the more plausible position, one that better accounts for the epistemic circularity of certain belief-forming mechanisms. Moreover, just because externalism allows room for "outrageous" beliefs does not mean that one cannot sensibly disagree with them. One way to disagree is to show how some beliefs do not meet the necessary and sufficient conditions for justification and warrant.[32] Again, this answer will not be intellectually satisfying to everyone, especially to skeptics who accept infinite regress as a reason for skepticism, and the dispute may show that the interlocutors have arrived at the limits of philosophy. Yet, the externalist position is a permissible one, one that does not commit the externalist to accept all views as equal.[33]

In terms very similar to Smith, Bergmann argues that such disputes may "bottom out."[34] Philosophy may not "resolve radical disagreements."[35] In such circumstances, Andrew Moon argues that means other than rational persuasion should be pursued. This does not mean that everyone should be agnostics. Absent defeaters, one can justifiably hold that one's beliefs are formed reliably. At least with religious beliefs, such beliefs could include that the other's religious beliefs are not formed reliably, thereby discounting agnosticism as the default position in such a state of disagreement.[36]

Interestingly, Moon makes this argument based on epistemic circularity. A reason one can justifiably hold a Christian belief is by coming to faith in the usual way one becomes a Christian: listening to a sermon, praying, experiencing God, and so on. Coupled with pneumatological intervention, one can justifiably hold that if Christianity is true, then her Christian beliefs are probably true. Even if some religious beliefs are partly caused by some unreliable mechanism, if Christianity is true and given the usual manner she took to coming to her beliefs (e.g., she did not consult a magic 8-ball), her beliefs are probably formed reliably with the aid of the Holy Spirit. This belief is epistemically circular because she formed the belief that her Christian beliefs are probably true based on the ways she came to believe and inferred from the inner testimony of the Holy Spirit to conclude that her beliefs are probably true. That is, the process through which she came to believe played a role in providing justification for the beliefs she holds. This is not malignant circularity because she does not doubt the reliability of her belief-forming process. If she doubted it, then she would have a defeater for her Christian beliefs and could not have used them as a premise to justify her beliefs. In this way, Christianity can be an epistemically self-promoting proposition; if a particular person justifiably holds a Christian belief, then one has good evidence of the reliable formation of one's beliefs.[37]

Ultimately, all beliefs arise from ontological commitments. Beliefs are ultimately based on reliable processes whose reliability must be circularly assumed rather than questioned if skepticism and malignant circularity are to be avoided. Moreover, such circularity should be expected between incommensurable worldviews given their different language games. Even if language games hold similar ontological commitments, the rules of the game are not univocal and rational disputes will bottom out.

In the end then, only faith is left; everyone is a believer. In the vein of Dooyeweerd, everyone is religious.[38] What is the externalist to do once she arrives at this terminus? Even if one reaches the limits of philosophy, one need not terminate the dialogue. Perhaps new arguments may arise, or one might engage in forms of communication that is not predominantly propositional. What Plantinga and Smith have shown is that knowledge and the means to knowledge are not reducible to propositional statements. Even if propositional statements end, embodied communication and persuasion can continue. A performative aesthetics is always already involved in communication, and it will be pronouncedly more important when such gridlock occurs. Importantly, if breakthrough occurs in this gridlock, it could be due to the work of the Spirit, pointing to the reality that moving from one language game to another at such a fundamental level is nothing short of a conversion.

Does this admission to faith reduce Reformed epistemology to fideism? Given Plantinga's painstaking effort to construct rational arguments for the warrant of Christian belief, he cannot be identified as an extreme fideist, which "disparages and denigrates reason."[39] Is he a moderate fideist? Not so. Moderate fideism takes any basic belief on faith. Plantinga rejects this relation between basic beliefs and faith. Faith is part of the deliverances of reason; faith is knowledge. Lest one mistake this claim as an intellectualization of faith, Plantinga is clear on the affective role of the Spirit and faith, as will be shown in following pages. And even if faith is not entirely noetic, it is necessarily noetic, and part of the deliverances of reason is that original noetic equipment, the *sensus divinitatis*:[40]

[A] capacity to apprehend God's existence is as much part of our natural noetic equipment as is the capacity to apprehend perceptual truths, truths about the past, and truths about other minds. . . . But then the belief that there is such a person as God is as much among the deliverances of reason as those other beliefs.[41]

Even if all ultimate worldview beliefs reduce to faith positions, this claim is not fideist.

THE EXTENDED A/C MODEL

As a Christian, Plantinga is not satisfied with the A/C model, as it only accounts warrant for generic theistic belief. Could Christian belief be warrant-basic? The answer to this question is the aim of the extended A/C model. The details of the model need not detain us, however. Rather, I will provide a brief summary and focus on those relevant aspects that pertain to Smith's epistemology.

Summary of the Extended A/C Model

Per the extended A/C model, God created humanity with intellect; will, both executive and affective; intimate knowledge of and affections toward God; and the *sensus divinitatis*. Human entrance into sin had deleterious cognitive and affective effects, disorders that have no natural cure. Sin destroyed intimate knowledge and affections. Not only do people no longer know God, they hate the good and love evil and themselves above all. In fact, this affective impact leads Plantinga to state that sin is "perhaps primarily an *affective* disorder or malfunction."[42] Noetically, the *sensus divinitatis* also suffered damage. Humanity no longer desires to know God and actively suppresses the deliverances of the *sensus divinitatis*. While remedy is not naturally possible, God created a means of salvation, which is pneumatologically accessible through the belief-producing tripartite process of faith. This broad conception of faith is similar to other belief-producing processes like perception and memory.[43] This process is comprised of Scripture, an "extraordinary cognitive process or belief-producing mechanism" called the internal instigation of the Holy Spirit (IIHS), and the resulting belief called faith.[44] The resulting belief meets the conditions of warrant and becomes knowledge when held with sufficient strength.

Nous and Affect

The supernatural work of the Spirit enlivens the gospel message and convicts its recipient of its truth.[45] This supernatural cognitive process produces faith. Although Smith charges Plantinga of being overly cognitive, Plantinga is not reductively cognitive. His focus on the *nous* is due to the aim of his project, which is to argue for noetic warrant and the Spirit's role in producing such belief since he considers nonbelief in God as sin's greatest cognitive consequence.[46] Yet, not only does he present an analog of warrant for affect, he clearly claims that faith involves the (affective function of the) will and intellect.[47] Moreover, he turns to the Heidelberg Catechism's affective description of faith as "deep-rooted assurance."[48] Plantinga reinforces this reciprocal relationship when he investigates the supposed priority that intellect or will may have over one another and concludes that faith is the healing of both. Plantinga also views the relationship between pretheory and theory as integrationist.

Remarking on their dialectical process, he argues that the affections aid one's perception of God, which further heightens these affections. Affections thus act as conditions of possibility of knowledge. On the other hand, one may not develop these affections without noetically perceiving God's moral qualities. Therefore, part of God's redemptive act involves curing the wayward affective will so that one can love the good and hate evil and renewing the mind so that one can perceive the majestic attributes of God and God's plan of redemption.[49] The relationship between affect and *nous* are reciprocal for Plantinga. "These truths must be sealed to the heart, as well as revealed to the mind."[50]

Despite this, Robert Roberts and W. Jay Wood argue that Plantinga's epistemology needs supplementing with passional-intellectual virtues because the will and the intellect are still too separated in Plantinga's account. Whether their critique is correct, they rightly demonstrate that emotion is a type of perception, a disposition to "see" and understand. Although they do not use the term emotional disposition to know well is a skillful know-how that can be cultivated. Epistemic virtues, especially emotional virtues, are not merely faculties akin to equipment, but are dispositions that form personalities. Having or lacking relevant virtues have epistemic consequences, such as knowing good and evil at a deeper, affective level. Some beliefs will not form without these virtues, and their presence and absence can affect a belief's degree of warrant.

Relatedly, the will is not merely an equipmental faculty. The will represents the epistemic agent, allowing one to "see" what others who have not cultivated their emotional dispositions cannot see. In this expanded account of Reformed epistemology, intellect and will overlap.[51] "Emotion is a peculiar and indispensable mode of *knowing* something. The 'will' is crossing over into the area of the 'intellect,' supplying a kind of 'cognition' that the 'intellect' by itself cannot produce."[52]

Affective Analog of Warrant

Warrant is not the sole property of cognitive belief. Because Plantinga's philosophical pursuits are informed by his theological commitments, he takes seriously the holistic nature of faith. Although analytic epistemology's main focus is noetic beliefs, Plantinga's theological commitments drive him to the critical role affections play in the completion of knowledge. To illustrate this important role, Plantinga compares the epistemic status of theistic belief between Christians and demons. Although demons have cognitive beliefs about God, they hate and reject God, seeking to dethrone God while knowing the futility of this aim. Plantinga rightfully points out that this behavior is due to the affective effects of sin. Sin damages not only the intellect but also the affective function of the will.[53] People love evil and reject the good. This reality illustrates that there are objectively right and wrong affections.[54]

Like the warrant conditions for belief, Plantinga argues that affections also have an analogous warrant model. First, right affections rely on properly functioning faculties. If a person feels happy when witnessing grave disaster, the person is likely suffering from affective malfunction. Misdirected affections result from the malfunctioning of the affective faculties. Second, affections require appropriate maxi- and mini-environments for their right operation. If one receives gossip that is not entirely true, which elicits affections that are misconstrued, a narrative, affective construal (NAC) will arise that will color the person's view of that particular reality. However, due to something amiss in this environment, her NAC will not qualify as NAK. Third, the design plan must be aimed at affections that are appropriate to their objects, and this design plan must be a good one, with high objective probability that the affections will be appropriate for their objects.[55] If these conditions are met, then the corresponding affection would be warranted. Plantinga's analog of warrant for affections is a robust prescriptive criteria that already contains Smith's lone prescriptive criterion of right-ordering of desire for NAK. Misdirected, malfunctioning affection disqualifies a construal from warrant. But just as proper function is insufficient for warrant, Smith's epistemology requires the supplementation of the entirety of Plantinga's warrant criteria. Importantly, the realist features, especially the reliability clause, shield NAK from DF's critiques. Although Plantinga does not attribute epistemic qualities to affections, nothing is lost or modified by augmenting Smith's NAK to Plantinga's view on affections. In this way, Plantinga's affective analog of warrant can inversely augment Smith's epistemology as a criteria for embodied knowledge.

CONCLUSION

The A/C models represent the philosophical theology of Plantinga's warrant model. Important to this project is the hermeneutic, *pistic* aspect of Reformed epistemology, the externalist response to the question of truth in the face of ultimately *pistic* commitments, the important epistemological role of the affections, and the affective analog of warrant. These elements provide a compatible picture between Reformed and postmodern epistemologies. The applicability of externalist warrant to *pistic* commitments and the seamless augmentation of the affective analog of warrant for NAK are clear. The next chapter further explores the reciprocal relationship between Smith and Reformed epistemology and demonstrates the postmodern side of Reformed epistemology before outlining the areas that converge, areas where Reformed epistemology can assist Smith, and areas that Reformed epistemology can critique Smith for repair.

NOTES

1. Plantinga, *Warranted Christian Belief*, viii–ix.
2. Plantinga, 152.
3. Plantinga, 198.
4. The value of theistic arguments is pragmatic. See Alvin Plantinga, "Two Dozen (or so) Theistic Arguments," in *Alvin Plantinga*, ed. Deane-Peter Baker (New York: Cambridge University Press, 2007), 203–27 (209).
5. See Smith, *Introducing Radical Orthodoxy*, 143.
6. Plantinga, *Warranted Christian Belief*, 173. More specifically, the theistic beliefs that it creates are not belief in God's existence, but belief in God's attributes or actions, such as "God is speaking to me" or "God forgives me." Plantinga, "Reason and Belief in God," 81. Andrew Moon makes an important argument that the number of these belief-producing faculties are unimportant as long as some faculty or faculties can produce properly basic theistic beliefs. See Moon, "Recent Work in Reformed Epistemology," 884. Some have criticized Plantinga's interpretation of the *sensus divinitatis*. For their critique and Plantinga's response, see Michael C. Sudduth, "Plantinga's Revision of the Reformed Tradition: Rethinking Our Natural Knowledge of God," *Philosophical Books* 43, no. 2 (2002): 81–91; R. Douglas Geivett and Greg Jesson, "Plantinga's Externalism and the Terminus of Warrant-Based Epistemology," *Philosophia Christi* 3, no. 2 (2001): 329–40; Georg Plasger, "Does Calvin Teach a Sensus Divinitatis?: Reflections on Alvin Plantinga's Interpretation of Calvin," in *Plantinga's Warranted Christian Belief: Critical Essays with a Reply by Alvin Plantinga*, ed. Dieter Schönecker (Dordrecht: De Gruyter, 2015), 169–89; John Beversluis, "Reforming the 'Reformed' Objection to Natural Theology," *Faith and Philosophy* 12, no. 2 (1995): 189–206; James P. Moreland and William Lane Craig, *Philosophical Foundations for a Christian Worldview* (Downers Grove: InterVarsity Press, 2003), 168–69; Craig, "A Classical Apologist's Response," 285–86; Plantinga, *Warranted Christian Belief*, 177; Plantinga, "Internalism, Externalism, Defeaters, and Arguments for Christian Belief," 382–83; Plantinga, "Reply," 134–35; and Plantinga, "Replies to My Commentators," 254–57.
7. Plantinga, *Warranted Christian Belief*, 184–86.
8. He specifically cites the moderate evidentialism of Paul Moser and the externalist sensible evidentialism of Stephen Wykstra. See Plantinga, "Internalism, Externalism, Defeaters, and Arguments for Christian Belief," 396; and Plantinga, "Reply," 124–28. For his positive remarks on evidence, see Plantinga, *Warrant and Proper Function*, 185–93; and Alvin Plantinga, "Rationality and Public Evidence: A Reply to Richard Swinburne," *Religious Studies* 37, no. 2 (2001): 215–22. His proper functionalism is compatible with other evidentialist theories, such as evidentialist reliabilism and phenomenal conservatism. See Martin Smith, "The Epistemology of Religion," *Analysis Reviews* 74, no. 1 (2014): 135–47 (140–43). Horace Fairlamb's argument that evidentialism is not necessarily tied to classical foundationalism shows how evidence and Reformed epistemology are not antithetical. See Horace Fairlamb, "Sanctifying Evidentialism," *Religious Studies* 46, no. 1 (2010): 61–76 (63–71). Insofar as Plantinga, Smith, and presuppositionalism are

Reformed and share similarities, it is important to point out that presuppositionalism is also positive about evidence understood apart from neutral epistemology. See Thom Notaro, *Van Til & the Use of Evidence* (Phillipsburg: P&R Publishing Company, 1980).

9. Linda Zagzebski disagrees with this argument because it disqualifies internalism if Christianity is true. However, Zagzebski does not take into consideration that preceding Plantinga's argument is his critique of internalism. He had already provided the groundwork to show that externalism is a better representative of general epistemology. See Linda T. Zagzebski, "Plantinga's Warranted Christian Belief and the Aquinas/Calvin Model," *Philosophical Books* 43, no. 2 (2002): 117–23 (118, 122–23).

10. Plantinga, *Warranted Christian Belief*, 186–90.

11. Plantinga, 190.

12. Plantinga, 191. Dieter Schönecker provides helpful clarification that *de jure* objections with regard to deontological justification and internal rationality "do *not* presuppose the falsity of theism." Yet, because they do not contribute toward warrant, Plantinga is right that there are no *decent* independent *de jure* objections. Dieter Schönecker, "The Deliverances of Warranted Christian Belief," in *Plantinga's Warranted Christian Belief: Critical Essays with a Reply by Alvin Plantinga*, ed. Dieter Schönecker (Berlin: De Gruyter, 2015), 1–40 (15).

13. Plantinga, *Warranted Christian Belief*, 191.

14. Kelly James Clark agrees, stating that the starting point determines the conclusion. Highlighting this perspectivity of reason, Clark presents Reformed epistemology as postmodern apologetics. See Kelly James Clark, "Reformed Epistemology Apologetics," in *Five Views on Apologetics*, ed. Steven B. Cowan (Grand Rapids: Zondervan, 2000), 266–84 (283). Cf., Smith, "The Epistemology of Religion," 141.

15. Alvin Plantinga, "Reliabilism, Analyses and Defeaters," *Philosophy and Phenomenological Research* 55, no. 2 (1995): 427–64 (444). Even God cannot demonstrate the reliability of God's belief-forming processes without relying on those belief-forming processes. Plantinga, "Internalism, Externalism, Defeaters, and Arguments for Christian Belief," 390. Kevin Diller argues that the mere act of knowing without noncircular argument or independent verification is not a liability, but "the strongest demonstration that knowledge is possible." Diller, *Theology's Epistemological Dilemma*, 31. While disagreeing, Richard Fumerton argues that direct acquaintance, such as pain, is self-justificatory. See Richard Fumerton, "Epistemic Internalism, Philosophical Assurance and the Skeptical Predicament," in *Knowledge and Reality: Essays in Honor of Alvin Plantinga*, ed. Thomas M. Crisp, Matthew Davidson, and David Vander Laan (Dordrecht: Springer, 2006), 179–91 (188–90). However, belief via direct acquaintance can be the result of cognitive malfunction.

16. Plantinga, *Warranted Christian Belief*, 170. This view is implicit in his charge to Christian philosophers. Since they have right to their pre-philosophical views, they should display more autonomy, integrity, and boldness. See Alvin Plantinga, "Advice to Christian Philosophers," in *The Analytic Theist: An Alvin Plantinga Reader*, ed. James F. Sennett (Grand Rapids: William B. Eerdmans Publishing Company, 1998), 296–315. Cf., Smith, *Who's Afraid of Relativism?*, 174.

17. Diller, *Theology's Epistemological Dilemma*, 171.

18. Bergmann, *Justification without Awareness*, 184. On the circularity of the reliability of sense perception, see Alston, *Perceiving God*, 107–8. Alston illustrates that such circularity involves no epistemic dependence on the part of the warrant and truth of a metaphysical thesis. If the epistemic status of a metaphysical thesis is brought into question, then mutual epistemic dependence occurs between the epistemological and metaphysical thesis, which rightfully becomes viciously circular. Alston charges Plantinga with this vicious circularity because Christian metaphysical commitment is supported by warranted Christian belief, illustrating that a mutual dependence between metaphysical belief and epistemological belief exists. However, Alston misinterprets Plantinga. While Christian metaphysical belief can be warranted, it does not demonstrate the truth of itself. Alston seems to misidentify an implicit internalist awareness move on Plantinga's part. My retort is supported by Richard Swinburne's objection to Plantinga that Plantinga has not demonstrated the actual warrant of Christian belief. Additionally, Oliver Wiertz answers negatively against the charges of circularity leveled at Plantinga. See William P. Alston, "Epistemology and Metaphysics," in *Knowledge and Reality: Essays in Honor of Alvin Plantinga*, ed. Thomas M. Crisp, Matthew Davidson, and David Vander Laan (Dordrecht: Springer, 2006), 81–109 (91–99); Richard Swinburne, "Plantinga on Warrant," *Religious Studies* 37, no. 02 (2001): 203–14 (206–7); and Oliver Wiertz, "Is Plantinga's A/C Model an Example of Ideologically Tainted Philosophy?," in *Plantinga's Warranted Christian Belief: Critical Essays with a Reply by Alvin Plantinga*, ed. Dieter Schönecker (Dordrecht: De Gruyter, 2015), 83–113 (87–93); and Plantinga, *Warranted Christian Belief*, 351–52.

19. Andrew Moon, "Circular and Question-Begging Responses to Religious Disagreement and Debunking Arguments," *Philosophical Studies* 178, no. 3 (April 25, 2020): 785–809 (792–93).

20. Bergmann, *Justification without Awareness*, 198–203.

21. Cf., Bergmann, 207–11; Plantinga, *Warrant and Proper Function*, 97, 183–84; and Wolterstorff, "Can Belief in God Be Rational If It Has No Foundations?," 149–50.

22. For a good survey of this criticism, see Schönecker, "The Deliverances of Warranted Christian Belief," 10–13. Andrew Moon helpfully pointed out in correspondence that this supposed criticism is less a critique than the acknowledgment of the incompleteness of Plantinga's project. One cannot fault Plantinga for limiting his project. He answers somewhat exasperatedly to Paul Moser's criticism that he should have provided some arguments for Christianity's truthfulness: "It was already, as Moser points out, a 500 page tome; I should have made it longer yet?" Even then, he is resolute that he knows of no successful arguments. Citing Richard Swinburne's probabilistic argument as one of the best arguments for God's existence, he comments that it still fails to prove God's existence. Moreover, if Plantinga believes that metaphysical views cannot be proven, then his A/C model is neither trivial nor incomplete. See Plantinga, "Internalism, Externalism, Defeaters, and Arguments for Christian Belief," 397–98.

23. To answer this apparent weakness, Deane-Peter Baker augments Plantinga's theory with Charles Taylor's moral transcendental argument. See Baker, *Tayloring Reformed Epistemology*, 87–98, 192–210.

24. For example, see David W. Tien, "Warranted Neo-Confucian Belief: Religious Pluralism and the Affections in the Epistemologies of Wang Yangming (1472–1529) and Alvin Plantinga," *International Journal for Philosophy of Religion* 55, no. 1 (2004): 31–55.

25. Wiertz, "Is Plantinga's A/C Model an Example of Ideologically Tainted Philosophy?," 95.

26. See Plantinga, "Reason and Belief in God," 74–82; and Plantinga, *Warranted Christian Belief*, 342–51. Cf., Plantinga, "Reply," 130–31.

27. Beilby, "Plantinga's Model of Warranted Christian Belief," 150.

28. Plantinga, *Warranted Christian Belief*, 248. A deeper reading of Calvin's view on faith would have aided Plantinga. Nicholas Wolterstorff helpfully shows Calvin as desiring certainty of faith, but not requiring such certainty as necessary for faith. See Nicholas Wolterstorff, "The Assurance of Faith," in *Practices of Belief: Selected Essays*, ed. Terence Cuneo, vol. 2 (New York: Cambridge University Press, 2010), 289–312 (305–12).

29. Plantinga, *Warranted Christian Belief*, 248n14.

30. Although Bergmann utilizes the term "justification," it is a "modified version of Plantinga's account of warrant" without the environmental and reliability conditions and is appropriate to use in this context. Bergmann, *Justification without Awareness*, 133.

31. Bergmann, 229.

32. Cf., Tyler D. McNabb, "Closing Pandora's Box: A Defence of Alvin Plantinga's Epistemology of Religious Belief" (University of Glasgow, 2016), 56–158, ProQuest Dissertations & Theses Global.

33. Bergmann, *Justification without Awareness*, 231–33. Besides the employment of natural theology, one way to navigate through epistemic disagreement in an externalist manner is through epistemic demotion. See Bergmann, "Religious Disagreement and Rational Demotion," 21–57.

34. Bergmann, *Justification without Awareness*, 231.

35. Bergmann. The end of philosophy is evidence that one's commitment to a position is often more than theoretical. Recall the Social Intuitionist Model.

36. Moon, "Circular and Question-Begging Responses," 806.

37. Moon, 793–96.

38. See Dooyeweerd, *In the Twilight of Western Thought*, 23–29.

39. Plantinga, "Reason and Belief in God," 87

40. Plantinga also counts "self-evident propositions... basic perceptual truths (propositions 'evident to the senses'), incorrigible propositions, certain memory propositions, certain propositions about other minds, and certain moral or ethical propositions" as part of the deliverances of reason. Plantinga does not indicate that this list is exhaustive. See Plantinga, 89.

41. Plantinga, 90.

42. Plantinga, *Warranted Christian Belief*, 208.

43. Plantinga, 256.

44. Plantinga. James Beilby argues that describing the IIHS as a nonnative (i.e., supernatural) process allows the believer to reject the belief due to its unfamiliarity

and recommends that the IIHS must reflect some similarity with the natural cognitive faculties. Beilby, "Plantinga's Model of Warranted Christian Belief," 151–53. James Anderson has proposed such a model in which the IIHS is understood as part of a properly functioning belief-forming *system*. This system includes the natural faculties and the IIHS, such that, even if the IIHS remains supernatural, it is a "natural" part of the design plan. Moreover, the IIHS utilizes natural means such as testimony and Scripture reading. James Anderson, *Paradox in Christian Theology: An Analysis of Its Presence, Character, and Epistemic Status* (Milton Keynes: Paternoster, 2007), 184–85. If so, the Spirit's work would "be phenomenologically similar *from the perspective of the cognizer*." Beilby, "Plantinga's Model of Warranted Christian Belief," 153.

45. Plantinga, *Warranted Christian Belief*, 250–51.
46. Plantinga, 217.
47. Plantinga, 206.
48. Plantinga, 247.
49. Plantinga, 303–4. In fact, *eros* toward God is one of the most important ways to display God's image and to participate in God. See Plantinga, 311–23.
50. Plantinga, 269.
51. Robert C. Roberts and W. Jay Wood, "Proper Function, Emotion, and Virtues of the Intellect," *Faith and Philosophy* 21, no. 1 (2004): 3–24 (5–21).
52. Roberts and Wood, 9.
53. Plantinga, *Warranted Christian Belief*, 291–92.
54. Plantinga, 309.
55. Plantinga, 310–11.

Chapter 9

Reformed Epistemology, Postmodernism, and a Way Forward

INTRODUCTION

This chapter pulls the relevant materials covered in the previous chapters on Plantinga for the purpose of identifying areas of Reformed epistemology that converge with Smith and areas that can provide assistance and critique. Through assistance and critique, repair is undertaken to build on and modify areas of Smith's epistemology that are incomplete or problematic. This threefold task of identifying areas of convergence, assist, and critique is important because Smith claims that Reformed epistemology is compatible with his non(classical) foundationalist postmodernism. However, his claim is brief and undeveloped. He mentions Reformed epistemologists such as Plantinga and Wolterstorff as examples of a Reformed tradition that rejects neutral reason, but he does not rely on them in the construction of his epistemology. Given Smith's confession of a congeniality between postmodernism and Reformed epistemology, investigating this supposed congeniality to determine the accuracy of this claim and taking on the constructive work to develop this claim are important. The first section investigates postmodernism in relation to Plantinga before moving to the second section on Wolterstorff's postmodern Reformed epistemology.

PLANTINGA AND POSTMODERNISM

In the latter section of *Warranted Christian Belief*, Plantinga counts postmodernism as a possible defeater to Christian belief. His position seems problematic for this work. Is synthesizing Smith and Plantinga akin to forcing a square peg into a circular hole? However, Plantinga does not reject postmodernism as such and definitely not the non-nihilistic version I have presented.

Plantinga correctly understands postmodernism as a variegated phenomenon. Even more importantly, he acknowledges congenial elements with postmodernism, such as its emphasis on equality and justice, the deconstruction of hidden prejudices under supposed universal normativity, and its rejection of classical foundationalism. He also acknowledges possible incompatibilities and investigates whether they are what postmoderns claim and if they act as defeaters. For Plantinga, the difficulty with this task is postmodernism's seeming obscurantism and lack of clear arguments.[1] In good analytic fashion, he identifies ideas that can act as possible defeaters for Christian belief.

First, Plantinga considers whether historical perspectivity acts as defeaters for Christian belief. According to the charge of historical conditionedness of belief, a belief could be unwarranted since being born in a different time and place would have led to different beliefs. While arguing that this critique is self-defeating since one who brings this charge may also not believe in it if one were to exist in a different time and place, Plantinga reiterates that warrant is circumstance-specific.[2] Social and historical location matter in belief-formation. Thus, while Plantinga dismisses the charge, he acknowledges some doxastic perspectivity.

Second, Plantinga tries to understand Rorty's seemingly anti-realist and social constructionist view of truth through Gary Gutting's sympathetic reading of Rorty. According to Gutting, Rorty does not view truth as social construction but is rejecting certain theories of truth. The truths he wants to maintain are commonsense truths. Plantinga finds this interpretation dubious. If Rorty is taken in the usual manner as a social constructionist of truth, then he represents an extreme nominalism that places the dependence of God's existence on the human mind. Plantinga finds fault in Rorty's (possible) argument for social constructionism. With this view, truth depends on sentences and, since sentences are human creations, truth depends on human language. The fault in this argument is that Rorty seems to presuppose that "beliefs, assertions, claims, suggestions, and so on are themselves sentences."[3] Plantinga shows its falsity by demonstrating the difference between propositions and sentences. The proposition $2 + 1 = 3$ exists as a necessary truth even if the sentence $2 + 1 = 3$ is not necessary. If the sentence is never uttered, then the sentence would not have been true, but the lack of utterance does not affect the truth of the proposition. If Rorty is taken as a metaphysical anti-realist, then Rorty would be incompatible with Christian belief. Does his anti-realism make Plantinga incompatible with Rorty?

First, one can interpret Rorty as a realist. Although Plantinga thinks this interpretation "implausibly emasculates Rorty," it is a possible reading given the difficulty of interpreting Rorty, coupled with Plantinga's own admission that "Rorty is a bit standoffish about arguments."[4] Second, if one insists on reading Rorty as an anti-realist, I can jettison Rorty as a representative of the postmodernism that is amenable with Christianity. Since Plantinga acknowledges the variegated characteristic of postmodernism, Plantinga can accept the metaphysically and epistemologically realist postmodernism of Smith.

However, does such realism make postmodernism uninteresting and platitudinous? Of course not. One reason why postmodernism is concerned with diversity and justice for the marginalized and uncovers the hidden powers that perpetuate injustice in the name of universal reason is due to its emphasis on finitude, contingency, embodiment, perspectivism, and pretheoricity. This emphasis on situatedness has great theoretical and practical implications and is far from being uninteresting and platitudinous. Yet, because Plantinga does not emphasize the contextuality of embodiment and knowledge, he can glean much from Wolterstorff, whose own version of Reformed epistemology highlights the postmodern theme of situatedness while remaining faithful to the overall vision of Reformed epistemology on the proper basicality of belief in God.

WOLTERSTORFF'S SITUATED RATIONALITY

Wolterstorff's contribution to Reformed epistemology is illuminating because he attends to the postmodern themes of contingency and situatedness. Wolterstorff argues that such themes are already embedded within (Dutch) neo-Calvinism.[5] According to Nathan Shannon, modernism still besets Plantinga because proper function is a static notion that lacks a sense of historical conditionedness.[6] The matter is different for Wolterstorff, who views the design plan as "developmentally basic."[7] According to Wolterstorff, the design plan is the original "operating system" that allows historicized persons to become aware of the "doxastic habits, customs, and responsibilities" through continual social experience.[8]

This contingent and situated epistemology can be labeled as "situated rationality."[9] Labeling situated rationality as postmodern is not an abstraction from Wolterstorff's epistemology. He himself acknowledges Reformed epistemology to be postmodern in the Kuyperian tradition, which rejects the epistemic neutrality of classical foundationalism and the evidentialist objection to Christian belief.[10] In their stead, Wolterstorff (and the Reformed tradition) turns toward trust as "one's fundamental stance."[11]

Trust is the result when God's view of the world is eliminated. The descent from that abstract ideality into situatedness and contingency leads to the destruction of indubitable certainty. Situatedness and interpretive perspectivity form the human condition, and Wolterstorff is highly cognizant of it.

Not only does he propose that "we must *historicize* our understanding of the belief-forming self," he is also critical of those who prioritize "necessarily true universalizations" and homogenous epistemic nature.[12] Wolterstorff fittingly calls such modernist epistemology the "epistemology of an *immobile* solitary reactor."[13] Against such universalization, Wolterstorff strongly emphasizes particularity. This emphasis dates to his training at Calvin College where he learned to probe the presuppositions of philosophical claims. This realization, in turn, led him to understand that "philosophy, at bottom, is a perspectival enterprise."[14] Like Smith, Wolterstorff's situated rationality rests on his anthropology, namely, a "Reidian *doxastic anthropology* . . . [that] represents a blending of the natural and the historical."[15]

Historicized Self: Developing Dispositions and Design Plan

While Plantinga makes passing remarks on the maturation of the design plan, Wolterstorff elaborates on contingent belief-formation in respect to the design plan.[16] For Wolterstorff, production of beliefs by proper functioning faculties is not dynamic enough to capture the way belief-formation actually occurs. He draws from David Hume and Thomas Reid to argue that belief-formation occurs through the particularities of life experiences of particular people in particular situations. Not only do beliefs arise from life experiences, but more importantly, life experiences modify the belief-dispositions that govern belief-formation. Modification of belief-dispositions points to the existence of innate or natural belief-dispositions, such as the disposition to believe people (the credulity disposition) or the disposition to form inductive dispositions (the inductive principle).[17] He writes, "We human beings are all hard-wired for belief; we all have an innate dispositional constitution that, when activated by one event or another, yields belief."[18]

Epistemic modification is part of the human design plan. The design plan not only matures, as Plantinga mentions, but the design plan itself cannot explain the modification and formation of belief-dispositions because many belief-dispositions are not part of the design plan. The design plan is the bare necessity that makes possible further modification and formation. The creation of new belief-dispositions acts as evidence that the design plan does not contain all belief-dispositions.[19]

For the historicized self, no life experience is univocal. The modification or creation of belief-dispositions is not based on universal human experience. For example, particular situations enable inductive belief-dispositions. Even if all people have the inductive belief-disposition, the formation of the disposition is based on personal history.[20] If based on personal history, it is possible that one's disposition is programmed rightly or wrongly. For example, never verifying the straightness of a stick in water, thus creating the belief-disposition to believe that sticks change shape when dipped in water is logically possible. Additionally, beliefs formed through personal history become part of the programming of further belief-formations. Belief-dispositions are programmed through the cycle of various life experiences and beliefs.[21]

Tradition plays an important part in doxastic programming. The historicized formation of belief-dispositions governs how belief-formation ought to occur in tradition. Wolterstorff provides two interrelated concepts, "ways of finding out" and "practices of inquiry," to illumine how tradition shapes doxastic programming and belief-dispositions.

Ways of finding out are

a sequence of actions such that, for some sort of human being in some sort of situation, were a person of that sort in a situation of that sort to employ that sequence as an action-plan for finding out X, the consequence would ensue that the agent found out X–assuming that all goes well.[22]

Thus, ways of finding out are action plans one implements in order to get to know something.

Practices of inquiry are socially acquired practices that seek to find something out. The difference between practices of inquiry and ways of finding out is that the latter is conducive to success. In this way, ways of finding out is a practice of inquiry, but practice of inquiry may not be a way of finding out. Wolterstorff gives divination as an example of a practice inquiry that is not a way of finding out.[23] Furthermore, utilizing the relevant practice of inquiry rightly entitles a belief, even if it is not ultimately true.[24] Conversely, failure to employ a practice of inquiry despite being obligated to do so (e.g., not looking into the evidence of a crime scene as a police investigator) or performing a practice of inquiry when one should not have done so leads to the loss of epistemic entitlement.[25] As such, practice of inquiry and entitlement to belief are situation-specific.

The situated contingency of ways of finding out and practices of inquiry is easy to see. Particular situations dictate the obligation of utilizing practices of inquiry. Wolterstorff highlights this contingency by drawing attention to three ways in which ways of finding out can be utilized. First, historical location dictates the social availability of a way of finding out. Particular situations dictate the availability of particular ways of finding out. Some are not just available, but obligatory. This situated reality is especially true for religious traditions, as they have "developed a whole array of practices of inquiry whose employment is regarded by members of the community as obligatory in one and another situation."[26] Second, not all socially available ways of finding out are personally accessible for many reasons. This inaccessibility could be due to limitations based on finances, knowledge, skill, or strength. Relatedly, entitlement can come and go, as one could be entitled at one time, but become unentitled later after failing to utilize a newly accessible way of finding out. Third, socially acceptable and personally accessible ways of finding out may nevertheless be personally unacceptable. The reasons are legion but highlighting tradition's great power in dictating the acceptability of a way of finding out is important. For example, certain Christian traditions find embryonic stem cell research unacceptable even if it's socially available and personally accessible.[27] Additionally, practices of inquiry shape doxastic programming. Programming contains certain beliefs, epistemic obligations, and particular options for ways of finding out based on context. Also, context will bring about inevitable glitches, that is, false beliefs and processes, into one's doxastic programming.

Like Smith, behind Wolterstorff's situated rationality is a situated anthropology. Epistemic actions and norms are inextricably tied to contingent situatedness, a view succinctly summarized by Wolterstorff:

> The proper question is always and only whether it is rational for this or that particular person in this or that situation, or for a person of this or that particular type in this or that type of situation, to believe so-and-so. Rationality is always *situated* rationality.[28]

Wolterstorff's Assist to Plantinga

The compatibility between situated rationality and Smith's postmodern epistemology is clear. However, how does Wolterstorff relate to Plantinga? No principled difference exists between their doxastic anthropology and epistemology.[29] Wolterstorff merely provides a fuller anthropological account than Plantinga without contradiction. Their epistemological concerns are similar. Plantinga is providing a general overview of the human epistemic situation whereas Wolterstorff provides a more focused picture of the epistemic process. His situated rationality is an account of people's normal epistemic operation and the status of their entitlement, not warrant.[30] Therefore, Wolterstorff is representing the typical believer in lieu of Plantinga's idealized believer. In this way, Wolterstorff is giving account of the "analogical extensions" and "belt of vagueness and imprecision" that lie outside the paradigm cases of warrant.[31] Not only is Wolterstorff's situated rationality compatible with Plantinga, Wolterstorff rightfully argues that there is no Reformed epistemology *tout court*. Instead, there are Reformed epistemologies of various concerns.[32] Plantinga's Reformed epistemology concerns warrant. Wolterstorff's project concerns entitlement. They are all part of a harmonious project with minor disagreements. Even when Wolterstorff recommends the inclusion of doxastic programming into Plantinga's theory of warrant, nothing is altered or erased, but merely enhanced. What does this inclusion look like?

Wolterstorff argues that there are cases in which an unwarranted false belief results from properly functioning cognitive faculties that meet all the other warrant conditions. The culprit of this false belief is not anything in the warrant conditions, but another false belief that operates as a background belief. Wolterstorff calls this "a *glitch* in the person's *doxastic programming*."[33] Wolterstorff considers whether one should take the glitch as part of a defective mini-environment, but finds including beliefs and feelings in the environment as nonsensical because such inclusion radically unites the self with the environment. Rather than fitting doxastic programming as part of the environment, he suggests including doxastic programming as part of the warrant conditions.[34] He writes,

> Our belief-forming faculties are designed in such a way that much of their output functions as programming for subsequent operations of the faculty, the output of those subsequent operations functioning as programming for yet later operations.[35]

The weakness of Plantinga's warrant model is its picture of the ideal believer that ignores the complexities of everyday epistemic situations of which most humans find themselves. Wolterstorff's concept of doxastic programming better represents the typical believer's epistemic situation and should be incorporated into the warrant model to "historicize" Plantinga. Because there is no incompatibility between Wolterstorff's postmodern Reformed epistemology and Plantinga, there is no incompatibility between Plantinga and certain types of postmodernism. Having completed the exposition of Reformed epistemology, I will now turn to critical analysis. This section is divided into three subsections: areas of convergence with Smith; areas of assist; and areas of critique.

CONVERGENCE

Plantinga's rejection of classical foundationalism and epistemic certainty, his defense of *pistic* commitment, and his account of warrant opened Plantinga, perhaps unknowingly, to the hermeneutic tradition. Merold Westphal concurs: "In the abandonment of the ideal of philosophy as presuppositionless science, philosophers from 'analytic,' 'continental,' and American pragmatist traditions, have more common ground than their vocabularies or habits of reading and conversation might suggest."[36] Smith's and Plantinga's common Dutch-Reformed tradition makes this compatibility unsurprising. Both are mining the tradition from different philosophical traditions, utilizing different methods and language, but finding themselves on the same trajectory.

First, they both share the same commitment to the epistemology of faith. Plantinga develops this view through externalist proper functionalism and likens Christian belief with other properly basic beliefs, such as perceptual and memory beliefs, which are beliefs that cannot, and need not, be justified. Plantinga's commitment to faith is demonstrated in his argument that Christian belief is warranted only if Christianity is true. Smith begins from embodied situatedness, contingency, and perspectivity to highlight the failure of Enlightenment objectivity and calls for a turn to contextual, embodied knowledge. He does not succumb to nihilistic relativism insofar as he follows Lindbeck's postliberalism (and Van Til's presuppositionalism) and grounds knowledge and truth in the being of God. The shared Augustinian heritage of Smith and Plantinga lead them to consider all knowledge as hermeneutically rooted in faith. For Smith, this means that apologetics must be one of out-narration rather than demonstration. For Plantinga, natural theology has pragmatic value, but it does not prove the truth of Christianity.

Second, although Plantinga admits to focusing on the noetic, he is neither unaware of the epistemic role of affections nor dismissive of affections altogether. Doxastic experience, the feeling of the rightness of belief, provides important evidence for internal rationality. If one lacks this feeling, one will likely reject the belief at hand. Affect, therefore, plays an important role in noetic formation and regulation. The Pentecostal affective-testimonial claim, "I know that I know that I know," is an instance of a particularly acute case of doxastic experience in one's belief-formation that is both affective, pretheoretical, and properly basic. Such testimony is Spirit-inspired and given Plantinga's argument that the IIHS has an affective component in producing faith, his epistemology of the Spirit converges with the Pentecostal view that the Spirit's inward witness leads to affective personal knowledge.[37]

Third, Smith and Plantinga share their emphasis on pretheoretical knowledge. Narratives and affections are ways of understanding the world apart from theoretical justification. Properly basic beliefs can be warranted apart from theoretical justification. However, Plantinga is more open to the possibility of induction and background experiences and beliefs directing and shaping pretheoretical beliefs.

Fourth, they see the importance of the epistemic role of communities. Due to the prominent place, cultural-linguistic situatedness plays in Smith, worrying about the lack of tradition's role in Plantinga's epistemology is natural. Beilby makes this critique. Although he recognizes that Plantinga mentions the importance of community in belief-formation in a footnote, he wonders whether this relegation undercuts its importance. A few observations can be noted.

First, like Plantinga's retort to Paul Moser's request for natural theological arguments, Plantinga is bound by the scope of his project. One can always ask Plantinga to address another topic. That so many lines of inquiry can arise from his work is a testament to the importance of his work. Second, Diller answers Beilby's charge, by explaining that Plantinga "is sketching an intentionally minimalist structure to give account of the principal way in which Christian belief receives warrant" and by associating community with congenial environment and proper function.[38] Third, testimony is by nature a communal act that is a pneumatologically enacted, essential occasion for faith.[39] Since Christian belief often occurs through testimony, the importance of community is implicitly present in Plantinga. Beilby also recognizes that nothing in Plantinga contradicts or diminishes the epistemic role of community.[40] Moreover, even if the importance of community is muted in Plantinga, Wolterstorff's situated anthropology holds it higher in regard. For to be situated as historicized persons means that they are located in community. Moreover, community conditions the availability and acceptability of ways of finding out and practices of inquiry. The creation and modification of beliefs and belief-dispositions are based on one's communal location, indicating that interpretation and perspectivism are inevitable human conditions. Relatedly, the formation of narrative, affective knowledge (NAK) depends on social, communal locations and particular experiences.

Clearly, any worry over the incompatibility between Smith and Reformed epistemology is misplaced. Understanding postmodernism as a variegated phenomenon is helpful. If postmodernism is essentially nihilistic, then the divide between Reformed epistemology and Smith would be unbridgeable. However, the epistemologically and metaphysically realist postmodernism of Smith that I have described and refined finds no incompatibility with Reformed epistemology. Even if there are conflicts that may have been missed, the central ideas—pretheory and proper basicality; *pistic* and hermeneutic knowledge; warrant, *nous*, and affect; traditioned and situated beliefs—are compatible, and any conflicts are minor.

ASSIST

Now that their compatibility has been established, how can Reformed epistemology aid Smith? Starting with Wolterstorff's situated rationality and then moving to Plantinga's prescription for affective warrant, I will demonstrate how Smith's descriptive epistemology benefits from their prescriptive conditions and show how broadening the IIHS beyond mere knowledge of God helps in understanding God's epistemic activity in cultural-linguistic frameworks that maintain the objective truth of Christianity.

First, Wolterstorff's theory of entitlement provides situation-specific justification for NAK. Wolterstorff has shown the dynamic nature of belief-formation and design plan, which does a better job than Plantinga in capturing the picture of the historicized self. The historicized self is always already part of a tradition which governs the available and acceptable means toward belief-formation. The historicized self matches Smith's situated knower. Wolterstorff provides an analysis of entitlement based on the workings of various innate and gained belief-dispositions and particular and appropriate ways of finding out. The beliefs produced through such means may not be warranted but can be entitled. If the Pentecostal tradition views testimony and experience as valid practices of inquiry, then it does not necessarily need to accommodate the internalist demand for philosophical or evidential verification. DF's demand for independent verification of NAK can thus be seen as foreign practices of inquiry, an inquiry undergirded by modernist assumptions about objective knowledge that is alien to the Pentecostal narrative tradition.

Entitlement claims are judged by tradition. Not all testimonies and affections will be deemed entitled. Pentecostal churches regulate the appropriateness of the gifts of the Spirit and testimonies, testing whether they are divinely inspired. Not all testimonies, prophecies, and interpretations are accepted as genuine. NAK's justification is dependent on the appropriate authorities of particular traditions. Importantly, the specter of cultural relativism is stemmed by previously outlined tests—categorial adequacy, intrasystematic coherence, immanent critique, transcendental argument, and *phronesis*—that allow for non-neutral rational adjudication between incommensurable language games.

Justification's value is pragmatic as it acknowledges the variegated epistemic situation of the everyday knower in tradition. Ultimately, however, justification is inadequate in meeting the loftier epistemic goal of warrant. One can be individually and communally justified but lack knowledge due to epistemic malfunction. What ultimately matters isn't justification, but warrant. This account is what Smith lacks and one which Plantinga can assist.

Hence, the second area of assist is the augmentation of the affective warrant criteria. Smith's epistemology includes the *ordo amoris* as its sole prescriptive criterion for knowledge. The relevance of Plantinga's noetic and affective warrant models is unmistakable. Rightly ordered desire can be reimagined as a notion of proper function. Narrative, affective construal (NAC) must meet the affective analog of warrant to become NAK.

The ease of assimilating the *ordo amoris* into the warrant criteria is evident due to its externalist character. Smith's claim that narrative and affect just are knowledge assumes the rejection of internalist verification. NAK needs no independent verification to overcome the supposed problem of narrative relativism and arbitrary story-ism, even if open to defeaters. That Plantinga does not view affect as knowledge is not a hindrance either since nothing is lost by adding epistemic value to it. Because Plantinga acknowledges the important role that affect plays in belief, Smith's claim to the epistemic nature of narrative-affect is not incompatible with Plantinga's view. Their merger is a natural development.

Third, merging the affective analog of warrant should also include Wolterstorff's doxastic programming. Situated knowers are not ideal knowers. One's doxastic programming is dependent on one's life experiences. Inevitably, false beliefs will creep into one's doxastic programming that will lead to more false beliefs even if Plantinga's warrant criteria are met. Relatedly, the narratives and affections one traffic in could affect the warrant status of those and others in the future. From a noetic perspective, false beliefs and processes act as glitches in one's doxastic programming. Narratively and affectively, they could be false narratives and wayward affections. For both, the cure is not merely true beliefs, true narratives, and correct affections. Following Roberts and Wood, the healing of these glitches will require moral and intellectual virtues. These virtues form the belief- and affective-dispositions that can draw one away from developing false beliefs and irrational affections.

Fourth, the truth condition of warrant is critical to repair Smith's descriptive epistemology. The goal of a postmodern Christian epistemology (PCE), and Christian epistemology in general, must be alethically aimed. This *telos* is not merely ostensive. Truth is performative because the goal of the Christian life is not mere noetic knowledge of God, but union with the Father in Christ through the Spirit. Such union is not purely passive. It requires active participation in the divine life. Therefore, knowledge of God must include noetic belief, narrative-affect, and practice. Yet, mere noetic belief, narrative-affect, and practice will not achieve knowledge of God. All knowledge, to be properly aimed at and participate in truth, must comprise of the integration of orthodoxy, orthopathos, and orthopraxis. Achieving the "ortho-" requires prescriptive criteria, which Smith lacks. For Smith, pretheoretical understanding *is* knowledge. While pretheoretical understanding (NAC) is meaningful construal, it cannot achieve the vaunted positive epistemic status of ("ortho-") knowledge (NAK) without a more robust warrant criteria, which Reformed epistemology provides. These prescriptive criteria, when coupled with Smith's nonpropositional epistemology, deliver a more full-orbed picture of knowledge.

Fifth, Reformed epistemology provides an externalist defense against the charges of relativism and arbitrariness that is motivated by the Either/Or dichotomy of Cartesian anxiety. Behind the Cartesian anxiety is the awareness requirement of internalism, which raises skeptical worries. I argued that postliberalism's epistemological and ontological realism and methods of rational adjudication were means to stem the encroachment of these worries. Plantinga's warrant provides further defense. If Smith's epistemology is externalist as I have argued, then such charges must first address the answers provided by externalism.

Sixth, the epistemic role of the Spirit in Plantinga can address how pretheoretical knowledge can be truth-aimed. The Spirit heals and guides epistemic faculties, working as the universal Spirit within the particularities of given cultural-linguistic communities of beliefs, narratives, and practices. If the epistemic role of the Spirit is broadened beyond just knowledge of God, then the Spirit's healing of the noetic and affective effects of sin, both individual and communal, can be seen as a wider work of restoring proper function.[41] Because the IIHS is truth-aimed, the Spirit's revelational activity in the human mind, heart, and practice can work through (positively) and overcome (negatively) immanent cultural-linguistic frameworks without bypassing any cultural-linguistic frameworks. To utilize Amos Yong's cultural-linguistic notion of pneumatological imagination, the Spirit's epistemological work brings together "multiculturality" (human plurality) and "interculturality" (human discourse) into a Spirit-mediated "transculturality" that maintains the immanence of cultural-linguistic knowledge and the transcendent work of divine speech that invades situated human knowledge.[42] Postliberalism is thus freed from radical immanence and makes divine interaction possible within cultural-linguistic communities as transcendence becomes enfolded in immanence.

Not only does a broadened epistemological role of the Spirit open the voice of the Spirit outside Christianity, Christians can be confident in the objective truth of Christian beliefs despite their various cultural-linguistic locations. In addition, all knowledge becomes dependent on divine grace, and all epistemic elements within cultural-linguistic frameworks become the means of pneumatological revelation.[43] This view is consistent with the Reformed commitment to *pistic* knowledge, being grounded in a realism that overcomes relativism—because the Spirit works through the diversity of cultural-linguistic communities without affirming every view as legitimate—and skepticism—because the Spirit heals the epistemic effects of sin and is truth-aimed.

CRITIQUE

Having already critiqued Smith's subcognitivism, his thin criterion for knowledge, and his misunderstanding of postliberalism, this section will focus on Smith's anti- or nonfoundationalism. Smith considers Reformed epistemology as nonfoundationalist.[44] Wolterstorff agrees, arguing that Reformed epistemology "does not commit those who embrace it to any form of foundationalism whatsoever."⁴⁵ Wolterstorff maintains that his verbiage of immediate/mediate beliefs corresponds with Plantinga's basic/nonbasic beliefs and that one cannot repudiate the division. However, he argues that the basic/nonbasic verbiage is saddled with foundationalist assumptions, leading to the assumption that Reformed epistemology merely broadens what counts as foundational beliefs. The immediate/mediate verbiage does not necessitate foundationalism since coherentists also admit of such division.

Foundationalists maintain that certain doxastic merit attaches to basic beliefs and argue how such merit transfers from basic to nonbasic beliefs. Wolterstorff calls this foundationalist position a bipartite account. Plantinga's warrant criteria contain no such bipartite requirement. Wolterstorff rightly describes Plantinga's warrant criteria as a unified account about the warrant of both basic and nonbasic beliefs. However, he concludes from this that Plantinga's warrant criteria do not qualify as an expanded foundationalism.⁴⁶

I contend that Wolterstorff misunderstands Plantinga's foundationalism. First, Michael Bergmann provides a picture of generic foundationalism that contradicts Wolterstorff's description. Bergmann argues that foundationalism is motivated by the infinite regress argument, which argues as follows: if the justification of belief does not terminate, justification is saddled with infinite regress, is achieved via circular reasoning, or is impossible. The acceptance of a doxastic terminus leads to the distinction between basic and nonbasic beliefs and what Bergmann calls the "Generic Foundationalist Epistemic Principle," according to which

> a belief has positive epistemic status E if and only if *either*: (i) it is not inferred from another belief and it satisfies conditions C [for proper basicality]; *or* (ii) it is inferred in way W from another belief with positive epistemic status E.⁴⁷

This principle provides the impetus for foundationalism, and Bergman considers the basic/nonbasic distinction as central to foundationalism.

Bergmann provides six different views about justified beliefs. Besides the properly basic (PB) view, there are JJ (justification of belief is inferred from another justified belief), UF (justification of belief can be inferred from unjustified belief), CR (circular reasoning can justify belief), IR (infinite regress can justify belief), and RS (there is no justified belief) views. UF, CR, IR, and RS are intuitively implausible. JJ is in no better place because JJ entails either CR, IR, or RS views that accept unjustified belief.⁴⁸ If pretheoretical belief is basic, and more importantly, properly basic, then it accepts a PB view and foundationalist structure and contradicts the other five views. In fact, Smith's distinction between the prereflective doxological confessions of theology¹ and theology² follows this foundationalist structure.

Second, Wolterstorff misunderstands Plantinga's project. While Plantinga's warrant conditions do not imply a basic/nonbasic distinction, his project is not merely about warrant, but the warrant of Christian belief. The A/C models are PB with respect to warrant. Although the warrant conditions do not require proper basicality, Christian belief illumines how proper basicality is importantly related to warrant. The basic belief language allows for distinction between proper and non-proper basic belief. PB belief is a basic belief that "meets some other condition C."[49] Importantly, Plantinga states that "differing choices for C [leads] to different varieties of foundationalism."[50] Once one accepts *proper* basicality, one accepts foundationalism. This concept is not apparent in Wolterstorff's immediate/mediate verbiage. He does not speak of properly immediate belief, which is not surprising because his project is about justification. One can be entitled to a belief, but such belief may be unwarranted. Ultimately, the question of Christian belief is not about epistemic rights, but whether Christian belief has warrant sufficient for knowledge.[51]

Plantinga himself defines generic foundationalism as "a family of views" about normative noetic structures that distinguish between basic and non-basic beliefs.[52] The normativity can be deontological, axiological, *aretaic*, or functional, with Plantinga's theory following a (proper) functionalist structure.[53] As a foundationalist, Plantinga argues that the basing relation between beliefs cannot be circular.[54] With these descriptions, that Plantinga rejects JJ (because he is an externalist and accepts the basic/nonbasic distinction), UF (due to *proper* basicality), CR (rejects circular reasoning), IR (PB beliefs terminate the regress), and RS (warrant precludes this view) is clear. In Bergmann's typology, Plantinga is a PB foundationalist.

Even if, as Wolterstorff argues, coherentists use the immediate/mediate distinction, this argument does not negate Reformed epistemology's foundationalism. Plantinga modifies the popular view of coherentism as being typified by circular evidential support in a sufficiently large circle, arguing that coherentism is a theory about warrant in which "a belief *B* is *properly basic* for a person *S* if and only if *B* appropriately coheres with the rest of *S*'s noetic structure."[55] Plantinga recognizes that coherentism utilizes the immediate/mediate distinction through basic/nonbasic language. Defined this way, coherentism is not centrally about circular, inferential *reasoning* but about coherence as such. With coherence achieved through PB beliefs, Plantinga argues that coherentism is a "nonstandard [foundationalism] with unusual views about what is properly basic."[56]

Bergmann acknowledges Plantinga's description of coherentism and argues that such coherentism is not a competitor to foundationalism. "Linear coherentism," the position that circular reasoning is true, is a clear competitor to foundationalism, but he contends that it is not seriously defended by many. He also argues that Susan Haack's foundherentism, an alternative to coherentism and foundationalism, is still foundationalist in its acceptance of the basic/nonbasic distinction and rejection of UF, CR, IR, and RS, and he concludes that "defending either coherentism or foundherentism does not, in itself, amount to an objection to foundationalism."[57]

Insofar as the generic thesis of Reformed epistemology is that religious belief doesn't require undefeated evidence or argument, then it can be consistent with anti- or nonfoundationalism. However, Smith's pretheory-theory structure best suits foundationalism so it is best to augment Plantinga's foundationalist Reformed epistemology, especially since Bergmann confirms that the basic/nonbasic distinction is important for answering the regress problem.

How does PB foundationalism compare to Smith's antifoundationalism? Amos Yong's taxonomy of anti-, non-, post-, minimalist, and classical foundationalism is helpful for situating Smith appropriately. Using a spectrum, Yong places antifoundationalism, nonfoundationalism, postfoundationalism, minimalist/weak/soft (generic) foundationalism, and classical/hard foundationalism from left to right. Classical foundationalism follows the Cartesian requirement of epistemic certainty. Minimalist foundationalism, which Yong places Reformed epistemology in, insists on non-Cartesian foundations and sees proper basic beliefs emerging from doxastic practices. Postfoundationalism is a *via media* between Cartesian foundationalism and antifoundationalism, acknowledging the contextuality of all knowledge while maintaining the possibility of overcoming the radical contextuality of localized knowledge through "interdisciplinary, intercultural, and inter-contextual conversation."[58] Yong finds nonfoundationalism difficult to define due to differences in characterization by its proponents. On the one hand, nonfoundationalism is more like antifoundationalism in its repudiation of universal knowledge.[59] On the other hand, nonfoundationalism is like postfoundationalism in its interdisciplinarity. Antifoundationalism is coherentist, locating "all knowledge subjectivistically and, arguably, solipsistically, within a groundless web of beliefs."[60] Yong's spectrum can now be pictured in figure 9.1.

Even with Yong's descriptions, clarity of these theories is still lacking. There are overlaps and confusions of categorization. Two interesting notes can be made from this observation. First, Yong states that

> if foundations are equivalent to warrants, then all rationalities and epistemologies are foundational in that sense. The question, then, is not whether or not any particular rationality is foundational, but what kind of foundations are being appealed to and how they operate.[61]

Although he is using "foundation" equivocally, Yong is right that each theory carries its own criteria for ultimate appeal, whether webs of belief,

| Anti- Foundationalism | Non- Foundationalism | Post- Foundationalism | Minimalist Foundationalism | Classical Foundationalism |

Figure 9.1   A Spectrum of Foundationalisms According to Amos Yong's Schema. Author Created.

narratives, and epistemic practices of a community, interdisciplinary dialogue, or PB beliefs of various sorts. This statement aligns with Plantinga's argument that even coherentism, except for linear coherentism, can be foundationalist since it is about (nonstandard) PB beliefs for which appeal is made. Second, there are similarities between non-, post-, and minimalist foundationalism. Both Plantinga's and Wolterstorff's Reformed epistemology reject the epistemic certainty of classical foundationalism and affirm the particularities of beliefs arising from different contexts, narratives, and worldviews. Moreover, non- and postfoundationalism do not necessarily repudiate the basic/nonbasic distinction. Therefore, instead of differentiating the three views, integrating non- and postfoundationalism into minimalist foundationalism as its particular instantiations is best.[62] At minimum, they can be seen as sharing family resemblances of foundationalism. Thus, Yong's spectrum can be condensed this way as shown in figure 9.2.

Having described these various theories, to which position does Smith belong? He clearly rejects classical foundationalism and aligns himself with "the antifoundationalism of the postliberal approach."[63] Yet, Lindbeck and Smith have misunderstood antifoundationalism and foundationalism as such. First, they equate foundationalism with Cartesian foundationalism.[64] Smith also weds foundationalism with the ostensive correspondence of Cartesian subjective/objective dualism.[65] Nothing in foundationalism necessitates Cartesianism or ostension. Second, and relatedly, they describe foundationalism as purporting a universal foundational structure, an "'absolute' standpoint."[66] Once again, this characterizes classical foundationalism. Third, they affirm antifoundationalism for its rejection of "universal norms of reasonableness . . . [that] can be formulated in some neutral, framework-independent language."[67] Yet, non-, post-, and minimalist foundationalism reject such neutrality. The reason for their misunderstanding can be attributed to Lindbeck's own admission of an inadequate treatment of antifoundationalism and the relationship between truth and justified belief.[68] Given Lindbeck's own clarification about correspondence as ontological truth and categorial and intrasystematic "truths" as necessary conditions for ontological truth, he isn't an antifoundationalist linear coherentist. For justification

| Anti- Foundationalism | Minimalist (Non- Post-) Foundationalism | Classical Foundationalism |

Figure 9.2   A Modified Spectrum of Foundationalisms. Author Created.

is not based on circular reasoning or groundless webs of belief. Instead, postliberalism is minimalist foundationalist. It acknowledges the contextuality of language, practice, and belief, recognizes the plurality of foundations, and views reality and its experiences as grounds and occasions for belief. If postliberalism is minimalistically foundationalist, then Smith's postmodern epistemology must be foundationalist unless Smith decides to break away from Lindbeckian postliberalism.

CONCLUSION

This chapter explored the compatibility of Reformed epistemology with Smith's postmodern epistemology and offered constructive assistance and repair through critique. While Plantinga is compatible with postmodernism, Wolterstorff accentuates the compatibility by highlighting the historicized self and knowledge. Although this idea is implicit in Plantinga, Wolterstorff highlights its importance. Wolterstorff's situated rationality also assists Smith with an account of tradition-dependent, situated entitlement that shows how traditioned NAK can be justified. However, Wolterstorff's theory of entitlement should be supplemented by Plantinga's externalist warrant criteria, which is itself augmented by Wolterstorff's theory of doxastic programming. Their combined warrant criteria reinforce Smith's thin criterion of *ordo amoris* and in turn provides an externalist defense against internalist critique of postmodern epistemology without sacrificing the importance of truth. This Plantinga-Wolterstorff warrant criteria can augment Smith's epistemology without any loss or contradiction. Reformed epistemology also provides a stronger connection to truth, emphasizing that a Christian epistemology should not be satisfied with mere belief (NAC) but seek right understanding (NAK). Furthermore, the Spirit's reparative work on the epistemic faculties can be broadened out beyond religious knowledge so that cultural-linguistic communities do not remain radical immanent. God can guide and direct cultural-linguistic communities through these immanent means, such that transcendence becomes enfolded in immanence. Finally, I provided an extensive critique and commentary on Smith's anti- or nonfoundationalism through Yong's taxonomy. After modifying the taxonomy, I argued that Smith and Reformed epistemology, along with PCE, is minimalistically foundationalist.

NOTES

1. Plantinga, 422–27.
2. Plantinga, 428–29.

3. Plantinga, 434.
4. Plantinga, 432, 433.
5. Wolterstorff, "Reformed Epistemology," 343.
6. Shannon, *Shalom and the Ethics of Belief*, 53–54. Shannon also finds the principle difference between Plantinga and Wolterstorff in the inadequate role volition plays in belief-formation in Plantinga. Shannon, 54. However, this criticism is not valid since Plantinga's view aligns with Wolterstorff on this matter. See Plantinga, "Reason and Belief in God," 34–38.
7. Shannon, *Shalom and the Ethics of Belief*, 51.
8. Shannon, 52, 53.
9. Shannon states that this term appears consistently throughout Wolterstorff's works even though Wolterstorff never adopts it as an official term. Shannon, 11n29. For example, see Wolterstorff, "Thomas Reid on Rationality," 65; and Wolterstorff, "Can Belief in God Be Rational If It Has No Foundations?," 155.
10. Wolterstorff, "Reformed Epistemology," 343.
11. Wolterstorff, 344.
12. Nicholas Wolterstorff, "Historicizing the Belief-Forming Self," in *Practices of Belief: Selected Essays*, ed. Terence Cuneo, vol. 2 (New York: Cambridge University Press, 2010), 118–43 (119, 127–29); and Nicholas Wolterstorff, "Entitlement to Believe and Practices of Inquiry," in *Practices of Belief: Selected Essays*, ed. Terence Cuneo, vol. 2 (New York: Cambridge University Press, 2010), 86–117 (104).
13. Wolterstorff, "Entitlement to Believe and Practices of Inquiry," 86.
14. Nicholas Wolterstorff, "Postscript: A Life in Philosophy," in *Practices of Belief: Selected Essays*, ed. Terence Cuneo, vol. 2 (New York: Cambridge University Press, 2010), 409–25 (421).
15. Wolterstorff, "Historicizing the Belief-Forming Self," 120.
16. See Plantinga, *Warrant and Proper Function*, 22, 26.
17. Wolterstorff, "Historicizing the Belief-Forming Self," 129–32; and Wolterstorff, "Can Belief in God Be Rational If It Has No Foundations?," 150–51. Furthermore, Wolterstorff differentiates between belief-dispositions and reasoning-dispositions. The former produces immediate beliefs and the latter produces mediate beliefs. See Wolterstorff, "Thomas Reid on Rationality," 47.
18. Wolterstorff, "Historicizing the Belief-Forming Self," 136. Some innate dispositions are not present at birth but emerge at a later time. See Wolterstorff, "Can Belief in God Be Rational If It Has No Foundations?," 150.
19. Wolterstorff, "Historicizing the Belief-Forming Self," 132.
20. Wolterstorff, 130–31.
21. Wolterstorff, 136–37.
22. Wolterstorff, "Entitlement to Believe and Practices of Inquiry," 91.
23. Wolterstorff, 92.
24. Entitlement is a deontological concept of justification. "Entitlement does not imply truth." Nicholas Wolterstorff, "On Being Entitled to Beliefs about God," in *Practices of Belief: Selected Essays*, ed. Terence Cuneo, vol. 2 (New York: Cambridge University Press, 2010), 313–33 (316). Wolterstorff even makes the provocative suggestion that non-alethic and nonrational obligations may at times

have precedence over alethic obligations. See Wolterstorff, "Can Belief in God Be Rational If It Has No Foundations?," 156–57. Thus, Wolterstorff's project must be seen as complementing Plantinga without being equated.

25. Wolterstorff, "Entitlement to Believe and Practices of Inquiry," 105.
26. Wolterstorff, "On Being Entitled to Beliefs about God," 322–23.
27. Wolterstorff, "Entitlement to Believe and Practices of Inquiry," 93–98.
28. Wolterstorff, "Can Belief in God Be Rational If It Has No Foundations?," 155.
29. Shannon, *Shalom and the Ethics of Belief*, 52n96.
30. Nicholas Wolterstorff, "Epistemology of Religion," in *Practices of Belief: Selected Essays*, ed. Terence Cuneo, vol. 2 (New York: Cambridge University Press, 2010), 144–72 (145).
31. Plantinga, *Warranted Christian Belief*, 156. Plantinga's acknowledgment of the complexity of the epistemic situation indicates that his warrant model is not necessarily beset by a trace of modernism. That his project does not explore these analogous extensions does not equate his epistemology with modernism. Thus, Shannon's critique that Plantinga's doxastic anthropology retains a "removed and idealized character" reminiscent of modernism, especially in light of his admission of the alignment between Wolterstorff and Plantinga, is thus questionable and puzzling. See Shannon, *Shalom and the Ethics of Belief*, 53–54.
32. Wolterstorff, "Reformed Epistemology," 337. Even the internalist phenomenal conservatism can qualify as Reformed epistemology. See Logan Paul Gage and Blake McAllister, "Phenomenal Conservatism," in *Debating Christian Religious Epistemology: An Introduction to Five Views on the Knowledge of God*, ed. John M. DePoe and Tyler Dalton McNabb (London: Bloomsbury Academic, 2020), 61–81.
33. Wolterstorff, "Historicizing the Belief-Forming Self," 141.
34. Wolterstorff, 140–43.
35. Wolterstorff, 143. Through highlighting John Locke's own admission, Wolterstorff demonstrates the power of doxastic programming by showing how it steers reason. He even argues that "programmed . . . affects and beliefs . . . affect the outputs of the faculties employed." Wolterstorff, "On Being Entitled to Beliefs about God," 328.
36. Westphal, "Taking Plantinga Seriously," 175.
37. J. Aaron Simmons, "Philosophy: Inspiration for Living Relationally and Thinking Rigorously," in *The Routledge Handbook of Pentecostal Theology*, ed. Wolfgang Vondey (New York: Routledge, 2020), 399–409 (404).
38. Diller, *Theology's Epistemological Dilemma*, 158.
39. Diller, 157.
40. Beilby, "Plantinga's Model of Warranted Christian Belief," 140–41.
41. Plantinga alludes to communal and affective malfunctions or sins in various places. See Plantinga, *Warranted Christian Belief*, 207, 216, 213.
42. Amos Yong, "The Pneumatological Imagination: The Logic of Pentecostal Theology," in *The Routledge Handbook of Pentecostal Theology*, ed. Wolfgang Vondey (New York: Routledge, 2020), 152–61 (157).
43. Cf., Diller, *Theology's Epistemological Dilemma*, 50, 52, 57–58. This argument is congenial with Amos Yong's foundational pneumatology. Cf., Yong, *Spirit-Word-Community*, 102–3.

44. Smith, *Thinking in Tongues*, 108; and Smith, *Introducing Radical Orthodoxy*, 180n109.
45. Wolterstorff, "Reformed Epistemology," 340.
46. Wolterstorff, 347.
47. Michael Bergmann, "Foundationalism," in *The Oxford Handbook of the Epistemology of Theology*, ed. William J. Abraham and Frederick D. Aquino (Oxford: Oxford University Press, 2017), 253–73 (254).
48. Bergmann, 255–59.
49. Plantinga, *Warrant*, 70.
50. Plantinga.
51. Plantinga, *Warranted Christian Belief*, 179.
52. Plantinga, *Warrant*, 68.
53. Plantinga, 73.
54. Plantinga, 74.
55. Plantinga, 78. Emphasis mine.
56. Plantinga, 79.
57. Bergmann, "Foundationalism," 260. Peter Tramel argues similarly about foundherentism's reliance on basic beliefs to stop the regress problem. See Peter Tramel, "Haack's Foundherentism Is a Foundationalism," *Synthese* 160, no. 2 (2008): 215–28 (220).
58. Yong, *Spirit-Word-Community*, 98.
59. Yong also likens it to minimalist foundationalism, but his description of Ronald Thiemann's nonfoundationalist theology does not match the foundationalism of Plantinga. See Yong.
60. Yong, 97.
61. Yong, 100.
62. For stylistic reasons, it's also appropriate to designate nonfoundationalism as antifoundationalism since the prefix alludes to the repudiation of foundations.
63. Smith, *Who's Afraid of Relativism?*, 173.
64. Smith, 80n6. This equation is a common misunderstanding. For example, see Thiel, *Nonfoundationalism*, 1–37. Nancey Murphy makes this same connection but also links epistemic justification with foundationalism. Murphy, "Introduction," 9–12. Bergmann argues that many have unjustifiably moved from foundationalism to nonfoundationalism after the demise of Cartesian or classical foundationalism. Yet, this move is a non sequitur. Rejecting Cartesian foundationalism and its requirement for epistemic certainty does not require adopting an alternative to generic foundationalism. In fact, given that certain forms of coherentism are categorized as special forms of foundationalism, some of these alternatives are merely non-Cartesian varieties of foundationalism. See Bergmann, "Foundationalism," 269.
65. Smith, *Who's Afraid of Relativism?*, 80.
66. Smith, 173; Smith, *Who's Afraid of Postmodernism?*, 118; and Lindbeck, *The Nature of Doctrine*, 130.
67. Lindbeck.
68. Lindbeck, "Foreword to the German Edition of The Nature of Doctrine," 197–99.

Conclusion

Contours of a Postmodern Christian Epistemology

The aim of this book was to construct a postmodern Christian epistemology (PCE) through the principal investigation of James K. A. Smith's Pentecostal, postmodern epistemology with the assistance of Reformed epistemology in what J. Aaron Simmons calls mashup philosophy. The voice of Smith is predominant and the epistemology is more "Smithian" than "Plantingian," but the construction does not merely reiterate his epistemology. Major areas of repair involved his subcognitivism and his misunderstanding of postliberalism, anti-realism, and foundationalism. Reformed epistemology provides important assistance by reinforcing Smith's thin epistemic criterion and situating him under externalism. The product is a PCE that triperspectivally integrates *nous* (basic and nonbasic), narrative-affect, and kinesthetics. It remains postliberal and hermeneutic without eliminating its ontological and epistemological realism.

This chapter summarizes the constructive work by outlining the characteristics of this PCE. If the following descriptions are brief, it is because much of the materials were covered throughout the book. The aim of this chapter is to draw the materials together to provide succinct descriptions of a non-nihilistic PCE.

First, this epistemology acknowledges the integral relationship between pretheory and theory. Smith is essentially correct about the quantitative primacy of narrative, affective know-how. Knowledge *is* predominantly pretheoretical, narrative, and affective. One predominantly embodies knowledge and navigates and judges reality through performative actions and embodied means rather than propositional or theoretical beliefs. Theoretical noetic beliefs always arise from embodied know-how. There is no theoretical thought that is unaccompanied by tacit knowledge. Postmodernism is right: knowledge is always already interpreted and interpreting because embodied persons are situated in particular contexts, inhabiting particular rules of various language games in embodied liturgies.

Theoretical noetic beliefs also play a qualitatively important role. Knowledge may be predominantly pretheoretical, but theory often steers or corrects pretheoretical knowledge, even as it is shaped by pretheory. Beliefs, knowledge, and construal are greatly shaped by reflective thinking. Many background beliefs and PB beliefs were once theoretical beliefs that have sedimented down to the pretheoretical. Not recognizing this indirect or direct influence of theory on pretheory leads to the (ironic) loss of communicating the power of pretheoretical practice and understanding. Theory can play a directing role, uncovering pretheory's power and discerning its proper ordering. Without theory's aid, investigating the categorial adequacy and coherence of truth claims becomes impossible. Such functions point to their design. Within the framework of good creation, no incommensurable relationship exists between theory and pretheory. Each have their unique functions, and part of their designed function is to mutually inform one another. Without their proper functioning, one will either be beholden to the Charybdis of hyper-rationalism or the Scylla of deformative cultural liturgies.

In this way, the relationship between pretheoretical affect and *nous* is strengthened. As Haidt and Solomon have shown, emotion is cognitive. Affect is cognitive judgment that can be rational or irrational. It must be rightly ordered and properly functioning for warrant. This affective proper functionalism provides the necessary concepts and language to understand how pretheoretical emotional judgment can be justified, rational, and warranted.

Second, and relatedly, it is externalist, proper functionalist, and minimalistically foundationalist. Warrant is achieved through external states of affairs that do not require internal awareness. All forms of knowledge are subject to the Plantinga-Wolterstorff warrant criteria, whether noetic or affective. Even kinesthetic knowledge is subject since embodied knowledge participates in God's truth when it is functioning properly according to God's design and purposes. And as noted earlier, it maintains the foundationalist structure with the pretheory/basic and theory/nonbasic structure. But unlike Smith's affective foundationalism, the direction of influence is not unilateral, and background experiences and beliefs, including prior theoretical beliefs that sedimented into pretheoretical status, influence pretheoretical knowledge. It also rejects neutral reason and recognizes that foundational beliefs and understandings are much wider than the set of self-evident, empirical, and incorrigible beliefs.

Third, despite Smith's self-proclaimed relativism, this epistemology is epistemologically and ontologically realist. The *telos* of knowledge is the being of God who embodies truth, and participation in God's truth occurs through ostensive belief, narrative-affective performance, and kinesthetic performance. This performative realism bridges the subject-object dualism and seriously takes the reality of being-in-the-world in the pursuit of embodying and participating in truth. Being-in is to always already participate in epistemic activities as embodied beings. But as embodied and necessarily situated, knowledge is hermeneutic. This perspectivalism of hermeneutic situatedness is undergirded by a creational hermeneutic that proclaims the goodness of interpretation. As a God-ordained mode of knowledge, embodied hermeneutic knowledge cannot be anti-realist that fails to deliver truth. Moreover, the truth condition of warrant requires this realism. Thus, without negating the epistemic reality of NAC as meaning-making understanding, NAK is necessarily realist.

Fourth, despite the differentiation between NAC and NAK, PCE doesn't endorse a hierarchy between truth and meaning. I emphasized truth over meaning to secure epistemological realism. However, I want to be vigilant against the specter of objectivism that might haunt my emphasis on truth. Performative correspondence does not view ostensive propositional reference as the highest epistemic goal. Objective data-fact is not the primary mode and *telos* of being-in-the-world. People do not primarily operate in the mode of the data-fact. Even the seemingly pure objective fact of mathematical truths is not memorized for memory's sake, as if the goal of existence is to embody the game Trivial Pursuit. Data-facts are utilized and performed in meaning-making activities. If I must cross a 100 feet bridge, the data-fact of distance, which is always already interpreted through particular language involving various units and perspectives, is not merely memorized, but performed for the sake of some purpose. Even if warrant is more important than entitlement for certain purposes, entitlement is important in factical experience. Sometimes, even the obligation to truth becomes secondary to other obligations, such as relational and *shalomic* obligations, that may not be achievable through the sharing of the naked truth. This is just how humans operate. Human lives are colored by meaning and many, even if not all, beliefs require justification, which is pursued through situated ways of finding out. Therefore, performative correspondence is not another mode of truth that lords over meaning but integrates meaning and truth in performance while making room to distinguish between legitimate and illegitimate meaning.

Fifth, while truth ultimately terminates in the being of God, this truth cannot be proven ultimately without circularity. Knowledge is thus ultimately *pistic*. PCE repudiates neutral reason because it begins from faith. It is not another prolegomenon for knowledge but is itself dependent on the reality of God. For without God's act in the world, embodied, perspectival knowledge befalls the tragedy of originary violence. What qualifies this postmodern epistemology is its Christian ground.

However, even though *pistic* knowledge is ultimately unprovable, it can be justified, rational, and warranted. Rational adjudication is possible. First, immanent critique and transcendental arguments investigate the categorial adequacy and intrasystematic coherence of incommensurable language games. Second, apologetics is possible, but its *telos* and methodology are changed. The purpose of apologetics, whether as defense, offense, or proof, should principally aim for the establishment of plausibility and warrant. Apologetics thus becomes primarily about persuasion, an "out-narration," an effort to show how Christianity provides the best explanation of the relevant data or narrative. Given that truth must also be performed, PCE promotes a performative apologetic that invites the Other to participate in the *shalomic* community through radical hospitality and guesting in each other's presence. This method is an affective-cognitive exercise in empathy and participation.

For example, apologetics as proof would eschew classical arguments for God's existence for the most part and turn to testimonies and *shalomic* relationships that seek to rewrite the Other's narratives and social imaginary. Philosophical arguments, even the classical proofs, can be utilized but under a postmodern epistemological framework that aims to persuade the Other to appreciate the plurality of knowledge and meaning-making narratives and language games that guides. Apologetics as offense could attempt to criticize the plausibility of non-Christian worldviews by demonstrating their categorial inadequacy, intrasystematic incoherence, or their inability to meet the warrant conditions.[1] Again, such demonstration is not merely ratiocinative. One can call attention to inadequacies that occur between beliefs, experiences, and actions. Defensive apologetics can provide defeater-defeaters to maintain PB Christian beliefs' warrant or epistemically promote one's beliefs while demoting others' beliefs.[2] Given that most Christians are not trained apologists, PCE reminds them that turning to their lived Christian experiences, narratives, and the IIHS are appropriate epistemic defenses given that humans all function in incommensurable language games.[3]

If Plantinga is right that metaphysical views are not demonstrable, then apologetics as often conceived cannot deliver what it promises. Alternatively, PCE apologetics invites the Other to try on the hermeneutic lens of Christianity to see its plausibility for warrant. This plausibility is not merely noetic. Plausibility arises from performance because perception of God in encounter requires passional and participative involvement. Apologetics is thus noetic, affective, and performative. Rational plausibility is reenvisioned through holistic embodiment.

Sixth, the confession of *pistic* knowledge points to the pneumatological basis of all knowledge. Not only is knowledge of metaphysics *pistic*, with God as the Creator, creation acts as the medium of pneumatological revelation. All knowledge is a response to pneumatological revelation and must be rightly ordered. There is no secular realm that remains autonomous from the reaches of God's pneumatological revelation. Although reception of revelation is pluralistic and variegated, one can have confident trust that the Spirit utilizes cultural-linguistic communities to communicate God's truth.

Seventh, inasmuch as knowledge (*yada*) is holistic, mere noetic belief without participating in the truth is ultimately a lie. Response to pneumatological revelation ultimately requires participating in the life of God through divine grace. Therefore, the goal of PCE is not the promotion of the epistemic nature of belief, action, and affect. The goal of knowledge is the goal of spirituality, the participation in God the truth through orthodoxy, orthopraxis, and orthopathos. NAC is unconcerned with achieving "ortho" status. NAK, on the other hand, is alethically aimed by participating in God and God's will for the world. The repeated theme of the necessity of participation and performance for knowledge thus promotes the necessity of growing in virtuous character. The active sanctified life, which always takes on the posture of receiver of God's work, is more apt to achieve the epistemic status of orthodoxy, orthopraxis, and orthopathos. Therefore, knowledge is, from beginning to end, a journey of virtue; knowledge made into wisdom and understanding.

CONCLUSION

PCE presents a multidimensional picture of embodied, hermeneutic knowledge. Such is to be expected to capture the biblical picture *yada*. The findings accord well with Dru Johnson's excellent work on biblical epistemology, evidencing its fit with the Christian faith. According to Johnson, the Bible provides the following characteristics of knowledge: embodiment (know-how), perception (PB beliefs and know-how), sociological-prophetic-authorial (community), history-diachronic (situatedness), personal knowledge (affective know-how), intimate knowledge (affective know-how), ritual (community, embodiment, narrative, affect), ethics, and participatory-realist.[4]

The Christian aspect of this model, that which fits comfortably in the trajectory of biblical revelation, cannot be nihilistic about truth. As I have argued, postmodernism is not a monolithic reality that essentializes nihilistic relativism. Despite Smith's mistaken acceptance of relativism and antifoundationalism, Smith is not a nihilistic postmodern and neither is the postmodernism that I presented. This "healing" of postmodernism is an important contribution by Smith, whose voice has gained critical influence in Reformed, Evangelical, and Pentecostal traditions. Since I also inhabit these traditions, this work has been an attempt to bring even more healing and clarity by critically building on Smith's epistemology in order to show that this "Smithian" PCE can clarify the epistemic reality of finite, contingent creatures. While I enlisted Reformed epistemology to assist and correct Smith, I also made the case for Reformed epistemologists to see a closer affinity with postmodernism (and Pentecostalism) and demonstrated how Reformed epistemology can apply in new contexts.

This project began with reflection on my cross-cultural identity and experiences. This mashup project reflects that hybridity. As a Korean-American (broadly) Reformed Pentecostal, my life experiences and beliefs were formed primarily in communal, embodied, narrative, and affective ways. As a child, I was immersed in the myths and legends of Korea and the history of my Pyeongsan Shin clan that cultivated in me a respect for virtuous character and the good and, conversely, disapproval for vice and evil. After immigrating to the United States, despite my desire and efforts to assimilate with what I believed to be "American" culture, I came to realize that difference marked not just my identity and thoughts, but the world as well. This realization hit me forcefully after I joined the US Navy and was surrounded by people whose beliefs and lifestyles were as diverse as the states and nations they came from. Especially impactful is my salvific encounter with God whose redemption placed me in a radically different narrative and lifestyle. This narrative bore down to my worldview as I placed the trajectory of my life in the biblical drama and began to view reality in a different light. These experiences paved the way for my openness to postmodernism.

When I became a new Christian, I knew that I knew that I knew that God was real, and God changed my life. My life and reality were to make a fundamental shift toward God's will. Inasmuch as God is ontologically true as one who exists and reveals God's will to me, I knew that God's truth could be known. And while I am convinced of this realist position, there were times that I knew that I knew that I knew that something was true only to find that I was mistaken. Those experiences also provided the lens to distinguish between NAC and NAK and the need for robust criteria for warrant. In this way, the PCE that I have presented is deeply rooted in my own hybrid experiences and beliefs.

This book is significant in various ways. First, it is an important reminder to the Reformed, Evangelical, and Pentecostal communities that postmodernism is not necessarily the disease of all societal evils. While those committed to cognitive-propositionalism and absolute truth will maintain their aversion to postmodernism presented in this work, I argued against such absolutist propositionalism without dismissing propositional knowledge or correspondence theory of truth. In fact, cognitive-propositionalism represents Bonhoeffer's notion of cheap grace since truth does not require its performance. Postmodern knowledge is like costly grace that requires much from people with its performative criterion. To know (*yada*) God requires the involvement of the whole person.

Second, this work was a fruitful dialogue between analytic and continental religious epistemology. Smith's epistemology was ensconced in the strength of externalism, such that critiques against it must also defeat externalism. This analytic assistance is a demonstration of the bridging of the divide between the two traditions. Smith and Plantinga are ideal partners for this endeavor due to their shared Reformed heritage that rejects epistemic neutrality and emphasizes the all-encompassing life-system of Christianity. This conversation also helped illumine the postmodern sensibilities of Reformed epistemology. Moreover, the analytic rigor applied to the prescriptive categories of justification and warrant provided valuable contribution to Smith's continental epistemology that was heavy on description, but light on prescription.

Third, developing out of Smith's outline of a Pentecostal epistemology, PCE remains consistent with Pentecostal epistemology. Moreover, if its arguments are sound and realism remains true, then the ontological grounding of PCE should provide some stability to any glocally developed Pentecostal epistemology. And as mentioned earlier, Pentecostal epistemology has fruitful dialogue partners in postmodern and Reformed epistemologies.

Finally, taking up Linda Zagzebski's and Dru Johnson's critique that much of epistemology neglects the non-propositional, this book contributed toward an appreciation of the importance of non-propositional knowledge and provided a prescriptive account for its warrant. It's high time that alternative modes of knowledge that better reflect the fleshly, situated embodiment of human being-in-the-world gain greater prominence in contemporary epistemology.

One might wonder whether postmodern studies are fruitful. If postmodernism is situated and contingent, will not a postmodern project be on the way toward its own eclipse? Indeed, this must be so. I hold no illusion that this PCE is a timeless, neutral epistemology that assumes a monolithic vision of knowledge or Christianity. With time, it too will fade away or be shaped according to one's particular epistemic milieu. Postmodernism thus faithfully lives out the Protestant dictum, *semper reformanda*. However, inasmuch as parts of it are faithfully responding to revelation of divine reality, PCE should have some enduring power even if not in its original form. For to be situated and embodied means to hold in tension historical and situated continuity with discontinuity. Even the antithesis of discontinuity is made possible by the thesis that came before. From a Christian, and especially Pentecostal view, such tension is not only the natural by-product of hermeneutic realism, dynamic change and development should be expected from the surprising work of the Holy Spirit. Come, Holy Spirit! Ever renew our knowledge!

NOTES

1. For example, see Tyler D. McNabb, "Warranted Religion: Answering Objections to Alvin Plantinga's Epistemology," *Religious Studies* 51, no. 4 (2015): 477–95 (485–92). McNabb argues that Advaita Vedanta Hinduism cannot account for proper function, design plan, or true beliefs.

2. Defeater-defeaters do not provide warrant for Christian beliefs. If they did, then Christian beliefs would no longer be basic. Instead, defeater-defeaters allows one to maintain the warrant of her original beliefs. See Plantinga, "Reason and Belief in God," 84. Michael Sudduth misses this point when he points to the reflective nature of defeater-defeaters as evidence that reflective rationality contributes toward warrant of theistic belief. See Michael C. Sudduth, "The Internalist Character and Evidentialist Implications of Plantingian Defeaters," *International Journal for Philosophy of Religion* 45, no. 3 (1999): 167–87.

3. This recommendation is an application of Andrew Moon's argument for circular self-promotion. See Moon, "Circular and Question-Begging Responses."

4. Johnson, *Biblical Knowing*, 187–200.

Glossary

Alethic: An adjective pertaining to truth. Derived from the Greek word *aletheia*, meaning truth.

ANTI-REALISM

Alethic: Anti-realism about truth in which truth and understanding are constructed by conceptual schemes. Truth statements do not correspond to reality but refer to other statements within conceptual schemes.

Conceptual: Anti-realism about concepts. That is, while mind-independent reality exists, reality is significantly dependent on conceptual schemes. So much so that kinds of entities, those entities, and their interrelations are dependent on conceptual schemes.

Creative: See internal realism. The properties of mind-independent reality are furnished by creative minds. While Hilary Putnam calls his view internal realism, Alvin Plantinga renames internal realism as creative anti-realism and argues that creative anti-realism is in the end equated with existential anti-realism since, on this account, properties of objects are dependent on creative minds.

Existential: The theory that denies the existence of mind-independent reality. Reality and its properties are furnished by the mind.

BELIEF

Basic: According to the foundationalist picture of beliefs, basic beliefs are non-inferential beliefs that belong in the epistemic foundation.

Nonbasic: According to the foundationalist picture of beliefs, nonbasic beliefs are inferential beliefs that receive their justification from other beliefs until the justificatory chain terminates in some justified basic belief.

Properly Basic Belief: A basic belief that has met some condition that makes it appropriate to hold and is self-justified. For example, the basic belief of seeing a tree is properly basic if a tree exists in front of the person. However, if one sees a tree that does not exist due to some cognitive malfunction, the belief may be basic but not properly basic.

Categorial Adequacy: Pertaining to pragmatic adequacy. Categories of a given cultural-linguistic form of life provide the conceptual framework for meaningful statements. A statement made within a form of life that lacks the categories is deemed categorially inadequate, *ad hoc*, and arbitrary within the form of life. For example, Christians who claim that humans have no free will due to absolute divine sovereignty lack the categories within their form of life, and the statement is deemed categorially inadequate.

Categorial/Categorical Truth: According to George Lindbeck, categorial truth is more accurately a necessary condition for ontological truth, specifically regarding pragmatic adequacy, and is not to be considered as a form of truth.

Cognitive-Propositionalism: A theory of doctrine often associated with Evangelicalism that considers doctrines as timeless propositional truth claims.

Correspondence Theory of Truth: The theory of truth that considers proposition as true if it refers accurately to a state of affairs.

Creator-Creature Distinction: The doctrine that emphasizes the ontological difference between God the Creator and God's creation.

Cultural-Linguistic Model: The postliberal theory of religion and doctrine in which they are understood not primarily as the dispenser of timeless truths or as the mediator of universal religious experience but should be seen as linguistically constructed culture or form of life that acts as comprehensive interpretive schemes.

De Facto Objection: An objection against the truth of theism.

De Jure Objection: An objection against the rationality or warrant of theism even if theism might be true.

Doxastic Experience: The phenomenal feeling that accompanies right or wrong belief.

Empirical Transcendental: James K. A. Smith's terminology for mind-independent reality that constrains the range of one's interpretation of reality.

Experiential Expressivism: A theory of doctrine often associated with modern liberal theological traditions that consider doctrines as subjective, nondiscursive symbols that express universal religious experience or feeling.

Externalism: An epistemological theory of justification or warrant that rejects the necessity of one's awareness of the justificatory elements of a belief for its justification or warrant. Rather, a belief is justified or warranted if it is produced in the right way, such as reliable processes or by properly functioning cognitive faculties.

Extratextuality: A postliberal term denoting extralinguistic external reality, especially in regard to meaning found outside immanent cultural-linguistic or intratextual systems.

Facticity/Factical: Martin Heidegger's notion of the given pretheoretical, situated experience prior to and even resistant to theoretical conceptualization.

Family Resemblance: Related to Ludwig Wittgenstein's idea of language games, family resemblance rejects essentialist definitions and replaces them with similarities in kind.

Fore-Structure: The pre-given structure of interpretation that reveals interpretation is never presuppositionless.

Formal Indication: A method of pretheoretical understanding that does not deliver conceptual knowledge or content of things but points to the concrete things themselves.

Form of Life: Related to language games, form of life refers to the totality of rule-governed social acts, including language games, of particular cultures. In this way, particular religions qualify as forms of life and language games.

FOUNDATIONALISM

Antifoundationalism: The coherentist rejection of foundationalism and its basic/nonbasic belief structure. A belief is justified when it coheres with the wider web of beliefs.

Classical/Strong/Universal/Cartesian: The foundationalist theory that endorses the justification of a belief if and only if it is self-evident, evident to the senses, or incorrigible.

Generic/Minimalistic: The bare foundationalist thesis about the basic/nonbasic belief structure.

Postfoundationalism/Nonfoundationalism: In this work, postfoundationalism and nonfoundationalism are taken to be the same theory, although they can be distinguished based on varying definitions. Post/

nonfoundationalism is a variation of generic foundationalism that rejects the one universal foundation and epistemic certainty of classical foundationalism and replaces it with multiple contextual foundations due to various conceptual schemes. Taking conceptual schemes and epistemic fallibility seriously, post/nonfoundationalism promotes interdisciplinary and inter-contextual dialogue for the advancement of knowledge.

Immanent Critique: A mode of non-neutral rational adjudication in which one hypothetically assumes the resources internal to another language game in order to test its categorial adequacy.

Internalism: An epistemological theory of justification or warrant that considers awareness of the justificatory element(s) of a belief as a necessary criterion for justification or warrant.

Intrasystematic Truth: According to George Lindbeck, intrasystematic truth is more accurately a necessary condition for ontological truth, specifically regarding a statement's overall coherence with its form of life.

Intratextuality: A postliberal term denoting meaning generated within cultural-linguistic communities as its frame of reference.

Justification: The status of a belief when it is held appropriately. A justified belief sometimes indicates that it is true but not necessarily so.

Know-How: Knowledge that is not noetic but embodied and pretheoretical, such as kinesthetic bodily judgments, emotive judgments, and narrative, affective knowledge.

Know-That: Noetic knowledge that can be pretheoretical or theoretical.

Language Game: Ludwig Wittgenstein's term denoting that the primary function of language is not to refer to external reality but to act according to the conventional rules of contextual communities or games. That is, the meaning of words is governed by how words are used in context. Each form of life is a language game with its own particular rules. This idea is motivated by Wittgenstein's repudiation of essentialist definitions.

***Lex Orendi, Lex Credendi*:** Latin phrase for "the law of prayer is the law of belief." That is, worship determines belief.

Metanarrative: An ultimate narrative or worldview that purports to be legitimized by neutral reason. What distinguishes a metanarrative from other ultimate narratives is the forgetting of its own *pistic*, contextual perspectivity.

Narrative, Affective Construal: Interpretive understanding elicited by and embedded in narrative and affect that lacks a truth component.

Narrative, Affective Knowledge: Interpretive knowledge elicited by and embedded in narrative and affect that has a truth component.

Noumenon: Associated with Immanuel Kant, the noumenon is the thing-in-itself, objective reality that is independent of sense perception.

Phenomenon: Associated with Immanuel Kant, the phenomenon is the world as it appears through sense perception.

Phronesis: Greek term for practical wisdom. A mode of non-neutral rational adjudication in the absence of epistemologically objective criteria.

Pistic: Greek term for faith. Used in this work to indicate that knowledge is ultimately grounded in faith due to the impossibility of epistemologically neutral objectivism.

Present-at-Hand: Martin Heidegger's notion in which an object is disentangled from its meaning and used through theoretical conceptualization. Because the primary mode of apprehending an object is through its use, this theoretical conceptualization of merely knowing the facts is a derivative mode of understanding.

Pretheoretical Understanding: Embodied knowledge that differs from propositional or inferential knowledge. This is the primary mode of knowing in its frequency.

Ready-to-Hand: Martin Heidegger's notion in which the meaning of an object is apprehended immediately and pretheoretically through its use. This is the primary and fundamental mode of apprehending the world.

REALISM

Ontological/Metaphysical: The theory that accepts the existence of mind-independent reality with intrinsic properties.

Epistemological: The theory that accepts the existence of mind-independent reality and its knowability.

Internal Realism: An ontologically realist theory attributed to Hilary Putnam. Reality does not have intrinsic properties independent of conceptual schemes, and access to that reality is only possible through conceptual schemes.

Regulative Theory: Postliberalism's theory of doctrine in which the primary role of doctrine is to regulate religious speech to correspond with first-order religious practice. A doctrine is deemed true if it's categorically adequate, intrasystematically coherent, and practiced in a way that corresponds with reality.

RELATIVISM

Benign: James K. A. Smith's version of relativism in which truth claims are understood merely as relative to a context.
Nihilistic: The form of relativism that denies any objectivity to truth and assigns truth value to the claims of individuals or cultures.

Sensus Divinitatis: Latin term for the sense of the divine. In Alvin Plantinga's usage, the *sensus divinitatis* is a divinely designed cognitive faculty or disposition to form theistic belief when triggered in various ways.
Social Imaginary: Charles Taylor's term for pretheoretical, inarticulate, and largely unstructured understanding, which acts as the interpretive scheme that makes reality coherent and meaningful.
Sub specie aeternitatis: Latin term denoting epistemic neutrality or "God's view of the world," the idea that one has achieved a perspectiveless view of reality.
Sui generis: Latin term denoting uniqueness.
Tacit Knowledge: Michael Polanyi's term for pretheoretical, primordial knowledge that guides and makes theoretical knowledge possible. It is gleaned not so much through propositional instruction but through embodied apprenticeship and mimesis.
Theoretical Knowledge: Inferential knowledge.
Thrownness: Martin Heidegger's notion that persons find themselves in their particular situations, having been handed over to it, which elicits the task of a response that is authentic to their selves.
Transcendental Argument: An argument introduced by Kant and popularized by presuppositional apologetics that argues for a particular reality, such as rationality for Kant or objective morality for presuppositionalists, by inquiring into the necessary precondition for the existence of that reality, such as the categories of understanding or God. While similar to an immanent critique, transcendental arguments can use resources external to the language game in question.
Triperspectival: John Frame's theory that a whole can be understood by looking at its three integrated perspectives: normative, situational, and existential perspectives. The triadic relationship presupposes their interdependence, such that correct and fuller knowledge is only possible when all three are integrated and not merely balanced. In this work, the triperspectival integration of orthodoxy, orthopathos, and orthopraxis is encouraged for achieving holistic knowledge and correspondent truth.
Warrant: The quality or quantity that turns mere belief into knowledge.

Bibliography

Adler, Mortimer J., and Charles Van Doren. *How to Read a Book: The Classic Guide to Intelligent Reading*. New York: Touchstone, 1972.

Albrecht, Daniel. *Rites in the Spirit: A Ritual Approach to Pentecostal Charismatic Spirituality*. Sheffield: Sheffield Academic Press, 1999.

Albrecht, Daniel E., and Evan B. Howard. "Pentecostal Spirituality." In *The Cambridge Companion to Pentecostalism*, edited by Cecil M. Robeck and Amos Yong, 235–53. New York: Cambridge University Press, 2014.

Alston, William P. "Epistemology and Metaphysics." In *Knowledge and Reality: Essays in Honor of Alvin Plantinga*, edited by Thomas M. Crisp, Matthew Davidson, and David Vander Laan, 81–109. Dordrecht: Springer, 2006.

———. *Perceiving God: The Epistemology of Religious Experience*. Ithaca: Cornell University Press, 1991.

Althouse, Peter. "Toward a Theological Understanding of the Pentecostal Appeal to Experience." *Journal of Ecumenical Studies* 38, no. 4 (2001): 399–411.

Anderson, Allan. *An Introduction to Pentecostalism: Global Charismatic Christianity*. New York: Cambridge University Press, 2004.

———. "Varieties, Taxonomies, and Definitions." In *Studying Global Pentecostalism: Theories and Methods*, edited by Allan Anderson, Michael Bergunder, André Droogers, and Cornelis van der Laan, 13–29. Berkeley and Los Angeles: University of California Press, 2010.

Anderson, James. *Paradox in Christian Theology: An Analysis of Its Presence, Character, and Epistemic Status*. Milton Keynes: Paternoster, 2007.

Anderson, Robert M. *Vision of the Disinherited: The Making of American Pentecostalism*. New York: Oxford University Press, 1979.

Baker, Deane-Peter. *Tayloring Reformed Epistemology: Charles Taylor, Alvin Plantinga and the de Jure Challenge to Christian Belief*. London: SCM Press, 2007.

Baker, Don. *Korean Spirituality*. Honolulu: University of Hawai'i Press, 2008.

Baker-Hytch, Max. "Epistemic Externalism in the Philosophy of Religion." *Philosophy Compass* 12, no. 4 (2017): 1–12.

Bartholomew, Craig G. *Contours of the Kuyperian Tradition: A Systematic Introduction*. Downers Grove: IVP Academic, 2017.

Bartholomew, Craig G., and Michael W. Goheen. *Christian Philosophy: A Systematic and Narrative Introduction*. Grand Rapids: Baker Academic, 2013.

Beilby, James. "Externalism, Skepticism, and Knowledge: An Argument against Internalism." *Philosophia Christi* 10, no. 1 (2008): 75–86.

———. "Plantinga's Model of Warranted Christian Belief." In *Alvin Plantinga*, edited by Deane-Peter Baker, 125–65. New York: Cambridge University Press, 2007.

Benson, Bruce Ellis. *Graven Ideologies: Nietzsche, Derrida & Marion on Modern Idolatry*. Downers Grove: InterVarsity Press, 2002.

Ben-Ze'ev, Aaron. "Emotion as a Subtle Mental Mode." In *Thinking about Feeling: Contemporary Philosophers on Emotions*, edited by Robert C. Solomon, 250–68. New York: Oxford University Press, 2004.

———. "The Logic of Emotions." In *Philosophy and the Emotions*, edited by Anthony Hatzimoysis, 147–62. Royal Institute of Philosophy Supplement: 52. New York: Cambridge University Press, 2003.

Berendsen, Desiree. "Religious Passions and Emotions: Towards a Stratified Concept of Religious Passions: Robert Solomon Versus Thomas Dixon." In *Encountering Transcendence: Contributions to a Theology of Christian Religious Experience*, edited by Lieven Boeve, Hans Geybels, and Stijn Van den Bossche, 201–12. Dudley: Peeters, 2005.

Berger, Peter L. *The Many Altars of Modernity: Toward a Paradigm for Religion in a Pluralist Age*. Boston: De Gruyter, 2014.

Bergmann, Michael. "Foundationalism." In *The Oxford Handbook of the Epistemology of Theology*, edited by William J. Abraham and Frederick D. Aquino, 253–73. Oxford: Oxford University Press, 2017.

———. "Internalism, Externalism and the No-Defeater Condition." *Synthese* 110, no. 3 (1997): 399–417.

———. *Justification without Awareness*. New York: Oxford University Press, 2006.

———. "Religious Disagreement and Rational Demotion." In *Oxford Studies in Philosophy of Religion*, edited by Jonathan L. Kvanvig, 6:21–57. New York: Oxford University Press, 2015.

Bernstein, Richard J. *Beyond Objectivism and Relativism: Science, Hermeneutics, and Praxis*. Philadelphia: University of Pennsylvania Press, 1988.

Beversluis, John. "Reforming the 'Reformed' Objection to Natural Theology." *Faith and Philosophy* 12, no. 2 (1995): 189–206.

Bird, Phyllis A. "'Male and Female He Created Them': Gen 1:27b in the Context of the Priestly Account of Creation." *Harvard Theological Review* 74, no. 2 (1981): 129–59.

Blosser, Philip. "God among the Philosophers." *New Oxford Review* 66, no. 9 (October 1999): 39–42.

Boersma, Hans. "Introduction: The Relevance of Theology and Worldview in a Postmodern Context." In *Living in the Lamblight: Christianity and Contemporary Challenges to the Gospel*, edited by Hans Boersma, 1–13. Vancouver: Regent College Publishing, 2001.

Bom, Klaas. "Heart and Reason: Using Pascal to Clarify Smith's Ambiguity." *Pneuma* 34, no. 3 (2012): 345–64.

BonJour, Laurence. "Externalism/Internalism." In *A Companion to Epistemology*, edited by Jonathan Dancy, Ernest Sosa, and Matthias Steup, 2nd ed., 364–68. Malden: Wiley-Blackwell, 2010.

Borgmann, Albert. *Crossing the Postmodern Divide*. Chicago: University of Chicago Press, 1992.

Bowald, Mark Alan. "Who's Afraid of Theology: A Conversation with James K. A. Smith on Dogmatics as the Grammar of Christian Particularity." In *The Logic of Incarnation: James K. A. Smith's Critique of Postmodern Religion*, edited by Neal DeRoo and Brian Lightbody, 168–81. Eugene: Pickwick Publications, 2009.

Boyce, Kenneth, and Alvin Plantinga. "Proper Functionalism." In *The Bloomsbury Companion to Epistemology*, edited by Andrew Cullison, 143–61. New York: Bloomsbury Academic, 2015.

Briggs, Richard S. "Humans in the Image of God and Other Things Genesis Does Not Make Clear." *Journal of Theological Interpretation* 4, no. 1 (2010): 111–26.

Butler, Christopher. *Postmodernism: A Very Short Introduction*. New York: Oxford University Press, 2002.

Calhoun, Cheshire. "Cognitive Emotions?" In *What Is an Emotion?: Classic and Contemporary Readings*, edited by Robert C. Solomon, 2nd ed., 236–47. New York: Oxford University Press, 2003.

———. "Subjectivity and Emotion." In *Thinking about Feeling: Contemporary Philosophers on Emotions*, edited by Robert C. Solomon, 107–21. New York: Oxford University Press, 2004.

Caputo, John D., and Michael J. Scanlon. "Introduction: Apology for the Impossible: Religion and Postmodernism." In *God, the Gift, and Postmodernism*, edited by John D. Caputo and Michael J. Scanlon, 1–19. Bloomington: Indiana University Press, 1999.

Castelo, Daniel. "Pentecostal Theology as Spirituality: Explorations in Theological Method." In *The Routledge Handbook of Pentecostal Theology*, edited by Wolfgang Vondey, 29–39. New York: Routledge, 2020.

———. *Pentecostalism as a Christian Mystical Tradition*. Grand Rapids: William B. Eerdmans Publishing Company, 2017.

———. *Revisioning Pentecostal Ethics: The Epiclectic Community*. Cleveland: CPT Press, 2012.

Cathey, Robert A. *God in Postliberal Perspective: Between Realism and Non-Realism*. Trascending Boundaries in Philosophy and Theology. Burlington: Ashgate, 2009.

Chisholm, Roderick M. *Theory of Knowledge*. Englewood Cliffs: Prentice Hall, Inc., 1966.

Clark, Gregory A. "The Nature of Conversion: How the Rhetoric of Worldview Philosophy Can Betray Evangelicals." In *The Nature of Confession: Evangelicals*

& *Postliberals in Conversation*, edited by Timothy R. Phillips and Dennis L. Okholm, 201–18. Downers Grove: InterVarsity Press, 1996.
Clark, Kelly James. "A Reformed Epistemologist's Closing Remarks." In *Five Views on Apologetics*, edited by Steven B. Cowan, 364–73. Grand Rapids: Zondervan, 2000.
———. "Reformed Epistemology Apologetics." In *Five Views on Apologetics*, edited by Steven B. Cowan, 266–84. Grand Rapids: Zondervan, 2000.
Clark, Mathew S. "Pentecostal Hermeneutics: The Challenge of Relating to (Post)-Modern Literary Theory." *Africa Journal of Pentecostal Studies* 1, no. 1 (2002): 67–92.
Clements, Keith W. *Freidrich Schleiermacher: Pioneer of Modern Theology*. San Francisco: Collins Liturgical, 1987.
Clouser, Roy A. *The Myth of Religious Neutrality: An Essay on the Hidden Role of Religious Belief in Theories*. Notre Dame: University of Notre Dame Press, 2005.
Conee, Earl, and Richard Feldman. "Internalism Defended." In *Epistemology: Internalism and Externalism*, edited by Hilary Kornblith, 231–60. Malden: Blackwell Publishing, 2001.
Conner, Benjamin T. *Disabling Mission, Enabling Witness: Exploring Missiology through the Lens of Disability Studies*. Downers Grove: IVP Academic, 2018.
Cox, Harvey. *Fire from Heaven: The Rise of Pentecostal Spirituality and the Reshaping of Religion in the Twenty-First Century*. Reading: Addison-Wesley Publishing Company, 1995.
Craig, William Lane. "A Classical Apologist's Response." In *Five Views on Apologetics*, edited by Steven B. Cowan, 232–35, 285–90. Grand Rapids: Zondervan, 2000.
Crouch, C. L. "Genesis 1:26-7 as a Statement of Humanity's Divine Parentage." *Journal of Theological Studies* 61, no. 1 (2010): 1–15.
D'Arms, Justin, and Daniel Jacobson. "The Significance of Recalcitrant Emotion (or, Anti-Quasijudgmentalism)." In *Philosophy and the Emotions*, edited by Anthony Hatzimoysis, 127–45. Royal Institute of Philosophy Supplement: 52. New York: Cambridge University Press, 2003.
Davis, Richard B., and Paul Franks. "Against a Postmodern Pentecostal Epistemology." *Philosophia Christi* 15, no. 2 (2013): 129–45.
———. "On Jesus, Derrida, and Dawkins: Rejoinder to Joshua Harris." *Philosophia Christi* 16, no. 1 (2014): 185–92.
Dedeke, Adenekan. "A Cognitive-Intuitionist Model of Moral Judgment." *Journal of Business Ethics* 126, no. 3 (2015): 437–57.
Deonna, Julien A., and Fabrice Teroni. *The Emotions: A Philosophical Introduction*. New York: Routledge, 2008.
DeRoo, Neal. "Introduction." In *The Logic of Incarnation: James K. A. Smith's Critique of Postmodern Religion*, edited by Neal DeRoo and Brian Lightbody, xv–xxvii. Eugene: Wipf & Stock, 2009.
Derrida, Jacques. *Of Grammatology*. Translated by Gayatri Chakravorty Spivak. Baltimore: Johns Hopkins University Press, 1997.

Descartes, René. *Discourse on Method and Meditations on First Philosophy*. Translated by Donald A. Cress, 4th ed. Indianapolis: Hackett Publishing Company, 1998.

DeYoung, Rebecca Konyndyk. "Pedagogical Rhythms: Practices and Reflections on Practice." In *Teaching and Christian Practices: Reshaping Faith & Learning*, edited by David I. Smith and James K. A. Smith, 24–42. Grand Rapids: Eerdmans Publishing Company, 2011.

Diller, Kevin. "Can Arguments Boost Warrant for Christian Belief?: Warrant Boosting and the Primacy of Divine Revelation." *Religious Studies* 47, no. 02 (2011): 185–200.

———. *Theology's Epistemological Dilemma: How Karl Barth and Alvin Plantinga Provide a Unified Response*. Downers Grove: InterVarsity Press, 2014.

Dooyeweerd, Herman. *In the Twilight of Western Thought*. Edited by James K. A. Smith. Studies in the Pretended Autonomy of Philosophical Thought. Grand Rapids: Paideia Press, 2012.

Fairlamb, Horace. "Sanctifying Evidentialism." *Religious Studies* 46, no. 1 (2010): 61–76.

Fales, Evan. "Proper Basicality." *Philosophy and Phenomenological Research* 68, no. 2 (2004): 373–83.

Faupel, D. William. "Whither Pentecostalism?" *Pneuma* 15, no. 1 (1993): 9–27.

Feldman, Richard. "Plantinga, Gettier, and Warrant." In *Warrant in Contemporary Epistemology: Essays in Honor of Plantinga's Theory of Knowledge*, edited by Jonathan L. Kvanvig, 199–220. Lanham: Rowman & Littlefield Publishers, 1996.

Fennell, Jon. "On Authority and Political Destination: Michael Polanyi and the Threshold of Postmodernism." *Perspectives on Political Science* 42, no. 3 (2013): 154–61.

Ferraris, Maurizio. "Transcendental Realism." *The Monist* 98, no. 2 (2015): 215–32.

Fine, Cordelia. "Is the Emotional Dog Wagging Its Rational Tail, or Chasing It?: Reason in Moral Judgment." *Philosophical Explorations* 9, no. 1 (2006): 83–98.

Fletcher, Jeannine Hill. "As Long as We Wonder: Possibilities in the Impossibility of Interreligious Dialogue." *Theological Studies* 68, no. 3 (2007): 531–54.

Fodor, James. "Postliberal Theology." In *The Modern Theologians: An Introduction to Christian Theology since 1918*, edited by David F. Ford and Rachel Muers, 3rd ed., 229–48. Malden: Blackwell Publishing, 2005.

Frame, John M. *Cornelius Van Til: An Analysis of His Thought*. Phillipsburg: P&R Publishing Company, 1995.

———. "Presuppositional Apologetics." In *Five Views on Apologetics*, edited by Stanley N. Gundry and Steven B. Cowan, 207–31. Grand Rapids: Zondervan, 2000.

———. *The Doctrine of the Knowledge of God*. Phillipsburg: P&R Publishing Company, 1987.

Frestadius, Simo. "In Search of a 'Pentecostal' Epistemology: Comparing the Contributions of Amos Yong and James K. A. Smith." *Pneuma* 38, no. 1 (2016): 93–114.

———. *Pentecostal Rationality: Epistemology and Theological Hermeneutics in the Foursquare Tradition*. London: T&T Clark, 2020.

Fumerton, Richard. "Epistemic Internalism, Philosophical Assurance and the Skeptical Predicament." In *Knowledge and Reality: Essays in Honor of Alvin Plantinga*, edited by Thomas M. Crisp, Matthew Davidson, and David Vander Laan, 179–91. Dordrecht: Springer, 2006.

Gage, Logan Paul, and Blake McAllister. "Phenomenal Conservatism." In *Debating Christian Religious Epistemology: An Introduction to Five Views on the Knowledge of God*, edited by John M. DePoe and Tyler Dalton McNabb, 61–81. London: Bloomsbury Academic, 2020.

Geivett, R. Douglas, and Greg Jesson. "Plantinga's Externalism and the Terminus of Warrant-Based Epistemology." *Philosophia Christi* 3, no. 2 (2001): 329–40.

Genderen, J. van, and W. H. Velema. *Concise Reformed Dogmatics*. Translated by Gerrit Bilkes and Ed M. van der Maas. Phillipsburg: P&R Publishing Company, 2008.

Gettier, Edmund L. "Is Justified True Belief Knowledge?" *Analysis* 23, no. 6 (1963): 121–23.

Gill, Jerry H. *Deep Postmodernism: Whitehead, Wittgenstein, Merleau-Ponty, and Polanyi*. Amhert: Humanity Books, 2010.

———. *The Tacit Mode: Michael Polanyi's Postmodern Philosophy*. Albany: State University of New York Press, 2000.

Goldie, Peter. "Emotion, Feeling, and Knowledge of the World." In *Thinking about Feeling: Contemporary Philosophers on Emotions*, edited by Robert C. Solomon, 91–106. New York: Oxford University Press, 2004.

———. "Narrative and Perspective; Values and Appropriate Emotions." In *Philosophy and the Emotions*, edited by Anthony Hatzimoysis, 201–20. Royal Institute of Philosophy Supplement: 52. New York: Cambridge University Press, 2003.

———. "Narrative Thinking, Emotion, and Planning." *The Journal of Aesthetics and Art Criticism* 67, no. 1 (2009): 97–106.

González, Justo L. *The Mestizo Augustine: A Theologian between Two Cultures*. Downers Grove: IVP Academic, 2016.

Greene, Joshua D. "Dual-Process Morality and the Personal/Impersonal Distinction: A Reply to McGuire, Langdon, Coltheart, and Mackenzie." *Journal of Experimental Social Psychology* 45, no. 3 (2009): 581–84.

Greene, Joshua D., and Jonathan Haidt. "How (and Where) Does Moral Judgment Work?" *TRENDS in Cognitive Sciences* 6, no. 12 (2002): 517–23.

Greene, Joshua D., Leigh E. Nystrom, Andrew D. Engell, John M. Darley, and Jonathan D. Cohen. "The Neural Bases of Cognitive Conflict and Control in Moral Judgment." *Neuron* 44, no. 2 (2004): 389–400.

Greene, Joshua D., R. Brian Sommerville, Leigh E. Nystrom, John M. Darley, and Jonathan D. Cohen. "An FMRI Investigation of Emotional Engagement in Moral Judgment." *Science* 293 (2001): 2105–8.

Greenspan, Patricia. "Emotions, Rationality, and Mind/Body." In *Philosophy and the Emotions*, edited by Anthony Hatzimoysis, 113–25. Royal Institute of Philosophy Supplement: 52. New York: Cambridge University Press, 2003.

Guignon, Charles B. *Heidegger and the Problem of Knowledge*. Indianapolis: Hackett Publishing Company, 1983.

———. "Moods in Heidegger's Being and Time." In *What Is an Emotion?: Classic and Contemporary Readings*, edited by Robert C. Solomon, 2nd ed., 180–90. New York: Oxford University Press, 2003.

Haidt, Jonathan. "The Emotional Dog and Its Rational Tail: A Social Intuitionist Approach to Moral Judgment." *Psychological Review* 108, no. 4 (2001): 814–34.

———. "The Emotional Dog Gets Mistaken for a Possum." *Review of General Psychology* 8, no. 4 (2004): 283–90.

———. *The Righteous Mind: Why Good People Are Divided by Politics and Religion*. New York: Vintage Books, 2012.

Haig, Albert. "Modernity, 'Radical Orthodoxy,' and Cornelius Van Til: A Journey of Rediscovery of Participatory Theism." *Colloquium* 47, no. 2 (November 2015): 257–73.

Harris, Joshua Lee. "Who's Truth? A Response to Davis and Franks's 'Against a Postmodern Pentecostal Epistemology.'" *Philosophia Christi* 16, no. 1 (2014): 175–84.

Hart, Hendrik. "The Articulation of Belief: A Link between Rationality and Commitment." In *Rationality in the Calvinian Tradition*, edited by Hendrik Hart, Johan Hoeven, Van Der, and Nicholas Wolterstorff, 209–48. Eugene: Wipf & Stock, 1983.

Hauerwas, Stanley. *The Peaceable Kingdom: A Primer in Christian Ethics*. Notre Dame: University of Notre Dame Press, 1983.

Hauerwas, Stanley, Richard Bondi, and David B. Burrell. *Truthfulness and Tragedy: Further Investigations in Christian Ethics*. Notre Dame: University of Notre Dame Press, 1977.

Heidegger, Martin. *Being and Time*. Translated by Joan Stambaugh. Albany: State University of New York Press, 2010.

Hensley, Jeffrey. "Are Postliberals Necessarily Antirealists? Reexamining the Metaphysics of Lindbeck's Postliberal Theology." In *The Nature of Confession: Evangelicals & Postliberals in Conversation*, edited by Timothy R. Phillips and Dennis L. Okholm, 69–80. Downers Grove: InterVarsity Press, 1996.

Hess, Richard S. "Equality with and without Innocence: Genesis 1-3." In *Discovering Biblical Equality: Complementarity without Hierarchy*, edited by Rebecca Merrill Groothuis and Ronald W. Pierce, 79–95. Downers Grove: InterVarsity Press, 2005.

Heywood, David. *Divine Revelation and Human Learing: A Christian Theory of Knowledge*. Explorations in Practical, Pastoral and Empirical Theology. Burlington: Ashgate, 2004.

Higton, Mike. "Reconstructing the Nature of Doctrine." *Modern Theology* 30, no. 1 (2014): 1–31.

Hill Fletcher, Jeannine. *Monopoly on Salvation?: A Feminist Approach to Religious Pluralism*. New York: Continuum, 2005.

Hunsinger, George. "Postliberal Theology." In *The Cambridge Companion to Postmodern Theology*, edited by Kevin J. Vanhoozer, 42–57. New York: Cambridge University Press, 2003.

Huyssteen, J. Wentzel van. *Essays in Postfoundationalist Theology*. Grand Rapids: Eerdmans Publishing Company, 1997.

———. *The Shaping of Rationality: Toward Interdisciplinarity in Theology and Science*. Grand Rapids: William B. Eerdmans Publishing Company, 1999.

Jacobsen, Douglas. *Thinking in the Spirit: Theologies of the Early Pentecostal Movement*. Bloomington: Indiana University Press, 2003.

Janz, Paul D. *The Command of Grace: A New Theological Apologetics*. New York: T&T Clark, 2009.

Johnson, Dru. *Biblical Knowing: A Scriptural Epistemology of Error*. Eugene: Cascade Books, 2013.

———. *Knowledge by Ritual: A Biblical Prolegomenon to Sacramental Theology*. Winona Lake: Eisenbrauns, 2016.

Johnson, Mark. *Moral Imagination: Implications of Cognitive Science for Ethics*. Chicago: University of Chicago Press, 1993.

Kärkkäinen, Veli-Matti. "Pentecostalism and Pentecostal Theology in the Third Millennium: Taking Stock of the Contemporary Global Situation." In *The Spirit in the World: Emerging Pentecostal Theologies in Global Contexts*, edited by Veli-Matti Kärkkäinen, xiii–xxiv. Grand Rapids: Eerdmans Publishing Company, 2009.

———. *Toward a Pneumatological Theology: Pentecostal and Ecumenical Perspectives on Ecclesiology, Soteriology, and Theology of Mission*. Edited by Amos Yong. New York: University Press of America, 2002.

Kay, William. *Pentecostalism*. London: SCM Press, 2009.

Kelly, Stewart E., and James K. Dew Jr. *Understanding Postmodernism: A Christian Perspective*. Downers Grove: IVP Academic, 2017.

Kennett, Jeanette, and Cordelia Fine. "Will the Real Moral Judgment Please Stand Up?: The Implications of Social Intuitionist Models of Cognition for Meta-Ethics and Moral Psychology." *Ethical Theory & Moral Practice* 12, no. 1 (2009): 77–96.

Klaus, Byron. "The Holy Spirit and Mission in Eschatological Perspective: A Pentecostal Viewpoint." *Pneuma* 27, no. 2 (2005): 322–42.

Koons, Jeremy Randel. "Plantinga on Properly Basic Belief in God: Lessons from the Epistemology of Perception." *Philosophical Quarterly* 61, no. 245 (2011): 839–50.

Kornblith, Hilary. "Internalism and Externalism: A Brief Historical Introduction." In *Epistemology: Internalism and Externalism*, edited by Hilary Kornblith, 1–9. Malden: Blackwell Publishing, 2001.

Land, Steven J. *Pentecostal Spirituality: A Passion for the Kingdom*. Cleveland: CPT Press, 2010.

Lawler, Peter Augustine. *Postmodernism Rightly Understood: The Return to Realism in American Thought*. Lanham: Rowman & Littlefield Publishers, 1999.

Leithart, Peter J. *Solomon Among the Postmoderns*. Grand Rapids: Brazos Press, 2008.

Lindbeck, George A. "Atonement & the Hermeneutics of Intratextual Social Embodiment." In *The Nature of Confession: Evangelicals & Postliberals in Conversation*, edited by Timothy R. Phillips and Dennis L. Okholm, 221–40. Downers Grove: InterVarsity Press, 1996.

———. "Confession and Community: An Israel-like View of the Church." In *The Church in a Postliberal Age*, edited by James J. Buckley, 1–9. Grand Rapids: Eerdmans Publishing Company, 2002.

———. "Foreword to the German Edition of The Nature of Doctrine." In *The Church in a Postliberal Age*, edited by James J. Buckley, 196–200. Grand Rapids: Eerdmans Publishing Company, 2002.

———. "George Lindbeck Replies to Avery Cardinal Dulles." *First Things*, no. 139 (2004): 13–15.

———. "I Pray That They Might Be One as We Are One." In *Postliberal Theology and the Church Catholic: Conversations with George Lindbeck, David Burrell, and Stanley Hauerwas*, edited by John Wright, 55–75. Grand Rapids: Baker Academic, 2012.

———. "Response to Bruce Marshall." *The Thomist: A Speculative Quarterly Review* 53, no. 3 (1989): 403–6.

———. "Scripture, Consensus and Community." In *The Church in a Postliberal Age*, edited by James J. Buckley, 201–22. Grand Rapids: Eerdmans Publishing Company, 2002.

———. *The Nature of Doctrine: Religion and Theology in a Postliberal Age*. Louisville: Westminster John Knox Press, 1984.

Lints, Richard. "The Postpositivist Choice: Tracy or Lindbeck?" *Journal of the American Academy of Religion* 61, no. 4 (1993): 655–77.

Löffler, Winfried. "An Underrated Merit of Plantinga's Philosophy." In *Plantinga's Warranted Christian Belief: Critical Essays with a Reply by Alvin Plantinga*, edited by Dieter Schönecker, 65–81. Dordrecht: De Gruyter, 2015.

Lyotard, Jean-François. *The Postmodern Condition: A Report on Knowledge*. Minneapolis: University of Minnesota Press, 1984.

MacIntyre, Alasdair. *After Virtue: A Study in Moral Theory*, 3rd ed. Notre Dame: University of Notre Dame Press, 2007.

Madison, Gary B. *The Politics of Postmodernity: Essays in Applied Hermeneutics*. Boston: Kluwer Academic Publishers, 2001.

Marshall, Bruce D. "Aquinas as Postliberal Theologian." *The Thomist: A Speculative Quarterly Review* 53, no. 3 (1989): 353–402.

Marty, Martin E. "James K.A. Smith's 'Cultural Liturgies.'" *Sightings*, November 12, 2018. https://divinity.uchicago.edu/sightings/articles/james-ka-smiths-cultural-liturgies.

Mather, Hannah R. K. "Affect, Ethics, and Cognition: A Renewal Perspective on the Spirit's Role in the Interpretation of Scripture." *Journal of Pentecostal Theology* 29, no. 2 (2020): 179–93.

McClymond, Michael J. "Charismatic Renewal and Neo-Pentecostalism: From North American Origins to Global Permutations." In *The Cambridge Companion to Pentecostalism*, edited by Cecil M. Robeck and Amos Yong, 31–51. New York: Cambridge University Press, 2014.

McGrath, Alister E. "An Evangelical Evaluation of Postliberalism." In *The Nature of Confession: Evangelicals & Postliberals in Conversation*, edited by Timothy R. Phillips and Dennis L. Okholm, 23–44. Downers Grove: InterVarsity Press, 1996.

———. *Christian Spirituality: An Introduction*. Malden: Blackwell Publishing, 1999.

McNabb, Tyler D. "Closing Pandora's Box: A Defence of Alvin Plantinga's Epistemology of Religious Belief." University of Glasgow, 2016.

———. "Warranted Religion: Answering Objections to Alvin Plantinga's Epistemology." *Religious Studies* 51, no. 4 (2015): 477–95.
Menzies, Robert P. *Pentecost: This Story Is Our Story*. Springfield: Gospel Publishing House, 2013.
Meyer, Birgit. "Pentecostalism and Globalization." In *Studying Global Pentecostalism: Theories and Methods*, 113–30. Berkeley and Los Angeles: University of California Press, 2010.
Michener, Ronald T. *Postliberal Theology: A Guide for the Perplexed*. New York: Bloomsbury T&T Clark, 2013.
Middleton, J. Richard, and Brian J. Walsh. *Truth Is Stranger than It Used to Be: Biblical Faith in a Postmodern Age*. Downers Grove: InterVarsity Press, 1995.
Milbank, John. "Foreword." In *Introducing Radical Orthodoxy: Mapping a Post-Secular Theology*, 11–20. Grand Rapids: Baker Academic, 2004.
———. *Theology & Social Theory: Beyond Secular Reason*, 2nd ed. Malden: Blackwell Publishing, 2006.
Mitchell, Mark T. "Michael Polanyi, Alasdair MacIntyre, and the Role of Tradition." *Humanitas* 19, no. 1 (2006): 97–125.
Moon, Andrew. "Beliefs Do Not Come in Degrees." *Canadian Journal of Philosophy* 47, no. 6 (2017): 760–78.
———. "Circular and Question-Begging Responses to Religious Disagreement and Debunking Arguments." *Philosophical Studies* 178, no. 3 (2020): 785–809.
———. "Recent Work in Reformed Epistemology." *Philosophy Compass* 11, no. 12 (2016): 879–91.
Moreland, James P., and William Lane Craig. *Philosophical Foundations for a Christian Worldview*. Downers Grove: InterVarsity Press, 2003.
Moyaert, Marianne. "Postliberalism, Religious Diversity, and Interreligious Dialogue: A Critical Analysis of George Lindbeck's Fiduciary Interests." *Journal Of Ecumenical Studies* 47, no. 1 (2012): 64–86.
Murphy, Nancey. *Beyond Liberalism and Fundamentalism: How Modern and Postmodern Philosophy Set the Theological Agenda*. Valley Forge: Trinity Press International, 1996.
———. "Introduction." In *Theology without Foundations: Religious Practice and the Future of Theological Truth*, edited by Stanley Hauerwas, Nancey Murphy, and Mark Nation, 9–31. Nashville: Abingdon Press, 1994.
Murphy, Nancey, and James Wm. McClendon, Jr. "Distinguishing Modern and Postmodern Theologies." *Modern Theology* 5, no. 3 (1989): 191–214.
Murray, Paul D. *Reason, Truth and Theology in Pragmatist Perspective*. Leuven: Peeters, 2004.
Naugle, David K. *Worldview: The History of a Concept*. Grand Rapids: Eerdmans Publishing Company, 2002.
Neumann, Peter D. *Pentecostal Experience: An Ecumenical Encounter*. Eugene: Pickwick Publications, 2012.
———. "Spirituality." In *Handbook of Pentecostal Christianity*, edited by Adam Stewart, 195–201. DeKalb: Northern Illinois University Press, 2012.

Nimmo, Paul T. "Karl Barth." In *The Oxford Handbook of the Epistemology of Theology*, edited by William J. Abraham and Frederick D. Aquino, 523–34. Oxford: Oxford University Press, 2017.
Noel, Bradley Truman. *Pentecostal and Postmodern Hermeneutics: Comparisons and Contemporary Impact*. Eugene: Wipf & Stock, 2010.
Notaro, Thom. *Van Til & the Use of Evidence*. Phillipsburg: P&R Publishing Company, 1980.
Oden, Thomas C. *After Modernity... What?: Agenda for Theology*. Grand Rapids: Zondervan, 1992.
Okholm, Dennis L. *Learning Theology through the Church's Worship: An Introduction to Christian Belief*. Grand Rapids: Baker Academic, 2018.
Oliverio, L. William, Jr. "Theological Hermeneutics: Understanding the World in the Encounter with God." In *The Routledge Handbook of Pentecostal Theology*, edited by Wolfgang Vondey, 140–51. New York: Routledge, 2020.
Olson, Roger E. "Pietism and Postmodernism: Points of Congeniality." *Christian Scholar's Review* 41, no. 4 (2012): 367–80.
———. "Pietism: Myths and Realities." In *Pietist Impulse in Christianity*, edited by Christian T. Collins Winn, Christopher Gehrz, G. William Carlson, and Eric Holst, 3–16. Cambridge: James Clarke and Company, 2012.
———. *Reformed and Always Reforming: The Postconservative Approach to Evangelical Theology*. Grand Rapids: Baker Academic, 2007.
Olthuis, James H. "On Worldviews." *Christian Scholar's Review* 14, no. 2 (1985): 153–64.
Oppy, Graham. "Natural Theology." In *Alvin Plantinga*, edited by Deane-Peter Baker, 15–47. New York: Cambridge University Press, 2007.
Pappas, George. " Stanford Encyclopedia of Philosophy." Edited by Edward N. Zalta. *Internalist vs. Externalist Conceptions of Epistemic Justification. The Stanford Encyclopedia of Philosophy*, 2017. https://plato.stanford.edu/archives/fall2017/entries/justep-intext/.
Paxton, Joseph M , and Joshua D. Greene. "Moral Reasoning: Hints and Allegations." *Topics in Cognitive Science* 2, no. 3 (2010): 511–27.
Pecknold, C. C. *Transforming Postliberal Theology: George Lindbeck, Pragmatism and Scripture*. New York: T&T Clark International, 2005.
Penner, Myron B. "Introduction: Christianity and the Postmodern Turn: Some Preliminary Considerations." In *Christianity and the Postmodern Turn: Six Views*, edited by Myron B. Penner, 13–34. Grand Rapids: Brazos Press, 2005.
Perkins, Tasi. "Beyond Jacques Derrida and George Lindbeck: Toward a Particularity-Based Approach to Interreligious Communication." *Journal of Ecumenical Studies* 48, no. 3 (2013): 343–58.
Perrin, David B. *Studying Christian Spirituality*. New York: Routledge, 2007.
Phillips, Timothy R., and Dennis L. Okholm. "The Nature of Confession: Evangelicals & Postliberals." In *The Nature of Confession: Evangelicals & Postliberals in Conversation*, edited by Timothy R. Phillips and Dennis L. Okholm, 7–20. Downers Grove: InterVarsity Press, 1996.

Placher, William C. *Unapologetic Theology: A Christian Voice in a Pluralistic Conversation*. Louisville: Westminster John Knox Press, 1989.

Plantinga, Alvin. "Advice to Christian Philosophers." In *The Analytic Theist: An Alvin Plantinga Reader*, edited by James F. Sennett, 296–315. Grand Rapids: William B. Eerdmans Publishing Company, 1998.

———. *God and Other Minds: A Study of the Rational Justification of Belief in God*. Ithaca: Cornell University Press, 1967.

———. "How to Be an Anti-Realist." *Proceedings and Addresses of the American Philosophical Association* 56, no. 1 (1982): 47–70.

———. "Internalism, Externalism, Defeaters, and Arguments for Chrsitian Belief." *Philosophia Christi* 3, no. 2 (2001): 379–400.

———. "On Heresy, Mind, and Truth." *Faith and Philosophy* 16, no. 2 (1999): 182–93.

———. "On 'Proper Basicality.'" *Philosophy and Phenomenological Research* 75, no. 3 (2007): 612–21.

———. "Rationality and Public Evidence: A Reply to Richard Swinburne." *Religious Studies* 37, no. 2 (2001): 215–22.

———. "Reason and Belief in God." In *Faith and Rationality*, edited by Alvin Plantinga and Nicholas Wolterstorff, 16–93. Notre Dame: University of Notre Dame Press, 1983.

———. "Reliabilism, Analyses and Defeaters." *Philosophy and Phenomenological Research* 55, no. 2 (1995): 427–64.

———. "Replies to My Commentators." In *Plantinga's Warranted Christian Belief: Critical Essays with a Reply by Alvin Plantinga*, edited by Dieter Schönecker, 238–62. Dordrecht: De Gruyter, 2015.

———. "Reply." *Philosophical Books* 43, no. 2 (2002): 124–35.

———. "Respondeo." In *Warrant in Contemporary Epistemology: Essays in Honor of Plantinga's Theory of Knowledge*, edited by Jonathan L. Kvanvig, 307–78. Lanham: Rowman & Littlefield Publishers, 1996.

———. "Two Dozen (or so) Theistic Arguments." In *Alvin Plantinga*, edited by Deane-Peter Baker, 203–27. New York: Cambridge University Press, 2007.

———. *Warrant and Proper Function*. New York: Oxford University Press, 1993.

———. *Warrant: The Current Debate*. New York: Oxford University Press, 1993.

———. *Warranted Christian Belief*. New York: Oxford University Press, 2000.

———. *Where the Conflict Really Lies: Science, Religion, and Naturalism*. New York: Oxford University Press, 2011.

———. "Why We Need Proper Function." *Noûs* 27, no. 1 (1993): 66–82.

Plasger, Georg. "Does Calvin Teach a Sensus Divinitatis?: Reflections on Alvin Plantinga's Interpretation of Calvin." In *Plantinga's Warranted Christian Belief: Critical Essays with a Reply by Alvin Plantinga*, edited by Dieter Schönecker, 169–89. Dordrecht: De Gruyter, 2015.

Polanyi, Michael. *Personal Knowledge: Towards a Post-Critical Philosophy*. Chicago: University of Chicago Press, 1974.

———. *The Tacit Dimension*. Chicago: University of Chicago Press, 2009.

Pollock, David C., Ruth E. Van Reken, and Michael V. Pollock. *Third Culture Kids: Growing Up Among Worlds*, 3rd ed. Boston: Nicholas Brealey Publishing, 2009.

Poloma, Margaret M. *The Assemblies of God at the Crossroads: Charisma and Institutional Dilemmas*. Knoxville: University of Tennessee Press, 1989.

———. "The Future of American Pentecostal Identity: The Assemblies of God at a Crossroad." In *The Work of the Spirit: Pneumatology and Pentecostalism*, edited by Michael Welker, 147–65. Grand Rapids: Eerdmans Publishing Company, 2006.

———. "The 'Toronto Blessing' in Postmodern Society: Manifestations, Metaphor and Myth." In *The Globalization of Pentecostalism: A Religion Made to Travel*, edited by Murray W. Dempster, Byron D. Klaus, and Douglas Petersen, 363–85. Eugene: Regnum Books International, 1999.

Polt, Richard F. H. *Heidegger: An Introduction*. Ithaca: Cornell University Press, 1999.

Pust, Joel. "Warrant and Analysis." *Analysis* 60, no. 1 (2000): 51–57.

Quinton, Anthony. "Continental Philosophy." In *The Oxford Companion to Philosophy*, edited by Ted Honderich, 161–63. New York: Oxford University Press, 1995.

Rambo, Shelly. *Spirit and Trauma: A Theology of Remaining*. Louisville: Westminster John Knox Press, 2010.

Ranaghan, Kevin Mathers. "Rites of Initiation in Representative Pentecostal Churches in the United States, 1901-1972." Ph.D. Dissertation, University of Notre Dame, 1974.

Reardon, Bernard M. G. *Religion in the Age of Romanticism*. New York: Cambridge University Press, 1985.

Robeck, Cecil M. "Taking Stock of Pentecostalism: The Personal Reflections of a Retiring Editor." *Pneuma* 15, no. 1 (1993): 35–60.

Robeck, Cecil M., and Amos Yong. "Global Pentecostalism: An Introduction to an Introduction." In *The Cambridge Companion to Pentecostalism*, edited by Cecil M. Robeck and Amos Yong, 1–10. New York: Cambridge University Press, 2014.

Roberts, Robert C., and W. Jay Wood. "Proper Function, Emotion, and Virtues of the Intellect." *Faith and Philosophy* 21, no. 1 (2004): 3–24.

Rorty, Richard. *Philosophy and the Mirror of Nature*. Princeton: Princeton University Press, 1979.

Saltzstein, Herbert D., and Tziporah Kasachkoff. "Haidt's Moral Intuitionist Theory: A Psychological and Philosophical Critique." *Review of General Psychology* 8, no. 4 (2004): 273–82.

Salzman, Todd A. "Experience and Natural Law: A Universal Method for Approaching Particular Values." In *Encountering Transcendence: Contributions to a Theology of Christian Religious Experience*, edited by Lieven Boeve, Hans Geybels, and Stijn Van den Bossche, 185–200. Leuven: Peeters, 2005.

Schner, George P. "The Appeal to Experience." *Theological Studies* 53, no. 1 (1992): 40–59.

Schönecker, Dieter. "The Deliverances of Warranted Christian Belief." In *Plantinga's Warranted Christian Belief: Critical Essays with a Reply by Alvin Plantinga*, edited by Dieter Schönecker, 1–40. Berlin: De Gruyter, 2015.

Schrag, Calvin O. *The Self after Postmodernity*. New Haven: Yale University Press, 1997.

Sexton, Jason S. "The Imago Dei Once Again: Stanley Grenz's Journey toward a Theological Interpretation of Genesis 1:26–27." *Journal of Theological Interpretation* 4, no. 2 (2010): 187–206.

Shannon, Nathan D. *Shalom and the Ethics of Belief: Nicholas Wolterstorff's Theory of Situated Rationality*. Cambridge: James Clarke and Company, 2015.

Sheehan, Paul. "Postmodernism and Philosophy." In *The Cambridge Companion to Postmodernism*, edited by Steven Connor, 20–42. New York: Cambridge University Press, 2004.

Sim, Stuart. "Postmodernism and Philosophy." In *The Routledge Companion to Postmodernism*, edited by Stuart Sim, 3–11. New York: Routledge, 2001.

Simmons, J. Aaron. "Introduction: The Dialogical Promise of Mashup Philosophy of Religion." *The Journal for Cultural and Religious Theory* 14, no. 2 (2015): 204–10.

———. "Philosophy: Inspiration for Living Relationally and Thinking Rigorously." In *The Routledge Handbook of Pentecostal Theology*, edited by Wolfgang Vondey, 399–409. New York: Routledge, 2020.

———. "Prospects for Pentecostal Philosophy: Assessing the Challenges and Envisioning the Opportunities." *Pneuma* 42, no. 2 (2020): 175–200.

Sire, James W. *Naming the Elephant: Worldview as a Concept*, 2nd ed. Downers Grove: IVP Academic, 2015.

Smith, Christian. *Moral, Believing Animals: Human Personhood and Culture*. New York: Oxford University Press, 2003.

Smith, David I., and James K. A. Smith. "Introduction: Practices, Faith, and Pedagogy." In *Teaching and Christian Practices: Reshaping Faith & Learning*, edited by David I. Smith and James K. A. Smith, 1–23. Grand Rapids: Eerdmans Publishing Company, 2011.

Smith, James K. A. "A Little Story about Metanarratives: Lyotard, Religion, and Postmodernism Revisited." In *Christianity and the Postmodern Turn: Six Views*, edited by Myron B. Penner, 123–40. Grand Rapids: Brazos Press, 2005.

———. "A Principle of Incarnation in Derrida's (Theologische?) Jugendschriften: Towards a Confessional Theology." *Modern Theology* 18, no. 2 (2002): 217–30.

———. "Alterity, Transcendence, and the Violence of the Concept: Kierkegaard and Heidegger." *International Philosophical Quarterly* 38, no. 4 (1998): 369–81.

———. *Awaiting the King: Reforming Public Theology*. Grand Rapids: Baker Academic, 2017.

———. "Between Predication and Silence: Augustine on How (Not) to Speak of God." *The Heythrop Journal* 41, no. 1 (2000): 66–86.

———. "Continuing the Conversation." In *The Logic of Incarnation: James K. A. Smith's Critique of Postmodern Religion*, edited by Neal DeRoo and Brian Lightbody, 203–23. Eugene: Wipf & Stock, 2009.

———. *Desiring the Kingdom: Worship, Worldview, and Cultural Formation*. Grand Rapids: Baker Academic, 2009.

———. "Determined Violence: Derrida's Structural Religion." *The Journal of Religion* 78, no. 2 (1998): 197–212.

———. *How (Not) to Be Secular: Reading Charles Taylor*. Grand Rapids: Eerdmans Publishing Company, 2014.

———. *Imagining the Kingdom: How Worship Works.* Grand Rapids: Baker Academic, 2013.

———. *Introducing Radical Orthodoxy: Mapping a Post-Secular Theology.* Grand Rapids: Baker Academic, 2004.

———. *Jacques Derrida: Live Theory.* New York: Continuum, 2005.

———. "Keeping Time in the Social Sciences: An Experiment with Fixed-Hour Prayer and the Liturgical Calendar." In *Teaching and Christian Practices: Reshaping Faith & Learning*, edited by David I. Smith and James K. A. Smith, 140–56. Grand Rapids: Eerdmans Publishing Company, 2011.

———. "Liberating Religion from Theology: Marion and Heidegger on the Possibility of a Phenomenology of Religion." *International Journal for Philosophy of Religion* 46, no. 1 (1999): 17–33.

———. "Natural Law's Secularism?—A Response to Christian Smith." *Christian Scholar's Review* 40, no. 2 (2011): 211–15.

———. *On the Road with Saint Augustine: A Real-World Spirituality for Restless Hearts.* Grand Rapids: Brazos Press, 2019.

———. "Pentecostalism." In *The Oxford Handbook of the Epistemology of Theology*, edited by William J. Abraham and Frederick D. Aquino, 606–18. New York: Oxford University Press, 2017.

———. "Questions About the Perception of 'Christian Truth': On the Affective Effects of Sin." *New Blackfriars* 88, no. 1017 (2007): 585–93.

———. "Re-Kanting Postmodernism?: Derrida's Religion within the Limits of Reason Alone." *Faith and Philosophy* 17, no. 4 (2000): 558–71.

———. *Speech and Theology: Language and the Logic of Incarnation.* New York: Routledge, 2002.

———. "Taking Husserl at His Word: Towards a New Phenomenology with the Young Heidegger." *Symposium* 4, no. 1 (2000): 89–115.

———. *The Fall of Interpretation: Philosophical Foundations for a Creational Hermeneutic*, 2nd ed. Grand Rapids: Baker Academic, 2012.

———. "The (Re)Turn to the Person in Contemporary Theory—A Review Essay." *Christian Scholar's Review* 40, no. 1 (2010): 77–92.

———. "The Spirit, Religions, and the World as Sacrament: A Response to Amos Yong's Pneumatological Assist." *Journal of Pentecostal Theology* 15, no. 2 (2007): 251–61.

———. "Thinking in Tongues." *First Things* 182 (April 2008): 27–31.

———. *Thinking in Tongues: Pentecostal Contributions to Christian Philosophy.* Grand Rapids: Eerdmans Publishing Company, 2010.

———. *Who's Afraid of Postmodernism?: Taking Derrida, Lyotard, and Foucault to Church.* Grand Rapids: Baker Academic, 2006.

———. *Who's Afraid of Relativism?: Community, Contingency, and Creaturehood.* Grand Rapids: Baker Academic, 2014.

———. "Worldview, Sphere Sovereignty, and Desiring the Kingdom: A Guide for (Perplexed) Reformed Folk." *Pro Rege* 39, no. 4 (2011): 15–24.

———. *You Are What You Love: The Spiritual Power of Habit.* Grand Rapids: Brazos Press, 2016.

Smith, Martin. "The Epistemology of Religion." *Analysis Reviews* 74, no. 1 (2014): 135–47.

Solomon, Robert C. "Emotions and Choice." In *What Is an Emotion?: Classic and Contemporary Readings*, edited by Robert C. Solomon, 2nd ed., 224–35. New York: Oxford University Press, 2003.

———. "Emotions, Cognition, Affect: On Jerry Neu's A Tear Is an Intellectual Thing." *Philosophical Studies* 108, no. 1 (2002): 133–42.

———. "Emotions, Thoughts, and Feelings: Emotions as Engagements with the World." In *Thinking about Feeling: Contemporary Philosophers on Emotions*, edited by Robert C. Solomon, 76–88. New York: Oxford University Press, 2004.

———. "Emotions, Thoughts and Feelings: What Is a 'Cognitive Theory' of the Emotions and Does It Neglect Affectivity?" In *Philosophy and the Emotions*, edited by Anthony Hatzimoysis, 1–18. Royal Institute of Philosophy Supplement: 52. New York: Cambridge University Press, 2003.

———. *The Passions: Emotions and the Meaning of Life*, 2nd ed. Indianapolis: Hackett Publishing Company, 1993.

———. "The Philosophy of Emotions." In *Handbook of Emotions*, edited by Michael Lewis, Jeannette M. Haviland-Jones, and Lisa Feldman Barrett, 3rd ed., 3–16. New York: The Guilford Press, 2008.

Solomon, Robert C., and Kathleen M. Higgins. *A Short History of Philosophy*. New York: Oxford University Press, 1996.

Sousa, Ronald De. "The Rationality of Emotion." In *What Is an Emotion?: Classic and Contemporary Readings*, edited by Robert C. Solomon, 2nd ed., 248–57. New York: Oxford University Press, 2003.

Spector-Mersel, Gabriela. "Narrative Research: Time for a Paradigm." *Narrative Inquiry* 20, no. 1 (2010): 204–24.

Spencer, Lloyd. "Postmodernism, Modernism, and the Tradition of Dissent." In *The Routledge Companion to Postmodernism*, edited by Stuart Sim, 125–34. New York: Routledge, 2001.

Spittler, Russell P. "Pentecostal and Charismatic Spirituality." In *Dictionary of Pentecostal and Charismatic Movements*, edited by Stanley M. Burgess, Gary B. McGee, and Patrick H. Alexander, 804–9. Grand Rapids: Zondervan, 1988.

Stern, Robert. "Introduction." In *Transcendental Arguments: Problems and Prospects*, edited by Robert Stern, 1–11. Oxford: Oxford University Press, 1999.

Stump, Eleonore. "Orthodoxy and Heresy." *Faith and Philosophy* 16, no. 2 (1999): 147–63.

Sudduth, Michael C. "Plantinga's Revision of the Reformed Tradition: Rethinking Our Natural Knowledge of God." *Philosophical Books* 43, no. 2 (2002): 81–91.

———. "Reformed Epistemology and Christian Apologetics." *Religious Studies* 39, no. 3 (2011): 299–321.

———. "The Internalist Character and Evidentialist Implications of Plantingian Defeaters." *International Journal for Philosophy of Religion* 45, no. 3 (1999): 167–87.

Swinburne, Richard. "Plantinga on Warrant." *Religious Studies* 37, no. 2 (2001): 203–14.

Taylor, Charles. *Modern Social Imaginaries*. Durham: Duke University Press, 2004.
Thiel, John. *Nonfoundationalism*. Minneapolis: Fortress Press, 1994.
Thiselton, Anthony C. *Hermeneutics: An Introduction*. Grand Rapids: William B. Eerdmans Publishing Company, 2009.
Tien, David W. "Warranted Neo-Confucian Belief: Religious Pluralism and the Affections in the Epistemologies of Wang Yangming (1472–1529) and Alvin Plantinga." *International Journal for Philosophy of Religion* 55, no. 1 (2004): 31–55.
Til, Cornelius Van. "Introduction." In *Christian Apologetics*, edited by William Edgar, 2nd ed., 1–15. Phillipsburg: P&R Publishing Company, 2003.
Tilley, Terrence W. "Incommensurability, Intratextuality, and Fideism." *Modern Theology* 5, no. 2 (1989): 87–111.
Toit, Cornel W. du. "Emotion and the Affective Turn: Towards an Integration of Cognition and Affect in Real Life Experience." *HTS Toelogiese Studies/ Theological Studies* 70, no. 1 (2014): 1–9.
Tóth, Beáta. *The Heart Has Its Reasons: Towards a Theological Anthropology of the Heart*. Cambridge: James Clarke and Company, 2016.
Tracy, David W. "Fragments: The Spiritual Situation of Our Times." In *God, the Gift, and Postmodernism*, edited by John D. Caputo and Michael J. Scanlon, 170–84. Bloomington: Indiana University Press, 1999.
———. "Lindbeck's New Program for Theology: A Reflection." *The Thomist: A Speculative Quarterly Review* 49, no. 3 (1985): 460–72.
Tramel, Peter. "Haack's Foundherentism Is a Foundationalism." *Synthese* 160, no. 2 (2008): 215–28.
Trenery, David. *Alasdair MacIntyre, George Lindbeck, and the Nature of Tradition*. Eugene: Pickwick Publications, 2014.
Vanhoozer, Kevin J. "Lost in Interpretation?: Truth, Scripture, and Hermeneutics." *Journal of the Evangelical Theological Society* 48, no. 1 (2005): 89–114.
———. "Pilgrim's Digress: Christian Thinking on and about the Post/Modern Way." In *Christianity and the Postmodern Turn: Six Views*, edited by Myron B. Penner, 71–103. Grand Rapids: Brazos Press, 2005.
Velleman, J. David. "Narrative Explanation." *The Philosophical Review* 112, no. 1 (2003): 1–25.
Volf, Miroslav. "Theology, Meaning & Power: A Conversation with George Lindbeck on Theology & the Nature of Christian Difference." In *The Nature of Confession: Evangelicals & Postliberals in Conversation*, edited by Timothy R. Phillips and Dennis L. Okholm, 45–66. Downers Grove: InterVarsity Press, 1996.
Vondey, Wolfgang. *Beyond Pentecostalism: The Crisis of Global Christianity and the Renewal of the Theological Agenda*. Grand Rapids: Eerdmans Publishing Company, 2010.
———. *Pentecostal Theology: Living the Full Gospel*. New York: T&T Clark, 2018.
———. *Pentecostalism: A Guide for the Perplexed*. New York: Bloomsbury T&T Clark, 2013.
Warrington, Keith. *Pentecostal Theology: A Theology of Encounter*. New York: T&T Clark International, 2008.

Westphal, Merold. "Appropriating Postmodernism." In *Postmodern Philosophy and Christian Thought*, edited by Merold Westphal, 1–10. Bloomington: Indiana University Press, 1999.
———. "Must Phenomenology and Theology Make Two?: A Response to Trakakis and Simmons." *The Heythrop Journal* 55, no. 4 (2014): 711–17.
———. *Overcoming Onto-Theology: Toward a Postmodern Christian Faith*. New York: Fordham University Press, 2001.
———. "Taking Plantinga Seriously: Advice to Christian Philosophers." *Faith and Philosophy* 16, no. 2 (1999): 173–81.
Wiertz, Oliver. "Is Plantinga's A/C Model an Example of Ideologically Tainted Philosophy?" In *Plantinga's Warranted Christian Belief: Critical Essays with a Reply by Alvin Plantinga*, edited by Dieter Schönecker, 83–113. Dordrecht: De Gruyter, 2015.
Wittgenstein, Ludwig. *Philosophical Investigations*. Edited by P. M. S. Hacker and Joachim Schulte. Translated by G. E. M. Anscombe, P. M. S. Hacker, and Joachim Schulte, 4th ed. Malden: Wiley-Blackwell, 2009.
Wolterstorff, Nicholas. "Are Religious Believers Committed to the Existence of God?" In *Practices of Belief: Selected Essays*, edited by Terence Cuneo, 2:350–71. New York: Cambridge University Press, 2010.
———. "Can Belief in God Be Rational If It Has No Foundations?" In *Faith and Rationality*, edited by Alvin Plantinga and Nicholas Wolterstorff, 135–86. Notre Dame: University of Notre Dame Press, 1983.
———. "Entitlement to Believe and Practices of Inquiry." In *Practices of Belief: Selected Essays*, edited by Terence Cuneo, 2:86–117. New York: Cambridge University Press, 2010.
———. "Epistemology of Religion." In *Practices of Belief: Selected Essays*, edited by Terence Cuneo, 2:144–72. New York: Cambridge University Press, 2010.
———. "Historicizing the Belief-Forming Self." In *Practices of Belief: Selected Essays*, edited by Terence Cuneo, 2:118–43. New York: Cambridge University Press, 2010.
———. "On Being Entitled to Beliefs about God." In *Practices of Belief: Selected Essays*, edited by Terence Cuneo, 2:313–33. New York: Cambridge University Press, 2010.
———. "Ought to Believe-Two Concepts." In *Practices of Belief: Selected Essays*, edited by Terence Cuneo, 2:62–85. New York: Cambridge University Press, 2010.
———. "Postscript: A Life in Philosophy." In *Practices of Belief: Selected Essays*, edited by Terence Cuneo, 2:409–25. New York: Cambridge University Press, 2010.
———. "Reformed Epistemology." In *Practices of Belief: Selected Essays*, edited by Terence Cuneo, 2:334–49. New York: Cambridge University Press, 2010.
———. "The Assurance of Faith." In *Practices of Belief: Selected Essays*, edited by Terence Cuneo, 2:289–312. New York: Cambridge University Press, 2010.
———. "The World Ready-Made." In *Practices of Belief: Selected Essays*, edited by Terence Cuneo, 2:12–40. New York: Cambridge University Press, 2010.

———. "Thomas Reid on Rationality." In *Rationality in the Calvinian Tradition*, edited by Hendrik Hart, Johan Van Der Hoeven, and Nicholas P. Wolterstorff, 43–69. Eugene: Wipf & Stock, 1983.

Wynn, Mark R. *Renewing the Senses: A Study of the Philosophy and Theology of the Spiritual Life*. Oxford: Oxford University Press, 2013.

Yong, Amos. "The Pneumatological Imagination: The Logic of Pentecostal Theology." In *The Routledge Handbook of Pentecostal Theology*, edited by Wolfgang Vondey, 152–161. New York: Routledge, 2020.

———. *Renewing Christian Theology: Systematics for a Global Christianity*. Waco: Baylor University Press, 2014.

———. *Spirit-Word-Community: Theological Hermeneutics in Trinitarian Perspective*. Eugene: Wipf & Stock, 2006.

———. *The Dialogical Spirit: Christian Reason and Theological Method in the Third Millennium*. Cambridge: James Clarke and Company, 2014.

———. "Whither Systematic Theology?: A Systematican Chimes in on a Scandalous Conversation." *Pneuma* 20, no. 1 (1998): 85–93.

Zagzebski, Linda T. *On Epistemology*. Belmont: Wadsworth Cengage Learning, 2009.

———. "Plantinga's Warranted Christian Belief and the Aquinas/Calvin Model." *Philosophical Books* 43, no. 2 (2002): 117–23.

Index

A/C model. *See* Aquinas/Calvin model
Adler, Mortimer, 76n14
"Advice to Pentecostal Philosophers" (Smith, J.), 4
affect: Christian belief with, 180–81; cognition with, 76, 77n25; extended A/C model with, 171–82; *nous* with, 180–81, 210; warrant with, 180–81
affection: belief and, 50–51; narrative and, 45, 46, 54–55; in Pentecostalism, 47; Plantinga on, 196
Albrecht, Daniel, 15
Alston, William, 9n6, 143n41, 185n18
Althouse, Peter, 17–18
anterior dorsolateral prefrontal cortex (anterior DLPFC), 63–64
anthropology, 43, 46, 95–97
antifoundationalism, 31, 120, 174, 203, 204
anti-realism, 111, 143nn44–45, 143n48
Aquinas, Thomas, 112–13
Aquinas/Calvin model (A/C model), 8; against, 173–77; of Christian belief, 173–77; circularity of, 177–79; F&M on, 171–74; truth in, 173–74; warrant in, 171–77. *See also* Calvin, John; extended A/C model
Aristotle, 74
Audi, Robert, 163

Augustinianism, 3, 28, 92–95, 137
authority, 24, 31, 122n41
autonomy, 24; of reason, 38n103; in referentialism, 106–7; tradition contrasted with, 23

Bacon, Francis, 23
Baker, Deane-Peter, 175, 185n23
Baker, Don, 15
Baker-Hytch, Max, 167n43
Beilby, James, 155, 196; Diller answering, 197; IIHS described by, 186n44; inferentialism of, 176–77; on justification, 156
belief: affection and, 50–51; basic, 80n71; Bergmann distinguishing, 201; in cultural-linguistic model, 109–10; design toward, 168n56; doxastic programming disrupting, 195; as doxological practice, 18; emotion differentiated from, 78n49; Gettier on, 158; Great Pumpkin opposition to, 175–76; incorrigible, 165n14; with justification, 201; knowledge contrasted with, 3, 30; objectivism compared with, 29–30; reason juxtaposing, 165n17, 206n17; Reformed Christians emphasizing, 18–19; *sensus divinitatis*

243

differentiated from, 172–73; theory basing, 170n87; tradition influenced by, 193; truth contrasted with, 213; warrant compared with, 20, 216n2. *See also* Christian belief; justified true belief (JTB); properly basic belief; religious belief
Ben-Ze'ev, Aaron, 68, 80n66, 81n94
Bergmann, Michael, 154–55, 174, 186n35; Audi compared with, 163; belief distinguished by, 201; externalism with, 169n67, 177–78; Plantinga contrasted with, 186n30
Bernstein, Richard, 130–31
Bertrand, Russell, 154
bias, 18–19, 31, 60
body, 96
Boersma, Hans, 34n51
Bom, Klaas, 50, 51
Bonhoeffer, Dietrich, 214
Borgmann, Albert, 22, 23
Bourdieu, Pierre, 95–96
Bowald, Mark, 97n1
Brandom, Robert, 107–8, 121n27
Briggs, Richard, 146n88
Brunner, Emile, 147n89

Calhoun, Cheshire, 78n49
Calvin, John, 186n28
Calvinism, 1–2, 176, 191
Cartesianism, 18, 23–24, 52, 90–91, 130, 199–200. *See also* Descartes, René
Castelo, Daniel, 17, 72–73, 142n19
category, 112, 134
Cathey, Robert, 114
CCK. *See* cross-cultural kid
Chisholm, Rodrick, 165n14
Christian belief: A/C model of, 173–77; with affect, 180–81; circularity in, 177–79; with extended A/C model, 179–82; Moon on, 178; with *nous*, 180–81; in pistic commitment, 174–75; Plantinga considering, 190; of truth, 173–74; warrant of, 160, 162, 171–82

Christianity: diversity of, 121n38; Penner on, 31; Pentecostal spirituality contrasted with, 17; postmodernism with, 5–6, 8. *See also* postmodern Christian epistemology; Reformed Christians
circularity, 177–79, 185n18, 211
Clark, Kelly James, 184n14
Clark, Mathew, 40n149
Clouser, Roy, 35n52
cognition, 74–75; affect with, 76, 77n25; with emotion, 67–69, 78n47; intuition unified with, 63; judgment with, 70; moral psychology and, 59–65; philosophy of emotion with, 65–72. *See also sensus divinitatis*
cognitive-propositionalism, 109, 114, 116
coherentism, 202–3
communion, 140–41
Conee, Earl, 155
construal, 68, 79n57, 80n82. *See also* narrative, affective construal (NAC)
correspondence: of DF, 129; with God, 112–13; postliberalism rejecting, 115–16; truth as, 118, 142n22. *See also* performative correspondence
Cox, Harvey, 17
creation, 138–41
cross-cultural kid (CCK), 1, 8n1
Crouch, C. L., 146n88
cultural-linguistic model, 109–10, 117

DA. *See* Derrida's Axiom
Dasein (immersion), 96, 131
Davis, Richard, 7
Davis with Franks (DF): analysis of critique, 129–31; correspondence of, 129; against NAK, 127–41; presuppositionalism misrepresented by, 144n54. *See also* Franks, Paul
degree, 159, 168n58
dependence relations, 161–64
Derrida, Jacques, 62, 88–89, 98n3, 143n40
Derrida's Axiom (DA), 128, 129

Index

Descartes, René, 18–19, 23–24, 52, 90–91, 96, 131
desires, 65–66
Desiring the Kingdom (Smith, J.), 19, 73
Dew, James K., Jr., 38n103
DF. *See* Davis with Franks
Diller, Kevin, 174, 184n15, 197
diversity, 121n38
doctrine, 73, 108–10, 113
Dooyeweerd, Herman, 91, 179
doxastic programming, 193, 195, 199
doxological practice, 2, 18, 20, 31, 35n52, 41–42
dual-process theory, 64

EAAN. *See* Evolutionary Argument against Naturalism
embodiment, 94, 97
emotion: awareness and, 80n73; belief differentiated from, 78n49; Ben-Ze'ev on, 80n66; cognition with, 67–69, 78n47; feeling distinguished from, 78n50; Goldie on, 71; judgment and, 65, 66, 70–72, 79n5; logic in, 69, 80n80, 81n94; rationality and, 69, 71–72; with reality, 66; reason with, 67; reflection eliminating, 81n94; with reflective thinking, 68; with thought, 66–67; wayward, 70–72. *See also* philosophy of emotion; reason-emotion interface
Enlightenment, 62
Enlightenment modernism, 22–25, 30, 36n68
environment, 158–59, 195
epistemology: anthropology and, 43, 46; of faith, 196; hermeneutics overlapping with, 99n21; over ontology, 24; postmodern, 94; of Smith, J., 51–53, 94. *See also* Pentecostal epistemology; postmodern hermeneutic epistemology; Reformed epistemology

Evangelicalism, 57n61
evidentialist objector, 153
Evolutionary Argument against Naturalism (EAAN), 168n54
experience, 96, 121n31
extended A/C model: with affect, 171–82; Christian belief with, 179–82; *nous* in, 180–81; summary of, 180; warrant in, 179–82
externalism: Bergmann with, 169n67, 177–78; internalism juxtaposing, 7, 155–56; justification in, 165n17; Plantinga on, 154–57; proper function representing, 167n43; Reformed epistemology on, 154–57; warrant preferred by, 155, 198–99

facticity, 43, 131, 136, 138
Fairlamb, Horace, 183n8
faith: epistemology of, 196; with postmodernism, 88; as pretheoretical understanding, 53–54; Truth with, 25; with undecidability, 90–91
Faith and Rationality (Plantinga), 152
Fales, Evan, 161–63
The Fall of Interpretation (Smith, J.), 97n1, 129
F&M. *See* Freud with Marx
feeling, 78n50
Feldman, Richard, 155–56
Fine, Cordelia, 63
finitude, 99n16, 99n25
fMRI. *See* functional magnetic resonance imaging
Fodor, James, 124n66
formal indication, 135–36
foundationalism, 73, 208n64; with coherentism, 202–3; with normativity, 153–54, 202; of Reformed epistemology, 200–201; of Smith, J., 61, 204–5; Yong on, 203–4, *204*. *See also* antifoundationalism
Frame, John, 2, 16, 34, 53–54
Franks, Paul, 7
Frestadius, Simo, 9n6, 50–51
Freud, Sigmund, 171–72

Freud with Marx (F&M), 171–74. *See also* Marx, Karl
Fumerton, Richard, 184n15
functional magnetic resonance imaging (fMRI), 63–64

generality problem, 167n41, 167n43
Gettier, Edmund, 154, 158
gift, 140–41, 146n88, 147n90
Gill, Jerry, 3–4, 27, 39n131
glocalization, 2, 9n5
God, 68, 89; beyond category, 112; correspondence with, 112–13; embodiment knowing, 94; image describing, 146n88; knowledge of, 16–17, 42, 82n110; Land on, 118; with the Other, 138–39, 141; reality of, 142n19; reference with, 137–38; revelation of, 121n25; time as, 99n16; truth actualizing, 113–14. *See also imago Dei*
God and Other Minds (Plantinga), 152
Goldie, Peter, 71
Gonzalez, Justo, 6
Great Pumpkin opposition, 175–76
Greene, Joshua, 64
Greenspan, Patricia, 79n57, 80n80
Gutting, Gary, 190–91

Haack, Susan, 203
habits, 92–93
habitus (disposition), 95–96
Haidt, Jonathan, 55, 59, 63–65, 67, 76, 76n12, 77n21
Haig, Albert, 9n3
Harris, Joshua, 128, 129, 143n48
Hauerwas, Stanley, 45, 123n61
Heidegger, Martin, 43, 69, 88–89, 96, 100n78, 135
Hensley, Jeffrey, 115–16
hermeneutics: epistemology overlapping with, 99n21; with experience, 121n31; humans as, 88–89; interpretation with, 91; relativism with, 104; religion in, 109–10; undecidability and, 90.

See also postmodern hermeneutic epistemology
Hess, Richard, 146n88
Heywood, David, 48
Hill Fletcher, Jeannine, 144n51
humans, 88–91
Hume, David, 192
Hunsinger, George, 124n67
Husserl, Edmund Gustav Albrecht, 62
van Huyssteen, J. Wentzel, 21, 37n85
hybridity, 8n1

identity, 44–45
IIHS. *See* internal instigation of the Holy Spirit
image: as gift, 141; God described by, 146n88; with incarnation, 146n87; revelation with, 139. *See also imago Dei*
imagination, 44, 54, 95
Imagining the Kingdom (Smith, J.), 74
imago Dei (God's image), 140, 146n88, 147n90
incarnation, 136, 139, 146n87
induction, 163
inferentialism, 169n68, 176–77
intentionality, 92
internal instigation of the Holy Spirit (IIHS), 180, 186n44
internalism: externalism juxtaposing, 7, 155–56; JTB accepted by, 154–55; Plantinga on, 154–57; Reformed epistemology on, 154–57
interpretation, 122n39, 122n52; with hermeneutics, 91; by humans, 88–91; in postmodern hermeneutic epistemology, 87–91; of reality, 132; with schema, 99n43; of Smith, J., 87–88; truth intertwining with, 123n60; worldview impacted by, 97
intersubjectivity, 90
Introducing Radical Orthodoxy (Smith, J.), 73, 94
intuition: cognition unifying, 63; judgments with, 64–65; moral psychology and, 59–65; reason

influencing, 59–60, 63. *See also* social intuitionist model
Irenaeus, 82n110

Jesus Christ, 16, 19, 46, 109, 113, 146n81
Johnson, Dru, 113–14, 168n62, 215
JTB. *See* justified true belief
judgment: with cognition, 65, 70; construal as, 80n82; emotion and, 65, 66, 70–72, 79n5; know-how yielded by, 70; moral, 59, 64–65, 78n41; with reason, 61
justification: Beilby on, 156; belief with, 201; deontological, 152–54; in externalism, 165n17; for NAK, 198; with obligation, 206n24; with postliberalism, 134–35; tradition acknowledged by, 198; truth with, 125n88; warrant differentiated from, 151–52, 165n17, 169n64
justified true belief (JTB), 154–55

Kant, Immanuel 5, 66, 81n94, 100n78, 143nn44–45
Kantianism, 128. *See also* neo-Kantianism
Kelly, Stewart E., 38n103
kinesthetic emotion, 70
know-how, 27, 39n129; as anthropology, 95; concepts as, 108; judgment yielding, 70; know-that contrasted with, 28; primacy of, 209
knowledge: authority granted by, 24, 122n41; belief contrasted with, 3, 30; embodiment situating, 97; of God, 16–17, 82n110; inferential, 161; language needed for, 27; narrative, 27, 44; in non-nihilistic postmodernism, 28–31; objectivism destroying, 30; personal, 28–31, 48; as pistic, 212–13; in postmodernism, 25–26, 209–10; practical, 28–29; with pragmatism, 115; reality depending on, 131; with reason, 78n44; reference and, 135–41;

relativism and, 106; schematic, 47–49; scientific, 27, 44; Smith, J., viewing, 69; Spirit renewing, 215; tacit, 28–31, 42; *telos* juxtaposing, 212; trauma embodying, 46–47; truth included by, 51. *See also* narrative, affective knowledge
know-that, 28
Konyndyk DeYoung, Rebecca, 74
Koons, Jeremy, 170n87
Kuhn, Thomas, 117

Land, Steven, 16–17, 46, 49–50, 77n25, 118, 119
language: agency in, 114; knowledge needing, 27; meaning in, 104–5; rationality tied to, 107; society requiring, 26; trauma and, 47
language games, 26, 105, 133–34
legitimation, 26–27, 39n114
Leithart, Peter, 22
Lindbeck, George A., 7, 28, 103, 123n61, 196; Bernstein juxtaposing, 130–31; on doctrine, 108–9; Hill Fletcher on, 144n51; Hunsinger on, 124n67; language games with, 133–34; MacIntyre juxtaposing, 123n58; Michener describing, 125n89; on truth, 113, 116–17
linguistic pragmatism: Brandom and, 107–8; relativism with, 104–8; with Rorty, 106–7; Smith, J., and, 104–8; with Wittgenstein, 104–6
linguistics, 1
liturgies, 92, 95
Locke, John, 23, 165n17, 207n31
logic, 69, 81n94, 136, 139
love, 92–93
Lyotard, Jean-François, 25–28, 38n103, 44, 98n3, 107

MacIntyre, Alasdair, 123n58, 123n61
Marshall, Bruce, 113, 125n88
Marx, Karl, 171–72
meaning: in language, 104–5; narrative organizing, 43–46; as ostensive,

104–5; in postliberalism, 110–11; as pragmatic, 105–6; in relativism, 105, 110–11; Smith, J., and, 110–11; truth with, 211
Merleau-Ponty, Maurice, 96
metanarrative, 38n103; legitimizing of, 26–28, 39n114; in non-nihilistic postmodernism, 25–28; reason legitimizing, 39n114; science as, 26; worldview contrasted with, 26–27. *See also* narrative
Michener, Ronald, 125n89
Middle Age, 23
Middleton, J. Richard, 31
Mitchell, Mark, 28
modal aspects, 91
modernism, 36n60, 50; Middle Age and, 23; Pentecostal spirituality and, 22–25; Plantinga with, 207n31; postmodernism compared with, 22, 25, 48; religious belief viewed by, 24. *See also* Enlightenment modernism; postmodernism
modernity. *See* modernism
moods, 65–66
Moon, Andrew, 168n58, 178, 183n6, 185n22
moral psychology: cognition and, 59–65; intuition and, 59–65; pretheory and, 59–65; rationalist model of, 60; reason and, 59–65; SIM of, 60–63; theory and, 59–65
Moser, Paul, 183n8, 185n22
Moyaert, Marianne, 144n51
Murphy, Nancey, 208n64
myth, 91

NAC. *See* narrative, affective construal
narrative: affection and, 45–46, 54–55; identity driven by, 44–45; imagination in, 44, 54; meaning organized by, 43–46; worldview in, 45
narrative, affective construal (NAC), 52, 55, 142n24, 182, 199, 214

narrative, affective knowledge (NAK): arbitrariness with, 127–35; DF against, 127–41; with formal indication, 135–36; as hierarchical, 74–75; justification for, 198; NAC distinguished from, 52, 55, 142n24, 182, 199, 214; neo-Kantianism with, 127–35; with non-neutral rational adjudication, 133–35; Pentecostal epistemology with, 43–49, 51–52; Pentecostalism with, 20; primacy of, 43; with realism, 131–33; with reference, 136–38; relativism with, 127–35; as schema, 47–49; with Smith, J., 131–33, 138–41; theoretical knowledge compared with, 46–47; as triperspectival, 51; truth and, 51–52; in worldview, 31, 54, 55n12
The Nature of Doctrine (Lindbeck), 111–12
Naugle, David, 19, 20
neo-Kantianism, 127–35
Neumann, Peter, 17
non-neutral rational adjudication, 133–35
non-nihilistic postmodernism: knowledge in, 28–31; Lyotard in, 25–28; metanarratives in, 25–28; Polanyi, M., in, 28–31; Smith, J., with, 103
normativity, 153–54, 202
nous (intellect): with affect, 180–81, 210; Christian belief with, 180–81; in extended A/C model, 180–81; intellectualism with, 34n51; warrant with, 180–81

objectivism, 29–30, 39n131
obligation, 153, 206n24
O'Donovan, Oliver, 121n21
Oliverio, L. William, Jr., 10n17
Olson, Roger, 17
Olthuis, James, 18
ontology, 24

Oppy, Graham, 169n72
the Other, 136, 138–39, 141, 212

Pannenberg, Wolfhart, 99n16
The Passions (Soloman), 65
PCE. *See* postmodern Christian epistemology
Pearlman, Myer, 73
Pecknold, C. C., 117
Penner, Myron, 21, 31, 40n151
Pentecostal epistemology: critique of, 49–51; with NAK, 43–49, 51–52; primacy of, 52–54; with schematic knowledge, 47–49; truth and, 51–52
Pentecostalism, 2, 9n4; affection in, 47; doctrine and, 73; doxological practice of, 20, 31, 41–42; Evangelicalism juxtaposed with, 57n61; family resemblance describing, 21; glocalization of, 9n5; NAK with, 20; with postliberalism, 118–19; postmodern, 4–5; Smith, J., and, 6–7, 97; spirituality and, 13–15; worldview in, 20, 21; worship in, 55n6
Pentecostal spirituality: Christianity contrasted with, 17; modernism and, 22–25; postmodernism with, 13–31, 42; rationalism comparing, 49; as triperspectival, 49–50, 75; worldview in, 18–20
Pentecostal Spirituality (Land), 16
performative correspondence: with reality, 114–15; relativism with, 117; Smith, J., and, 112–19
Perkins, Tasi, 144n51
Perrin, David, 15
perspectivism, 1, 30–31
phenomenology, 135
philosophy of emotion: with cognition, 65–72; cognitive emotion and, 67–69; kinesthetic emotion and, 70; pretheory and, 65–72; with reason, 65–72; reason-emotion interface and,
70–72; theory and, 65–72; wayward emotion and, 70–72
phronesis (practical wisdom), 7
pietism, 17, 33n35
pistic commitment, 174–75, 182
Placher, William, 122n51
Plantinga, Alvin, 2–3, 7, 110, 186n40; on affection, 196; Alston misinterpreting, 185n18; Bergmann contrasted with, 186n30; Christian belief considered by, 190; on dependence relations, 161–64; EAAN by, 168n54; on externalism, 154–57; on induction, 163; on internalism, 154–57; on justification, 152–54; on knowledge, 161; modernism with, 207n31; postmodernism and, 189–91; on properly basic belief, 159–64; Reformed epistemology of, 151–64, 189–91; Smith, J., contrasted with, 5, 133; Smith, J., convergence with, 195–97; Soloman juxtaposing, 80n71; on warrant, 157–59, 167n37; Wolterstorff and, 8, 194–95, 201–2; Zagzebski on, 184n9. *See also* Aquinas/Calvin model; extended A/C model
Plato, 154
Platonism, 94, 100n57, 106, 126n99, 127, 135; rationalism with, 41–42; of Smith, J., 138; theory failing, 138
Polanyi, Karl Paul, 42–43, 48
Polanyi, Michael, 28–31, 39n131
Poloma, Margaret, 37n73, 48–49
postliberalism, 28, 97n1, 103, 112–14, 117; cognitive-propositionalism juxtaposing, 116; correspondence rejected by, 115–16; justification with, 134–35; Land resembling, 119; meaning in, 110–11; Pentecostalism with, 118–19; postmodernism juxtaposing, 120n1; relativism juxtaposing, 108–10, 118–19; Smith, J., and, 108–10, 118–19

postmodern Christian epistemology (PCE), 199, 209, 212
postmodern hermeneutic epistemology: affective, kinesthetic formation and, 91–93; anthropology and, 95–97; Augustinianism and, 93–95; interpretation in, 87–91; myth in, 91; transcendental condition and, 95–97; worldview in, 91
postmodernism, 2, 36n60; characterization of, 21; with Christianity, 5–6, 8; critique of, 200–205; Enlightenment contrasted with, 62; faith with, 88; family resemblance in, 21; Gill on, 39n131; knowledge in, 25–26, 209–10; modernism compared with, 22, 25, 48; with Pentecostal spirituality, 13–31, 42; pietism compared with, 33n35; Plantinga and, 189–91; postliberalism juxtaposing, 120n1; rationalism rejected by, 42; with rationality, 191–95; Reformed epistemology connected to, 164n2, 189–205; with RO, 6; science unveiled by, 25–26; Wolterstorff with, 191–95; in worldview, 18–21, 214. *See also* non-nihilistic postmodernism
postmodernity. *See* postmodernism
postmodern Pentecostal epistemology (PPE), 128
poststructuralism, 143n40
posture, 61
PPE. *See* postmodern Pentecostal epistemology
pragmatism: knowledge with, 27, 115; revelation with, 107; Smith, J., highlighting, 108. *See also* linguistic pragmatism
prayer, 16
present immediacy model, 88–89
presuppositionalism, 143n49, 144n54
pretheoretical understanding, 53–54; theoretical knowledge contrasted with, 43, 49, 50, 52, 57n66, 58n77

pretheory: Haidt and, 63–65; philosophy of emotion and, 65–72; primacy of, 138; reason as, 64, 73–74; Smith, J., and, 72–75; Spirit as, 200; theory relationship with, 59–76, 138, 141, 210
primacy: egalitarian, 52–54; of know-how, 209; NAK of, 43; of Pentecostal epistemology, 52–54; of pretheory, 138; qualitative, 53, 75, 147n98; quantitative, 53, 147n98
proper function: externalism represented by, 167n43; generality problem of, 167n41; of warrant, 157
properly basic belief, 6, 183n6; as dependent, 160; Plantinga on, 159–64; Reformed epistemology on, 159–64; warrant differentiated from, 162
Pust, Joel, 168n58
Putnam, Hilary, 110

Radical Orthodoxy (RO), 1, 126n99; dichotomy eradicated by, 93; postmodernism with, 6; postmodern Pentecostalism with, 4–5; secularism rejected by, 94
Rambo, Shelly, 46–47, 90, 115
Ranaghan, Kevin, 16
ratiocination, 81n94
rationalism, 22; knowledge foiled with, 30; Pentecostal spirituality compared with, 49; with Platonism, 41–42; postmodernism rejecting, 42
rationality: concepts in, 107–8; in cultural-linguistic model, 117; emotion and, 69, 71–72; language tied to, 107; postmodernism with, 191–95; Reformed epistemology with, 191–95; the Self and, 192–94; of Wolterstorff, Nicholas, 191–95
Rational Romanticism. *See* Romanticism
realism: NAK with, 131–33; perspectivism contrasted with, 1; relativism compared with, 5, 111–12;

with Rorty, 110; Smith, J., and, 111–12, 117–18, 127–28, 131–33, 210–11; truth questioned with, 111–12. *See also* anti-realism

reality: emotion with, 66; of God, 142n19; interpretation of, 132; knowledge depended on by, 131; performative correspondence with, 114–15

reason, 77n21; autonomy of, 38n103; belief juxtaposing, 165n17, 206n17; bias with, 60; with emotion, 67; intuition influenced by, 59–60, 63; judgment with, 61, 78n41; knowledge with, 78n44; legitimation provided by, 39n114; metanarrative legitimized by, 39n114; moral psychology and, 59–65; perspectivism relativizing, 30–31; philosophy of emotion with, 65–72; with posture, 61; as pretheory, 64, 73–74; private moral, 62–63; reflection of, 74–75; Smith, J., viewing, 73–74; with theory, 73–74

"Reason and Belief in God" (Plantinga), 152–53

reason-emotion interface, 70–72

reference: with God, 137–38; knowledge and, 135–41; NAK with, 136–38

referentialism, 106–7, 110, 122n43

reflection: emotion eliminated by, 81n94; lack of, 82n114; of reason, 74–75; Smith, J., on, 74

reflective thinking, 68

Reformed Christians, 18–19, 34n51, 35n52, 54

Reformed epistemology: Cartesianism defending against, 199–200; critique of, 200–205; dependence relations in, 161–64; on externalism, 154–57; foundationalism of, 200–201; on internalism, 154–57; Johnson on, 168n62; with justification, 152–54; pistic commitment in, 182; of Plantinga, 151–64, 189–91;

postmodernism connected to, 164n2, 189–205; properly basic belief in, 159–64; with rationality, 191–95; Smith, J., assisted by, 197–200; warrant in, 157–59; of Wolterstorff, 191–95

Reid, Thomas, 175, 192

relativism, 122n51; with anti-realism, 111; Brandom and, 107–8; with hermeneutics, 104; with linguistic pragmatism, 104–8; meaning in, 110–11; with NAK, 127–35; narrative, 127–29; nihilistic, 105, 106; with performative correspondence, 117; postliberalism juxtaposing, 108–10, 118–19; realism compared with, 5, 111–12; Rorty and, 106–7; Smith, J., with, 103–20; truth in, 111–12, 130; Wittgenstein and, 104–6

reliabilism, 167n43, 185n18

religious belief, 109–10; Clouser defining, 35n52; modal aspects of, 91; modernism viewing, 24; secularization contrasted with, 37n85

representationalism, 106, 110, 122n43

Rescher, Nicholas, 125n87

revelation: of God, 121n25; with image, 139; perpetual, 147n89; with pragmatism, 107

ritual, 82n114

RO. *See* Radical Orthodoxy

Roberts, Robert, 181, 199

Romanticism, 36n68, 65

Rorty, Richard, 122n51; Gutting differentiated from, 190–91; linguistic pragmatism with, 106–7; realism with, 110; Smith, J., compared with, 106–7

Saussure, Ferdinand, 89
schema, 47–49, 99n43
Schönecker, Dieter, 184n12
Schrag, Calvin, 24, 30
science, 25–26, 29
secularism, 94

secularization, 37n85
the Self, 192–94
self-evidence, 165n14
sensus divinitatis (divinity), 172–73, 179, 180
Sexton, Jason, 146n87
Shannon, Nathan, 152, 191, 206n6, 206n9
Sheehan, Paul, 30
SIM. *See* social intuitionist model
Simmons, J. Aaron, 4
Sims, Stuart, 31
Sire, James, 19
Smith, Christian, 44–45, 126n97
Smith, James K. A., 1, 3, 9n3, 37n85, 97n1; assistance for, 72–75; Augustine of Hippo illuminated by, 137; Brandom contrasted with, 107–8; with Brunner, 147n89; correspondence truth rejected by, 118; creational-redemptive model juxtaposing, 140; creation and, 138–41; critique of, 200–205; curriculum vitae of, 98n2; DA committed to by, 129; epistemology of, 51–53, 94; foundationalism of, 61, 204–5; Haidt compared with, 62–63; as hierarchical, 82n124; interpretation of, 87–88; knowledge viewed by, 69; linguistic pragmatism and, 104–8; meaning and, 110–11; NAK with, 131–33, 138–41; with non-nihilistic postmodernism, 103; with PCE, 209; Pentecostalism and, 6–7, 97; performative correspondence and, 112–19; Plantinga contrasted with, 5, 133; Plantinga convergence with, 195–97; Platonism of, 138; postliberalism and, 108–10, 118–19; pragmatism highlighted by, 108; presuppositionalism of, 143n49; pretheory and, 72–75; realism and, 111–12, 117–18, 127–28, 131–33, 210–11; reason viewed by, 73–74; on reflection, 74; Reformed epistemology assisting, 197–200; with relativism, 103–20; representationalism rejected by, 106; Rorty compared with, 106–7; Smith, C., criticized by, 126n97; Solomon compared with, 68–69, 78n50; sub-cognitivism and, 72; on *telos*, 92; theory and, 72–75; as triperspectival, 51–52; truth and, 111–12, 121n21; Wittgenstein compared with, 104–6; worldview clarified by, 34n42
social intuitionist model (SIM), 59–63
society, 26
Solomon, Robert, 55, 65, 67–70, 76, 78n50, 80n71
Spector-Mersel, Gabriela, 44
Speech and Theology (Smith, J.), 21, 97n1
Spencer, Lloyd, 21, 22
Spirit, 200, 215
spirituality, 13–15, 72–73. *See also* Pentecostal spirituality
Spittler, Russell, 15
sub-cognitivism, 74–75
Sudduth, Michael, 169n68

Taylor, Charles, 18, 37n85, 54, 185n23
telos (vision), 92, 93, 212
Theaetetus (Plato), 154
theology, 72–73, 82n114, 169n72
theoretical knowledge, 46–47; pretheoretical understanding contrasted with, 43, 49, 50, 52–53, 57n66, 58n77
theory: belief based on, 170n87; moral psychology and, 59–65; philosophy of emotion and, 65–72; Platonism failed by, 138; pretheory relationship with, 59–76, 138, 141, 210; reason with, 73–74; Smith, J., and, 72–75; with sub-cognitivism, 74–75

Thiel, John, 23
Thinking in Tongues (Smith, J.), 19, 87, 94
thought, 66–68
Tilley, Terrence, 121n38
time, 99n16
totality, 22, 25, 30
Tóth, Beáta, 50, 78n47
Tracy, David, 22, 121n31
tradition: autonomy contrasted with, 23; belief influenced by, 193; category of, 134; as doxastic programming, 193; intersubjectivity indicating, 90; justification acknowledging, 198; practical knowledge passed with, 28–29; of Reformed Christians, 54
transcendental condition, 95–97
trauma, 115; knowledge embodied by, 46–47; language and, 47; with undecidability, 90
Trenery, David, 123n58
triperspectival, 51–52
truth: in A/C model, 173–74; belief contrasted with, 213; Christian belief of, 173–74; circularity of, 211; as correspondence, 118, 142n22; of doctrine, 110; with faith, 25; God actualized with, 113–14; interpretation intertwining with, 123n60; with justification, 125n88; knowledge including, 51; Lindbeck on, 113, 116–17; with meaning, 211; NAK and, 51–52; Pentecostal epistemology and, 51–52; realism questioned with, 111–12; in relativism, 111–12, 130; Rescher on, 125n87; Smith, J., and, 111–12, 121n21; Vanhoozer on, 124n67; warrant with, 159, 173–74

undecidability, 90–91

Vanhoozer, Kevin, 21, 123n60, 124n67

Van Til, Cornelius 'Van Tillian,' 1, 9n3
Velleman, David, 45, 46
Vondey, Wolfgang, 9n4

Walsh, Brian J., 31
warrant: in A/C model, 171–77; affect of, 171–82; belief compared with, 20, 216n2; of Christian belief, 160, 162, 171–82; circularity in, 177–79; core of, 167n38; degree of, 159; with design, 168n53; doxastic programming included by, 199; environment of, 158–59; in extended A/C model, 179–82; externalism preferring, 155, 198–99; Feldman on, 156; inference boosting, 169n68; justification differentiated from, 151–52, 165n17, 169n64; with *nous*, 180–81; with pistic commitment, 174–75; Plantinga on, 157–59, 167n37; proper function of, 157; properly basic belief differentiated from, 162; in Reformed epistemology, 157–59; theology increasing, 169n72; with truth, 159, 173–74
Warranted Christian Belief (Plantinga), 171, 189
Wenger, Etienne, 73–74
Westphal, Merold, 5, 23, 31, 40n153, 125n90, 195
Who's Afraid of Relativism (Smith, J.), 88, 97n1, 103, 104
Wittgenstein, Ludwig, 21, 26, 104–6
Wolterstorff, Nicholas, 2–3, 5, 143n44, 151, 165n17, 169n64; on Calvin, 186n28; Plantinga and, 8, 194–95, 201–2; postmodernism with, 191–95; rationality of, 191–95; Reformed epistemology of, 191–95; the Self historicized by, 192–94; Shannon on, 206n9
Wood, W. Jay, 181, 199

worldview: as bias, 18–19; interpretation impacting, 97; intersubjectivity equated with, 90; metanarrative contrasted with, 26–28; as myth, 91; NAK in, 31, 54, 55n12; in narrative, 45; in Pentecostalism, 20; Pentecostal spirituality in, 18–20; in postmodern hermeneutic epistemology, 91; postmodernism in, 18–21, 214; with Reformed Christians, 19, 35n52; Smith, J., clarifying, 34n42
worship, 55n6
Wykstra, Stephen, 183n8
Wynn, Mark, 68, 70

Yong, Amos, 18, 20, 53, 58n77, 203–4, *204*

Zagzebski, Linda, 184n9, 215

About the Author

Yoon Shin (PhD, University of Aberdeen) is associate professor of philosophical theology at Southeastern University. He is a Pentecostal philosophical theologian and has published in *Pneuma* and *Constructive Pneumatological Hermeneutics in Pentecostal Christianity.* He also coleads the Philosophy Interest Group in the Society for Pentecostal Studies.

www.ingramcontent.com/pod-product-compliance
Lightning Source LLC
Chambersburg PA
CBHW020113010526
44115CB00008B/818